Collected Poems

AUSTIN CLARKE was born in Dublin in 1896, [...] College Dublin where he became an assistant l[...] which his first collection of poems, *The Vengeance* [...] subsequently lost the lectureship and in 1922 went to England, where he worked as a journalist and book reviewer. In 1932 he won the National Award for Poetry at the Tailteann Games in Dublin and became a foundation member of the Irish Academy of Letters at the invitation of W.B. Yeats and George Bernard Shaw. A playwright (the author of over twenty verse plays), as well as a poet, he returned to Dublin in 1937. He received the Casement Award for Poetry and Drama from the Irish Academy of Letters in 1938. Austin Clarke was the co-founder (with Robert Farren) of the Dublin Verse-Speaking Society which made its first broadcast in 1940, on Radio Éireann. In 1944 he co-founded the Lyric Theatre Company (again, with Robert Farren) which performed verse plays twice-yearly at the Abbey Theatre until 1951, when a fire rendered the theatre unusable. Austin Clarke was president of Irish PEN in 1942, 1946–9, 1952–4 and 1961. He was the author of three novels, three memoirs and some twenty collections of poetry. In 1966 an Honorary D.Litt. was conferred on him by Trinity College Dublin; in 1968 the Irish Academy of Letters awarded him its highest honour, the Gregory Medal; in 1972 he received the first American Irish Foundation Literature Award and in the same year was nominated for the Nobel Prize by Irish PEN. Austin Clarke died in 1974.

R. DARDIS CLARKE is a journalist and the youngest of Austin Clarke's three sons.

CHRISTOPHER RICKS is the William M. and Sara B. Warren Professor of the Humanities at Boston University, where he is Co-Director of the Editorial Institute. He was elected Professor of Poetry at the University of Oxford in 2004.

Irish Poetry from Carcanet Press

Eavan Boland
Selected Poems
Outside History
In a Time of Violence
Night Feed
The Lost Land
Code
New Collected Poems
Domestic Violence
Three Irish Poets (ed.)

Moya Cannon
Carrying the Songs

John F. Deane
Toccata and Fugue
Manhandling the Deity
The Instruments of Art
A Little Book of Hours

Greg Delanty
The Blind Stitch
The Ship of Birth
Collected Poems

Padraic Fallon
A Look in the Mirror
*The Vision of MacConglinne
and other plays*

Thomas Kinsella
Collected Poems
Selected Poems

Paula Meehan
Dharmakaya
Painting Rain

Peter McDonald
Pastorals
The House of Clay

Sinéad Morrisey
There Was Fire in Vancouver
Between Here and There
The State of the Prisons

Mary O'Malley
The Boning Hall
A Perfect V

Justin Quinn
The 'O'o'a'a' Bird
Privacy

John Redmond
Thumb's Width
MUDe

AUSTIN CLARKE

Collected Poems

Edited by R. Dardis Clarke

with an introduction by
Christopher Ricks

CARCANET

with

The Bridge Press

First published in Great Britain in 2008 by
Carcanet Press Limited
Alliance House
Cross Street
Manchester M2 7AQ

with The Bridge Press, 17 Oscar Square, Dublin 8

The publisher acknowledges financial assistance from Arts Council England

Published with the support of University College Dublin

Additional financial support for this publication from the following organisations
is gratefully acknowledged:
Arts Council Ireland
Dublin City Council Arts Office
Bord na Móna Real Fires – the ideal book reading companion
The Irish Times

      BORD NA MÓNA   THE IRISH TIMES

Typeset by XL Publishing Services, Tiverton
Printed and bound in England by SRP Ltd, Exeter

Contents

For the links of those boastful manacles
That hold back meaning, but I prefer it
To being a silent Englishman
Who cannot untie his tongue.

Who cannot untie his tongue? As against holding it a moment.

For an Englishman who is a criticus or criticaster (and whose name is Christopher and initials C.R.), this may be more than usually salutary.

Why *boastful*, the manacles? Because the London pavement-performer makes it his boast that he will be able to escape. And why is it a good thing to *hold back meaning*? Because, if the poet isn't careful, *meaning* has a way of too insistently shouldering its way in, so that we readers then have the meaning but miss the experience. Did it really become too supple by half, Mr Clarke's escapologistical skill? No doubt not. How intricate the chains of thoughts and sounds prove themselves, in his unmanacled hands. His are the displacings and enlacings of rhyme: *remarked / Mr Clarke was*. And *Irishman* into *manacles* and then with calculated anticlimax into *Englishman*. 'A Jocular Retort' concludes with a characteristic caveat (Clarke is a warner), with *snake-dance* off-stress rhyming with *half-naked*, and finally an anti-climax that is no kind of let-down, being instead a well-judged reservation that is by no means unthankful:

Whenever Circe has a night-party
And entertains with her famous snake-dance
Clubbable guests that show the kind
Of wallowers they are, when she's half-naked,
She forgets to give us our fill. But I
Have liked her and sometimes she is kind.

First, an expected Muse: Circe. Second, a surprising rhyme (albeit not a start-ling one in Clarke, who delights in *rime riche* and all its shapes and sizes): *kind / kind*. And last, the refreshing coolth of understatement (*liked! sometimes!*) in the close:

But I
Have liked her and sometimes she is kind.

For all its humane directness, the Frost anecdote is an involuted one with its links, its manacles, its untying. Within it, there is the sense of getting away as well as of getting away with something (by way of audacious ambidexterity, happy to be openly ostending, a great show). Escape is the key. And yet how unsimple *escape* may be.

The escapologist is at the opposite pole from an escapist (and I speak as the father-in-law of Zippo, a former escapologist who subsequently escaped into the related world of the circus). The two poles may be one reason why the words arrive in the language at about the same time.

> *escapologist*: A performer skilled in extricating himself from knots, handcuffs, confinement in a box, etc. (From 1926)

As for *escapist*, one of its odd features is that the figurative sense is to be found (if we are to believe the *Oxford English Dictionary*) just earlier than the literal sense:

> 1. One who escapes or who tries to escape, from captivity, prison etc. 1934
> 2. *fig.* Esp., one who seeks distraction from reality or from routine activities. 1933

The first figurative citation for the noun (1933: 'Do you take me for an escapist?') is from an Ulsterman, C.S. Lewis, whereupon the year 1942 supplies a description of the Irish as 'Turning their backs on the world of effort and action. Fortunate islanders... happy, drab escapists.' (Evelyn Waugh, needling to say.) A few years *earlier*, again oddly, there had been 'Hence *attrib.* or as *adj.*, that proves escape from reality or routine; pertaining to escapism' (1930). *Hence* is bizarre if the *attrib.* really is the earliest of the cognate words. Something must be escaping me.

A contrast of the escapist with the escapologist is central to Clarke's sense of it all. His firm praise for the *Collected Poems* of William Empson prompts a reminder of Empson's persuasive unwinding of what was at issue within all the talk in the 1930s and 1940s about escapism and the arts.

> *escapism*: The tendency to seek, or the practice of seeking, distraction from what normally has to be endured.

This is from 1933, the first two instances being about poetry, and the third about abstract art. In 1940, Empson wrote in a note to one of his poems, 'Your Teeth are Ivory Towers':

> Critics often say that modern poetry retires into an ivory tower, doesn't try to make contact with a reader, or escapes facing the problems of the time. I try to defend it by saying that there is a good deal of defence in ordinary life (talking or biting). A critic like

Editor's Foreword and Notes on the Text

Austin Clarke was born in Manor Street on the north side of Dublin city in 1896. He was educated at Belvedere College and won a scholarship to University College Dublin, then in St Stephen's Green, where he obtained a first class honours BA (1916) and a first class honours MA in English with a thesis on the plays of John Ford (1917). In 1917 he was appointed assistant lecturer in English at UCD, replacing Thomas MacDonagh, who had taught him there and had been executed in 1916 as one of the leaders of the Easter Rising. On 31 December 1920 Clarke was married in the Dublin Registry Office. The marriage lasted ten days and was unconsummated. In 1921 he lost his position at UCD, apparently (according to Maurice Harmon in a special Irish University Review issue on him in 1974), 'because of his civil marriage'. Clarke himself believed this. (Interestingly, in *The UCD Aesthetic: Celebrating 150 Years of UCD Writers*, edited by Anthony Roche, Harmon writes: 'Although he was appointed Assistant Lecturer in English at UCD to replace Thomas MacDonagh, who had been executed for his part in the Easter Rising, Clarke suffered a nervous breakdown and eventually had to leave his position.')

After his UCD days had ended, Clarke went to London (1922), where he earned his living at reviewing in various papers and literary magazines. He made frequent visits back to Dublin during his exile, which lasted until 1937 when, fearing the outbreak of war, he returned with his second wife and two children to settle at Bridge House, Templeogue, Co. Dublin, where he was to live until his death there on 19 March 1974. Back in Dublin he began writing and reviewing books for the *Irish Times*, to which he continued to contribute until the end of his life, apart from a period during the 1960s when he reviewed for the *Irish Press*.

In 1940 Clarke and Robert Farren had founded the Dublin Verse-Speaking Society, which broadcast on Radio Éireann. Clarke continued to work for Radio Éireann until the mid-60s, presenting a weekly poetry programme with a team of trained verse-speakers. During the 1940s he had also devoted considerable time to verse drama and, as co-founder (with Farren) of the Lyric Theatre Company, hired the Abbey Theatre twice a year for a couple of

Sunday nights to put on plays by Yeats, George Fitzmaurice, Padraic Colum, T.S. Eliot and himself, amongst others. These performances came to an end with the Abbey Theatre fire in 1951, which became the subject of two poems.

A foundation member of the Irish Academy of Letters, Clarke won many awards in his long career, including the Academy's Gregory Medal, its supreme award for distinction in literature. He received the first American Irish Foundation Literary Award in 1972. Irish PEN nominated him for the Nobel Prize in the same year.

After the death of Yeats in 1939, Clarke had become concerned that verse drama would be neglected by the Abbey Theatre. He set about to make sure that this did not happen by forming the Dublin Verse-Speaking Society, and also the Lyric Theatre Company, to perform poetry readings and verse plays at the Abbey Theatre. He felt, correctly as it turned out, that with the death of Yeats the directors would neglect verse and concentrate on 'popular' drama. He established the Bridge Press to publish his plays and poetry (the actual printing was carried out by jobbing printers). The first volume published was *As the Crow Flies*, a lyric play for radio produced in a limited edition of 175 copies in 1973. In all, there were twelve publications, of which six were poetry, five plays and one essays. His last Bridge Press publication was his own last book, *Tiresias* (1971). Since then there have been two further Bridge Press publications: F.R. Higgins, *The 39 Poems* (1992), selected and edited by R. Dardis Clarke, and *Austin Clarke Remembered* (1996), essays, poems and reminiscences to mark the centenary of Clarke's birth (1996), edited by R. Dardis Clarke, with an introduction by Seamus Heaney.

Notes on the Text

Austin Clarke's *Collected Poems* was last published by Dolmen Press in 1974, just after the poet's death in March of that year. Since then there have been two editions of Clarke's Selected Poems, one edited by Thomas Kinsella (Dolmen Press, 1976) and one edited by Hugh Maxton (W.J. McCormack; Lilliput Press, 1991). Since then Clarke has effectively been out of print.

Clarke did not tend to change his poems once they had been published, and he did little revision except to his early long poems. In his epic work *The Vengeance of Fionn* only a few words were changed. However, with his volume *The Sword in the West* he did make drastic changes, outlined below. *The Fires of Baäl* and *The Cattledrive in Connaught* were also revised.

In compiling this *Collected Poems* my principle has been to order the poems chronologically by the publication dates of the original collections, from the *Vengeance of Fionn* (1917) to *Tiresias* (1971). The only poem here which was not published in any of these volumes, apart from the Dolmen *Collected Poems*, is 'The Wooing of Becfola', Clarke's last published poem. The poems appear in the order in which they appeared in the original volumes and the text has been checked against the original editions. The Dolmen *Collected Poems* had a number of typographical errors and incorrect titles; one poem was included twice and one was out of sequence; the author's notes were incomplete. The intention has been to correct these errors in this *Collected Poems*.

In his *Later Poems* (1961), which consisted of five volumes already published – *Pilgrimage* (1929), *Night and Morning* (1938), *Ancient Lights* (1955), *Too Great a Vine* (1957) and *The Horse-Eaters* (1960) – Austin Clarke included notes, some of which had been included in the original volumes although some of the collections, *Ancient Lights*, for instance, had not originally contained notes. In the *Collected Poems* (1974) the notes included most of those from the original collections. In this present volume I have restored some notes that were omitted from both the *Later Poems* and the 1974 *Collected Poems*.

Clarke's first volume, *The Vengeance of Fionn* (1917), was extremely well received and went to a second edition. The *Times Literary Supplement* reviewer wrote: 'Like Keats, the poet scatters his treasures with a lavish hand... its general workmanship... shows a jewelled richness of surface that is thoroughly Irish... it is as original in conception as it is refined in execution.' The *Irish Times* declared: 'Not since Mr Yeats first put on his singing robes has any Irish poet appeared with such decisive claim to be in the bardic succession.' These quotations, together with one from the *Freeman's Journal*, were printed on the cover of the second edition.

The Sword of the West (1921) consisted of two sections. The first, 'Concobar', covers events before Cuchullin's birth, at the end of which we have 'Black Valley (1918). The second section, 'The Death of Cuchullin', relates events prior to Cuchullin's death, at the end of which we have 'Bloody Foreland' (1920–21). Clarke was unhappy with the book, and indeed tried to have it suppressed. When he came to prepare *Collected Poems* (1936) he revised and cut the volume extensively. 'Concobar' became 'Concobar in Uladh' and was only about a third the length of the original. In *Collected Poems* (1974) the poem became 'Concobar' again. 'The Death of Cuchullin' became 'The Music-Healers' (dedicated 'To Hellé Flecker') in *Collected Poems* (1936). It retained the title in *Collected Poems* (1974) but it was revised so much that effectively there are now three poems. The version here is that which appeared in *Collected Poems* (1974). (Maurice Harmon has discussed the revisions in '"The Sword of the West" (1921, 1936, 1974)', *Études Irlandaises*, 10, n.s., December 1985.) 'O Love, There Is No Beauty' appears in *Collected Poems* (1936) and is in fact taken directly from 'The Death of Cuchullin'. The only difference between the two poems is the last line, which in the original was: 'That dance with bloody feet'. This became: 'That dance with bloodied feet', and was used unchanged in *Collected Poems* (1974).

The Fires of Baäl (1921) was dedicated: 'To A.E. In deep respect' and included nine extracts of press notices of *The Vengeance of Fionn*.

The Cattledrive in Connaught and Other Poems (1925) was dedicated: 'To Josephine' and included the note: 'Several lyrics, which have appeared in *The Nation*, *The New Statesman*, *The New Witness*, *The Irish Statesman* and *The Dublin Magazine*, are by courtesy of the respective Editors, re-printed in this book.'

Pilgrimage and Other Poems (1929) was dedicated: 'To my mother' and included the note: 'This Edition is limited to five hundred copies, of which twenty-five have been numbered and signed by the Author.'

Collected Poems (1936) had an introduction by Padraic Colum and was dedicated: 'To A.E. Who sustained the cause of Irish poetry, giving imaginative courage and hope to all of us, I dedicate this Collection in sadness and memory'. In this volume *The Vengeance of Fionn* was dedicated: 'In memory of my father' and *The Music-Healers* was dedicated: 'To Hellé Flecker'. *Collected Poems* (1936) also included two plays, *The Flame* and *The Son of Learning*. The only poems not already included in previous volumes were 'Wandering Men' and 'Six Sentences' – 'Black and Tans', 'Civil War' I and II, 'To James Stephens', 'No Recompense' and 'The Tales of Ireland'. 'To James Stephens' was published in *The Shamrock and Irish Emerald* (11 December 1920). 'Wandering Men' was first published in the *Spectator* (8 October 1932).

Night and Morning (1938) was the first of the third series of Tower Press Booklets published by the Orwell Press and included the note: 'This edition is limited to three hundred copies.' It consisted of new poems and 'No Recompense'.

Ancient Lights (1955) was published in a limited edition of two hundred copies. 'The Blackbird of Derrycairn' is taken from the play *As the Crow Flies*, first broadcast on Radio Éireann (6 February 1942).

Too Great a Vine was first published in November 1957, limited to two hundred copies, and went into a second impression in April 1958.

The Horse-Eaters (1960), the third in the Poems and Satires Series, the only hardback of the three, was published in an edition of two hundred copies.

Forget Me Not (1962) includes the note: ' "Forget Me Not" by Austin Clarke was commissioned by the Arts Council of Great Britain for the Poetry at the Mermaid Festival, London, 1961 and is set in Poliphilus and Blado Italic

Hurrying from the dark-lit pines beneath
The Fenians scattered on the sunbrowned heath,
Bronze-girt Oscar, Caoilte and Oisin
Hailing Fionn and Diarmuid on the green
Hilltop. The poet musically lipped:
'As I came hither O Fionn I heard the sounds
Of otters swimming lakeward and glad calls
From height to height and sweetly belling hounds
Till louder than the roaring of the falls
At Assaroe the anger of your words
Foamed against the wind. O be not rash
Of tongue lest quicker than the silver flash
Of salmon leaping there, unscabbarded swords
Lighten between ye!'
                              But Fionn did not hear.
He stood knee-deep in ferns; boar-like, his eyes
Glinting. He saw above the forest's verge
The black blunt precipice of Gulban rear
Skyward, the clouded mountain tops and three
Eagles in the high blue air like flies
Flickering around a solitary peak.
Below; the windy hillocks dropped to the sea –
A blue-green-shadowed plain, and salt-white surge
Pawed round black capes. Then he heard Oisin speak
To the Fianna, 'Watch ye like a cloud
Of seamews hovering with drooped pink claws
Over the green-hollowed waves for prey?
Begone!' Caoilte laughing and Diarmuid say
Slowly mouthed 'O maker of the loud
War words that drive the foe like rooks and daws
From creaking elms, of songs that pluck out wrath
Even as a harper a rusted string, not you
But him whose taunts to me are as the froth
On a boar's hot fangs, I spurn, I spurn.' A raven flew
Like a black thought into the forest trees
Above and from the sun-green bracken Fionn stared
At its slow flight till like the sea-born breeze
Soughing through the pines below he heard
The voice of Diarmuid 'and if I no more
Come from the forest's jaws when yonder sun is red

O make for me a song, Oisin, lest men
That loved me once, wrong me when I am dead;
Friend, friend, a song of laughter and of tears,
Of the glad sunlight and the glittering spears
Of springtime rain, my fights and wanderings
Conquest and love and sleep.
Tell that the clay of age could never creep
Coldly around my heart nor did I sit
Mumbling at a turf fire half blind with rheum
And maybe groping feebly in the gloom
Finger the leather breasts of a dumb hag
That once, O Gods, was the white Grainne. Tell
That as the lightning dancing on the crag
I snatched the joy of very life from doom.
Farewell!'

III

*It is nightfall of the same day. At the river beneath Rath Ghrainne two boys may be
vaguely seen in the dim changing twilights. They are speaking.*

'I heard a trout leap
Under the bulrushes. I hear 't again.'
'No. That was a waterhen
Diving. But I am hungry. Let us go,
It is dark and the linnets are asleep
But we will waken at the dawn and steal
Upon Beann Gulbain with the hound and spear
And we will pull ripe blackberries and peel
Hazel nuts and hunt among the pines until
The sun is red. Let you now string the trout.'
'No, I will take the quicken rod.'
                                        'I will.
Hasten! Hasten! For the stars are out
And we must go.'
                    'Ainnle! as you stooped
To watch the roach hidden in the deep
Waters, I ran up to the crooked hill.
A rabbit bobbed out of a burrow and ran

Behind a tussock; a great hawk flew
Slowly above the alder tops and drooped
Into the night, then I saw torches creep
Along Beann Gulbain through the darkened trees.'
'It was the moonrise, maybe,'
                              'Hist!
Do you not hear a stir?'
                              'It is the breeze
Going about the reedy lake.'
                              'A cry?'
'I hear a curlew crying near the sky.'
'Look! Ainnle, look! The fairy mist
Is round us and the grass is wet. A fear
Is on me.'
            'Be quiet now. Here is the path.'
'Ainnle! What is that still thing in the night?'
'Where, Youngling? I can only see the white
Mushrooms i' the grass.'
                         'Upon the rath.'
'A misty willow.'
                   'But it turned and faced
Us, and when the moon shone out I saw'…
'It is some woman who has come to draw
A pitcher of water from the well. But here
Is the gap beneath the sallies. Let us haste!'

IV

From the rath upon the darkened height
A woman gazed into the lonely night.
Long since the lowing of the unmilked cows
And the faint bleat of lambs lost from their ewes
On cold grey hills had ceased. The far off cries
Of herds and hunters plashed i' grassy dews
With barking dogs, eager for the hearth fire,
Draughts of thick mead, the swine flesh and goat cheese
And sweet sleep by their wives, had gone. No stir
– Silence and night, only beneath the trees
The river flowing into silence. Once arose

The pattering of feet along a path
Mingling with childish voices sweetly shrill
As the river on the pebbles. 'O too fast
Ainnle, Ainnle!' floated beyond the hill.
The woman moved and listened as they passed
Moaning. Hour after weary hour went by.
The moon was clouded. Seaward, far away
Beyond the iron mountains, blackly cragged,
Beann Gulbain loomed.
Through the night the sound of feeble feet
Stumbled slowly, and a withered crone,
A rushlight in her claw-thin fingers, came
To the woman. 'Child, child, ye are wet,'
She muttered, hobbling near and in the flame
Saw for a moment the white face. 'Ye fret
And fret, poor child, and your two hands like stones
Lying in a cold pool. O childeen, come
From the damp air of night time. Those young drones
Are sleeping in their beds, and I stayed up
To find you.' But the woman sat there dumb
And motionless. 'O Grainne, I am old
And these poor withered paps once gave you suck
And those old arms have nursed you. It is cold
And wet out here.' She wailed, remembering
How she had seen the girlish Grainne gaze
Even as now on the cold silver moon
With slender fingers clasped round her white knees
Shadowed in her hair, a sleepy croon
Upon her lips; or on the summer days
Dance whitely through the daisies on the grassy lands
Of Temair where the great dewlapped cows grazed
Or stood in waters under elm trees
Staring. 'O child, I have a gold-graved cup
Brimmed with sweet milk. It was drawn by a girl's white hands
From the full udders of the red-brown cow
Grass-deep at lowing time and it is mixt
With honey sucked from clover by wild bees.
Come to the hot turves and put its taste betwixt
Your lips.' She wrung her hands and keened 'O dead!
O sorrow, sorrow this night, what will I do?

Child... child.' The woman slowly raised her head
And spoke 'Hush! I will go with you.'

Under the dark rafters candlelight
Flickered uneasily and the shadows woke
And moved about the floors on noiseless feet.
But the two women crouched by the flame
Upon the hearthstone knew not. A murmur broke
The stillness. 'O child, child, I'll put on peat
For the fire's ashy and you are wet and cold.
It is late, sleep a little, sleep, and I will sleep
Too' and as she slumbered Grainne leaned
Gently and covered her. 'The others keened
To-day' she thought, 'and someone would not weep,
Not weep. Their eyes are heavy and sleepy now,
Tired with the long sunlight and now the day
Is old. I will be quiet though it is old,
Though all these days are old, these quiet days
That flowing slowly seemed one summer's day
Undarkened nor disturbed by night and sleep
But even as shining waters calmed in deep
Pools, – and all the peaceful household hours
And the garden of grasses and of purple flowers,
The swarmy murmuring of the bees
Among the smoke-grey limes, the elm trees
Drowsing in the heat of the blue noon
Around the rath when the tired winds could pull
No leaf and from the grianan came the croon
Of spinning-women while the bundled wool
Turned on the droning spindle, sweet to me
As I sewed in the sunlight – and the prattled words
Of children and of waters at the fords.
Never on the hilltops shall I see again
Diarmuid and the antler-burdened men
Darkly speared against the saffron west
Homecoming. I will not look... it is some dream
That will go from me suddenly. No, no, no –
Yet I could almost weep that all these days
Are gone forever. Night from its flooded weir
Is rushing blackly on me and I must gaze

Into its gloom and I am full of fear.'
She leaned and slowly swayed,
'O little children of mine sleep, sleep, awhile
For it is night and all the birds are still.
O Connla of the dark curls do not stir,
The crickets sleep.' 'I see my children smile,'
She murmured, 'in their sleep. No, no, they are grown
And gone from me'... She drowsed then started up
'O Diarmuid, bitter it is
Through the long nights, lying awake, alone,
Stretching my arms to you in vain, in vain.
It was Fionn that hated you and betrayed
You. It was he pulled up the lonely tree
Of the tall windy nest and it is he
Brought sorrow and bitterness on me.
I am a woman, helpless, but if you were here
Diarmuid, you would rise up and catch a spear
And drive him though he were with his multitudes.
I do forget. Am I not beautiful?
Has not Fionn sought me lovingly all day?
There is sorrow more than a speary wound
To lure him to my lips and laugh and turn away.'
'O Diarmuid, my dark strong love, my love,' she crooned,
'We will go again, we will haste, to the lonely woods
Where the ripe red berries drop and quiet rain,
Where silver waters twinkle with swallow wings
And between the mountains every glen is full
Of sunshine and of little birds.
We will be there wandering and talking of love
By the streamy ways and putting off old thoughts
Of the dark moons in a little place of trees.
It is I, calling you, Grainne, the beautiful,
Grainne, the lonely.' She raised her proud head
As in the cold starlit air and the breeze,
She was shaken by old vehement
Joys till she forgot the summer days
Of a new hope, the quickening in her womb
That gave her heart sweet faintness and the throes
Of longed birth, the babes that sucked her paining breast
With soft closed lips and all the gentle kind

But I, who faltered long ago, must look
Only far-off as the desolate peaks
Forever gaze upon the Promised Land.'
He called forth mighty Josuë
Whose pale hands grasped the darkness like a sword
And gave him brasslike strength in fire and doom
To lead great Israel.
                         Then sadly voiced
He spoke to them with graver utterance:

'O men who are now aged in Jeshurun,
Following the lonely cloud of God
Across His wilderness, weep not. Rejoice,
O Levites, bear the Ark on gilded staves
Before the multitudes with bended song,
Timbrels and flowers that maidens gather, rich
With earth. O bear it as a king, the jewel
In his great shield against the sun; it gleams
Upon the blinded dwellers of the night
And they flee. Go down among their olive hills
With song and javelin, for your loud joy
Is bitter to them as strewn aloe blossoms,
Or the fox between their vineyard paths.
Bring in the corn and wheat, the bruised green oil
Bullocks, the gifts of kings and trembling doves
Of women that give birth, burned with all spices
To build sweet savours for the Lord. Go down,
For ye shall eat the wine-bulged grape and cloud
His praise in frankincense through Israel.
From the high mountains to the setting sun
In lands whose ancient voices are the sea
Your tribes shall grow as cedars. Mighty ones
In Reuben, lions of the race of Dan,
Rear your maned strength for the new days are yours,
The sorrow and exulting of our people
Whose wanderings shall pass away like smoke
Of desolated cities.'
                         He went from them
Quickly into the night. Only the lepers
Scraping their jewels of moonlight with a flint

And the last sentinels could hear the sands
That sighed around his feet. But in that square
Through all the star-long hours the patriarchs
Sorrowed.
                    Around them Israel lay close
In sleep. The young conceived in darkness
And aged men, the slaves of memory,
Still trod the sand, dragging onward the millstone
Of every mile or tricked by happiness
They lay deliciously in lush oases
On an unwrinkled belly, hearing a lioness
That raged among her cubs within the pit
And by the fig-trees where the locusts bite,
The mouthy camels stepping to the pool,
Crackle of driven whip and naked children
Plash in the green-palmed water. But the sick,
Dreaming the little doors of pyramids
Had shut them in, fled down unending steps,
Tore gum-cloths from their leaded genitals,
Tumbled as beetles in the scale of Judgment
And wakened in a sweat while trumpets blared
The dawn and multitudes outside were calling
'Wail, wail, for he is gone!'
                              And all that day
A little nation watched across the desert
Strange vultures passing into storm and God
Conceal the mountains of the Promised Land.

II

Thunder was throned among the desolate peaks
Above; but in a waste of rock that noon
Dazzled with undiscoverable metals,
Moses had toiled on, feeling in the far air
The eyes of unseen eagles watching him.
He came, at last, into an upper gorge
Where, huddled in the sallow beams of light,
The ancient trees clinging to precipices
Were juniper and, starting from a chasm,

Red-flowered as the mulberries that fed their silk
Twilled on the loom, tuned as a sounding-board
To sweetness, fashionable with sad tales
Of sylvan love and the tired hands that pull
The softer fruit of sleep; piled luxuries
From the world's wharf, told in the counting-houses
Of Tyre and three-harbour'd Sidon where men fish
For purple; the sea-scum of ambergris,
Breath-taking nacre from the sunlit sharps
Of ocean, Arabian flowers to sweeten,
To bestrew the beds of pale lascivious queens –
Not more luxurious Sodom and Gomorrah,
With smell of cooking, noise of gum and dish,
Until God's patient anger broke, angelic,
In burning brimstone, thunder and in might
That smote the lechery of young and old,
Finding in splint of painted furniture
And ewers of Egyptian glass, women
Whose bodies at the toilet, soaked in spikenard
And rubbed by the docile fingers of their slaves
In such obedience could despise the eye
Of Nubian eunuchs, holding their black toys,
And men, lust-maddened, taken in strange sin.
But the counted years wait with the unborn vulture
Upon the hills and Babylon, too, shall fall,
The proud, the mighty, be abashed and all
Her lofty ones crushed by a common wheel;
In ragged purple, as a harlot, she
Shall wail the instruments of her dead love.
Too soon the warnings of her gods are heard
At night in the rumbled temple. Capturings
Upon her terra-cotta walls are terrified
And in the mounting dreams of men take flight.
The voice of Israel that was despised
Calls through her populace in mockery
'Babylon, the mighty, is fallen, fallen, fallen!'
And vaulted echoes cry among themselves,
'O fallen, fallen!'
                    So shall her temples rock,
Her towers, her innumerable pillars, topple

Into the thoroughfare and all be still
As in the desolate regions of Gomorrah,
Where heron once had made her stilted nest
By the salt-glittering shores of the Dead Sea
Undesolated and blue, beautiful
Though there no tangled splash of net is heard
No children play.
                Beyond, the Jordan flows
Through gorges of wild palm: a narrowing land
Of wine and saffron. There on his rock of war
The ram still feeds the dreadful horn that locks
The gate of smaller cities. There in the grass
At early spring, the uncomplaining cows
Tethered by trickling milk can hear, far off
Happiness coming from the shelter, when
Night-dews are dropping through the olive leaves
Below.
       Amid the irrigated steps,
Orchards of sacred pomegranate, of prune
And citron, crouching on the granite hills,
He saw, changing or sullen in the sunlight,
Contemptuous with temple plat and tower,
A tiny traffic at each battlemented
Gate –
      the Cities of the Plain.
                Anguished
He gazed on that sun-guarded land, finding
No promise of his peace. But faint and clear
As a leaf-shadow where the young vine tends
Her house, scarce-breathed on the gentleness
Of distance, he could see at last the hills
Of Giliad. For there are little valleys
Odorous with balsam boughs and fair
As those ravines beneath the steeper pines
That hide Caucasian peaks of star-blue ice
Where the red cliffs of rhododendron are
A lasting sunset – milder those with sound
Of enshrined water and the merry chime
Of anklets, as the Gentile women spread
A dance beneath the almond-blossom trees

Concobar

Dectora, the sister of Concobar, King of Ulster, disappears into the Invisible Land. Druids are consulted and on their advice an unarmed stranger sets out to find tidings of her.

I

                                      Mighty the land
Of Concobar.
                 As when a sudden gale
Breaks light from rock to bracken, water-dug
By rain-black bogland or by cataracts
In the ground-rumbling glens, a dawn-fed eagle
Huddled upon a whistling cliff, half-winged
Against the rise of air, can fiercely watch
Through storm-red eye, the tops of every crag
Jutted like capes into the floating gloom,
The dismal sleeted tarns and branch-crashed forests
Herded by frightened elks, but far below the pinefall –
A land of vast rain-overshadowed plains
Stripped by the ploughing rivers, barren rocks
Warted with iron raths and wooded slopes
Changed into pasturing clouds, or grass-green fields
That follow swiftly in the yellow storms
Of racing sunlight as the miles of wheat;
Beyond the boglands glittering with water,
The purplish mountain-peaks against the world
Brooding with clouded thunder – and seeing at last
Suddenly that kingdom vanish into blackness,
With spike-reared wing roars on the blast, its mate
Eyried in storm –
                Yet mightier was seen
By spies the land of Concobar.
                      Seaward
It spread with milder shows of common cloud

Into the four winds from the sunned waters
Of Toraige, where the clan of boatheads bobbed
As seals around the reefs and gusts were white
Upon the wave-top, while barefooted girls
Worked in the ebb amid gleam-dripping weed
And men pitchforked all day the slabby kelp
Burning in fogs of sunlight down the shore
Of sea-lost bays to bless the night with fire;
Beyond, the rocky seagull-flighted headlands
Where in tough grasses, held in the wind's notch,
Spearmen of Concobar that had pursued
A phantom shadow legging from the glens
Have seen the pale green ocean, far below,
Sworded with wavering gold and sunset isled
Along the shoal of its forgotten cloud
And hurrying down into a narrow pinewood,
Skylighted, in the sedge of the starred glens
Took eels by hand or dreamed of white-maned waves
Neighing round Tirnanogue; remote sea-mountains
Behind Slieve League, where bolted by that cliff
Against the sky's edge, the wintering winds
Scream; in the east the hidden isle
Of Rathlin, where through blackening waves the sunlight
Lurches in icy spray along the crags
Even to the chill, dark, swan'd waters
Of Shruth-na-Mwaol.
                          Men told of other regions,
Remoter reed-lands hidden in the mist
Where the pale drift of ceannavaun
Hangs in the turf-black waters and no curlews
From Errigal will pick within that glen
Where stones have overgrown their shape; the coast
Of the wind's kingdom – there on the ultimate headlands,
Plunged in the moaning voices of the sea,
The pillar-stones of ancient warrior-kings,
That fell in their last battle with the gods,
Crumbled, there on the desolate capes of death
Long buried in storm and cloud.
                          His reign was bound

Along the powerful west by far-seen cairns
Across a stone-strewn plain. But hidden there
By her own land Maeve ruled, and that proud queen
Obeyed the gods in flight of birds or dream
Yet wrangled with their messengers by wheel-rim
Or carven pillar. In her iron houses
Riveters leaped from fire to blow, tightening
The pincers, in her halls by night and day
The roar of talking men, of argument,
The women stitching leather into folds,
The clattering of looms, the deep tense murmur
Of coming war. Far-off outlandish clans,
Routing the hills with cattle forays, saw
The mountain gap, where Dorcha, the usurper,
Mated fierce women of his tent, the sea
Narrow beyond the lower glen; cantreds
Beyond Slievemore, where in a sunset fume
Below the topmost crag the smelters work
By trough and gully; and the forest regions
No man has wandered, where Fearcu, the Hounded,
Rules monstrous clans; southward a stranger kingdom
For there, Curoi, last of the earthing gods,
Still barred and stepped his mountain-dwelling with
Atlantic cloud and thunder.
                   Fertile the land
Of Concobar.
               His power was furrowed in the soil
At dawn, and he had grasslands swept by rains
Of forests, pasture of the shadowed hawk.
In every field lambs tugged the slapdash dug
And milch cows lowed at noon. In summer time
Heather-brown honey dripped on mountain trees,
Sky-blue in tangled cords the giant salmon
Would drag the boathead down; the harvest came
With blackbirds to the wild-red-appled glens,
The breezes pushed knee-deep through barley, droves
Of swine tramped in acorn-fattened oakwoods,
And the shake of a nut-clustered hazel filled
Pattering vats.
           Fruitful his reign.
                The seed

And crop of those uncounted acres gave
To Concobar the might that poets praise,
For, brighter than his mass'd head-hair, the gold
Of those gigantic curls which glorified
His godlike loins. But when embossed by rage
And knobbed as baser metal by such strength,
Enringed, ell-ridged, the mounting vein had burned
From blue to angrier purple, that Queen Maeve,
Who guards her substance as the rounded hills
Of Connaught, could alone, scorning the help
Of serving-women, bring the champion low.
Seen from the rampart of his dwelling-house
Along a plain the herd of his prize bulls
Roamed, slow in summer as the sedging Boyne;
The plain of Emain Macha – named from her
Who stood, a goddess, tall and virginal
In sudden sunlight once, her hair unbound
As yellow brass upon her ample breast,
Before stern Duvtha as he watched his goats
Upon the crags above a brooked glen
Where scarce a magpie came or the late bud
Upon the thorn – and for a summer kept
His jealous bed until in a wayside camp,
Braggart with ale, he mouthed abundant praise
Of her long supple body and its speed,
Thence, dragged by mocking men before the King,
And she, grey-smiled, unwomaned by her love,
Though heavy burdened in her womb, outran
The uncharioted mares of Concobar.
Fainting beyond the bloodied dust, she dropped
Unshaped twins and from a distant cloud
A holy voice across the plains called down
The curse of Dana on the sombre host,
In their most dangerous hour at rath or ford,
Weakness of women in the childbed.
                                    Long
Had Concobar ruled all the land of Ulster
Twixt door and steamy cauldron; for his dead mother
Gave him, grown of her bone, in her fierce milk
Rage of forged iron to unseat his foes

And hurl their axles in the ravens' dyke,
And kinghood who in her wine-hot flesh had stayed
The love-sick Fergus with a woman's guile,
Unkingdomed him and throned her stripling. He,
Gathering strength as the ringed sap of oaks
Against the unskied storms, in after years
Gave battle on the ridges of the glens.
But Fergus fled into the rain-grey dawn,
White-lipped, slack-rein'd, with a score broken horsemen,
Grey phantoms galloping through greyer mist
All day across the boglands where no tree
Clouded a gleam of green in the ceaseless rain
And the Twelve Pins drizzled by the scudding west;
Too fiercely rowelling the jaded side
And floundering through narrow lakes of sunset
Blood-red against the reeds, unbridled with night,
They stumbled down a plashy glen of cromlechs
Stark in the starlight, and with starven cries
Clamoured against the sullen catch of Maeve's
High house, and she, armed queen among the rays
Of that wide threshold, scorning an outcast lover,
Succoured him, smiling; as the grinding stone
To the blade's sparky top he bent, long brooded
Vengeance and dried the faggots of unkindled hate.

So rose at length the great war in the north.

II

High in the whitish speckling of the dawn
Above undarkening bog the skylark's song
Thrilled dew out of the air and by the lakes
Ripple of osiers rustled. A light rain crossed
The grey gap of the wind and down in glens
New leaves of sally were stirring where hidden bees
Fat wintered honey and the streamlets swam
Around the inches, snow-blossomed by the sloe,
Into every creek.
                    Soon from the vales

Of Uladh came the joyous song of hunters
Calling above the drench of branches –

'Oro!

Brighten, bring the spears o' the Spring
And while the thrushes sing, good women sweep
Your floors, gather for your mats the morning reeds
And spin your wool: for over Slieverea
Hawked sunrays hover in the water-light
Beyond the grousy heather and herons wade
From river gravel. Who twist the heavy fish
With sallies peeled from Druim-da-leish, who steal out
To chase bewildered wings when they can hear
The mountain boar? O then the giollas whisk
Their beagles through the grass when the rain souses
The boughs of hazel and clambering the rocks
Climb nearer the drowsing eagle.

O the clean green spears
O' the Springtime!'

Far away their voices hunted
Along the sky while women at their half-doors
Sat turning their spindles. There on a fine day
Dectora, the sister of the King, hurried with
A song to spin an April dream on her distaff
And when at dusk the stars and corncrakes came
And candles were lit within her broidered grianan
She sweetly called:

'My women, tell old ranns
Of love around me, now children are abed,
And tell of kings, and warriors long ago
That loved.'

And to herself she said: 'I'll think
Of Sualtem, sworded he is, and his brave voice
Deep as a hound's and fierce: perhaps he rules
Beyond his galloping men to swerve aside and
Wonder about me. To-morrow I will bind
My hair with an ornamental brooch, come out
Into the sun and look on him, if he be king'd
Above his clan.'

And so they told
Old ranns their spinning-wheels heard long ago –

How Aongus sang and sorrowed for his love
A hundred years in a forgotten wood
Beside the Boyne and saw through leafy ways
Her mournful gaze and how they sweetly flew
By lake and hazelwood as sad white swans
Seeking an island creek where sallies hang
Above the floating stars, these ancient tales
Of love; how Etaun came from a sidhe-mound
When the dawnlight in the pale cold east
Drew the frail watery blossom through the bare
Branch of the sloe and gave her love to rouse
Grave Eochaid Baun with joy — but sorrow came;
Midir, her fairy spouse hid in Moymell,
Climbed like a falcon the ridge of the world
And standing in the royal dún, a proud
Tall yellow-bearded king from a strange land,
Claimed her, sweet-named, and her red hungered lips
Knew his, how unsighted by tears she ran to him
Murmuring fears and into their own past
They vanished from the cry of rowdy spears,
And staring crowds heard in the raftered air
Sorrowful laughter following them; tales
Of the great Danaan kings, of silver Nuada
Isled in a southern lake, of Lugh the proud,
The lonely, wandering through the woods; and Dectora
Knowing she was most beautiful in Ulad,
Laughed lowly and murmured with the beading rushlight
For companies who walked in rain-green woods
And raised her head with pride; for these were the days
When Deirdre, the sorrowful, was unborn;
She, too, in a stray glen would hear these tales
And cry for the old loves nor know herself
More beautiful and that cold woman would heap
Treasure of kings around her naked feet,
Raiment of grass-green wool and silver deerskin,
And lift a lonely jewel on her brow
To be a queen, nor how in torchlit Emain
Fearing her beauty more than Concobar
Between his leering spears and wild with love
She would know the sorrow of a leaning sail

Upon brown waters and, in her love and weary,
Trouble the piteous spears of goodly clans
And bring them death and Uladh's mighty kingdom,
Ruin, but these were the showery days of spring
When Dectora was beautiful in Uladh,
Dectora who was now proud and drowsed with ranns
Of the Sidhe and murmuring:
                                        'These are
Old stories of the woods and of old loves
And some, though kings, unhappy, unbeloved,'
Being half asleep.
                        But in the darker hour
Her bed growing strange with dreams of man, she got up,
Washed, bathed her flowers, then wandered, tall, long-legged,
Amid the royal ferns...
                              'Where has she gone?'
Her women came out into the grassy morning
Calling her and hawklings rose from the wood
Beyond them. Rushing down the rocky valley
They sobbed among the grumbling kerns and pulled
Their uncombed hair, moaning, 'Mavrone!
Mavrone!'
                  A man looked from thin trees, his thin eye
Green as a crow's and cried:
                                    'Wailing women,
At dawn the toilers in their stony furrows
Along a hillside saw your mistress borne in
A litter towards the south.'
                                    A tumult rose
For through the rumble of air a great car
Drove and a voice resounded through the glen:
'Who are these women keening by the woods?'
A soldier saluted from his post:
                                        'Arch-druid,
They wail for Dectora, the sister of the King!'
And on the heights of Emain Macha weapons
Flashed evil light far away.
                                    At darkfall,
Wrapped in their bratta, the chieftains assembled
And tows at the unsteady edge of the gusts

In the last light of day the darting winds
Rippled the loughs into trickle of silver.
But far beyond the gravel, sink of glen
And rain of ridges that came near, I saw
A haze of peaks that had been secreted
By day and drawn their paleness from the sea;
And all that night I dreamed of messengers
Too great for thought that hides itself in time
And all night heard the murmuring of new waters
That go within the tide.
                          At break
Of day I heard below the crags a stir
Of forest rains. I clambered down, unharmed
As runnels; there the gnarled clans of the oak
Gloomed with their green moons and the last boars
Sank in old mast and under midnight yew
Where no bird sleeps. Far down the rainy glades
At twilight in the slush the feeding doe
Eared silence and faded from the misting ways.
Sometimes as hawk along the birching daylight
I wandered with a troubled shadow. Sometimes
I snared the rabbit at my feet. I broke
Into a riper shade on the third day
Still seeking the lost Dectora; and there,
Among such leaves as none might pillage, I knew
The graspings of great nuts would stand unprized
By human eye. But I had seen for sign
The sunlight grassing near a thunder-oak
That aired young leaves –
                          I had come to the wood's
Green shore.
            At sunset a druid mist
Crept from the mountains like grey sleep. All night
I dreamed, and in my dream came to the ledges
Of early dawn and far below me lay
Another valley rivering through mist;
And as I wandered, One passed by with eyes
Brighter than sunlight on a hawk's poised wings
Above the bracken, and a frightened blackbird
Scuttered out of the brambles with guttural sobs.

I lay beneath a cairn all day and watched
The heather-darkened gleam of water-fire
Between the mountain-rocks, and far below
Weir-silver flowing through the sallow tops –
All day. But when the red-sea-dreaming sun
Was darkly wooed in the west, I sank
Below the curlew cry into the dew,
Into the misting valley, and I saw
A crumbling well where nine old hazels swayed
And in the waters the nine shadows. I
Flung as a thirsted stag the louder leaves
Into the darkness and drank where the waters
Stumbled upon the stones. A river flowed
Beyond that sacred well into the night,
And with its hazel murmur, dark in wisdom
I crossed the fiery mearing of the sunset.

Because the mind has many changes, time
Has shut my memory. I cannot tell
The day that I had hidden in the heather,
Storing the honey of thought in the sun
And dreaming of Uladh. But rain-purple ridges
Came nearer and the air was welled
With smallness of sun-hidden larks. I knew,
O Concobar, that iron is unwrought
When the last gods withdraw themselves from earth
And sky, but those who dream of them again
Shall be the holders of our darkened mind.
But now grey berries of evening grew in the woods
And the cuckoo of the softness had left
His branch to a low soughing; I made stir
And went with starlit brows into the night...
The river slipped the hollows of its echo
And poured the dawn from dark-green-wooded rocks
Into the Valley of the Wandering Voices
Where many sang:
                    'In the ring of day
I was above the flighting of the clouds
And saw the dewy, dark-blue pinewoods reel
From mist below.'

VI

Voice of the stranger rose. The red stone eyed him
From the breast of Concobar.
                                'As a kittiwake
Driven, in sleet from two thousand feet of cliff
With feeble screams, bewildered by a tumult
Of seaward mountains silent in the night,
I fled in a dream beyond the soundings, the forelands,
Into our forgetful past. There, King after King
With white-bronze-hammered shield that seemed to mourn
Their misery, despair, led the defeated
Fomorian hosts, mocked by iron harp-note
By far-off laughter.
                        Vision hurried me backward,
Vision hurried me onward. I saw in confusion
The Battle of Moytura. I heard a clamour
Of shoring waters surge below me: a King
Passed, mantling the tide, tip of his spear,
A sea-green star. Within my vision, appeared
The demi-gods, Midir the Proud, Iuchar,
Bore Derg, clapped in thunder, Diancecht,
Erc, Len. I counted the assembly of those heroes
In wars, too terrible for the annals of men, as
Leaning on sword-hilts, their great paps dark as warts
Within the gleam of breast, their scrota bulged
In shadow.
                Vision hurried me on, vision hurried me back.
Out of the tidal glimmer, Mannanan rose
Again from the shallows of bladder-weed, his cloak-hem
Rolled slower than the lengthening billow lifting
A curl of incoming spray on Carrig-na-rón.
There I saw Losrem, fierce-born from the womb
Upon a cold flagstone, among his attendants
Greasing a targe of leather bull-hide, there,
Balor – his baleful eye was fleshed with sleep,
Cuoch, the harper, fretted by gull-cries, Tethra
Whose nameless sea-children move in clumsy flight
Slower than bull-seals carried on the billows.
Dream within dream.
                        In a confusion of brightness,

Appeared the Tuatha da Danaan, godlike.
Their brows were glibbed with overlocks, their bratta
Dyed sunlight from the ample ochre vats.
Ready with spears, their gilded shields embossed
And graven – with a woman's name.
                                        Enemy
Clans marched with lifted spear, coarse bratta fastened
By massive brooches of iron, in each brooch
A rough-hewn stone of eager fire. They held
Flat blades. Far off I spied another clan
With tussle of head-manes loading their rough shoulders,
Aprons of hide, septs from Tory, half hidden
By wash of tide and knobbled as their cliffs.
North of the shelving shore, clans with flails
To thresh the iron crop of battle, clans whose
Outlandish weapons were lean with hunger. Far
Away I saw the billow-riding champions
In whistling mantle shaped from the glossy skin
Of sharklets, damp with brine. Flotilla
Of men at the thwart; low as cormorants,
They ruddered their way to shore:
                                        The Eye of Balor
Stared through the freezing clouds. Losrem,
His locks unfluttered by the fatal ray,
Lifted his war cap, crying:
                                'Beware, beware,
The blanching of the moon!'
                                        Gobain, the armourer,
Heard clangour. Sparks on his sooty skin, he sprang from
The anvil horn, plunged the hiss of a blade,
Scarce forged, into sudden steam of a cauldron,
Then, as he gored a moaning way into the darkness
A thickness stood before him. When the rattle
Of blade was flung back by his answering shield,
He hurled his pike through quick expanding echoes,
Caverned himself and grasping his adversary,
Strangled him to a scream.
                                Far off, a bale-fire,
He saw the eye of Ruadan: two shafts
Pierce deeply through the gaps of breasting wolf-skin

Tearing the tender pap. Backward he staggered
Fearfully swaying like a charioteer
Tilted by speed above the plunge of fetlock,
Thudding of track, then doubling his hurt arm
He raised his blade and, with a heaving groan, cleft
The Fomor through the groin.

                    Out of the night
Came Brifé, the mother of slain Ruadan
And crouching like a she-wolf from the forests
Above her dead, she raised so long a howl
Into the night that distant warriors hushed
Their weapons and looked at one another, gray
With fear; while Goibniu by a flooded river
Washing the heavy gouts stained black in the moonlight
From his deep holes, trembled.

                    Uala, hearing,
Outleaped his leapy shadow from rock to rock, but
Luoch cast down his angled harp, sworded
Himself. They fought against the defiance
Of their own breathing; nethers close
As lovers on the first night.

                    Within the valley
Heroes lay warring against death, eyes closed,
While Diancecht, the druid, with wonderful hands,
Laid on their burning brows the drip of glass
Grown i' the chill of woods and poured softness
Into their wound-holes; and from under the boughs
Slumber came mothering through the dew.

                    Once more
The Eye of Balor stared – a vacant moon
Risen above the sky-line. Midir aimed spear.
Gathering a mile from the leather thong it soared, then
Falconing over a tilt of lake, it swooped –
And, moaning, the unmooned monster sank into
Nothingness.

            As the rock-beaten rain
Comes lately, dragging night, so the Fomorians
Attacked a press of cars. Axles went awry,
Rims cracked. But the fugitives had changed
Into a herd of elk, plunging from river bed

Through forest, tossing back the waves of leaves
With swimming antlers more than five miles
Beyond.
        Their King fled through the pathless gloom
Between cloud-oozing defiles, his seven wound-holes
Pursuing him like a wolf-pack in the raining
Darkfall, then fought his rival. So a boar would
Charge when he heard the quicker baying of hounds.
Then crashing through the leafy forest lairs
Of Liathdruim-na-Lir, he lurks, hearing
The scenters scrubbing closer; unthicketing,
He turns with snarl of tusk.
                    A voice cried:
                            'Where

Is Mannanaun MacLir?'
                  And others clamoured
That sea-name:
                'Mannanaun, O Mannanaun!'

Then dark against the sky a form
Arose. As when our fishermen are blown
With the last light of day towards a fiord
Of Lochlinn, tossed on the billow tops, they see
Between the storm-rents of sails and cordage
A headland loom from the east, the blue-haired god
Walked through the waves; he held in readiness
A brace of javelins and on his forearm
A shield of copper like a blood-red moon
Clotted in sea-fog. At every stride of his,
The shore changed to brine and the Fomors became
A raft of tern, a row of rocks.
                      Vision
Of good and evil hurried me, hurried me on. I
Saw, then, the ray of Lu lengthening in the dawn.
The clouds rolled backwards as it hurled the void
Of gods into the void.

VII

Beyond the bogland where, at a step, the heather
Blackens into turf, I wakened, quick-eared
As a leveret and heard outside the pale
Of a wood, half tuning to the blackbird note,
A voice come sweetly:

       'Pleasant it was in Uladh,
Choosing the wool in a comfortable grianan,
When floor had been strewn at an early hour with fresh reeds
And mats of fern from Derrybawn, to hear
Rain in the thickets, the sparrows picking grain,
Croon of the quern at the doorstep and the kerns
Grinding their gaffs to string the self-flung salmon
Above the weir at Cloon.

       Pleasant the hoof-knock
Of the foals beneath the Dún, gleaning
Of harvest. Poets came with rann, with staff
In their coloured cloaks along the hill-paths. Supper
Steamed at the red o' the sun: plenty:
A hero's portion, ale in the crumpled horns
By waxlight, double-stops of music to pluck up
Stories of long ago.'

      A woman walked slowly,
Sun-lighting from the birches.

       'Brightness,' I stammered,
'Over the water that seeps at this early hour,
Singing, Woman of the Western Sidhe,
Having no grief...'

      As I bowed, she answered, smiling:
'I am a woman of the kindly Gael,
An exile still in the hidden country where fruit
And flowers are gathered at the same time. You see me
In a vision. Far away, I am longing now
For Uladh, dew on the run-the-hedge, rain-drops tipping
The barley, household clatter, dish-washing, pot-wallop,
My women caught up in the arms of song, as I was,
At night when the last smouldering brands had left
The shadows alone.'

     Her words were softer.

       'Tell them

I shall come back after the salmon have gone down
The Falls of Assaroe. This bigness that shares
My breast, slowing my feet, is the son of our god.'
The stranger bowed to the throne.

'Concobar, much as been hidden, for the mind is thronged
Within the cast of thought.'
The stranger had vanished.
                              But the chieftains
Half stirred out of their intoxication
For in the south the Wave of Cliodna slowly
Lifted and the royal shield, awakening with
The long surf-thickened roar of the ocean,
Thrice rumbled danger to the throne
And on the heaving breast of Concobar
The precious stone from Balbec bickered, waned.

The Music-Healers

*'This now being so resolved among them together, come women and maids, wise men
and poets, reciters and all various professors that were in the fort, and into the house
where Cuchullin was they entered. Cathva also, with Concobar's harper and foster-
brother of the sweet strains, making melody, and music. Ferceirtne, too, being on the
couch beside Cuchullin, guarding and beguiling him.'*

I

Westward for many nights the routed army
Fled under the flare of pitch with rattle of wheel-rim,
Yoke, car-pole, closer where a woman sat
With staring eyes behind the tilt of the weapons
That knew their passing cantreds as the marron
Whistled them onward and the pillar-stones
Loomed – each like a fabled king; until that long ridge
Where the Brown Bull – whose horns had brought the Great War –
Climbed into cloud, was nearer. From gap after gap,

The wests blew in, just lit with brine. The woman heard,
League beyond league, the misery of harps.

Soon in a glen of scoria,
Pit-falling, furies of ill-fire sprang up
To wrestle with the night. Before his divisions
Were camped, Maine Olgarech strode, stood
Before Queen Maeve.

      'Half of our men, land-loose,
Stumble to mountain-doors with wild halloes,
Unused to the emptiness. In the south-west,
Erc and his tumblers go down the slopes, terror
Biting their heels. Son o' the rock leaps on
From height to height, while triumph with burdens
Lashes to Emain Macha. Beyond us, only
The salt, unalterable air!'

      Fergus,
With exiled brows, spoke then:

      'Command in the west
Has scattered to the islands. Screeching, shrills
Of the seagulls blown by the rabble of stories
Knock back from Knocknaree. The lobsterers,
The cockle-men who left their daily pickings
For the inland war, the men I loved, have fallen.
I mix with nothing around me. Heap cairns midway
The sky and hill. Let cloud, snow-eagle, pass,
Goffering sails below. What legend is left
To cut on stone?'

      'War-stricken men,'

      Cried Maeve,
'Who have outrun my messengers, cast off
The weight of battle, eased your shoulder-blades, reddened
By iron. Already your wives, your servants, have prepared
The heroes' portion for you. All's on the broil.
Quick to the surrender, spurt, flow.
Get me a hardier breed. Forget that our armies
Were thrown about by their Laeg, trick-driver o'
The North, when his eight spokes were shielded in speed
That snaffled, left, right, as he circused among
Them – shank to leg – while that young acrobat,

Cuchullin, changed into a juggler, encircled
By swordlets. Ring-a-ruddy with their fresh
Supply of crania, the bob-and-wheel
Went widdershins.'
                        At night in her simple shelter
The Queen remembered how she had driven one day
Across the plain and seen another horse-car
Come towards her. The woman-driver stopped. She wore
A leaf-green mantle. Two plaits were bound about
Her head: a third sunbeaming to her knee.
Maeve recognised that woman from the sidhe-mounds:
Fedelm, the prophetess, heard the future in
Her warning voice,
                 'I see the northern armies
Through a blood-red mist, weak from the curse of Macha.
Within his fort Concobar lies, Coscraige
His son droops, weak-legged as a winter fly. The son
Of Dorcha crawls in Rath Aerthier. The champion,
Celtar Mac Uthecar, mopes at Dun-le-glas,
Fergus Mac Rory rouses his army chiefs
In vain.'
        'What of the coming war?'
                         Pale-faced
The Prophetess had turned. Above the rein-strap
Immortal hand was raised. Her lips were red-struck.
'Setanta, lad of Lu, will defend by himself
The Gap o' the North
               I see, I see, the fallen
Through a blood-red mist.'
                   Swift car was speck.
Queen Maeve remembered that story of the past.
Ochill, King of the Western Sidhe, Bove
Bearg, the ruler of the Southern Sidhe,
Had banished their quarrelsome swineherds from royal sty
And midden. Throughout the ages, that bad pair, Root and
Riccney, had fought in many a phantom shape: two
Elderly ravens, heard croaking somewhere nor'ard
Of Cruachan, then sou'west, then croaking from
The Sidhe-mound at Feven. Soon they became
Blod, Bled, caverned water-beasts under the Suir,

The tidal Shannon. They surfaced, yawing fire
Across the eskers, the invers, changed their shapes
Again, sharp, Thin Edge, fighting in the foggy
Fields. Men could hear at darkfall ding of metal,
Randan of conflict. Stag-like, with antlers locked,
They pushed year against year. Sky-dragoning,
They weathered the midlands from Slieve Bloom. Men saw them,
Two whitenesses that stopped all going, sank
The axle-tree in snowdrift. Big to small,
They ruffianed backward in time, until they wriggled
As water-worms; one in the well men call Glas Fead
Near Cooley, the other in the spring of Garad
Uarán at Cruachan. Their names, then, Crimnious, Timmius.
Maeve pondered to herself:
                              'I heard the tiny
Whimpering of the worm, then dipped a pitcher
Into the well, caught Timmius, saw him changing
In hue from green to purple, to black. The glug-glug
Was gone, the pitcher dry. The swineherds grew
From puny to huge again, tried on ill-fitting
Fantasies, pick-me-ups of air, new twists
Of anatomical variety,
Glottis, liver and lights, obscurer glands
Until they were completely bollocksed. At last
Their hate became prize-bulls, Findbenna, Pride
Of Connaught, roaming the plain, a mighty sire
Among my cows. His rival, the Brown of Cooley,
Was haltered by my ranchers. They drove him by green road,
Blue road, brown road, after our army had crossed
The Border that I might graze him in my pastures.
So why should I fear now that get of a god
Slipping along a car-pole, showing off in
His trewes the heavenly bulge of his father, pretending
To light o' loves the upshot is his own?'

Armed with a spear, she went beyond the smouldering
Stones of the cooking pits, and leaving the last
Look-out out below, climbed up from ledge to ledge,
Came under a wood topographers have never
Notched on a stave. A wild boar glinted past her

With sidelong glance out of an upper glen.
Three times, three times, on high, she called to the distant
Daughters of Calitin, dealers in omen
And spell, who set the wisps of madness alight,
In the domicile of reason, to revenge her, felt the
Beat of their pins. Hallucinatory figures
Of coming-and-going, the Furies taloned, bore
Her into the unknown world. When the chill
Of dawn had brought her body back and she saw
The broken spear-shaft lying at her feet,
Maeve wept.

II

In that ill-lighted house among the mountains,
Before dream-fighters came to tilt his feet
And the skilled women lap his head, Cuchullin
Brooded on the third day, for he had heard
Storm break about the anvils that have forged
Themselves, nor could he find the sweets of metal
That iron hides in the last sound. In vain
Did men turn air to thought and women patch
The fire that he might know the comforting
Of ear and eye. In vain did Gennan turn
His wonder to untruth:
           'Lift the great horn,
For day has laid a burning blade
Upon the waters, thunder no more sounding
Under the capes.
        I looked into the west
And the claw had gone.
          But I saw blue-men heave
Their backs in struggle, for they bore a seawoman
Who prized the very shore. Bled, bled by scale
Or fin, they fought for that unreal breast
Because of her comb-breaking hair, and I
Could hear her shrieking thinly for the sea.
These things I saw from Malinmore.
           Drink, drink,

For ale is clearer at the sunset. Thought
Returns, but far beyond the lift of sail
The Reddener still burns upon the wave.'

Cuchullin stirred.
                        'The rivets are red-hot
And iron swims the trough. We live by hate
And what we hold. See! See, the black men draw
The roaring damper that the inner fire
May cook my instruments and thunderbolts
Of war.'
                    'O do not listen to the door
Or creaking bolt. Dear, I am Emer, your
Own wife. Three days these companies have played
To entertain your fancy and they are tired.
They drink the unheathered ale that has been taken
From stone and do not know whether to laugh
Or moan.'
                    But every chink became a fife
And blew itself in that ill-lighted house
Until he got the tune into his nod
And toe.
            We dance, we dance from the rock to grass
And hold our hands together as we pass
The mountain heather, the rock, the grass...
                                    'He has heard
Maybe, the daughters of Mainey,' she said,
                                        'For they,
Being lazy in the house, grew crazed together
And ran into the dew, and now they dance
Forever in the hazes of heather.
                            When she
Was young, my grandmother heard them at her door,
Dancing out of Dunlewy.
                            Alas that he should hear that reel,
For it is a foolish thing and put a stop
To many a fine wheel!
                        But I hear in the house
My women catching as they iron the clothes.

Hush now.'
         'I have seen Cerb.'
                  'O golden top-knot!'
'Apple that breaks the branch!'
                'I know an herb
To cure a common ill.'
           'The night is cold,
O let me in!'
        'She took that secret plant.'
'She hid it next her skin.'
            'He was my darling
Among all men.'
         'Happiness comes and goes.'
'The starlings leave the glen.'
           'Ah Cu,
Listen, for they sing and here is one
Who, knowing we are far from court, has brought
A rustic song.'
        'O I will leave the island
Where they haul the fish to cut them on the stone
And leave their guts, a goodly due
Under the beak of seamew, cormorant
Or scavenger.
        Then I will lift a sail
And lean towards Gortahork where many a torc
Lies hid in the grass and cold dark water
That never saw the sun – and find the woman
Who put her hand upon my heart and take
No word but, close as hole in corner, lie
With her again, wherever be her bed.'

Ferceirtne sang:
        'As I went far, O men,
From Carrowmore I heard the seagulls cry
And trail the clumsy feathers of their young
Around that rock where banished Malachi
Was swollenheaded by such pain, he cracked
The bladder-weed to get him wine.
           No slop
Or poultice now could draw the fiery blister,

Too big in gullet for those parching lips
Were thicker than his thumbs.

                             He dreamed of a ship
Hulling the waves, lashed heavily with cask
And broaching, while his wife, with dull red locks,
Lying at his feet, began to sigh and bare
Herself again that she might squeeze out for him
The last tittle of her milk.'

                          Some cried
Or laughed because the ale was strong. But Emer
Turned to them.

                'These are sad tales
That hold the fire, and there is no song can mend
A woe that had so sorrowful an end
Too long ago.'

              She was uneasy
Thinking how men have been too long in pain
Or love and said to them that they should sing
Of peace in the heart, seeing she had so much
To do with grief. Before a head could turn,
A young man had come in although the door
Was barred. His voice was kind and sly; he gave
A riddle to the old.

                 'Men pare the nails
Of that beast at the root, for the sacred boughs
Are a well of light. But when the moon has passed
Behind the sea and unseasonable apples
Ripen, O gather them at midnight, lest
The eaters from the air have swifter wings.

I lie on the dark beds of song. I warm
Myself at the fire before a pot is on,
But in the summer I will walk through grass
Into the west, my ear to the little cuckoo
Over the grey hazes where seven isles
Bramble the waters.

                   There will be clouds on Nephin,
Higher than the ram may clamber to the grass
Where the loose stone-wall topples in the gap
Of the wind.'

              'Then make a song, for one

Is sorrowful here this night.'
                                And to a string
He sang these pleasant words:
                                'There was a king
That had nine lands and ale outside the door
And he had happy pine-lands to snare the song
Of birds. So far below the showery peaks
And falling gleams of water, shouting men
Climbed out and drove the cowering eagles back
With empty claws.
                        And they looked down and told
Of twigging tops and hazel ways where sunlight stays
All day, and heard the early cuckoo calling
From the green brink of May.
                                And so that King
Grew great of heart with his extravagance,
And hearing far below the watery noise
Of dancing branch, the cry of summer bird
Around the isles.
                    He called for every comer
Whose wandering words, much like the mountain herds
Of sheep, are lost in quiet days, to spill
Their mellow praise into his cup and dropped
Asleep, when thrushing woods were yellow-topped
With sunset.'
                    'I'll have no music pass my head.
What is reality, since everything
That had been hidden up the mighty Sleeve
Is turning inside out? I hear, I hear
The stockmen, stonemen, listening behind
That door.
                There is a sound can change the mind
Another – and it puts a treacherous hand
Upon the bolt.'
                    'O do not answer him,
Cuchullin, for they say he has a foot
In every household, big or small, who runs
As riddle can. Have you not clapped the wall
Back, when the skipping-rope was quicker than
A head or heel to cup the acrobats

From Greece?'
        'Run up to him sweet voice
Jostle among their praises, for such a man
Can whistle a married woman to his bed,
Having the blackbird throat.'
          'Listen to that,
Cathva! His mind is near and a sharp tongue
Has touched the shaky tooth I know so well,
Let everybody go to bed that I
May nurse him, lest the fearful dream come back,
For never was I jealous of my husband
Until to-night.'
      After the company
Was gone, she sat in patience. But the fire
Fell with a sound that angered him.
          'I hear
Old thunder rutting in his Atlantic cave.'

And near her heart she sighed:
        'O little Hound,
That never more will know the running gleam,
Dew of the morning-tide on shores of grass,
Lie down and slumber for the things of storm
Walk with blind eyes within the staggering wood.'

But he half-hearing said:
        'There are no stags
In the wood. I hear a lonely woman
Crying in the night out there. They cut
Her name, fourfold on stone, for every wind
To spell.'
    'Come back, dear mind, master of eye
And word, come back.'
        She prayed until her heart
Went wild...
      'Now I could almost laugh, seeing
That I must have the sweet craft of a woman,
Enticement on my lips as though I drank
Oldness of wine before bed, yet when there is laughter
The rafters will grouse, and if there are women

Come to the house, it may be they will turn
Away, if a man is ill and there is no herb,
No foolish herb that could be pulled under the full moon
In the welling hour, for cure... And a wild one ran out
Into the rain, for, being childless, she grew tired
Of the long hall and the wet smother of smoke
Upon the flags... And, though I disremember,
She might have come upon the airy people
Who help the young in their trouble... Yet having many
A word run to my head I know the court-women
Whisper that I am proud because I have
Fine clothes. But their eyes will never take him away
From me. No... no... no. How will they take him,
Seeing I am his wife? Nor will they make him
Forsake me. Had I not fought them with a dagger
Who gazed in his face and thought him least, when Briccriu
Held feast and the wine was braggart. But he, being sick,
Grew haggard. I have been dutiful to him
And silent... and I know that sorrow like mine
Can cruddle a mild-white skin, for all
The raddling of the high cheekbone.'

        Her tears
Had hidden him.

      'Cuchullin, it is I
Without lie, though I cry. Remember Emer,
How she would dream herself too brave, although
I seem her shadow now. O grief, his eyes
Gaze through me into the roomy darkness
As though he never knew me. Come back to him,
Come back, dear mind, to the grey-green and blue pupil
That stand so wide apart.'

       She turned
And whispered to herself.

        'I would cross the mearing
When shadowy strikers have wearied of the flame
By the weir, I would run within hearing and call
A few men from the glen, for to-night I am fearing
For him I love. O I would cross the mearing
Though many a stone fall.'

        But he looked up

And said:
> 'When mountain-rocks are red with bracken,
> The fox may run unseen!'

And she:
> 'Women
> Who know the little mists of Lackan, wean
> Their children in the chilly sun and go
> Indoors, when the wooding hawk has dropped
> Below the hungry hill.

O we will hurry
> South where the squirrels run a mile through boughs
> From isle to isle, and in the hazels
> The sunlight dances with green heels.

We will be happy,
> For there the cuckoo is whiling over the waters
> An hour from dawn and in the sapping woods,
> When summer has gone, the apples in their soft falling
> Ripen the grass again.

And there
> Through the rushes no stepping-stones go.'

He shook
And cried.
> 'Bear sun in every speckle, hawk!
> Cross water by no ford!'

But she, remembering
Her dread, began to comfort him again.
> 'Happy was I and the women sorted wool
> Until the twilight took the seven hues
> Away, but candle brought them back again.
> I went down to the river by myself
> And saw a sedging moon. It was the night
> That I had heard your name for the first time
> And someone said though I would not believe him,
> That when you were a boy you left the playgreen,
> The school-war, and you ran a hundred miles
> To guard big Cullan's house and so became
> The Hound of Ulster.'

Then she thought:
> 'There is much good in lullabies, and I
> Will make one now to quiet him! —

Little Hound,

Little Hound, I weary of seeing the days
Come and go, the women who talk at nightfall
When you are away with the men and every sound
Is a catching of my breath. I weary myself
And I vex my heart with its longing. O would I were she
Who went after dark, without fear, without slip
Over the weir of the otter, with open red lips
To run and cry through the grass as a misting plover
On her wild one, her lover.

                      O would we were as free,
For he stood beside her cry and carried her with laughter
Through fluttered woods and the glens without a name,
And married her in a pleasant land where they
Lived happy ever after.

                 Sleep, sleep, little Hound,
And sleep now, for drowsily under Slieve Fews
The heavy dews creep on the bough, while I weep,
While I weep. Let you yawn and grow weary
And slumber. I would take off my shoes and move
On bare feet through the house lest he wake,
Lest he wake. I would lie down beside him and give
My own sleep. For clearly I see now the morrow,
Grey dawn on the lake, and sorrow with me, while around
Every island wings drip.'

               Then in despair
She whispered.

          'He does not know me,
What can I do, who am a lonely woman
With no child of our own to please his knee
But sit down here and cry poor eyes out
Lest any illness take him far from me?
How will they ever know I lie awake
In bed, hearing the wind become a river,
Crying for a little thing, a childeen of our own.
Why should they all have children?... I am
A lonely woman and he does not know me,
And what, now, can I do?'

              'The smoke of prayer
And knife is low upon the stone, but far
Inland, the nations drive the haltered bullock

That adoration steam upon the altar
Our fathers raised.'

                    'Ah, Cu, I am to blame.
What is my grief to yours?'

                              'All yesterday
I fought the waves until a demon-smith
Went by with rivets in his mouth. O then
I saw beyond my hand a dim red sun
Burn on the anvil of the water-storm,
Alone.'

              'Now I will ready the fire,
Put bread and ale upon the table, dear,
And a tall light, lest the idle servants
Come – and we will eat.'

                          'The gods look down
Somewhere or other, – the ridge of the world –
Whenever, wherever the smoke of a cooking pot
Drifts out from isle to isle.

                        Men double the back
For the yearly thrift of rye. They wive and rear
Children and die. But should they squabble for
A spit of rock; that blow is handed down
Because the story-tellers have so little
To do.'

            As she went
About the smouldering shadow, he said:

                                        'I
Have dreamed too wildly and there is no room
Can hold more than a foolish thought. Seeing
That bread is at my elbow, candlelight
And simple things, a heavy waterish jewel
Some man has kindled in itself because
He wished. There has been too much crying
Inside my head. The wise have seen the fires
Going down and have gone to bed. I am
Tired, but they left an aching in my joints
That will not let me rest.'

                        Her busy heart sang louder:

                                        'He is freed.

We will be happy for they say that the evil

Will empty at dawn and go into the air.'
The bread fell from his hand.
                                    'No, No,
I have been wrong. The minds of many men
Make greatness, take fire and tumult of their dreams.
A spacious land is ploughed by sun and rain;
The seasons are their yoke. But when the breeze
Runs with the barley like the steady pouring
Of grain into the copper, jealousy
Must keep that delicate shore.
                                    Alas! They grind
Again the implements and thunderbolts
Of war, who have despised their strength, thinking,
If quietness come like a summer shower
To idle in the tops of the woods, that peace
Has mellowed in the vats of all that land.
Yet peace is the counting of ungathered wool
Along the crag, sound in the little bay
Where sails may flounder and men in a sunny hold
Forget to dream of wealth beyond the wave;
Slow days; a woman burdened in her womb
Might wind and rewind from the bobbin, weave
On rackets of the loom a winter cloth
Piecemeal and dream it cast-off in the gloom
With wear and tear, before the last fiery threads
Of parting wings break in the west.
                                    I hear,
I hear within the darkness many an axe
Unhafted by the timbers we have known.
Hazel and hollywood fall down, for song
Is hedged no more. Only a naked wind
Is shivering by the river.'
                        'You are cold
And will not eat. See, I have drawn a faggot
Across the fire-top.'
                        'As I lay in camp
Last night, I dreamed that a great maggot came
Out of the river to attack me. But
The famous strength that has afflicted me
Because it is not mine, sprang into fury

That hacked and hacked the monster into pieces:
But all those pieces were a living brood
And each one wriggled, hurrying by itself,
Into the suck beyond. O then I knew
Man may destroy all things but war. And I,
Who feared no danger, was afraid.'

                        A third voice
Spoke in the hall:
                 'Cuchullin, why do you dream
In an ill-lighted house where only the smoke
Of hillside twigs and damp can fight old wars
In wintertime? This is the melancholy
Of a lovesick youth who has tied his feverish hands
To the bedpost because of an affliction
That makes him weak. I hear the men
Of Connaught marching and the rock-hid spies
On the stagbeetle's track.
               Fergus MacRoy
Has fled again to that stone-fort where wits
Are crazed by the skirling and whirling of seagulls
Pale as their droppings, Conal ridden out
With seven hundred horse. A storyteller
Has seen the brand-new fires that banqueted
At Emain – and the bedsticks of a king
Beneath the Black Hag's pot.
                 Ride, ride with me
Into our camp, for here is treachery
In every corner and a creeping sound
Of body-knives below the skirting. Tallows
Flare in the dún and the doors are barred.'
                    The Fury
Was treading air.
             'O listeners in this house,
Tiptoe upon the yewen-seasoned floors
Lest a foolish crack cry treason!'
                  'Have you forgotten Niav
Who warmed the left side of your camp-bed, cut
Her hair that she might swagger among men,
Laughed as she straddled the car-pole at every bump
Of hub, knowing that her little hand at night

Was closer on your thigh than the great weapon
All feared but she? Have you forgotten Niav
Who loves you still?'
                              'The voice is older than
Your words, harsh as an iron sheet.'
                                            'You have
Betrayed me by your fears.'
                                    'Why are those eyes
Bloodshot and furious?'
                              'Your cowardice
Has dried my tears.'
                        But Emer beat the air
That was tormenting him, held candle up
Because the grey-green and blue pupil stared
So wide apart.
                  'Why are you fighting sleep,
My pet, when I would keep you from all harm?
This night is dangerous, but O to-morrow
You will be better. Cathva whispered me
That Calitin might cast his ugly daughters
Upon the air, each one alike in claw
And dug. Three years they were in Babylon,
And they went down into that fiery shop
Where Vulcan works, braining his horrible
Designs; and with his help they taught man how
To shape the instruments and thunderbolts
Of war.'
            The phantom mocked
His drumming ear.
                        'Will he not dare to look
On me? Will he not turn from any comfort
Though Connaught men hurdle the livestock, cook
Their mess by day and fill themselves with talk
Of fabulous conquest? Will he run into the air
Bare-necked who was a dreaded man, before
The stitchers with their comic chalk have yoked
A shirt too big for him? Must I go bare,
Pleasing a common eye, forget a taste
Upon my tongue that cannot sport again
With him all night.
                        O now let war take top

And cut, the hillside camp give messages
That light can carry, men dig deeper than
The mole they blind; Nature replenish all
And habit vanish from reality –
Fantastic as famine that sleeps i' the weak sun;
So when the defeated are gone, abandoned women
May gape at doors that hold a dreadful sight
And, for all their fear, have rape to bed, before
The fires upon their hearth are trampled out.
O now let war take high and low!'

       Beware!
Though we are air, poor air, though we pass
And the mountain grass cannot stir, O beware!

Who is it that is crying out there all night?
Is there no lover's sleep but I must dream
That music crossed the ford although the blowman
Was lost?

    O Cuchullin, beware, beware
The knottings of her hair! No man has knife
Can cut them to the worm.

       'What are your names?'
We are the three who lay in Glenmacnass,
And though we have no bodies now, believe
That we are men.

     But Emer said to him:
'O do not listen, dear one, for the moon
Is dangerous at night and when a small cloud
Comes over it, they say the chatterers
Hide from the glint of wet fur in the heather
As some beast goes by.'

      The wrangle
Had faded, for Cuchullin lay again
In an uneasy slumber. With a sigh
She looked on his distorted face and turned
Away. O she had too much grief that night
And all her love was vain. It was high time
That the dream-fighters came to tilt his feet
And women lap his head, having much skill
To help the great.

      When she was gone

He stirred to find a minute in the gloom
And, hearing but the creak of his arm muscle
And kneecap, called:
                    'Women are whirled as leaves.
They drift against our dreams.'
                              And he bent down
Beside the hearth.
                    Inside of sleep
He was aware that his own cunning mind
Was listening at a door. His body put
A hand into the shadows. With a laugh
He felt along a wall, sharpening
With every memory, his instruments
And bolts of war.
                    There in the doorway,
Unsheltered by wind and rain, his Niav
Was standing.
                    With a cry she came
Breathless, as when she warned him of the ship
Below Dunseverick.
                    'Go back! Go back,
Cuchullin, for the air is dangerous
At midnight. As I waited in the fort
A young man came, whose voice was kind and sly,
To warn me. Down the secret path I ran,
I ran to you. The wind and rain have drenched me
To the very skin. Three times I slipped, I tumbled
By stone and rabbit-hole and I am black
Or blue all over.
                    See, see!'
                              – she smiled to comfort him –
'My clothes are torn and I must strip before
The fire now; though the women hate me, beg
Needle and thread.'
                    'Why did you leave me,
An hour ago?'
                    'I was not here to-night.
You know they have kept me from you, darling.'
                                        'Lies,
All lies. I saw you with my own two eyes

Behind that chair.'
        'But I was never here
Before. I swear, beloved, it is true.
Go back, go back, the air is dangerous
At midnight.'
        Desperate with every nail
She clung to him.
        'Ah, little fury, I know
You have deceived me.'
        'No. No. It is
A terrible mistake, and I can see
All clearly now. O that is why an hour
Ago, I had a shivering fit beside
The fire and I was not myself. And, then,
That young man came, whose voice was kind and sly,
With a warning riddle. But I will save you now,
For I can see all clearly in my head.
Go back, go back, the air is dangerous
At midnight.'
        'I know your trick of tongue,
For I let on to be asleep to-night,
But I heard every word you said
Behind my back. Aye, there is treachery
In this or that corner and a creeping sound
Of body-knives below the skirting. Tallows
Flare in the dún and every door is barred
But mine.
        Warn, warn the listeners again
To tiptoe on the yewen-seasoned floors
Lest a foolish crack cry treason!'
        She could not tell
The black from the purple pupil standing wide
Apart, so terrible with sight, where she
Had danced to many a candle-top until
She was too small. She could not tell the black
From purple, who with a cry for help
Had fled into the night.
        'All, all my comrades gone,'
He pondered,
        'Who were with me in the great war

Of Connaught, and though I call to Conal Cearnach,
Laery the open-handed, Ferdia
Or my poor Laeg who gave me every rein,
They cannot hear me now. The strong return
No more. The good, the gentle, whom I had
Protected, have been done to death, that I
Might snatch at sleep. But I will stay the North
And keep that border to the desolate end
Who thought to spend the uncounted years in peace,
Happily beside the fire, among new children
And memories.'
                    Far in the night, the voices
Of all those gentle friends whom he had loved
Cried out, and he was shaken by his tears:
Cuchullin, our Cuchullin, we are dead!
The sudden pain was mixed into our sleep
With light. We wander in the painful air,
We are emptied as cries into the storm.
Break wine and sleep, and now, poor women, weep,
For we were dreaming and the killers came.
Cuchullin, our Cuchullin, we are dead,
And all the westward land is smoke and flame!

What, what is man but a poor balancer
When time is pressing on his hands! He keeps
Appointment with the breath that must destroy
Him, wears in a last agony the pitchcap
Of thought. But now this story-man, Cuchullin,
Had armed his body even before his mind
Turned down in headless fury to clap on him
Gigantic strength, from pan to bone, shaking
The rafters with old challenge.
                         All the tumblers,
The breathers, in that house had run, half-dressed,
To watch him in the shadows clip the hook
And staylet of his battle-coat. Only
The cry of Emer rang back as she turned
To Niav, knowing that no mortal voice
Could keep him from the open door. All, all
Stood there, half-dress'd, and chill with fear, they heard

The madman mutter to his jacket, stared
At what was going on in that dark hall.

III

Spies came with tidings to the seven doorways
Of Emain Macha.
     'Too far at daybreak
Beyond the narrows of water, we saw
Cuchullin.'
     'Too far, too far, at night-rise
Beneath that anvil-horn, the sidelong moon,
We saw Cuchullin, crazed by unreal combat
Dust-going along the sea-roads, jetty locks
Mocking at flight. But in the glens we heard
Armies of Erc — and Maeve stirred in the West.'

The hall was silent as Conal Cearnach struck
The bench-row.
     'Concobar, you have called vainly on druids
For earth or sky-sign, weakened by an old curse
As women in the child-bed
     But who'll obey
When the Hound bays?'
     He laughed, left, and his horse-man
Outside set up a clatter.
     Across the plain
They cantered, bronze bit by bit.
     'Spur faster, faster,
Lest we be late, riding against the morrow.'
'Men, who will master fate?'
     Ye ride, ye ride
To your disaster.
     Turning, they saw the mocks and
The murk of timbering flame, heard a long cry
From Emain Macha as though the Firbolgs sacked
The inner fort. Then Conal rallied his riders,
Horns at his helmet bullocking against

The lie.
      'Men, night has cast up a handful of nothings,
Flame, sound or some suck out of her reedy pools
To terrify late-goers. Let those, who will,
Fix girth and follow me,'
                  And rode with horns
Under the drip of woods.
           Shadows
That brooded there looked around the tree-trunks, sank
Into marl-pits.
        Soon, as they went in gloom, they grew
Aware of many passing by their pommels
With icy breath and knew that the host of the dead
Were catching at their coldly-sweating horns;
And a fellow, crazing with the silence, cried:
'Look at that dim-and-grey-cloud-wandering-wolf:
The moon!' – And disappearing under the drip
Of woods.
      The pines were flitting by wild bushes
And past the furlong of paleness, shadowy flats,
They galloped into the Gap o' the North,
Hearing a clangour that rebounded from anvils
Within Slieve Gullion and the mile-long echoes
Hammered again from the mountain-gates, sea-bolted
Invers and estuaries of Muirthemne
And on their riding breath went murmur:
                'Cauldrons
Of strength overbrim. There, Cualann, the smith, forges
Terrible weapons for the heroes. Houndless,
He broods and reforges, rivets in flame, in down-roar,
Remembering how, long ago, the king
Had supped there late at night below the soot-curtain.
A cry spattered outside. There, in the hush,
Young Setanta stood before the farrow
Calling in pride: 'I am your Hound now.'
And swinging his hurley stick, skipped out again
To see the threshing moon gleam on the Border below
And measure his land, then coming down through ferns, he
Caught up the angles of a harp, tinkling
Till dawn, forehead against the pegs.'
              They rode

Scarce hearing hoof-beat on stone until their horses
Stopped, turned and, pawing softness, came to bogland,
Along a causeway raised – men tell – by giants
Unnumbered centuries ago, splashing
The paven moonlight from the fetlocks which
The granite waked out of its aged slumber,
Complaining far behind them. Coot dived, heron
Got up, reed-legged. Then all became aware
Of the Three that galloped in red mantles before them.
Deep drove the spurs and in a sudden flaring
Of marish light, Conal remembered how the doomed
King Conairé, slow, burdened with care of homeward
Tribute, saw long ago the Three who galloped:
Red motes, that throbbed to westward – and turning, knew by
The visionary smoke and flame on the eastern
Sky-rim, his reign was over. Then Conal, spurring on,
Called out:
              'Answer me, if you are men. What news
Has brought you here?'
                     But, laughing from the manes,
One of the Three sang out an ancient riddle:
'Ride, mortals, ride to the southeast, find
No shelter at the Brugh. Fire-wisps of madness
Have scattered the guests, there, downward the pots.
                                        Ride
For there is no gain.'
                  'And who are you that come
And go at night?'
                'No man can tell. We ride for the
Sake of a story.'
              'And is the Hound still
In the West?'
            The mockers had gone.
                              So Conal jingled
To himself.
          'By God, this is a crazy riddle
For lazy housewives when they griddle bread,
Squat, piddle, go to bed.'
                        Westward
They cantered through cold drops to softness of drizzle,

Not fortunate as the poets, the wand-men, who come in
Their speckled mantles by the meadow-paths to
A feast. They stumbled into a slough near cromlechs
That leaned against the centuries.
                                        A voice
Struck down from the heights, halting them.
                                                    'As I drove
My cattle home, I saw the Three Reds ride
Towards battle.'
                        A hugeing, hairy monster pranked
Himself from a dyke with bits of rags, foul goatskin
Across his paps and waggish seed-bag. Conal
Half shouted, backing into a roundabout of jangles,
His frightened mount.
                            'Drive, drive your shadowy herds
To crop among the vapours.
                                    Ulstermen look
For better faring –
                        Herdsman, shy stranger of
The Upper Glens!'
                        The riders gripped at the saddle
For all the dusk was a-click with phantoming horses
As, wrapping himself in a swirl of vapour, the Herdsman
Bewhistled his care through thunder.
                                            Lengthening
Under the fernshaw, the granite, all climbed from turn
To turn. Soon, Conal, reining on a brink,
Could see his fifty men below, rounding
The corner of the fernshaw. Shadowed firs
Were gaffing the salmon-moon in a rocky pool.
He heard the wheezing drop of needles, breezes
That swam through hazel softnesses, the swish
Of mountain ash; then trumpeting his troop
Together on that ridge, where a last larch
Strained at its windy tether, like a bitted stallion,
Led down the slidderers: from shade to moss,
Haunch after haunch, they went.
                                        Spoor of the wind
Scuttered across the waters; the old gusts
Ran, galloped by their left until they spied

Lifting, cloudless beyond the ridges, blanched
As snow and gullied by the moon, eleven peaks
Above a forest top.
>   They crossed a plain,
Prospecting for a camp.
>   Voices trebled
Along the slopes.

> *We dance, we dance, from rock to grass*
And hold our hands together as we pass
The mountain heather, the dew, the grass.

>   Lifting
His voice Conal called up to them:
>   'Lonely dancers
Who dance forever from mountain-rock to grass,
When stores of waterish blackberries are rotting
Softly below, remember this little band
Riding, riding, beyond marsh-flower and reed,
Crying of curlews; men that may return
No more.'
>   Legendary figures, they withied
And wove their night-camp.
>   When the herdless dawn
Came through the pure cold gap of the East,
They stretched from the passing woods to watch
Below the shelves of stone and the reed-beds, light
Fording a mile of water.
>   Soon
They cross between the mace-tops; as Athairne
And his people, Lochlann plunder on mules, wading
Like gull-men across the shallows of Maynalta
Behind a line of hurdles.
>   At noon, mounts
Were watered. The men, tearing at stale rations, heard
A woman keening by the ford:
>   *He is dead.*
My Hound is dead!
>   She looked at them
So sightlessly, her face was nothing
In the noon.
>   'It is the Washer of the Ford!'

The out-post cried.
        'Ride fast. Ride fast.'
                'No, no,
It is only the wraith of a woman bowed by grief
For an unrocked cradle.'
                They went from the ford,
Foreboding in their minds.
                Late that evening,
They came, weariful, headlong, to a land
Of stone.
        Beyond, the clouds were islands,
Rainbowing in a glen.
                Among the far-off hills,
As from a dazzling vat, whiteness was drifting
Upwards. Over a ridge, the gleam of broken
Water came.
        Ravens, far dots in the sky,
Sighted these human dots upon a hill-top
Preening their spears.
                There Conal and his men
Had halted in the last light; miles away
Across the plain, they could see a rout of riders,
Retreat of cars, along a level strand
And foam-line.
        Sky-belittled on a knoll,
Self-bound by gad against a pillar-stone
Cuchullin drooped. There he had fought despite
His mortal wounds.
                A vapour had come about
The brink, hiding the clearness of the ocean,
The pillar-stone.
        Storm slowly climbed
With gallic steps, the last desolate ridge
As a new legend darkened, lightened, that land.

O Love, There Is No Beauty

O Love, there is no beauty,
No sorrowful beauty, but I have seen;
There is no island that has gathered sound
Into dim stone from many reeded waters
But we have known.
              Heart of my sorrowful heart,
Beauty fades out from sleepy pool to pool
And there is a crying of wings about me
And a crying in me lest I lose you. Glimmer
Around me; sound, O weir, within my heart;
Bring calm on many waters, for I will be hearing
The salmon shatter the air into silver when
The chill grass ends their leaping.
                  As I was dreaming
Between the pines, she gleamed from windy heights
Pale-browed, in a dark battlemented storm
Of hair. Far down I wander in the woods,
Ankle-deep in autumn, who am light
And lost of the waters.
             I have no clan but her;
Being a dream, though the fierce incense burn,
Love, love me, as no woman ever loved
With intellect tense and more passionate
Than the heart, for when the hunger of ourselves
Is over, there is no joy but in the mind.
Think in me for I am become as water
Under the mountain-minds, and when the fire
Of intellect has taken me their minds
Reflect as thought reveals myself. Therefore,
My days are smoke and westward praise of god.
When I eat bread I choke with the fierce salt
Of dream. Therefore I have lived for the sun,
And looked from every cape, and I have been
A runner on swift feet that I might break
The tapes of life.
             Drag down your lonely hair
On breasts no child has ever known, for it

Will bring you happy sleep and peace. There is
No peace within my words. I will be secret
Lest the loud powers that move in wine and satire
Gathering themselves from me, the lonely gate
And fire, perplex you with the ancient storm
No woman can endure.
                          But O there was
No knowing her sad beauty that was made
For candlelight and sleep. Yet thinking I
Forego her, though she has left me bare; I sing
And the mountain hawk is sinking slower through glens
Of lonely air.
                          I know the steps of love.
Take hands with me, sad dancers in the glen,
For autumn leaves dance best when they are dead,
And we are less than they, O bitter dancers
That dance with bloodied feet.

The Cattledrive in Connaught and Other Poems

(1925)

Induction

I have a trick or two of tongue
May please, for I have been acquainted
With that most famous juggler, Mannanaun,
Who runs from lordly fire to fire, when he
Has wearied of the cold warrens of the wave,
To mend the table for a farthing's worth
Of praise from men by pulling a girl, a hound
Or music from his pocket: he's the patron saint
Of merry rogues and fiddlers, trick o' the loop men,
Thimblemen and balladmen that gild
The fair and his devotions are the crowd
For he looks on until the sun is red,
The tide turned, and the drink and the horses are gone.

Three Sentences

I
Ceilidhe

The red Armada of the sun burned down
From Magheraroarty, melodeons played
The Waves of Tory and the young girls sat
Upon the knees of men; I took my sup,
I kissed the mouth beside me and forgot
My sorrow on the cold dark tide.

II
Scandal

Though I have caught the knowledgeable salmon
Out of the unlighted waters at Cong,
Fasted on holy islands where the sail
Still bends a knee, I had not thought, O woman
Of the Dark Hair, that you would make the priest
Talk from the altar and our love as common
As holy water at the chapel door.

III
Blessing

O Woman of the House, no sorrow come
From the dark glen to leave your floor unswept,
When I was tired you gave me milk and bread
And I could sit down by the fire and dream
Of her who crazed my heart; when dew began
Behind the door and the lazy candle was lit,
I made this rann for sleep: no mouse creep out
Nor evil thing, O Woman of the House.

A Curse

Black luck upon you Seamus Mac-an-Bhaird
Who shut the door upon a poet
Nor put red wine and bread upon the board;
My song is greater than your hoard,
Although no running children know it
Between the sea and the windy stones.

Yet, Seamus of the Bards, when you are dead
And a curragh carries out the new coffin,
Heavy with you within, heavy with lead,
Because you let song go unfed,
The waves will roughen near Inisbofin
And moan around your lonely bones.

Praise

Macgillicuddy of the Reeks,
My praise upon the hilly, woody land
Where ruddy brambles are dark with feasting wings
There in the grass the wind runs as a filly,
Could I sing as freely — it is I
Would praise Macgillicuddy of the Reeks.

If There Was Nothing Noble

If there was nothing noble
In what seemed troubled beauty, I may wear down
My heels for song and craze myself again
With thinking of her ways and how I found
In every fault of her inconstant body
The sin her stripling has enjoyed.

                        It is,
Without lie, a common shame and will soon end
For I gave sleep for her and yet this boy
Can say to any man he had his fill
Of sleep who tasted her.

Secrecy

Had we been only lovers from a book
That holy men who had a hand in heaven
Illuminated: in a yellow wood,
Where crimson beast and bird are clawed with gold
And, wound in branches, hunt or hawk themselves,
Sun–woman, I would hide you as the ring
Of his own shining fetters that the snake,
Who is the wood itself, can never find.

Silver and Gold

Hammer the gold and silver into steel:
I have another metal that rings clear
To mind; the coining air knows, and I know,
That harp, thrown high, will turn a lucky head
And they that love once never have been loved.

She glittered in me as the twilight star
That like a patient crane haunts one bright pool
When sedge is bare. Now that we are awake,
Come with me, golden head, for every wood
Thickens again and the first callow light
Flutters around the hedges; we shall hear
The birds begin as sweetly as the chinking
Of few pence in my pocket. When the tides
Of sun are full and the salmon come up from
The south, Love, we shall hurry where the waves
Carry the heavy light into the shore
And see the marrying wings, for all the day
They are more silver than the lifting oar,
But in the evening they are gold again.

The Itinerary of Ua Clerigh

O men of Horn Head
May you reap black corn
For you drove me from your plantation,
But I know an isle
Where the fire does a step-dance
When the wind cannot land from the high surf,
And soon I was sailing
The pure tide with Norsemen
And I stayed a fortnight in Tory,
Though I was not acquainted
With the dark-haired women
For they gallop all day, there, on horseback.

At the heel of a cloud
I prayed on Croagh Patric
Above the islands of the bay;
I saw from a hilltop,
A mile to Clifden,
A hundred lakes upon a Sunday.
Were I safe in a glen,

Halfway through the rushes
When light was fishing the waters,
I would have good walking
From dewfall at evening
Beneath the little trees of Nephin.

I saw from Galway
A Spanish ship flaming
Beyond the phantom isles of Aran;
Grey stone for hedges
Has bound the green county
Around branchy Coole of the manor,
Where I halted with Yeats
To share the wise salmon
He grassed from the Lake of Jewels;
I dipped in his plate
Without praise, without wine,
Though he asked me to come to his Castle.

By Little Connaught
When sails were filling
And shadow danced like a balladman,
What should I hear
As I leaned on the counter
But the ferrule of O Conaire
Hitting the road
To Tirnanogue!
And, O Padraic, you did not know me,
Though we, for a week
In Baltinglass,
Were drinking with the Wicklow men.

Thoroughbreds and mares
Were sold at Ballinasloe
As I drew beside a crowd on the fair-day,
With drovers from Clare,
Horse-dealers over wave
And Volunteers that came in from Sligo.
Of brave Bonaparte
Street singers were droning

And, O boys, my money was a fire
When I heard the card-music,
The farmers at their drink
And the coloured kings and queens going by.

By the holy well,
And the honey house
Of stone, I read the Gospel
Until a bird called me
Over bright water
That was sapping the green miles of barley:
And when the chill rain
Was setting at night,
I met the great horsemen with plunder
And among black hills
I feasted with them,
In the royal house of Curoi Mac Dara.

The Pedlar

At the yellow house in Rathfarnham
The donkey fell asleep
And, leaping down, I gathered boughs,
I bound them to the harness
And when those airy leaves aroused her,
Backing the wheels of the cart,
She stared at me sadly, she brayed
And kicking the board up, started
To shorten the roadway.

In the town of Carlow
Shopkeepers ran out to look
And women called after the pedlar
When they saw the leaves blow,
Children were dropping their schoolbooks
And men were at work in the hayfield,
But we plucked the geese on the pools

As we galloped from stubble all day
By farmhouse, white barracks.

How can I deny that enchantment
When berries grew scarlet
And for twenty-six counties she went by
The halfway house at a canter,
Though I thought, had she sighted a barrel
Growing at a door, she would stop,
And the blackbird I carried for pleasure
Sharpening his beak on the sugar,
Sang to those branches?

Torchlight, in Tara
Had armed the rampart at night
And I heard the harp and crowds dancing
For a queen that had been married,
But the cold rain blew them away
As a story, and by the dark roads,
Where no farmer has strayed from the market
The berries, grown black in the moonlight,
Hurry us onward.

The Fair at Windgap

There was airy music and sport at the fair
And showers were tenting on the bare field,
Laughter had knotted a crowd where the horses
And mares were backing, when carts from the wheelwright
Were shafted: bargains on sale everywhere and the barmen
Glassing neat whiskey or pulling black porter
On draught – and O the red brandy, the oatmeal
And the whiteness of flour in the weighing scale!

Calico petticoats, cashmere and blouses,
Blankets of buttermilk, flannel on stalls there,
Caps of bright tweed and corduroy trousers

And green or yellow ribbon with a stripe;
The tanner was hiding, the saddler plied the bradawl;
Barrows had chinaware, knives and blue razors,
Black twisted tobacco to pare in the claypipe
And the halfpenny harp that is played on a finger.

Soft as rain slipping through rushes, the cattle
Came, dealers were brawling at seven-pound-ten,
On heifers in calf a bargain was clapped
When ewes that are nearer the grass had taken
Two guineas; the blacksmith was filing the horn in his lap
For the fillies called up more hands than their height,
Black goats were cheap; for a sow in the pod
O Flaherty got but the half of her farrow.

Balladmen, beggarmen, trick o' the loop men
And cardmen, hiding Queen Maeve up their sleeve,
Were picking red pennies and soon a prizefighter
Enticed the young fellows and left them all grieving —
While the marriageable girls were walking up and down
And the folk were saying that the Frenchmen
Had taken the herring from the brown tide
And sailed at daybreak, they were saying.

Twenty-five tinkers that came from Glentartan,
Not counting the jennets and barefooted women,
Had a white crop of metal upon every cart,
The neighbours were buying, but a red-headed man
Of them swearing no stranger could bottom a kettle,
Leaped over the droves going down to the ocean,
Glibbed with the sunlight; blows were around him
And so the commotion arose at the fair.

The Lad Made King

O storyteller do not tire
Between the fire and wall,
For hills are greener where the spade
Has been: though I ran with the bird-flocks
Until the fields were small,
And from wild grass that had no herd
But the wind and the gapping showers,
I came to the branches of the red fruit
And the water loud with stars.

In the glen of the blindmen
I was alone for a night,
With a stone in the flighty boughs
I gathered a bite;
On the road from Midluachra
I will come to an empty house,
Where a fire is, and cook
A handful of meal in new water
In the pot on the hook.

On the road of Fieries,
By the path of the blows,
To a lonely smithy I came;
Quarrymen dripped from the dark ferries
For they carried a strange tale,
But the farriers, lifting the bellows,
Heartened the horseshoe –
Yet how can they marry
The water and flame?

At the Feast of the Bullock
And the full of the night,
I heard the horsemen far away:
They snared me with light as a young bird
And hurried into Tara.
O hurlers that run after the ball
In the small fields I knew,

I am crowned by the wise with their red gold
Under rafters of black yew.

The Lost Heifer

When the black herds of the rain were grazing
In the gap of the pure cold wind
And the watery hazes of the hazel
Brought her into my mind,
I thought of the last honey by the water
That no hive can find.

Brightness was drenching through the branches
When she wandered again,
Turning the silver out of dark grasses
Where the skylark had lain,
And her voice coming softly over the meadow
Was the mist becoming rain.

The Son of Lir

Over the stony fields
That sharpen the hook in Connaught,
Alone with the drenching sky
Through cloudish grass, I ran
By the waters of black swimming,
Until the trees began:
I came under a wood
To water green as rye,
I heard in a place that was good for harps,
Where the sun dripped with the rain,
Carpenters in a green workshop
Elbowing the plane.

I wakened a land so quiet
The glens were herded by a horn,
But I followed far into the south
The bird-lakes of the morning:
I was awhile on an island
In a sunning mile of the Shannon
And in the golden sedge of corn
The men were rowing about
And women brought the blue-veined milk
For they turn the butter out.

Gold was wrecked against Kerry
On a day of wild fishing and oars
Gave the hags that curl the tide-tops
Wet money from the netting,
I rowed with the sail to one side
When light was salting from the harbour:
At the board of the Earl I would get
A share of the dish and the barrel
By swearing the fishermen spied
Where the shoal of mackerel ran
Sunward, beyond a black skerry,
The goldskin sails of Bran.

Last night in the house of Red Hugh
I tumbled, I juggled, I danced,
To-day on a fife I was stopping the music
For women in Skye and soon after
I talked with poor men in Cantyre.
I sprawl in blue rags and bad shoes
By the fire of a small king in Leinster,
I will play for his ease or I won't,
I will do what I will as my mind is pleasing
And if I am gone, I am here,
But when the tide whitens, I flame upon the seas
For I am the Son of Lir.

The House in the West

Where low rains are heavier
Than the sail in haze
And the cold sea is spread
On the soil to raise harvest,
Black calves are bred to reign over
The fair and behind their green tether,
In a bare land that halves every cloud,
There is a great house.

Men with the crowbar,
Breaking a road
From the spar of the dark land,
Have seen those far windows,
While unyoking a cart-load,
Take fire and a star
Coming over the water
Like Oisin after the heroes.

At darkrise the snipe
Strum on the rain;
But in that house, to the lighting
Of rushes, the air of the bagpipe
Blows a reel on the floor:
Big men strike in from a backward parish
And two of them carry a slain boar
Over the throating of greyhounds.

There is honey spitting from meat
And whitening of the ale there,
Brandy and wine that came from the seas,
Bright candles – and who that delight in
The mind, counting those companies
Of yellow-haired men or of women
That never had envy, would not be pleased
By the laughter, the music and chess-playing?

The Musician's Wife

The hour of the player
Begins with a star
And men built a blaze
To double the pillar
In the house of mead:
But the music of Craftinë
Was blown with the laughter
Of his wife as she fled.

Evening was paler
Than leaves of the foxglove,
When from sedges of forest,
It happened those lovers,
Who had come to the water
Where moonlight was mooring,
Unfastened the saddle
And thought to have rest.

Where the otter
Sank into jewels,
By the ferries of forest
They heard strange music
Cross: one of them wept
For, at Tara, she knew
Her husband was playing on
The hole-headed flute.

She wept, for her lover
Was drawn by the music
Halfway to the shore,
Where pebbles had thickened
The moonlight, and knew
That shadowy women,
With pale lips imploring
Him, rose from the lake.

They hurry, forever,
Where forests are felled
By lake-water, they
Have no rest from the fluting
And though they are shadows,
He dreams of strange beauty
And she weeps to herself
As they fade in the dew.

The Frenzy of Suibhne

Run, run to the sailmaker –
While I pluck the torn white hedges
Of sea to crown my head –
And tell him to bind hard the canvas
For the waves are unhorsed to-night;
I cracked a thought between my nails
That they will light a candle
When I swim from the loud grass
To the holy house of Kieran.

Storm is masted in the oakwood
Now and the fire of the hags
Blown out by the tide; in wet smoke
Mannanaun splashes by with a bagful
Of music to wager for the food
In a house where the women mull
Ale; workmen dream of their furnace
And the male jewels that are alive:
But I hear the hounds of the black queen race
As I nest in the drenching ivy.

The rain is drowning in Glenveigh
Where once the vats of brightness poured
Until the wet green branches hid
The black ridge of the boar:
Garlic was good there and the pignut;

Upon the clean tops of the wells
A tender crop was rooted
But the wild-eyed man of the water
Was feathered like a hawk to the foot.

I hurried at evening
From the glen of birches
When longer shadows
Were cropping
Their way: on a sudden,
Darkness was nearer,
Hazels had ripened,
I heard the rain drop.

Far down a dark hollow
Of sloe-trees, a bird
Cried and black swine
Ran under the fences
Of rain for a tall man
Followed, his one eye
Redder than grey turf
When it is stirred:
Far down the hollow,
Sloe-bushes ran.

A black drove of boulders
Was crossing the ford:
O to what household,
Swineherd, Red Swineherd,
Do you hurry unbidden
That men may carouse?
Breathe on their eye-lids
And bound to the rafters
May three naked women drip
Blood; in their hearing
Strange laughter and rapine

Of phantoms that tumble
From nothing, till fear
Empty the bladder,

Swineherd, Red Swineherd,
And shadows madden
The heart like a drum.

I hurried to the paddock
While stablemen were brawling
And under the bellies
Of horses I crawled:
Dark, dark was the harness,
(The wheelwright said I was mad)
But I flung back the lock
And I loosed forty hoofs to
The storm in the grass.

A juggler cried. Light
Rushed from doors and men singing:
'O she has been wedded
To-night, the true wife of Sweeny,
Of Sweeny the King!'
I saw a pale woman
Half clad for the new bed:
I fought them with talons, I ran
On the oak-wood – O Horsemen,
Dark Horsemen, I tell ye
That Sweeny is dead!

Stark in the rushlight
Of the lake-water,
I heard the heads talking
As they dripped on the stake:
Who runs with the grey moon
When ravens are asleep?
It is Sweeny, Little Sweeny
Looking for his mind.
When dogheads were barking in the wood,
I broke the horns of a goathead
For I heard them on the water
Call: *Sweeny, Little Sweeny*
Is looking for his mind.
But Robbers, dark Robbers, I tell ye
That Sweeny is dead!

If I sleep now, the hag
Of the haggard, will steal
My feathers though I drowned her
In the dark pool of Achill
That has no sound.

When tides were baying
The moon, in a glen
Of pools, I fed on
Grey cowdung: a hundred
Men hauling a slab
Upon the great dolmen
Of Sweeny the King,
From the shovels and barrow,

Fled. Nailing, I dug up
The gold cup and collar
And hid them in rain.
But how can mind hurry
As reeds without feet,
And why is there pain in
A mind that is dead?

I have heard the little music
Of Midna, I have seen
Tara in flame and a blooded moon
Behind the Ridge of Judgment…
But how can they find my name
Though they are crying like gulls
That search for the sea?
Nine years I hurried from mankind
And yet, O Christ, if I could sail
To the Island of the Culdees,
I would sleep, sleep awhile
By the blessing of the holy Kieran.

The Circuit of Cuchullin

Hurricane, lighting the last of the shattered lands, rang
Where the mountains are lifted, a handful of glimmering javelins
Flung far to the seaward, forever in cloud – as a horseman,
Galloping out of the gullies of sunlight,
Climbed, where the herds of the thunder lowed in black meadows:
Hillocky lands far below him grew dimmer – on red
Flooding oars the sun grated the uttermost islands – crossing
The momentary bridges that curdled in mist from the hoofs,
Far over the waterish valley of twilight, he saw
Tremendous gates hammered with copper, reforged in the sunset,
Guarded by clouds; he hung like a fiery drop, reined,
Disappeared, for loud laughter took flight to the rainy gulfs
Below, and he knew, as he galloped, that gods and their creatures
Drank, merry together.
              Far in the night he had heard
Strange hoofs, as the roar of the foaling tide raced in the glen,
Where the sea-mountains stable their clouds, and had ransacked the forge
Of Slieve Gullion, while farriers, leaping in fire and sea-fog,
Swung as they hammered speed into the fetlocks of war,
Half-naked: a hundred lit anvils belled in the glare
Of the furnaces, hurling night back on the ridges
Of mist, where the gullies roared past him, herding their weirs
To the forest below. He had seen the last precipice loom
Of the mountain-cupped lake and a grey mare, dimmer than cloud,
Grazing the water. They wrestled together, they fought
Deep in foam, till he vaulted upon her with bellying knees,
Saddled her, forced in the snaffle, clouding her nostrils and
Rearing upon her big haunches, the water-horse plunged
To the world.
           Muirthemnë reeled past, mountain-deep in the moonlight,
Gloom leaped from the ridges upon that new mane and the cry
Of the pine was cut down by the gale as faster yet faster
She fled from the bridle; the harder land stubbled in flame
From her pastern, over the racing plain, shafted with firs,
They saw the lake, weir'd in black reeds, where a queen long ago,
Hurried out with a wine-cup to open the well and a roar
Drowned the terrified rafters and over the meadow land
The idle bright grain of the moon poured; faster yet faster

They raced on, lengthening into the night where the waters
Of coldness are sown in the meadows of forest and, darker
With moorland, the miles dropped behind the cloud-hungering hoofs
As they rose, as they climbed, from a river-strewn valley, beyond
The last steps of the pinewood. Far, far, the bare rock
Trumpeted, lakes neighed and sank till the shivering mare
Stopped, for a stallion had bounded, black and gigantic,
To cover her. Plunging together from cloud-dwelling hollows
They fought in their dreadful espousals. The man had leaned down,
Turning the jaws of the noose. Backward the horses
Coiled and into the lowlands, as dragons, they dropped,
By river and wood, to the Valley of Terror, where camped
On the brink of a clearing, the outlaws of Calitin cooked
By their simmering fires and a daughter laid foot on a faggot
And ran on the flamy air crying:
                                        'Through the fingers of smoke
I have seen, I have seen, the horses of day and night
Plunging in cloud. Through the smoke and the flame I have seen,
I have seen!'
                    But the valley grew louder, for phantoms
Of battle, with glittering claws on their wings, climbed around him
That galloped, one hand locked in fire of the hard biting leather,
While thunder of horses, beneath him, was swayed, as by pole
And ground wheels, in their fury.
                                        Day rushed through the forests
Unseen and from darkening islands the sunset was heeled
By the wintering tides. Yet onward, far onward, they rode
Where the sail never lifted and only the northern wolves
Hear the whimpering pines or the Fomors, encamping, have piled
Their fires on the funeral isles, when the games and the wrestling
Are done. Heading the bridle in fury, they sounded
The ridge of the world, they climbed and the hare in a dream
Crawled by to the emptier grass, where the deer sheds a horn
They came; heavy clouds were asleep and the piebald moon
Was grazing below them.
                            Errigal, lifting a rusted
Spear, sank into cloud.
                            Far westward Nephin had gathered
Bright water and trees.
                            Softer than rain-hidden pools

Beyond the last leap of the salmon, the hushes of grass
Grew, air was lush with the hazel, by palings of cloud,
Dark inlets of pinewood, he rode to the glimmering sandhills,
There music fell down on the coast, and the horses becalmed
At the ocean. Caressing them, smoothing their haunches, he drove,
Without rein, into deepening silver and misty voices
Out of the dubious borders of Tirnanogue
Flowed to the saddle:
                            'Cuchullin, Cuchullin,'
                                      They murmured

About him.
            'Go with us, go,
For we know of a brightness beyond the lit blade: there, the hazels
Are nutting, day fades, and we move as the lifting gleam
To the steps of the tide.'
                        Shoreward he urged the great horses,
For he knew the pale foam was enchanted and loudly his heart
Had remembered the north, where men beat out the fire on the anvil,
Cast the spear, ride, leap, and are glad. By mountain and field
Where those hoofs ran, the farmers were turning in sleep as they dreamed
Of new war. Onward, far onward he rode by the ford
Of the stars; the horsemen of Mainë dragging their plunder
Leaped from a brink – and were gone; territories sank
Into forest; but onward, far onward, he rode and the plain
And the meadow were mown in silver, grew bare and wolves heard him
Galloping into the echoing gap of the north.

The Cattledrive in Connaught

How Maeve of Connaught disputed with her husband at an unreasonable hour regarding their respective possessions. How their cattle were driven in and counted. How a plenipotentiary was sent to Ulster to negotiate for a bull and a deal of ale consumed.

Queen Maeve sat up in bed and shook once more
Her snoring husband:
                'And I cannot sleep
An inch now for my head is full of words
That spoiled the chessboard, held the drinking cups
Half drained and climbed the more as candlelight
Ran low and is there any doubt that I
Had greater wealth when we were wed than you
Had bargained with my hand – have I not filled
The west with lowing herds, have I not fleeced
The hills, have I not brought the middlemen
From grassing plains to lift a wondering head
From seaward clouds and count a rout of horses
Graze beyond swimming where few island women
Gallop them, bareback, to the little seas
Of Connaught? Have I now or have I not?
Tell me, have I not hung this draughty house
From family looms and put a golden bit
Upon the winter, silence on the floor
With rushes that forget their dancing, kept
The churn in clotty buttermilk, the cauldron
In bubbling oatmeal, spun the heavy flower
Of wool?'
            'Your sheep go through my gap
And there is sleep on me.'
                    'You have not said
That I have greater wealth than you? Women
Can own their marriage-portion now-a-days
And is not mine the counterpane above
You, the door against the cold, has it not stored
The barn with oats and barley, ground white food

Out of the mill, cut down the heavy gleams
Within the woods and where the dawning smokes
From earthy skies driven the pale plough:
And rousing now, do you not hear my cows
Chewing in the new byre, the folded bleat
Of ewes that have been collied from the hills
In the red o' the year, while swine are in the oakwoods
And hookers riding by the hundred islands
Of Clew, heavy with running clouds or keeled
With wine – have I not brought into this kingdom
Larger wealth?'
                    Flattening out the bolster
He said:
            'Aye, but you brought it all
Upon your back.'
                    'That is a bitter word
To blame me. Am I not the daughter of
Eochaid Mor, whose house had overlooked,
As song, broad pasture-land, river and woods
In tilled blue acres near the clouds? Was I
Not bred within a plentiful home, my hand eyed
By troubling kings out of the north, lowering
Their blacker shields to sip the small red wine
Out of a mocking thimble while my women
Tattled that I slung in the woods and laughed
For all their meadows and could I not have reared
Them half a dozen sons: being so proud,
Desirable that I could yield a grazier
Contentment? Was I not raised upon the fat
Of cattle-lands?'
                    He turned upon his side
Again.
            'Husband, men of the north have said
To-night that I am wealthier and...'
                                        'Like
It is. A woman's ear is red for praise.
What of your wealth when you could never keep
The gate barred?'
                    'It was not so
For I had many hands to tether down

A jealous neighbour, empty out his haggard
And lay bare all his lands if he desired
To sow my field. I had required a farmer,
Wealthy, with seed in bag and barn, to lie
Beside me, easy-going for I am heady
But good in siring.'
                          'Aye I am to stand
While Fergus plays at king.'
                                    'Has he not said
My goods are greater?'
                            'I will do no more
Than sleep, for though you have your say, I have
More wealth than you.'
                            'Now from this minute
I will not sleep a foot until our wealth
Is gathered round the house and counted fleece
By skin, nor have it said that I have milk
By any man. I will not rest again
Till all is seen. Get up, get up and wake
The house at once. Call everybody in
To stir the hearth from ashes and ransack
What I have got.'
                    He bounced out of bed
Into the pot. He ran with candlelight
To waken up the household. All had heard
With fear that quarrel in the royal blankets
And filled the hall with yawny light and piled
Great smoke upon the flags and that proud queen
Came in before the women and sat down
Upon a carven chair in her white shift
And red strapping hair:
                          'Women, wash the sleep
Out of your eyes and bring the treasure that
I have within the house and pile together
Armfuls of jewels and rich draperies
Upon the settles, count with every rushlight
My furniture nor let a burning drop
Of grease spill. Hurry with my riches, chuck,
Run, Felm, run and gather emeralds
From fields of light. Unloosen all the bales

Of gorgeous stuffs, of oriental brocades
And golden silks that have been webbed with random
Fire.
          O from what deep and purple vats
Have these been wrung and reddened to the sound
Of dripping oars to dry upon the pillars
Of Tyre?
               Here rustles the yellow from the shuttle,
Long steeping in the tubs, the crotal has
Worked well.
             Unwind the sad embroideries:
Here are the fancies of young girls, for these
Many a white thumb has been pricked and eyes
Grown red... Here the young men follow hounds,
Drive with the javelin into green woods
Of the boar... Now the pale women sprawl
Heavy with rape and the sad tale ends
With the needle... Green offerings are sedged
On the steps of an island... Dimming swans
Reach out their necks to a star, the waters gloom
In threaded gales, the shining falls
From the loom.'
               'Good wife you have begun
To sneeze.'
             Hastily she threw a quilt
Brindled with purple round her shoulders:
                                    'Where
Is Fionnavar?'
               'Mother, here are pale
Sea-berries, cold as the moon.'
                         The queen had plunged
Her arms into piled jewels and a flame
Leaped over them:
                 'Ailill, here is a jewel
Beyond the telling. Red star of the west,
Light tramples from its seven doors. It shines
It blazes.'
             'I have as large a faggot
For that was quarried when you were the wife
Of Concobar.'
               At the red hearth of the jewel

Her hair fell down:
                    'I had forgotten. Break,
Blacksmith and quench it in the lake. I will
Revenge myself on Concobar. Had he
Not dared to scorn me for a watery chit
Half weaned out of the woods and when she sailed,
Trodden the white heel of the oars to fill
His bed? The shadows of the northern pines
Still ford these rivers from the sun to empty
The corners of my house. But I will plunder
His pasture-lands and break the feast that sits
Upon the rock and burn the rafters down
And brand my cattle in the flame.'
                        'Good wife,
Here are my treasures, cups and beaten pitchers
Mouthed with gold.'
                 'Bring in, bring in, my keeves
Of golden ware. Open the claws o' the torc,
The heading minn. O how light ripens
Within the knotted gold and with design
Touched by a rush flows in soft flowing waves
To the brim!
           Run, help the women bandied
Under the heavy drinking horns inlaid
With ancient feast.'
               'We bring the carven bronze
Polished until another sun swam out
Of sullen deeps.'
              'Their ruddy faces leap
Out of the brass.'
              'It brightens with the anger
Of the queen.'
           The floor was piled with dross
Of purple cloth, green hangings, golden shards
Of wool. Bare shadows ran unfolding them
Into a shimmering heap. There was a clatter
Of scullions putting cauldrons in a row,
Huge spits of iron tumbling from the chimney
And wenches hurried in with raw red chilblains
Upon their knuckles:
              'Queen, two dozen blankets

Stink in the vat of lye, but we have emptied,
O have we scoured, the pots beneath the hook
With sandstone.'
                        Fighters drove them back
With crockery, unhooked the swords: a score
Of them dragged in the massive golden shield
Carven with terrible heads that lift in storm
To a lost clan upon a peak – the queen
Guards her large body battled in its shadow,
Charioteering among blown ruddy tresses
Tangled in ravens.
                        All the brazen hall
Was studded with thick cauldrons that could feed
A county, rings, amber, bracelets, golden cups
So rounded that, being empty, they might seem
With grape, rich merchandise that had dragged down
New shipping to the beak, dapples of the fawn
And sun-white bedding, common wood as turned
Or carven into dragons as the harpwood
Aired with sweet music; among the costly bales
Cast up by that loud ebb of words the queen
Sat combing out her dandruff.
                                    'Keep the fire
In,'
      She said,
                  'Leave a rushlight at my elbow
And get you into sleep for I will sit
Until the dawn. But let the early herdsmen
Number the herds outside and drive far cattle
Into the lairs and send the barefoot runners
To dip their shins into the west, for I
Alone must have the greater wealth or die.

II

Harriers ran the roads
To the shadow-herded peaks
Of Connemara, by the hillocks lit
With handfuls of sharp water and they cried

At every farm:

               'Drive in the herds
Of Maeve and count them into rows.'

                               They called
At every holding:

                  'Peel the wattle now
On the cattle of the king.'

                     Men came to the stile
And the busy women, hanging out the clothes
On the currant bushes, cried

                      'Who are they
That are running?'

              But those heels
Had gone.

           Landowners at the door
Whittling the hours, whistled for the men
That mowed in the river field.

                    Down the beaten road
A band of horsemen galloped in a cloud
With following mares.

              'Whoa!'

                  'Steady!'

                    'Whoa!'
'Where do you go?'

              'To the Fair'

                  'To the Fair
Of Ballinasloe.'

          'Then call in all
The ready neighbours, for the thoroughbreds
And two-year-olds are counting and the drink
Runs as we run.'

            Along the heatherland,
The dark red bog, they hurried over fence
And steeping pool.

            'Dry the turf no more
But hurry to the spancel.'

             Down the glen
Of kelping where the silver share o' the sea
Lies idle, barelegged women in young waters,
Wrenching the sun out of the flannel, chased

The naughty ganders, hurried in for milk
Or griddle-bread into the house and called
The snoozing men.
                    In the turn
Of the glen, where by himself the black ram crops
A greener ring, mountainy folk came down
With sharpened pikes.
                    'Where is the fighting?'
                                        'At

What ford?'
            'O hurry to the cattle.'
                            In
A gap of cloud, men, larruping a herd
Through stumbling silver, came.
                            'What hoofs
Are these?'
            'Milk from the little grass
Of hunger.'
            'Bring them down.'
                        'Bring them down
To the green troughs of Inagh.'
                            They were climbing
The watery green flights of every glen
And sheep-men drove the barking lanes
Of rams into the pen and counted them
When light began to drizzle from the springs
Of air.
            And so the word ran west and came
Footsore upon the third day to the tides
Of light; men rowed the curraghs for a mile
And lifting the droppy sails to the islands
Gathered the sheep and ponies. Womenfolk
Quitting the patchwork quilts upon the shore
Had topped the family cauldron on the hook
With handy meal, gossiping of the far
Blue country when a king and red-haired queen
Fell out.
            Storm crowded in the far sea-mountains
Of Achill, broken into unploughed purple
Against the thundering herds of cloud driven

From the waterish hurdles of the west; by darkfall
Strange voices moved among the desolate peaks
Of war and the dim running islands gathered
Their brood of sails for men had seen the Bull
Of Connaught rage upon the shaken ridge
Of the world…

III

Fair of all fairings, sound the horn
In the delaying air and when the fires
Of branding scatter from the driven hoofs
Of war, praise then the happy, forest-belted,
The meadow-sunned and cattle-pasturing, plains
Of Cruachan; as ripe barley to the hook
My singing falls, for never Tailteann Fair
Fattening the red wattle with the noise
Of horseman and of dealers could surpass
The hosting of the cattle of the west:
The side of every glen had emptied out
Great droves into the highways and the cries
Of men hung on the cattle-clouded ridges
As showers in a gap; invading herds –
From every grazing land and hilly farm
Of boulders – even to the pools of Corran,
Bare inlets of the sky where the salt winds
Sow but themselves – small, firm in the hoof
Or fat and dappled, tail after dropping tail,
Thickened upon the plains until their steams
Had horned them in a rising of thick haze
Sun-beaten into gold.
            Queen Maeve
Surrounded by the yellow-haired tall sons
Of Mainë, lower rings of rough-browed men
With belts of red cowhide and hunting knives
Of horn, large-thoughted, gazed upon that plain
Of wealth nor heard the cursing cattlemen,
Boys walloping among the lairs, the roar
Of bulls humped on the slipping cows, the cud

Doubling the fodder and the happy sound
Of dropping dung.
                        Halfway from flowing haze
White milch cows moved upon the cobble road,
Bewildered, pawing for the soft rich grass.
'Whose herds are these?'
                        She said,
                                    'Sloughing their way
Through golden air?'
                        And Caoilte whistled
                                    'The king
Has more cattle than Maeve. I will sing of the flower of the herd
For they drove her with harps from the west,
Her salver was silver and O Hide of red gold,
The king has more cattle than Maeve.'
                                    A drove
Of bulls loomed out of fog dragging the ring
With blood-rimmed nostril.
                        'They are the king's and bred
Far in the Ox Mountains and their fence
Is the salt ocean...'
                        So the herds were told
And when the haze was red and dark came down
The folk made merry in the fields outside
The booths of drinking, barrels of sweet apples
And fiery rings of pitchlight where the tumblers
Rolled on a strip of mat as Mannanaun
Or caught nine mangolds from the air; the noise
Of cattle in the lairs as though men held
A yearly market in the west, skirling
Of pipes and ructions, where the islandmen
That carried knives cried for the king and women
Squabbled about his wife, had grown so loud
And wild among the shows that farming voices
Had come to sudden blows – for when the great
Fall out, what shall the people do? – but men
Hammered the boards and laughing girls tucked up
Red flannel petticoats around their forks
And footed to the reeds, as washerwomen,
The high-step jig; the boys tripped from the drink

And caught them into sixteen-handed reels
And grabbing hold of bolder wenches, big
Of bone, with coarse red hair, shouting, clapping
A gamey hand upon those buttocks loud
And shapely as a mare's, they danced them off
Their feet. Oro, the music squeezed below
The elbow!

        'Have you been upon Goose Green
And what saw you there?'

              'Men drinking black porter
And women gallivanting on their own
To any air.'

       Oro, the dancing at the fair and
The boozing!

       'Blow the pipes,
O bagman.'

       'Take a woman if you can.'
'I cannot dance. I may not dance
For I am married to the red-haired man.'
'O the droning.'

       'Sails were bobbing from the waves
To carry me.'

       'O swing her by the middle.'
'They drank upon the wedding night.'

          'They broke
The iron griddle.'

     'Turn'

       'The boys all sang
When the happy couple got into the bed:
"Good tailor, if the needle's eye is small,
Wet the thread."'

     'Hands round'

          'I will not dance,'
'She cannot dance, for she is married to
The red-haired man.'

      So merrily the legs
Were mixing and the concertina went in
And out...

     Within the brazen hall of Maeve
A Brehon rose:

       'The wealth of man and wife,

In pot and pan, in flock and herd, in cock
And hen, being cut upon the wood, is found
Alike, but for a bull who fiercely scorning
A woman's rule, trampled rebellious herds
And followed the king.'

                               Ailill got up in haste
And said:
                'I have disowned
The bull now. Geld him. Dip an iron brand
In tar. I give him back to her. The night
Burns low.'
                 'No, no, nothing will do
But that I have a like to size him,'
                                   Cried
The wife,
                'It is for me to give, not to
Receive. I am the owner of the house
Not he, and I believe for all these words
That I am wealthier; men counting fish
Into the barrels on an island when
The boats are shored had been as quick, flinging
The number and handfuls of the white salt,
The nets had been re-mended, codheads thrown
To stink i' the sun, the children on the knee
Before your words were done. Now I must have
Another bull and is there anybody
Can tell for praise, for such thanks as are shown
In bread, fire, sleep, of such a bull?'
                                Fergus
Replied:
                'I have heard tell there is a beast
As fierce and wild owned by a countryman
In Cualgne.'
                'I must have that bull.'
She called the royal messenger,
                              'Go, go,
MacRoth, with drovers, stable boys and food,
Hurry into his lands and know a queen
Follows your wind. Promise him what you will
So that you get the bull, nay fifty bloods

To stock his field or, if he would, the best
Of acreage in Connaught that has yielded
The sea no tribute. We give powers to you
For peace and war. If he is filled with greed
As such small farmers are, promise him more
Than a foolish head can hold and pinch the bargain
In the black o' the nail, or name the dreaded will
And majesty of the west, for empty or full,
I will not sleep until I have that bull.'
Half-witted Caoilte sang outside the door
Above the jigging:
                          'Hurry, boys, or lag
She will harry those lands and marry that bull
Yet for all that they say and for all that he gave
The king has more cattle and meadows than Maeve.'

IV

In the large house of Dara by the fire
The ruddy ale went round.
                          'A health, a health'
MacRoth replied:
                          'The loaning of the Bull.
That is a goodly bargain now, to drive him
Into the west, his praise to cross the fords,
He shall bring wealth and break the hurdles down
Between our lands and in a grassing year
For every calf dropped, you shall have the owning
Of a fine heifer, fatten as a chieftain
Beyond your neighbours when our mixing herds
Breed peace.'
                    MacDara drained the handed mug
And laughed so loud the flockbed under him
Shook:
          'That was a foolish talk of theirs
Upon the pillow for a happy ending.
I'd have no womenfolk to fill the house
With noise and smoke.'
                              He roared until the tick

Broke under him and dregged another cup
Walking the rushes:
                    'Aye, mighty is this Bull,
This Bull, and he has farmed the mountain-lands
With savage herds, dewlapped, fierce-sinewed, herded
In thunder, and I tell you now that he
Will stand for fifty cows within a morning
And rage for more. Only one herdsman can
Halter him. Boys could play hurley on his back,
They could.'
                    The neighbours had come in.
                                        He drank
The more.
                    'Aye, mighty is this Bull of mine,
Where is his fellow? There is not a bull,
Not one bred to withstand him. He will fling
Your bullock on a horn. His roar is louder
Than the lifting wave of Roary when the foam
Is throning. I stand at the door and men
Strike in. The board is plentiful. I make
His praise. They sit down by the fire and tell
Of wonders.
                    No, I will not lend the Bull.
There is none other. Let this woman turn
A wishing stone though she is queen. I'd have
No women in the herding.
                                        Mighty is
This Bull.'
                    'Remember, Dara, the great wealth
That you will have by road. You will become
A chieftain. Golden blinkers on the mules
That we shall send.'
                    'Neighbours, what will they say
In Ulster? He that bows to the west, may crop
The roadside grass!'
                    'But, man, they have a power
Of wealth.'
                    'Come west, MacDara. You shall have,
Bringing the Bull as broad lands he can roam
Within a day, a big car worth a score

Of women, brown land, early land and mowing
To spare, come west, MacDara, west.'
                                    He spat
Awhile.
            'But tell me of the grass
There,'
            'Sweet it is and hardy to the mouth
Now.'
            'Take a quart of ale, young man
And let me think. The bull is great, the prize
Greater. Why are those fellows making such
A noise?
            Hush there.'
                        Far down the hall
The Connaught herdsmen squabbled with the men
Of Ulster nor took heed while fleecy ale
Flocked through the gap:
                            'There is no grass
In the west.'
            'Our cattle are the hardier
In the hoof.'
            'Boys, they have drained the jug,'
'We have walked far.'
                        'This is our roof.'
'We have walked far.'
                        'We are the better men.'
'Black cattle of the west.'
                        'You lie.'
                                'Black cattle
Of the west, to sell.'
                        'This is no fair
To clap the bargain on a heifer's back.'
'Black cattle of the west.'
                        'We are no dealers.'
'We make no bid.'
                        'We'll take the bloody bull.'
'They cannot take the bullock.'
                                While they fought
Or wrestled, black-eyed Caoilte spilled the cups

And played —

> *'There are no men*
> *Can tether the fillies of Maeve*
> *For they have eaten such green oats*
> *They have grown heady*
> *Galloping on great wings*
> *About the glen.'*

Angrily MacRoth
Pulled out his sword and drove the harp and men
Beyond the door.

'Out, bad player, out
And if there is a river swim and peck
Your brood of gabbling wings.'

MacDara
Rushed from the farmers.

'By god, now, you have driven
My men out of my house but it was yours
That horned the knives. I see all clearly now
And you will never have this Bull of mine
On hire to fill your cows. Now take your money
Out of my lands for by the kindly laws
Of hospitality it is your own
To carry to that meddlesome red woman
In the west.'

'Good Dara, I but drove
The cups out of your house. Let us sit down
Again, put moves upon the board or count
This wealth.'

'Go to your ruly queen now.'

'Dara
Count up that store of labourable gold,
The lowing herds.'

Outside rough voices cursed
And fought but from the mountain acres rose
A bellowing that shook the rafters.

Dara
Bull-headed, blood-eyed, hurled the burly farmers
Back, scattering them as dice and shouted:

'The Bull

The Bull,
        They wull na' take the Bull.'
                         The men
Rushed in again. The house was filled with noise
Of breaking stools and heads.
                   'Be quiet now'
Cried Roth
        'Is this a country dance where boys
Take drink and fight for the women?'
                     MacDara
Heading the farmers, turned:
                'Now drive these herds
Back to their grey crops.'
            The Connaught man
Replied –
       'The new green withe is peeled
For breaking. Dara, you have scorned the will
That holds wide Connaught and the windy flock
Of island but the armies of Red Maeve
Shall bare these plains with hooks of fire and take
The Bull.' –
         And turning at the crowded door
Of parting flung his sword upon the floor.

Pilgrimage and Other Poems

(1929)

Pilgrimage

When the far south glittered
Behind the grey beaded plains,
And cloudier ships were bitted
Along the pale waves,
The showery breeze — that plies
A mile from Ara — stood
And took our boat on sand:
There by dim wells the women tied
A wish on thorn, while rainfall
Was quiet as the turning of books
In the holy schools at dawn.

Grey holdings of rain
Had grown less with the fields,
As we came to that blessed place
Where hail and honey meet.
O Clonmacnoise was crossed
With light: those cloistered scholars,
Whose knowledge of the gospel
Is cast as metal in pure voices,
Were all rejoicing daily,
And cunning hands with cold and jewels
Brought chalices to flame.

Loud above the grassland,
In Cashel of the towers,
We heard with the yellow candles
The chanting of the hours,
White clergy saying High Mass,
A fasting crowd at prayer,
A choir that sang before them;
And in stained glass the holy day
Was sainted as we passed
Beyond that chancel where the dragons
Are carved upon the arch.

Treasured with chasuble,
Sun-braided, rich cloak'd wine-cup,
We saw, there, iron handbells,
Great annals in the shrine
A high-king bore to battle:
Where, from the branch of Adam,
The noble forms of language –
Brighter than green or blue enamels
Burned in white bronze – embodied
The wings and fiery animals
Which veil the chair of God.

Beyond a rocky townland
And that last tower where ocean
Is dim as haze, a sound
Of wild confession rose:
Black congregations moved
Around the booths of prayer
To hear a saint reprove them;
And from his boat he raised a blessing
To souls that had come down
The holy mountain of the west
Or wailed still in the cloud.

Light in the tide of Shannon
May ride at anchor half
The day and, high in spar-top
Or leather sails of their craft,
Wine merchants will have sleep;
But on a barren isle,
Where Paradise is praised
At daycome, smaller than the sea-gulls,
We heard white Culdees pray
Until our hollow ship was kneeling
Over the longer waves.

Celibacy

On a brown isle of Lough Corrib,
When clouds were bare as branch
And water had been thorned
By colder days, I sank
In torment of her side;
But still that woman stayed,
For eye obeys the mind.

Bedraggled in the briar
And grey fire of the nettle,
Three nights, I fell, I groaned
On the flagstone of help
To pluck her from my body;
For servant ribbed with hunger
May climb his rungs to God.

Eyelid stood back in sleep,
I saw what seemed an Angel:
Dews dripped from those bright feet.
But, O, I knew the stranger
By her deceit and, tired
All night by tempting flesh,
I wrestled her in hair-shirt.

On pale knees in the dawn,
Parting the straw that wrapped me,
She sank until I saw
The bright roots of her scalp.
She pulled me down to sleep,
But I fled as the Baptist
To thistle and to reed.

The dragons of the Gospel
Are cast by bell and crook;
But fiery as the frost
Or bladed light, she drew
The reeds back, when I fought
The arrow-headed airs
That darken on the water.

The Confession of Queen Gormlai

Dawn, fielding on the mountains,
Had found that hovel
And in the dark she lay there,
Whom kings had loved,
Sharp on a shoulder-blade
Turning in straw and rags;
While, crossed from that clay threshold,
Her flesh became a dagger.

Monk, do not lift the hood
From black to hearing white;
The shadows of the schoolmen
That drift from fire to ice
Stoop, and my mind is stirred,
Remembering the books
I closed, for I am Gormlai
And she was beautiful.

With jewels and enamel
Men hammer in black gold,
In halls where feast was trampled
And camps the battle-axe
Had lit, I wore the crimson
My women worked in pattern;
And heard such flattering words,
That I bit to the kernel.

When companies came south,
I was in too much pride,
Counting the royal housework,
Vats of red-purple dye.
I had the light of linen,
Blue windows in the sun
To look from: I had thinness
Of white bread and Greek honey.

Starred airs were beaten fine
As silver when the craftsmen
Came; clergy graced the wine-cup
And scholars played at draughts.
But I laughed with grave Cormac
Above the candle-rows
And heard the string leap back
To men and women dancing.

His dogs had dashed a white stag,
The day that Cormac bared
Himself upon the flagstone
And was alone in prayer.
All night he turned to God
Because the body dies;
But had it been immodest
For him to rest beside me?

I had not read in book
That goodness can insult
The mind, that meeting looks
Are bright adultery.
Though I have lain in three beds
And many have blamed me,
No man has seen me naked,
Partaken in my shame.

O monk, when head is shaven –
Can grave be any less?
I count what Cormac gave me
No more than little blessing.
Our marriage was annulled,
The Mass bell rung by force,
The flesh that was made one,
Divided and divorced.

Flann, my own father, bargained
With Carrol, king of Leinster,
And joined our lands in marriage.
Black bridegroom of a sin,

He banished my musicians
And careful scribe. I feared
When Cormac was made bishop.
Could I stop war by tears?

He drank at posted fires
Where armies had been glutted
And he shrank bars of iron
Whenever his hand shut,
At night was it not lust,
Though I were fast in prayers,
For Carrol with his muscle
To thrust me in black hair?

He cropped the greener land
To Cashel top. He took
The bishop in his chapel
And wrung the holy mass-book.
But Cormac, in the fury,
Stumbled from crook to handbell –
And by the axe-red tonsure,
At his own font, he fell.

Unfooted light and rain
Were staked at Bealamoon;
The clergy fought in mail
Till Carrol had been wounded
And carried on a branch.
With my own hands I nursed
That big man in the blanket:
His wife took sweat and purge.

I have known politics
And tongue is tripped to blame.
The night I called him wicked,
Was I not quickly shamed?
Turning upon his sick-bed,
He kicked me with foul words
And my pale household fled –
O man within the cowl!

Fair Nial of the north,
The clerks may hold it sinful
To love the wife of Cormac,
For she was of your kin.
Good tent between the hostings
To bed me! O white Branch
Of Care – they sin the most
Who never broke commandment.

Two husbands had not fasted
With me – and they were slain.
One turned my soul at Cashel:
His powerful foe had shamed
The bed. All blame a widow
That rids herself of grief.
But, Nial, the day you rode back
I came with oils and mead.

Breaking in rain, the dayshine
Was driven against the glen
Where swineherds skulked in clay,
The sudden hail was fencing
Barley with oats and oakwood;
But you spoke, as we galloped,
Of farmers in housed smoke
As heavy as their crops.

For drizzling miles we kissed,
We clung to the glistening saddle
On roads that rang and misted
Below us, promised madly
To pray, but in cold heather
We broke the marriage ring,
Under your leathern cloak,
By thoughts that were a sin.

Smithied in gloom the low day
Had glowed upon the axle,
Southward along the causeways
The hilly clouds were backing:

We saw the drummers ride
The sands beside our kingdom,
And — as in sky — the tide stand
Amid a clan of wings.

But, husband, we repented
With penance on bare feet,
Received the sacraments
Within the holy week.
Happy in house and glen,
I turned the strap and silver,
Reading my books in Lent
Before I was a mother.

I lie in dock and fennel
Because my days were filled
With ease. I cast the linen
Upon my skin for silk.
I sent the babe to suck,
And with white pens I wrote.
But Cormac wore the shirt
Of fire, the shoes of stone.

At dark the doorkeepers
Are ragged in the draught:
Can they bar dreams from sleep
When spirits are unclad
And pitted in the air?
O Nial, that state of grace
Deceived us. Yearly parents,
Your pleasures are unchaste.

Tall ships have wharfed a town
Beside the south where Nial
Fell with the strange blue crowds
That cry in driven sleet.
Souls, dripping from the bulwark
That whistles sand through water,
Have drawn, where no suns dip,
Eel, otter and black swan.

Monk, if in matrimony
The pair that has been blessed
May please the lower limbs —
My third bed was not less.
I grieve our vessels shake
The soul and though I grovel
As Cormac in true shame,
I am impure with love.

At sun, she lay forsaken
And in red hair, she dragged
Her arms, around the stake
Of that wild bed, from rags
That cut the gleam of chin
And hip men had desired:
Murmuring of the sins
Whose hunger is the mind.

The Scholar

Summer delights the scholar
With knowledge and reason.
Who is happy in hedgerow
Or meadow as he is?

Paying no dues to the parish,
He argues in logic
And has no care of cattle
But a satchel and stick.

The showery airs grow softer,
He profits from his ploughland
For the share of the schoolmen
Is a pen in hand.

When midday hides the reaping,
He sleeps by a river
Or comes to the stone plain
Where the saints live.

But in winter by the big fires,
The ignorant hear his fiddle,
And he battles on the chessboard,
As the land lords bid him.

The Cardplayer

Had I diamonds in plenty, I would stake
My pocket on kings that walked out with Queen Maeve,
Or wager the acre that no man digs in Connaught;
And after the drinking I would cross my soul, there,
At the bare stations of the Red Lake.

They gave me hearts as my share of the dealing,
But the head that I like is not red and it is not black;
So I thought of the three that went over the water
And the earth they had when they brought Deirdre back;
For who break their money on a card that is foolish,
May find the woman in the pack.

Patric came, without harm, out of cold Hell…
A beggar nailed the black ace on the board.
I flung the game to the floor, I rose from their cursing;
And paler than a sword, I saw before me
The face for which a kingdom fell.

The Young Woman of Beare

Through lane or black archway,
The praying people hurry,
When shadows have been walled,
At market hall and gate,
By low fires after nightfall;
The bright sodalities
Are bannered in the churches;
But I am only roused
By horsemen of de Burgo
That gallop to my house.

Gold slots of the sunlight
Close up my lids at evening.
Half clad in silken piles
I lie upon a hot cheek.
Half in dream I lie there
Until bad thoughts have bloomed
In flushes of desire.
Drowsy with indulgence,
I please a secret eye
That opens at the Judgment.

I am the bright temptation
In talk, in wine, in sleep.
Although the clergy pray,
I triumph in a dream.
Strange armies tax the south,
Yet little do I care
What fiery bridge or town
Has heard the shout begin –
That Ormond's men are out
And the Geraldine is in.

The women at green stall
And doorstep on a weekday,
Who have been chinned with scorn
Of me, would never sleep

So well, could they but know
Their husbands turn at midnight,
And covet in a dream
The touching of my flesh.
Small wonder than men kneel
The longer at confession.

Bullies, that fight in dramshop
For fluttered rags and bare side
At beggars' bush, may gamble
To-night on what they find.
I laze in yellow lamplight —
Young wives have envied me —
And laugh among lace pillows,
For a big-booted captain
Has poured the purse of silver
That glitters in my lap.

Heavily on his elbow,
He turns from a caress
To see — as my arms open —
The red spurs of my breast.
I draw fair pleats around me
And stay his eye at pleasure,
Show but a white knee-cap
Or an immodest smile —
Until his sudden hand
Had dared the silks that bind me.

See! See, as from a lathe
My polished body turning!
He bares me at the waist
And now blue clothes uncurl
Upon white haunch. I let
The last bright stitch fall down
For him as I lean back,
Straining with longer arms
Above my head to snap
The silver knots of sleep.

Together in the dark –
Sin-fast – we can enjoy
What is allowed in marriage.
The jingle of that coin
Is still the same, though stolen:
But are they not unthrifty,
Who spend it in a shame
That brings ill and repentance,
When they might pinch and save
Themselves in lawful pleasure?

. . . . .

Young girls, keep from dance-hall
And dark side of the road;
My common ways began
In idle thought and courting.
I strayed the mountain fields
And got a bad name down
In Beare. Yes, I became
So careless of my placket,
That after I was blamed,
I went out to the islands.

Pull the boats on the roller
And rope them in the tide!
For the fire has got a story
That while the nets were drying,
I stretched to plank and sun
With strong men in their leather;
In scandal on the wave,
I fled with a single man
And caught behind a sail
The air that goes to Ireland.

He drew me from the seas
One night, without an oar,
To strip between the beach
And dark ribs of that boat.
Hard bed had turned to softness –

We drowsed into small hours.
How could I tell the glancing
Of men that awakened me,
When daylight in my lashes
Thickened with yellow sleep?

My fear was less than joy
To gallop from the tide;
Hooded among his horsemen,
MacWilliam bore me tighter.
The green land by Lough Corrib
Spoke softly and all day
We followed through a forest
The wet heel of the axe,
Where sunlight had been trestled
In clearing and in gap.

At dark a sudden threshold
Was squared in light. Men cast
Their shadows as we rode up
That fiery short-cut. Bench
And board were full at night.
Unknown there to the clergy,
I stayed with him to sin.
Companies of carousing –
Was I not for a winter
The darling of your house?

. . . . .

Women, obey the mission –
Be modest in your clothes
Each manly look and wish
Is punished but the more.
In king's house, I have called
Hurlers and men that fight.
It is my grief that time
Cannot appease my hunger;
I flourish where desire is
And still, still I am young.

I prosper, for the towns
Have made my skin but finer.
Hidden as words in mouth,
My fingers can entice
Until the sight is dim
And conscience lost in flame.
Then, to a sound of bracelets,
I look down and my locks
Are curtailed on a nape
That leads men into wrong.

Ships glide in Limerick
Between tall houses, isled
By street and castle: there
Are flighted steps to climb.
Soon with a Flemish merchant
I lodged at Thomond Gate.
I had a painted bedpost
Of blue and yellow ply,
A bright pot and rich curtains
That I could pull at night.

But in that corner house
Of guilt, my foreign face
Shook voices in the crowd,
As I leaned out to take
The twilight at my sill.
When tide had filled the boat-rings,
Few dealers could be tempted
Who drank upon the fair-day:
The black friars preached to them
And frightened me with prayers.

As I came to the Curragh
I heard how, at their ease,
Bands of the Geraldine
Gather with joy to see
The going of young horses
At morning on the plain.
A mile from Scholars Town

I turned to ask the way
And laughing with the chapmen,
I rode into the Pale.

The summer had seen plenty;
I saw but a black crop
And knew the President
Of Munster had come back.
All day, in high and low street,
His orderlies ran by.
At night I entertained him
Between the wine and map;
I whispered with the statesmen,
The lawyers that break land.

. . . . .

I am the dark temptation
Men know – and shining orders
Of clergy have condemned me.
I fear, alone, that lords
Of diocese are coped
With gold, their staven hands
Upraised again to save
All those I have corrupted:
I fear, lost and too late,
The prelates of the church.

In darker lane or archway,
I heard an hour ago
The men and women murmur;
They came back from Devotions.
Half-wakened by the tide,
Ships rise along the quay
As though they were unloading.
I turn a drowsy side –
That dreams, the eye has known,
May trouble souls to-night.

South-Westerly Gale

Haste, in the taffrail,
Had tightened every rope
And Inishturk drove back
From spray. Night on that shore
Maddened the bolt; and men
At fire or lighted table,
Heard, as the bishop prayed,
The shipwrecked cry of sinners –
The clang of bar and spike
Rolling the timbered wine.

Far waves came back at day
To double their white dances,
As though they were still breaking
On rock. Low skies outran
The rain; but Claremen played
Backgammon in the house
And squander of their crowns
Was molten as the haze,
Blowing from the foundries
Of storm within the south.

Calm of the evening
Brought companies to boat
Or step, when tide was greener
And flocked air lay on foam.
For they had seen a tall ship
Stand to the sun in flame
Between the cloud and wave,
Trimming her golden wicks –
And wagered that she came
From Portugal or Spain.

The Marriage Night

O let her name be told
At dusk – while fishermen
Take nobles on the oar
And pass the fiery dice
Of wineshops at the harbour,
That flush them in the haze:
There is a darker town
Of ships upon the wave.

The morning she rode down
Where topsails, that had brought
A blessing from the Pope,
Were scrolled in early water:
Such light was on her cheekbone
And chin – who would not praise
In holy courts of Europe
The wonder of our days?

All saw in that cathedral
The great Earls kneel with her;
The open book was carried,
They got up at the gospel.
In joy the clergy prayed,
The white-clad acolytes
Were chaining, and unchaining,
Fire-hearted frankincense.

Upon her night of marriage,
Confessions were devout;
Murmuring, as religion
Flamed by, men saw her brow.
The Spaniards rolled with flag
And drum in quick relays;
Our nobles were encamping
Each day around Kinsale.

But in deceit of smoke
And fire, the spoilers came:
Tower and unmortar'd wall broke
Rich flight to street and gate.
O she has curbed her bright head
Upon the chancel rail
With shame, and by her side
Those heretics have lain.

The Planter's Daughter

When night stirred at sea
And the fire brought a crowd in,
They say that her beauty
Was music in mouth
And few in the candlelight
Thought her too proud,
For the house of the planter
Is known by the trees.

Men that had seen her
Drank deep and were silent,
The women were speaking
Wherever she went –
As a bell that is rung
Or a wonder told shyly,
And O she was the Sunday
In every week.

Aisling

At morning from the coldness of Mount Brandon,
The sail is blowing half-way to the light;
And islands are so small, a man may carry
Their yellow crop in one cart at low tide.
Sadly in thought, I strayed the mountain grass
To hear the breezes following their young
And by the furrow of a stream, I chanced
To find a woman airing in the sun.

Coil of her hair, in cluster and ringlet,
Had brightened round her forehead and those curls —
Closer than she could bind them on a finger —
Were changing gleam and glitter. O she turned
So gracefully aside, I thought her clothes
Were flame and shadow while she slowly walked,
Or that each breast was proud because it rode
The cold air as the wave stayed by the swan.

But knowing her face was fairer than in thought,
I asked of her was she the Geraldine —
Few horsemen sheltered at the steps of water?
Or that Greek woman, lying in a piled room
On tousled purple, whom the household saved,
When frescoes of strange fire concealed the pillar:
The white coin all could spend? Might it be Niav
And was she over wave or from our hills?

'When shadows in wet grass are heavier
Than hay, beside dim wells the women gossip
And by the paler bushes tell the daylight;
But from what bay, uneasy with a shipping
Breeze, have you come?' I said 'O do you cross
The blue thread and the crimson on the framework,
At darkfall in a house where nobles throng
And the slow oil climbs up into the flame?'

'Black and fair strangers leave upon the oar
And there is peace,' she answered. 'Companies
Are gathered in the house that I have known;
Claret is on the board and they are pleased
By storytelling. When the turf is redder
And airy packs of wonder have been told,
My women dance to bright steel that is wed,
Starlike, upon the anvil with one stroke.'

'Shall I, too, find at dark of rain,' I cried,
'Neighbours around a fire cast up by the ocean
And in that shining mansion hear the rise
Of companies, or bide among my own –
Pleasing a noble ear? O must I wander
Without praise, without wine, in rich strange lands?'
But with a smile the secret woman left me
At morning in the coldness of Mount Brandon.

Collected Poems

(1936)

Wandering Men

When sudden night had trapped the wood,
We stumbled by dark earthing
To find a path we never knew
Though we went down on bare knee.
But as we prayed there came a sound
Of canticles upon the air,
A momentary flame that rounded
The bell-house of Kildare.

Among her women on the threshold
Great Brigid gave us welcome.
She had concealed in colder veil
Too soon the flaming of her forehead
That drew our eyelids in the wood.
By shadowy arch she led the way,
She brought us to a lighted room
And served each one at table.

I think it was the food of Eden
We shared, for that new ale,
Though brighter than the serpent-reed,
Was not indeed of summer's brew,
And drowsily we heard the calling
Of voices from an instrument –
Soft as the music that King Saul
Had feared beyond his tent.

And all that night I was aware
Of shapes no priest can see,
The centaur at a house of prayer,
The sceptred strangers from the East.
Confined in dreams we saw again
How Brigid, while her women slept
Around her, templed by the flame,
Sat in a carven chair.

We wakened with the early blackbird
Before the oaks had drawn
An old sun-circle in the grass:
The sightly house was gone.
Yet we gave praise to that sky-woman
For wayfare and a vision shown
At night to harmless men who have
No parish of their own.

Six Sentences

Black and Tans

No man can drink in any public-house
In Dublin but these roarers look for trouble
And break an open door in — Officer,
When spirits are at hand, the clock is moon:
Command these men, dreadful as what they hold,
Nor think the pockets of a pious poet
Have something worse in them than this poor curse.

Civil War

I

I could not praise too hot a heart
Or take a bellows to that blaze,
Yet, knowing I would never see him,
I gave my hand to Liam Mellowes.

II

They are the spit of virtue now,
Prating of law and honour,
But we remember how they shot
Rory O'Connor.

To James Stephens

Now that the iron shoe hangs by a nail
Once more and nobody has cared a damn,
Stick to the last of the leprechaun – I, too,
Have meddled with the anvil of our trade.

No Recompense

Quality, number and the sweet divisions
Of reason may forget their schoolmen now,
And door-chill, body's heat, a common ill,
Grow monstrous in our sleep: I have endured
The enmity of my own mind that feared
No argument; but O when truth itself
Can hold a despairing tongue, what recompense
To find my name in any mortal mouth?

The Tales of Ireland

The thousand tales of Ireland sink: I leave
Unfinished what I had begun nor count
As gain the youthful frenzy of those years;
For I remember my own passing breath,
Man's violence and all the despair of brain
That wind and river took in Glenasmole.

Night and Morning: Poems

(1938)

Night and Morning

I know the injured pride of sleep,
The strippers at the mocking-post,
The insult in the house of Caesar
And every moment that can hold
In brief the miserable act
Of centuries. Thought can but share
Belief – and the tormented soul,
Changing confession to despair,
Must wear a borrowed robe.

Morning has moved the dreadful candle,
Appointed shadows cross the nave;
Unlocked by the secular hand,
The very elements remain
Appearances upon the altar.
Adoring priest has turned his back
Of gold upon the congregation.
All saints have had their day at last,
But thought still lives in pain.

How many councils and decrees
Have perished in the simple prayer
That gave obedience to the knee;
Trampling of rostrum, feathering
Of pens at cock-rise, sum of reason
To elevate a common soul:
Forgotten as the minds that bled
For us, the miracle that raised
A language from the dead.

O when all Europe was astir
With echo of learned controversy,
The voice of logic led the choir.
Such quality was in all being,
The forks of heaven and this earth
Had met, town-walled, in mortal view
And in the pride that we ignore,
The holy rage of argument,
God was made man once more.

Mortal Pride

When thought of all our thought has crossed
The mind in pain, God only knows
What we must suffer to be lost,
What soul is called our own.
Before the truth was hid in torment,
With nothing but this mortal pride,
I dreamed of every joy on earth
And shamed the angel at my side.

Pray, how shall any bride discover
A husband in the state of bliss,
Learn in the curious arms of love
The ancient catechism
Man must obey? She never fears
He will forget the sacrament.
But thought is older than the years:
Before our doom, it came and went.

Tenebrae

This is the hour that we must mourn
With tallows on the black triangle,
Night has a napkin deep in fold
To keep the cup; yet who dare pray
If all in reason should be lost,
The agony of man betrayed
At every station of the cross?

O when the forehead is too young,
Those centuries of mortal anguish,
Dabbed by a consecrated thumb
That crumbles into dust, will bring
Despair with all that we can know;
And there is nothing left to sing,
Remembering our innocence.

I hammer on that common door,
Too frantic in my superstition,
Transfix with nails that I have broken,
The angry notice of the mind.
Close as the thought that suffers him,
The habit every man in time
Must wear beneath his ironed shirt.

An open mind disturbs the soul,
And in disdain I turn my back
Upon the sun that makes a show
Of half the world, yet still deny
The pain that lives within the past,
The flame sinking upon the spike,
Darkness that man must dread at last.

Martha Blake

Before the day is everywhere
And the timid warmth of sleep
Is delicate on limb, she dares
The silence of the street
Until the double bells are thrown back
For Mass and echoes bound
In the chapel yard, O then her soul
Makes bold in the arms of sound.

But in the shadow of the nave
Her well-taught knees are humble,
She does not see through any saint
That stands in the sun
With veins of lead, with painful crown;
She waits that dreaded coming,
When all the congregation bows
And none may look up.

The word is said, the Word sent down,
The miracle is done
Beneath those hands that have been rounded
Over the embodied cup,
And with a few, she leaves her place
Kept by a east-filled window
And kneels at the communion rail
Starching beneath her chin.

She trembles for the Son of Man,
While the priest is murmuring
What she can scarcely tell, her heart
Is making such a stir;
But when he picks a particle
And she puts out her tongue,
That joy is the glittering of candles
And benediction sung.

Her soul is lying in the Presence
Until her senses, one
By one, desiring to attend her,
Come as for feast and run
So fast to share the sacrament,
Her mouth must mother them:
'Sweet tooth grow wise, lip, gum be gentle,
I touch a purple hem.'

Afflicted by that love she turns
To multiply her praise,
Goes over all the foolish words
And finds they are the same;
But now she feels within her breast
Such calm that she is silent,
For soul can never be immodest
Where body may not listen.

On a holy day of obligation
I saw her first in prayer,
But mortal eye had been too late
For all that thought could dare.
The flame in heart is never grieved
That pride and intellect
Were cast below, when God revealed
A heaven for this earth.

So to begin the common day
She needs a miracle,
Knowing the safety of angels
That see her home again,
Yet ignorant of all the rest,
The hidden grace that people
Hurrying to business
Look after in the street.

Repentance

When I was younger than the soul
That wakes me now at night, I saw
The mortal mind in such a glory –
All knowledge was in Connaught.
I crossed the narrows of earthward light,
The rain, noon-set along the mountain,
And I forgot the scale of thought,
Man's lamentation, Judgment hour
That hides the sun in the waters.

But as I stumbled to the flint
Where blessed Patric drove a crowd
Of fiends that roared like cattlemen,
Until they stamped themselves out
Between the fiery pens, I felt
Repentance gushing from the rock;
For I had made a bad confession
Once, feared to name in ugly box
The growing pains of flesh.

I count the sorrowful mysteries
Of earth before the celebrant
Has turned to wash his mouth in wine.
The soul is confined to a holy vessel,
And intellect less than desire.
O I will stay to the last Gospel,
Cupping my heart with prayer;
Knuckle and knee are all we know
When the mind is half despairing.

No story handed down in Connaught
Can cheat a man, nor any learning
Keep the fire in, turn his folly
From thinking of that book in Heaven.
Could I unbutton mad thought, quick-save
My skin, if I were caught at last
Without my soul and dragged to torment,
Ear-drumming in that dreadful place
Where the sun hides in the waters?

The Lucky Coin

Collect the silver on a Sunday,
Weigh the pennies of the poor,
His soul can make a man afraid
And yet thought will endure.
But who can find by any chance
A coin of different shape
That never came from Salamanca
Or danced on chapel plate?

Though time is slipping through all fingers
And body dare not stay,
That lucky coin, I heard men tell it,
Had glittered once in Galway
And crowds were elbowing the spirit
While every counter shone,
Forgetting grief until the ages
Had changed it for a song.

Turning in cartwheels on the fairground,
The sun was hastier –
That strolling girls might have for dowry,
Two hands about a waist;
Men voted for the Liberator
After the booths were closed
And only those in failing health
Remembered their own souls.

On Nephin many a knot was tied,
The sweet in tongue made free there,
Lovers forgot on the mountain-side
The stern law of the clergy
That kiss, pinch, squeeze, hug, smack denied,
Forgot the evil, harm
And scandal that comes closer, lying
In one another's arms.

Not one of us will ever find
That coin of different shape
For it was lost before our rising
Or stolen – as some say.
But when our dread of the unseen
Has rifled hole and corner,
How shall we praise the men that freed us
From everything but thought.

The Straying Student

On a holy day when sails were blowing southward,
A bishop sang the Mass in Inishmore,
Men took one side, their wives were on the other
But I heard the woman coming from the shore;
And wild in despair my parents cried aloud
For they saw the vision draw me to the doorway.

Long had she lived in Rome when Popes were bad,
The wealth of every age she makes her own,
Yet smiled on me in eager admiration,
And for a summer taught me all I know,
Banishing shame with her great laugh that rang
As if a pillar caught it back alone.

I learned the prouder counsel of her throat,
My mind was growing bold as light in Greece;
And when in sleep her stirring limbs were shown,
I blessed the noonday rock that knew no tree:
And for an hour the mountain was her throne,
Although her eyes were bright with mockery.

They say I was sent back from Salamanca
And failed in logic, but I wrote her praise
Nine times upon a college wall in France.
She laid her hand at darkfall on my page
That I might read the heavens in a glance
And I knew every star the Moors have named.

Awake or in my sleep, I have no peace now,
Before the ball is struck, my breath has gone,
And yet I tremble lest she may deceive me
And leave me in this land, where every woman's son
Must carry his own coffin and believe,
In dread, all that the clergy teach the young.

Penal Law

Burn Ovid with the rest. Lovers will find
A hedge-school for themselves and learn by heart
All that the clergy banish from the mind,
When hands are joined and head bows in the dark.

Her Voice Could Not Be Softer

Suddenly in the dark wood
She turned from my arms and cried
As if her soul were lost,
And O too late I knew,
Although the blame was mine,
Her voice could not be softer
When she told it in confession.

Summer Lightning

The heavens opened. With a scream
The blackman at his night-prayers
Had disappeared in blasphemy,
And iron beds were bared;
Day was unshuttered again,
The elements had lied,
Ashing the faces of mad men
Until God's likeness died.

Napoleon took his glittering vault
To be a looking-glass.
Lord Mitchell, pale and suffering,
Fell to the floor in halves.
The cells were filling. Christopher
O'Brien, strapped in pain,
For all the rage of syphilis,
Had millions in his brain.

James Dunn leaped down the dormitory,
Thought has no stopping-place,
His bright bed was a corner shop,
Opening, closing, late.
Behind a grille, the unfrocked priest
Had told his own confession:
Accident in every street
Rang the Angelus.

Flight beyond flight, new stories flashed
Or darkened with affliction
Until the sweet choir of Mount Argus
Was heard at every window,
Was seen in every wing. The blackman
Kept laughing at his night-prayers
For somebody in white had taken
His photograph downstairs.

When sleep has shot the bolt and bar,
And reason fails at midnight,
Dreading that every thought at last
Must stand in our own light
Forever, sinning without end;
I pity, in their pride
And agony of wrong, the men
In whom God's likeness died.

The Jewels

The crumbling centuries are thrust
In hands that are too frail for them
And we, who squabble with our dust,
Have learned in anguish to dissemble;
Yet taken in the darkest need
Of mind, no faith makes me ashamed.
Whether the breath is foul or sweet
The truth is still the same.

If ordinary thought prevail
In all this knocking of the ribs
And the dead heat of mortal haste,
Why should I hesitate at morning
Or wake a memory of myself,
All eyes, terrible as the jewels
And carbons of the consciousness
That waste the night in falsehood?

The sanctuary lamp is lowered
In witness of our ignorance;
Greed of religion makes us old
Before our time. We are undone
Within the winking of an eyelid,
The very heavens are assailed
And there is nothing can be hidden:
Love darts and thunders from the rail.

The misery of common faith
Was ours before the age of reason.
Hurrying years cannot mistake
The smile for the decaying teeth,
The last confusion of our senses.
But O to think, when I was younger
And could not tell the difference,
God lay upon this tongue.

Ancient Lights
Poems and Satires: First Series

(1955)

Celebrations

Who dare complain or be ashamed
Of liberties our arms have taken?
For every spike upon that gateway,
We have uncrowned the past:
And open hearts are celebrating
Prosperity of church and state
In the shade of Dublin Castle.

So many flagpoles can be seen now
Freeing the crowd, while crisscross keys,
On yellow-and-white above the green,
Treble the wards of nation,
God only knows what treasury
Uncrams to keep each city borough
And thoroughfare in grace.

Let ageing politicians pray
Again, hoardings recount our faith,
The blindfold woman in a rage
Condemn her own for treason:
No steeple topped the scale that Monday,
Rebel souls had lost their savings
And looters braved the street.

Fashion

Now they have taken off their stockings
And bared the big toe like a monk,
Warned by the figuring of thin frock
And belt, modesty must look up –
Only to meet so pure a glance
The ancient sermon will not fit
Since right and wrong, though self-important,
Forget the long and short of it.

Marriage

Parents are sinful now, for they must whisper
Too much in the dark. Aye, there's the rub! What grace
Can snatch the small hours from that costly kiss?
Those who slip off the ring, try to be chaste
And when they cannot help it, steal the crumbs
From their own wedding breakfast, spare expense
And keep in warmth the children they have nourished.
But shall the sweet promise of the sacrament
Gladden the heart, if mortals calculate
Their pleasures by the calendar? Night-school
Of love where all, who learn to cheat, grow pale
With guilty hope at every change of moon!

Three Poems about Children

I

Better the book against the rock,
The misery of roofless faith,
Than all this mockery of time,
Eternalising of mute souls.
Though offerings increase, increase,
The ancient arms can bring no peace,
When the first breath is unforgiven
And charity, to find a home,
Redeems the baby from the breast.
O, then, at the very font of grace,
Pity, pity – the dumb must cry.
Their tiny tears are in the walls
We build. They turn to dust so soon,
How can we learn upon our knees,
That ironside unropes the bell?

II

These infants die too quick
For our salvation, caught up
By a fatal sign from Limbo,
Unfathered in our thought
Before they can share the sky
With us. Though faith allow
Obscurity of being
And clay rejoice: flowers
That wither in the heat
Of benediction, one
By one, are thrown away.

III

Martyr and heretic
Have been the shrieking wick!
But smoke of faith on fire
Can hide us from enquiry
And trust in Providence
Rid us of vain expense.
So why should pity uncage
A burning orphanage,
Bar flight to little souls
That set no churchbell tolling?
Cast-iron step and rail
Could but prolong the wailing:
Has not a Bishop declared
That flame-wrapped babes are spared
Our life-time of temptation?
Leap, mind, in consolation
For heart can only lodge
Itself, plucked out by logic.
Those children, charred in Cavan,
Passed straight through Hell to Heaven.

Offerings

Pity poor souls long suffering
In Purgatory, try to name
The living ones in crowded street.
What light can any stranger borrow
From them? Soon, very soon, we fade
As memory when our small savings
Are gone and every Mass is said.
And now in city churches, few
Pay little visits for our sake
At dusk. The candle-box is filled
With other pennies. In the morning,
Black alb is worn for eyelids that carry
In quiet tears the newly dead.

Bequests

When money burns in the last breath
Of frightened age, such bells are set
In air, their tongues will stick at nothing
Until religious institutions
Have storied every contribution.
Glad souls are in the signature
And yet God knows, despite our girders,
The spirit-level and the rule
Must witness to those shaking hands.

Ancient Lights

When all of us wore smaller shoes
And knew the next world better than
The knots we broke, I used to hurry
On missions of my own to Capel
Street, Bolton Street and Granby Row
To see what man has made. But darkness
Was roomed with fears. Sleep, stripped by woes
I had been taught, beat door, leaped landing,
Lied down the banisters of naught.

Being sent to penance, come Saturday,
I shuffled slower than my sins should.
My fears were candle-spiked at side-shrines,
Rays lengthened them in stained-glass. Confided
To night again, my grief bowed down,
Heard hand on shutter-knob. Did I
Take pleasure, when alone – how much –
In a bad thought, immodest look
Or worse, unnecessary touch?

Closeted in the confessional,
I put on flesh, so many years
Were added to my own, attempted
In vain to keep Dominican
As much i' the dark as I was, mixing
Whispered replies with his low words;
Then shuddered past the crucifix,
The feet so hammered, daubed-on blood-drip,
Black with lip-scrimmage of the damned.

Once as I crept from the church-steps,
Beside myself, the air opened
On purpose. Nature read in a flutter
An evening lesson above my head.
Atwirl beyond the leadings, corbels,
A cage-bird came among sparrows
(The moral inescapable)
Plucked, roof-mired, all in mad bits. O
The pizzicato of its wires!

Goodness of air can be proverbial:
That day, by the kerb at Rutland Square,
A bronze bird fabled out of trees,
Mailing the spearheads of the railings,
Sparrow at nails, I hailed the skies
To save the tiny dropper, found
Appetite gone. A child of clay
Had blustered it away. Pity
Could raise some littleness from dust.

What Sunday clothes can change us now
Or humble orders in black and white?
Stinking with centuries the act
Of thought. So think, man, as Augustine
Did, dread the ink-bespattered ex-monk,
And keep your name. No, let me abandon
Night's jakes. Self-persecuted of late
Among the hatreds of rent Europe,
Poetry burns at a different stake.

Still, still I remember awful downpour
Cabbing Mountjoy Street, spun loneliness
Veiling almost the Protestant church,
Two backyards from my very home,
I dared to shelter at locked door.
There, walled by heresy, my fears
Were solved. I had absolved myself:
Feast-day effulgence, as though I gained
For life a plenary indulgence.

The sun came out, new smoke flew up,
The gutters of the Black Church rang
With services. Waste water mocked
The ballcocks: down-pipes sparrowing,
And all around the spires of Dublin
Such swallowing in the air, such cowling
To keep high offices pure: I heard
From shore to shore, the iron gratings
Take half our heavens with a roar.

Respectable People

Thought rattles along the empty railings
Of street and square they lived in, years
Ago. I dream of them at night,
Strangers to this artificial light,
Respectable people who gave me sweets,
Talked above my head or unfobbed
The time. I know them by each faded
Smile and their old-fashioned clothes.
But how can I make room for them
In a mind too horrible with life?
This is the last straw in the grave,
Propping the tear in which grief burns
Away. Shame of eternity
Has stripped them of their quiet habits,
Unshovelled them out of the past.
Memory finds beyond that last
Improvidence, their mad remains.

Mother and Child

(Marian Year Stamp: 1954)

Obedient keys rattled in locks,
Bottles in old dispensaries
Were shaken and the ballot boxes
Hid politicians on their knees
When pity showed us what we are.
'Why should we care,' votes cried, 'for child
Or mother? Common help is harmful
And state-control must starve the soul.'
One doctor spoke out. Bishops mitred.
But now our caution has been mended.
The side-door opened, bill amended.
We profit from God's love and pity,
Sampling the world with good example.
Before you damp it with your spit,
Respect our newest postage stamp.

Inscription for a Headstone

What Larkin bawled to hungry crowds
Is murmured now in dining-hall
And study. Faith bestirs itself
Lest infidels in their impatience
Leave it behind. Who could have guessed
Batons were blessings in disguise,
When every ambulance was filled
With half-killed men and Sunday trampled
Upon unrest? Such fear can harden
Or soften heart, knowing too clearly
His name endures on our holiest page,
Scrawled in a rage by Dublin's poor.

Emancipation

That wretched girl still wakes me up
At night, for all she wore had been thrown
Away. I see her by O'Connell Bridge
And think: 'Yes, more than a century
Ago, religion went in such rags here.'
But pity is a kind of lust,
Although it stretch and turn. Have I
Not found at least what covers mine,
In the cast-off finery of faith?

An Early Start

Wide-awake, suddenly, as that new clang there,
I clapped my ears beneath the bedclothes, guessing
The Fathers of the Holy Ghost had bought
A bigger bell. Why should our blessed truth
Be measured by the mile? When I was humble,
My lies were quietly sung and never paid,
Yet they have made my bed. I will lie on,
Refuse to count a stroke. Troubler, your tongue
Is silver, though it rust. Strike if you must
And rattle every penny in the house.

The Blackbird of Derrycairn

Stop, stop and listen for the bough top
Is whistling and the sun is brighter
Than God's own shadow in the cup now!
Forget the hour-bell. Mournful matins
Will sound, Patric, as well at nightfall.

Faintly through mist of broken water
Fionn heard my melody in Norway.
He found the forest track, he brought back
This beak to gild the branch and tell, there,
Why men must welcome in the daylight.

He loved the breeze that warns the black grouse,
The shouts of gillies in the morning
When packs are counted and the swans cloud
Loch Erne, but more than all those voices
My throat rejoicing from the hawthorn.

In little cells behind a cashel,
Patric, no handbell gives a glad sound.
But knowledge is found among the branches.
Listen! The song that shakes my feathers
Will thong the leather of your satchels.

Vanishing Irish

Poverty drew lip down and yet there was laughter
In that raggedness of ours. Blind Raftery,
Who knew man's charges are both long and short,
Clapped heat to the touch-hole of the mighty mortar
Once – sent a young fellow, with shirt-tails flying the flag
Of his country, in search of bare toes and a shawl as bedraggled.
But how could he marry? His only belongings were longings,
Hugs, squeezes, kisses, a hundred thousand strong.
And how can I tell of his journey? Our silence now
Is beyond the aim of words and telltale frowned on.
Somewhere, the last of our love-songs found a refuge.
Perhaps in the hall of Rhadamanthus, the deaf
Can hear the comeback of its fol-de-rol
Skipping around the monstrous, unseen columns,
Free from our burden of bad thoughts and gloating,
Content as a flea in Connemara petticoat.

The Envy of Poor Lovers

Pity poor lovers who may not do what they please
With their kisses under a hedge, before a raindrop
Unhouses it; and astir from wretched centuries,
Bramble and briar remind them of the saints.

Her envy is the curtain seen at night-time,
Happy position that could change her name.
His envy — clasp of the married whose thoughts can be alike,
Whose nature flows without the blame or shame.

Lying in the grass as if it were a sin
To move, they hold each other's breath, tremble,
Ready to share that ancient dread — kisses begin
Again — of Ireland keeping company with them.

Think, children, of institutions mured above
Your ignorance, where every look is veiled,
State-paid to snatch away the folly of poor lovers
For whom, it seems, the sacraments have failed.

Return from England

Though every office stair
I climbed there, left me poorer,
Night after night, my wants
Toil down each step in selfsame
Dream; night after night, enduring
Such failure, I cast away
My body, on fire to reach
Mail-boat or train-from-Euston,
Catch up at last with smoke.
But mind, pretending pity,
Unslaves me in like haste,
Only to take me closer,

With some new tale of wrong here,
Holy retreat of tongue.
When I had brought my wife
And children, wave over wave,
From exile, could I have known
That I would sleep in England
Still, lie awake at home?

Too Great a Vine
Poems and Satires: Second Series

(1957)

Usufruct

This house cannot be handed down.
Before the scriven ink is brown,
Clergy will sell the lease of it.
I live here, thinking, ready to flit
From Templeogue, but not at ease.
I hear the flood unclay the trees,
Road-stream of traffic. So does the midge,
With myriads below the bridge,
Having his own enormous day,
Unswallowed. Ireland was never lay.
My mother wore no rural curch
Yet left her savings to the Church,
That she might aid me by-and-by,
Somewhere beyond the threatening sky,
What could she do, if such in faith
Be second nature? A blue wraith
That exquisites the pool, I mean
The kingfisher, too seldom seen,
Is warier than I am. Flash
Of inspiration makes thought rash.

Abbey Theatre Fire

Pride made of Yeats a rhetorician.
He would have called them knave or clown,
The playwright, poet, politician,
Who pull his Abbey Theatre down.
Scene-dock and wardrobe choked with rage,
When warriors in helmets saved
The auditorium and stage,
Forgetting our age, he waved and raved
Of Art and thought her Memory's daughter,
Those firemen might have spared their water.

Wolfe Tone

He called a conquered land his own
Although he never bowed at Mass
Behind locked door or knelt on grass.
But we are taught to disown
Him. Faith needs more than bite and sup.
What may we do but rattle his chains
At College Green despite cut veins?
We cannot blow his statue up.

The Trial of Robert Emmet

(To be re-enacted at Green Street Courthouse for An Tóstal, 1956)

Sentence the lot and hurry them away,
The court must now be cleared, batten and spot
Swung up with rope and ladder, lighting-plot
Rehearsed. No need of drop-scene for the play
To-night: bench, box and bar in well-mixed ray
Make do. Though countless miscreants have got
A life-term here, and some, the scaffold knot,
Forget the cells our safety fills by day.
See British greed and tyranny defied
Once more by that freethinker in the dock
And sigh because his epitaph remains
Unwritten. Cheer revolution by the clock
And lastly – badge and holy medal guide
Your cars home, hooting through our dirtiest lanes.

Past and Present

Although she went in pitiful tatters,
Her sons were trained in France and Spain.
But fashion in wear is all that matters
To-day. Our anguish was in vain.
Men find such grace in her good looks,
How can her conduct be too plain?
Better put by our history books
And gape, for now that lashings of pence
Are pounds, a word can give offence.

Nelson's Pillar, Dublin

No, let him watch the sky
With those who rule. Stone eye
And telescope can prove
Our blessings are above:
Capital for the few,
For patriots in queue,
The narrow way, turnstile
And shilling stair. His guile
Victoried. Let him stand
There, imaging our land.

Miss Marnell

No bells rang in her house. The silver plate
Was gone. She scarcely had a candle-wick,
Though old, to pray by, ne'er a maid to wait
At all. She had become a Catholic
So long ago, we smiled, did good by stealth,
Bade her good-day, invited her to tea
With deep respect. Forgetting her loss of wealth,
She took barmbrack and cake so hungrily,
We pitied her, wondered about her past
But her poor mind had not been organised;
She was taken away, fingering to the last
Her ivory decades. Every room surprised:
Wardrobes of bombazine, silk dresses, stank:
Cobwebby shrouds, pantries, cupboard, bone-bare.
Yet she had prospering money in the bank,
Admiring correspondents everywhere,
In Ireland, Wales, the Far East, India;
Her withered hand was busy doing good
Against our older missions in Africa.
False teeth got little acid from her food:
But scribble helped to keep much mortar wet
For convent, college, higher institution,
To build new churches or reduce their debt
The figure on her cross-cheque made restitution
For many sins. Piled on her escritoire
Were necessary improvements, paint-pot, ladder
And new coats for Maynooth, in a world at war,
Circulars, leaflets, pleas that made her madder
To comfort those who need for holy living
Their daily post: litterings, flyblown, miced
In corners, faded notes of thanksgiving,
All signed – 'Yours Gratefully, In Jesus Christ.'

Local Complainer

Their new Madonna at the quay-side,
Without a vessel in the tide-way,
White flower and stem of grace, but sea-ghost
When day and night are dim, has cost them
Eight hundred pounds: cut, dressed and chiselled,
The best Italian marble. In welcome
The clergy came, the Mayor with gownsmen,
Past derelicts of mill and warehouse
That bulge with emptiness. On feast-days
Shopkeepers string the Mall and Main Street
With Papal flags, mottoes in Latin.
No Protestant can call it sin that
They lead so reverent a high-life.
The nearest peak against the sky-line,
Believe me, has a tiny chapel
On top of it, much like the skull-cap
A monk wears. More of isles than hookers
In a bay the French have trawled. Our chequebooks
Are opened gladly for their statue,
Despite the Decalogue. So few can
Refuse to give or pray for lost souls:
The loyalist become Loyola,
Each week another Fontenoy won.
We scarcely know ourselves on Sunday.

The Loss of Strength

Farm-brooks that come down to Rathfarnham
By grange-wall, tree-stop, from the hills,
Might never have heard the rustle in barn dance,
The sluicing, bolting, of their flour-mills,
Nor have been of use in the steady reel
On step-boards of the iron wheel-rim,
For Dublin crowds them in: they wheeze now
Beneath new pavements, name old laneways,
Discharge, excrete, their centuries,
Man-trapped in concrete, deeper drainage.
Yet, littling by itself, I found one
That had never run to town.

No artificial fly or wet-hook
Could stickle it. Summer was cressing
Her mats, an inch from reeds. The brooklet
Ran clearly under bramble. Dressed
In the newest of feathers, black, trimmed
With white, a pair of waterhens dimmed
Away from me, with just a dot
Of red. Three visitors, one soul
Among them or not. Know-all can tot it
Up. Lesser bits of life console us:
Nature at jest in light and shade,
Though somewhat afraid.

I climb among the hills no more
To taste a last water, hide in cloud-mist
From sheep and goat. The days are downpour.
Cycle is gone, warm patch on trousers.
All, all, drive faster, stink without,
Spirit and spark within, no doubt.
When hope was active, I stood taller
Than my own sons. Beloved strength
Springs past me, three to one. Halldoor
Keeps open, estimates the length
To which I go: a mile to tire-a.
But I knew the stone beds of Ireland

Beclipped and confident of shank,
I rode the plain with chain that freed me.
On a rim akin to air, I cranked up
Standstill of gradient, freewheeled
Down glens beyond our national school,
Our catechism and British rule,
To find, thought I, the very roc's nest
A-spar on Diamond Hill; clouted
By wind, strawing the narrowest sea-lough,
A speck that saw a cloud put out
A goose-neck, counting far below
The Twelve Pins in a row.

The young must have a solitude
To feel the strength in mind, restore
Small world of liking. Saints have spewed
Too much. I wanted test of stories
Our poets had talked about, pinmeal
To potboil long ago. Cloud-feelers
Featherers, touched our restlessness.
Lost prosody restrained us. Summit
Showed valleys, reafforesting,
The Fianna, leaf-veined, among them.
Now only a wishing-cap could leave me
On the top of Slieve Mish.

Shannoning from the tide, a sea-god
Became our servant once, demeaned
Himself, a three-legged, slippery body:
Uncatchable, being submarine,
He spoke the hub. Now engineering
Machinery destroys the weirs,
Directs, monk-like, our natural flow:
Yet it was pleasant at Castleconnell
To watch the salmon brighten their raincoats.
The reeds wade out for what is gone:
That mile of spray faraway on the rapids
Is hidden in a tap.

My childish dreams were devildom.
Sleep rose and sank: the Great Flood waked me.
Reservoir at low level! Come,
Dear rain and save our Roundwood lake!
Should man complain of plans that curb
Torrent in turbine? Great disturbance:
The hush of light. Why keep with Fintan
The Falls of Assaroe, trample
Of transmigration, void of man
In shape of salmon? Those currents were ample.
Voltage has turned them riddle and all,
To a piddle and blank wall.

Thousands ply the wonted scissors,
Cut up the immaterial, take
Our measure. When the soul is body-busy,
Rhyme interferes for its own sake
But gets no credit. Late in the day,
Then, coasting back from Milltown Malbay,
I saw before bell rang a warning,
Scattery Island and its round tower.
A child was scorching by that corner
To hurl me back, unknottable power,
Hell-fire in twist and turn, grotesque:
Now, Celtic-Romanesque.

Abraham's Bosom was a coldness.
My companies got up from dust
In meditation. Granite unfolded
The Gospel, figured speech. Must bowed
To Shall in our Jerusalem:
Saintly acquaintance. John o' the Bosom
Inspired our quiet. Young disciples
Did their own field and house work: no women
Tattling, no infants there to wipe
And scold. Yet Devil mocked at hymnal:
His smoke annoyed our Kevin, itched
Heavenly nose in kitchen.

Celibacy is our best rule still,
Restraint increasing its adherents.
Stuck-honey embitters. Though the schoolmen
Denounce our senses, what can fear add?
Let women masculate with hair-cuts,
Piety hates their very guts
But makes no comment on what shortens.
Refrain, poor sight, for much goes bare:
Walking temptations, visible mortal
Sins, churched by fashion. Fewer stare now.
Layman watches the theologian,
Both, us. A cogent clan.

Too long near London, I broke in exile
Another bread. The nightingales
Naturalised my own vexation:
Yet, dearer on Inish Caltra, one boat-hail
At dawn. There Cummin learned to hum
Angelic breves and found the Thummin.
Illuminative centre, arc
By arc was circumscribed. A field
Too small, perhaps, in truth: the skylark
May hatch out cuckoo. Thought shielded
Sunnier pen-stroke. No friend of Alcuin's,
I saw God's light through ruins.

Blessing of staves, a-hurry on wave-top,
You gave to Europe; isle of fair hills.
Cure now my ills. Scholars, who shaved
The forehead, were often up in air,
Beautifying themselves by acts
Unrecognised at Rome. No pacts
With Nature diverted river, raised up
Lake. Miracles anticipated
Immoderate science of our days.
Clearly religion has never hated
A better world. Invention lies,
If truth can be surprised.

Too great a vine, they say, can sour
The best of clay. No pair of sinners
But learned saints had overpowered
Our country, Malachi the Thin
And Bernard of Clairvaux. Prodigious
In zeal, these cooled and burned our porridge.
(Later came breakspear, strong bow backing)
The arch sprang wide for their Cistercians.
O bread was wersh and well was brack.
War rattled at us in hammered shirts;
And Englishman had been the Pontiff.
They marched to Mellifont.

But time goes back. Monks, whom we praise now,
Take down a castle, stone by stone,
To make an abbey, restore the chain-light
Of silence. Gelignite has blown up
Too much: yet on the Hill of Allen,
The blasters are at work. Gallon
By gallon our roads go on. Stonecrushers
Must feed them. Fionn hunted here, Oisín
Complained of age. I think of rushed bones,
Bogland, in furnaces, grown greener,
The prophecy of Colmcille –
Car without horse – fulfilled.

Red, white and blue pegged up the pulley
When I ran to school, ready to snatch all,
Buckle and satchel. Holier colours
Look down. Our Easter Rising – a scratch
In empire, self-wounded by war and truce.
Last night, as if the screws were loose,
I heard high over Whitefriar Street
Din of a flyer, may be *St Kevin*,
St Brigid or *St Brendan*. Greeting
To overheads! Freedom will never
Rust here, as my poor pedal did.
Mould ran away with the medal.

See, faith and science reconciled:
Stepmother with child. Whispering of ward-screens,
Hope that no specialist has smiled on
Removes our corporal disorders.
Above the clouds where all is white
And blue, with nothing to alight on,
Annual pilgrimages, sprinkled
With blessings, go: flown hospitals.
Let Baily bow, Kish-i'-the-ship wink,
Poolbeg flash out to Rocklit-bill.
Through grottoes of cloud they come: few cured
At Lourdes: are reassured.

Loss but repeats the startling legend
Of time. A poet wants no more
To palliate his mind, edging
Worn cards behind a shaky door
Or tinting them until the puce
Shuffle the purple. May the Deuce
Take all of them and thought get better
While faith and country play a far hand!
Plod on, tired rhyme. The streams that wetted
Forgotten wheels push past Rathfarnham,
Half underground: slime steps on stone.
I count them – not my own.

Irish Mother

'My son will burn in the Pit,'
She thought. Making his bed
And glancing under it:
'He slept last night,' she said.

The Choice

Better to disobey
And keep her alive than pray
To scissors and rubber glove
So quickly again. Not love
But faith blesses our dust
In passing. Take cover: trust
No fit of Caesar. Knife
Killed him, brought to life.

War Propaganda

Neighbouring metal may summon the drum,
But ear, beware. They preach too well
Who choose the text of Kingdom come.
Rope-swung victims ring that bell.

Pilgrimage

No bed that walks is worth such pain:
The aeroplane that sinks from earth,
Arteries faster than railway train,
Ship-loads dipping with baggage, berth;
Sickness below and in the clouds:
Too many thousands are brought to pray
Because our wonder must have crowds
Purchasing trifles at stall and tray
To make a holiday of hope,
Then, stare at stretcher, limbs that grope.

Marian Chimes

Four times an hour the same peal
Casts up our appeal
And minutes that borrow a hood
Cloister the neighbourhood
And parish. Early to late,
Rings our apostolate
For Mary Immaculate:
Gratitude, counting aloud
Favours we are allowed.
So, while we work, buy, sell,
Let habit in its cell
Mechanically hymn
Her praise, who pleads with Him
To aid us. Street-laden note,
Reaching the sky, denote
Over and over again,
Our plight, our loss, our gain!

St Christopher

Child that his strength upbore,
Knotted as tree-trunks i' the spate,
Became a giant, whose weight
Unearthed the river from shore
Till saint's bones were a-crack.
Fabulist, can an ill state
Like ours, carry so great
A Church upon its back?

The Horse-Eaters
Poems and Satires: Third Series

(1960)

Intercessors

Our nuns come out to shop in the afternoon,
For holy fashion has decreed hold-alls.
Torchbearers sidle the clergy to their stalls
To share in the dark, huge hug, comic cartoon,
Forget awhile the morning fast in croon
Of saxophone. Free from the pledge of walls,
Passing the beggar-women who still wear shawls,
Capuchin pads in mediaeval shoon.
These are our intercessors. Strange that hotel
Lounge, cinema, shop-window can unbell
Them! Flattered by their numbers and display,
We break their vows with a smile. No rebel guessed
Prayer and retreat would sanctify unrest,
When Britain took the garrisons away.

Irish-American Dignitary

Glanced down at Shannon from the sky-way
With his attendant clergy, stayed night
In Dublin, but whole day with us
To find his father's cot, now dust
And rubble, bless new church, school buildings
At Glantworth, drive to Spangle Hill
And cut first sod, hear, answer, fine speeches,
Accept a learned gown, freedom
Of ancient city, so many kissing
His ring – God love him! – almost missed
The waiting liner: that day in Cork
Had scarcely time for knife and fork.

Knacker Rhymes

I

Don't ship, kill, can them
First — abattoirs pay —
Or chill the carcases
For hook and tray:
Packed, sacked, quay-stacked,
The neighless all saved
From wavetops, ill-treatment
Abroad. Our meat-trade
Respected: thousands
Bred yearly will fatten
Small farmers, browse,
Idle as cattle.
But why keep the raw hides
And none of the insides?
Let stomach be steady, then,
As hand that endorses
The bigger cheques. Irishmen,
Taste your own horses!

II

Forget the horse-slaughter,
Lies, argument, speeches,
And see that your daughter,
Expensively breeched,
Capped, jacketed, learn
How to ride in the suburb
And prove what you earn now
By showing her seat.
She'll do it, rub-dub,
Jogtrot, bob saddle
And straddle the meat
Dogs, foreigners, eat.

Fable

'I saw it all before,'
Cried Master Pupil,
'Good living, rush of orders:
Faith, shopsoiled…'

                'Sssh! For Heaven's
Sake,' Hold-your-Tongue
Put in.

       'They'll hear from me,
When I grow up,' bragged Scruple,
     But died too young.

Menai Strait

Hope shared that week-end ring
So long, the brass was cracked
By tide and side-track. Finger
Hid Fulham, the King's Road, all Chelsea.
Steam waved me. Green flag dipped.
But now that absence comes back
Over cloud-gap, Wales under wing-tip,
Tunnel, funnel, forgotten,
Fire-shovelled knots of slack:
       Her thoughts are elsewhere.

Christmas Eve

(Dublin: 1959)

Crack-up... crack-down. Guttering squib
Unhallowed the street-light of the Crib,
Our shops had bought for Mary and Son
In hope of larger benison.
Though every firework has been banned,
Student or reeler from a band
Flung it. Could fizzle-fazzle refuse
Merry, unlawful touch of fuse?
Go-bang alarmed, in the traffic, an
Elderly crosser, girl, African
Converted by us. Bar-clamouring booze
Came, mobbing O'Connell Street with boos,
Mocking the ancient jars of Cana,
So how could the Garda Siochana
Defend authority in pairs
From youths with thrown-out apples, pears,
Our goodness rotting in their teens?
Quick reinforcements from canteens,
They say, scoring with stripes and licks,
Batoned their fellow-Catholics,
Perhaps a running Protestant
Or two (not many are extant),
Piously making no arrest,
For bloody rioters need a rest
In hospital. Swayed by the mass,
Standers were late for Midnight Mass.

The Flock at Dawn

Rhyme, doting too near my pillow, hesitated,
Fled on a mocking note because I sleep
Alone now, having re-wooed her much too late
For open arms. Surprised on their own by Peep o'
Day, half of his old shirt on again, my dreams,
Moonlighters all, irised to blurs, blottings
Of vision: a young lot, most of them unseemly.
That hoarseness had come down the chimney pot.
Hearing mistook the spot. No rhyme but the jackdaw,
Who glosses a neighbourly fir-branch with his beak
And wants to be my tenant, left that caw.
Already the starling, tall as his twitter and tweak,
Was spangling himself, nearby, upon the gutter.
I turned, sheeting my doubtful self, and drowsed
While pinchbeck stims were inching past the shutter
Edges; then suddenly thought of that mighty unhousing
A mile away, rooks elming in a flock
Above Rathfarnham Castle, hunger in bits,
Whirring, time-struck, its own alarum clock:
Thousandfold call, not one, for Jesuits
In elmy, shadowy bedrooms, their birettas,
Soutanes off, spiritual weapons racked.
Soon I remembered foreign eyes of jet,
All staring at me, patient as the school-fact
Of afterlife – a portrait row of saints,
So much alike, they make the varnish dull,
Each holding up for the obedient painter
Or spanning with too sure a hand the skull
Of pauper, as though it were his astrolabe;
Then, dark in chapel, head-hung martyrs, nude
But for the loins. Multiplication Table
For parents now, emotion stalled, too shrewd.
The flock that comes from the appetising east,
To pilfer Dublin county or take to the hills,
Goes over our clumps of sleep, all one yet pieced,
Black as the cloth unrolling from the mills
At Blarney, Cork and Lucan; I see the looms

That drape unrisen bodies of the clergy.
Better a decent shabbiness for Doomsday:
Remnants, reversal, snippets of that serge.
A land of pious turncoats! Still in tatters,
The Penal Laws, half-mindless, mumble woes
Outside our city churches. Raise your hats
To money aisled a century ago.
The poor mouth is a purse now; humbleness
A lying pocket. Satire owns to pride
And poetry is what we dare express
When its neglect has been personified.
I wanted to get up in joy, unbolt
My dark room, see the wetness at Stepaside,
Tumble of chronicle, grass in revolt,
Forget that morning faith like the milk supplied
In bottles comes to us now with clatter and jolt.

Consider the wars of religion in old books.
We hated reformation. Bishop Bale
Of Ossory would put the unchristian pooka
To flight. Archbishop Browne stepped from a gale
Across the Irish Sea and, next day, carried
The staff of Jesus to Skinners' Row danging
Faggot and flame, declaring by his Harry
We reverenced a wand.
                    The English language
Was loopholed here for centuries. But the night
That Edmund jumped the wave-tops — faerie castle
A torch — our rivers ran with Thames to spite us.
We lost in that war of words. The syllables
Which measure all delight; mouth-exile. Scansion's
Our darling fondled over sea.
                    Who cares?
Our monks reside in eighteenth-century mansions
Now. Hell-fire rakes have spirited these heirs.
Always in debt to banks, they plan more buildings,
Made reckless by the vow of poverty,
Pile up the sums that burning souls have willed
To them in clock-tower, high walls, such debris;
Teach alms to gamble, while agents share the kitty.

Communities ply from abroad, new planters
Lording our land once more.
                                Hunger in bits,
The flock is flying from the dawn to scantle
Among the dairy farms. Tired of complaint,
I dream of revellers unvaulted, place-names
In County Dublin left by the unsaintly,
When few that crossed themselves had buckle or lace,
Mount Venus, Cupidstown, the Feather Bed...

Sleep nodded to life's nothing. Emptihead.

In the New Statesman Office

(Great Queen Street)

She waited humbly at the counter,
Beside me, stout, motherly, plain-faced.
'What name, please?'
                        'Dr Marie Stopes.'
Though Ireland shook in my veins, denouncing
The poor man's friend, I futured. Popes,
Far-seen in total white and lace,
Will pity our overbearing creed,
Somehow prevent the loss of grace –
And fewer orphanages need
Those begging letters (Mercy's fount)
Dispatched in plain envelopes.

The Dead Sea Scrolls

Why should our scholars try to save
The lost, because an Arab boy
Found too much goodness in a cave?
No looking back will change our Lot,
Make Paul a pry. Can bits destroy
Our great succession with blot and jot?
We know the gloss on a brown skin,
Many suspect that fire and sin
Have something in a bigger pot.

The Lower Criticism

How could Gallina sit,
Rounding and packing her grit,
Cackle for cardboard box,
Watched under by the fox?

Early Unfinished Sketch

Rosalind, in a negligée,
Began to sketch me as I lay
Naked and soon her serious touch
On sheet delighted me as much
In art as loving. Pencil drew,
Poised, measured again, sped downward, flew
Like love scattering clothes to greet
Itself. The outline was complete.
She pondered. Detail was different,
More difficult. She seemed intent
On what the ancients had adored,
Christian apologists deplored.

'Finish it, pet, how can I wait?'
'But, darling, I must concentrate.'
She failed, fled back to our caresses,
Sat up.
          'What's wrong?'
                              'The problem presses.'
'I have it! Yes. That group in bronze.'
'The satyrs?'
                    'Herrick would call them fauns.'
'Stock-still –'
                    'in the fountain spray at Florence.'
'All tourists showing their abhorrence!'
'But if that sculptor dared to limn it –'
'The nude, to-day, must have a limit.'
'And Rosalind –'
                    'obey the laws
Of decency.'
                    'In the line she draws?'

The Hippophagi

Up-to-date infant, rubbered, wheeled out,
I kicked up heels, soon took to them,
Learned the first premise of a race
Now lost in space. I was immortal,
Yea, so important that monks pursued me,
Similitudes of bygone ages.
Bodikin rages to be itself
When bookshelf fills with catechism.
The public schism makes Latin hoarser,
Scholastics coarsen the ignorants,
Sew up their pants. Single idea
Has circumscribed us, lyre'd Judea.

Frankincense, flowers of speech,
Small gifts, beseech us to be good;
Premature swoon of sense, globe-spurning,
Cup-borne; gums burn us, celestial lilies
Vase mortal chill. Soul fades, love-sick,
In rhetoric. But oh! those O's
And Ah's, glows, melts of me in sweet print.
I clasp my *Key of Heaven.* Cover
Be gold, let boy discover bine, grain,
Glues in that binding of desert tan
Mahommedan had palmed! A link went;
Beads, decades and all: self was delinquent.

Fond ones dozed with the patriarchs.
Afrits, darkening from Syria
In later myriads, saw dust-men,
Who rode in rust, guard wormwood, shoe-holes
Mad for Jerusalem. Sin shrouded
The plural couch, concubinage.
There was new vinage awash in ships:
Love without lips and night prolonged:
Our pallid Song o' Songs – her Talmud
In ghetto – rudded in slumber of don,
Aye, demijohn. Shall no cruse aid her?
Lickerish echo: 'no crusader.'

Would Padua find, Xavier miss
My prayer, Francis de Sales forget
In elegant letters, silk-knots of Dijon?
And, then those seizures and that gasp:
How often clasp was mortified;
Gonzaga laying in boyish state
That we might pray for happy death,
Give say to Saith, watching the flames
Roll by. All saints wore foreign disc.
Astonished, asterisked from waist down,
We starred and crowned lest we incite
Their Europe with immodest sight.

Liguori, early or late. Alphonsus
Carried the sconce, queried in Latin
The secret matrimonial code
Of laymen, showed their vice-in-virtue:
Sainted at thirty – but at four-score
And ten, the court held every night
By his own writings. Verba Turpia,
Mock-purple, judged base turn, touch, hot stuff
Misspent; buff witnessing by proxy,
Confession-boxed. How his stole fends
For aureole! Doting on hymn,
Hell snatched the stand from under him.

Cities remember ancient religion,
Signs, prodigies, fire coming up
And down, destruction in raised stone.
The streets I roamed in, suddenly horseless,
No tenderness in sky: terror
Of day was there, ready to strike out
A little likeness. Dodderers stop me
Often near shop or dissenting Church,
Mutter the world is in the wrong heads.
That makes me young again. Thought plays
The devil, unsought. Should the Almighty
Destroy it after All… might He?

Tables were breaking the Commandments,
For elements with a dreadful past
Were learning faster to obey
In little ways than I was. Door-bell,
A jar: electric shock containing
Delight, pain. Trolleys had reared in stable
Before I gave up safety pin, seized
Shirt-tail for decency. Objects
Were screwing, knobbing. Phonograph
Sang at me, laughed. But, once, noon stopped:
Eccentric gloom, fire-eddy. Sun
Eclipsed our dream of Edison.

The sky our guide-book. Man above
His own Jehovah – spreading out
Fire-hands on town-plan, chartered city:
No pore has pity. Quicker ends now
For daddies sending up their sons.
Death-dealing tons can fly alone;
Decimals known. What adder fidges
Within religion? Burnt offerings
For ageing scoffers? Wrangle of text
That shames the next world with a hell?
Be sure the aeon of ascent
Will have much spiritual assent.

I mitched from miracles. Older
Legends were bolder in type. I shinned
Our scullery window in horse-play, slithered
By wind to withers. How could I know
The future throwings of that mount,
Imagine the fount would be half mud,
A hydrant bursting in the street
For footless feet? Top gear took Wright up;
Blériot lightly cogged the spindrift.
Above the blue life go this and that,
Since boys were skirring with elastic,
And space is sending round a last tick.

Redcoat, blackcoat: I was willing
To bet that shilling was the same
When Ireland prayed, fought for a crown
Again. Thousands wore khaki; few
Revolted, knew what big guns meant.
Grey quickies bled the bioscope.
Rifle was rope. National good
Went bad: war-food. Crackshots of freedom,
Unbrothered, train greed to bow and shrug.
Beggar hugging his orthodoxy
And round of knocks, has bliss in sight:
His Church – another building-site.

Patting our dumb, why should we think,
To-day, of drinking-trough in streets
A-clatter with meat no butcher sold,
Regard that nose-bag in the dust,
When Europe, thrusting its bloody face
In ours, will pay for every snout?
Horses, in thousands, are out of work.
But, must we burke their past? Breed them
For lesser needs: our word will carry.
They galloped with Sarsfield, after Aughrim,
Kept Ballinasloe in decent trade.
Off course, old bets are soon betrayed.

Can jingle straighten the horse's mouth?
No monthly crowd forestalled this market
But men in the dark with hand-spit, chink
And rustle. Tinkers spilled the can
As quickly; tanglers seized the scruff
Of grazing stuff. 'Why should this dollop
Of ours be trolloped?' 'Wayside itchers
Become too rich now.' Deputies
Call out 'Feed France.' 'Are we beholden
To England?' Loaders at the North Wall
Hurrah for the Hippophagi.
Tots echo: 'Let's hip off a gee.'

Cockhorse is all aboard, child, with painter
And pulley, St George has lost a stirrup;
Paper knights galloped away with gold standard.
St Audeon stows the Channel, blesses,
They say, our business deals. Go, peep
Behind the clothes-horse, be my hurt.
Rhyme is no comforter. Learn later
How battened trade exposed by storm
Proved Lowry Lorc had pinched the ear-flaps
Of Tulyar. Mishap was ill-defended
In stall and Senate. Weather reports
Lay bare our soul in ancient ports.

The nasal syllable in Houyhnhnm
Brings rhyme-word. Minim, semibreve
Are here to grieve me with the last snap
Of silk string, clap of violin case.
Child sat, played in a self. Horse-hair,
Too scratchy in chair for calico,
Sprang with the bow-tip, rosin flew on,
Fingers grew up in centuries
Of grace-note. Unsure in time, as moth
Or behemoth, man steadies his wonders.
Backache, wing-thundered on its ledge, ends.
Fact stole, fell, goes beyond all legends.

The Irish Party bowed to carriage:
Hats were hard: Edward the Seventh
Our King. Shy de Valera taught
My sisters, chalked in classroom. Walls
Unscribbled. Royal Visitor
Had had good sport among the Bishops,
Eager to swish up their own steps
While flattery kept down the truth,
For at Maynooth, instead of skulls,
His racing colours were displayed.
Big wars bewildered our little one
And equity is still unwon.

Government has fine flesh to speed it,
Well-backed to breed in national stud-farm.
Let blood relations give employment,
Cut up, roast, boiled by French and Belgian.
Horse-eating helps this ill-fare state
To Sunday plate, has the same sauce.
The worst abroad is now our best.
Social unrest can bed in Britain.
Sham steed was spirited by dunlop;
I met with many a stop; what matter
If horse-shoe flattened a nail in tyre?
The near is distant now. Feet tire.

Hate, pale as peace, come, civilise all,
Unatomised! Earth goes a-mooning,
Word-specks are shooting the vapids, springs,
Long dampered, winging gush and jet.
Fire flies in wetness. Much abused,
But much amusing, vasty cod,
What good commodities you hold up
To mind! Old pet-names, meanwhile, teach
Mechanical species what we praised
In horse-power. Gage is overhead
For much has skied our hasty scene
Again. No shame, if overseen.

Bib shall obey the ever-known.
Why keep the grape-stone, leave the vine stock,
Sweet stain on frock? Could self have learned
In woody, ferny glen to choose
With Fionn the music of what happens,
Found in some Clapham an honest sect
Of intellect? Lastly a premise
That wants much phlegm: can polyglot,
Carried in snot so easily wiped
Away, decide? What dare we call
Our thought, Marcus Aurelius,
Unwanted void or really us?

Forget Me Not

(1962)

Forget Me Not

Up the hill,
Hurry me not;
Down the hill,
Worry me not;
On the level,
Spare me not,
In the stable,
Forget me not.

Trochaic dimeter, amphimacer
And choriamb, with hyper catalexis,
Grammatical inversion, springing of double
Rhyme. So we learned to scan all, analyse
Lyric and ode, elegy, anonymous patter,
For what is song itself but substitution?
Let classical terms unroll, with a flourish, the scroll
Of baccalaureate.
                    Coleridge had picked
That phrase for us – vergiss-mein-nicht, emblem
Of love and friendship, delicate sentiments.
Forget-me-nots, forget-me-nots:
Blue, sunny-eyed young hopefuls! He left a nosegay,
A keepsake for Kate Greenaway.

                              Child climbed
Into the trap; the pony started quick
As fly to a flick and Uncle John began
Our work-a-day, holiday jingle.
                              Up the hill,
Hurry me not.
            Down the hill,
Worry me not.
                  Verse came like that, simple
As join-hands, yet ambiguous, lesson
Implied, a flower-puzzle in final verb
And negative. All was personification
As we drove on: invisibility

Becoming audible. A kindness spoke,
Assumed the god; consensus everywhere
In County Dublin. Place-names, full of Sunday,
Stepaside, Pass-if-you-can Lane, Hole in the Wall.
Such foliage in the Dargle hid Lovers Leap,
We scarcely heard the waters fall-at-all.
Often the open road to Celbridge: we came back
By Lucan Looks Lovely, pulled in at the Strawberry Beds,
Walked up the steep of Knockmaroon. Only
The darkness could complete our rounds. The pony
Helped, took the bit. Coat-buttoned up, well-rugg'd
I drowsed till the clatter of city sets, warning
Of echoes around St Mary's Place, woke me;
But I was guarded by medal, scapular
And the *Agnus Dei* next my skin, passing
That Protestant Church. Night shirt, warm manger, confusion
Of premise, creed; I sank through mysteries
To our oblivion.

Ora pro nobis

Ora pro me.

'Gee up,' 'whoa,' 'steady,' 'hike.'

'Hike ow'a that.' Rough street-words, cheerful, impatient:
The hearers knew their own names as well. Horses,
Men, going together to daily work; dairy
Cart, baker's van, slow dray, quick grocery
Deliveries. Street-words, the chaff in them.
Suddenly in Mountjoy Street, at five o'clock
Yes, five in the evening, work rhymed for a minute with sport.
Church-echoing wheel-rim, roof-beat, tattle of harness
Around the corner of St Mary's Place:
Cabs, outside cars, the drivers unranked in race
For tips; their horses eager to compete,
With spark and hubbub, greet with their own heat
Galway Express that puffed to Broadstone Station.
They held that Iron Horse in great esteem
Yet dared the metamorphosis of steam.
Soon they were back again. I ran to watch
As Uncle John in elegant light tweeds
Drove smartly by on his outside car, talking
Over his shoulder to a straight-up fare
Or two, coaxing by name his favourite mare;

The best of jarvies, his sarcastic wit
Checked by a bridle rein; and he enlarged
My mind with two Victorian words. Grown-ups
Addressed him as Town Councillor, Cab
And Car Proprietor!

                Horse-heads above me,
Below me. Happy on tram top, I looked down
On plaited manes, alighted safely, caught
Sidelong near kerb, perhaps, affectionate glance
As I passed a blinker. Much to offend the pure:
Let-down or drench, the sparrows pecking at fume,
The scavenger with shovel, broom. But, O
When horse fell down, pity was there; we saw
Such helplessness, girth buckled, no knack in knee,
Half-upturned legs – big hands that couldn't unclench.
A parable, pride or the like, rough-shod,
Or goodness put in irons, then, soul uplifted
Bodily; traffic no longer interrupted.
Strength broadened in narrow ways. Champions went by,
Guinness's horse from St James's Gate:
Their brasses clinked, yoke, collar shone at us:
Light music while they worked. Side-streets, alleys
Beyond St Patrick's, floats unloading, country
Colt, town hack, hay-cart, coal-bell. Often the whip-crack,
The lash of rein. Hand-stitch in the numb of pain
At school. Religious orders plied the strap
On us, but never on themselves. Each day, too,
Justice tore off her bandage in Mountjoy Street.
The Black Maria passed, van o' the poor.
Weeks, months clung to those bars, cursed, or stared, mute.
Children in rags ran after that absenting,
Did double time to fetlocks. Solemnity
For all; the mournful two or four with plumes,
Hooves blackened to please your crape. The funerals
Go faster now. Our Christianity
Still catching up with All is Vanity.

Nevertheless,
Nature had learned to share our worldliness,

Well-pleased to keep with man the colours in hide,
Dappling much, glossing the chestnut, sunshading the bays,
To grace those carriage wheels, that *vis-à-vis*
In the Park. Let joy cast off a trace, for once,
High-stepping beyond the Phoenix Monument
In the long ago of British Rule, I saw
With my own eyes a white horse that unfabled
The Unicorn.

Mechanised vehicles;
Horse-power by handle-turn. My Uncle John
Lost stable companions, drivers, all. Though poor,
He kept his last mare out on grass. They aged
Together. At twenty-one, I though it right
And proper.

How could I know that greed
Spreads quicker than political hate? No need
Of propaganda. Good company, up and down
The ages, gone: the trick of knife left, horse cut
To serve man. All the gentling, custom of mind
And instinct, close affection done with. The unemployed
Must go. Dead or ghosted by froths, we ship them
Abroad. Foal, filly, farm pony, bred for slaughter:
What are they now but hundredweights of meat?
A double trade. Greed with a new gag of mercy
Grants happy release in our whited abattoirs.
'Gentlemen, businessmen, kill on the spot! O
That,' exclaim the good, 'should be your motto.
Combine in a single trade all profits, save
Sensitive animals from channelling wave,
Continental docking, knackering down.
We dread bad weather, zig-zag, tap of Morse.'
Well-meaning fools, who only pat the horse
That looks so grand on our Irish half-crown.

I've more to say —

Men of Great Britain
Openly share with us the ploughtail, the field-spoil,

Trucking in Europe what we dare not broil
At home.
                    Herodotus condemned
Hippophagy.
                    And Pliny, also.
                                        Besieged towns
Denied it.
                    Stare now at Pegasus. The blood
Of the Medusa weakens in him.
                                        Yet all the world
Was hackneyed once – those horses o' the sun,
Apollo's car, centaurs in Thessaly.
Too many staves have splintered the toy
That captured Troy. The Hippocrene is stale.
Dark ages; Latin rotted, came up from night-soil,
New rush of words: thought mounted them. Trappings
Of palfrey, sword-kiss of chivalry, high song
Of grammar. Men pick the ribs of Rosinante
In restaurants now. Horse-shoe weighs in with saddle
Of meat.
                    Horseman, the pass-word, courage shared
With lace, steel, buff.
                    Wars regimented
Haunches together. Cities move by in motor
Cars, charging the will. I hear in the lateness of Empires,
A neighing, man's cry in engines. No peace, yet,
Poor draggers of artillery.
                    The moon
Eclipsed: I stood on the Rock of Cashel, saw dimly
Carved on the royal arch of Cormac's Chapel
Sign of the Sagittary, turned my back
On all that Celtic Romanesque; thinking
Of older story and legend, how Cuchullin,
Half man, half god-son, tamed the elemental
Coursers: dear comrades: how at his death
The Gray of Macha laid her mane upon his breast
And wept.
                    I struggled down
From paleness of limestone.
                                        Too much historied

Land, wrong in policies, armings, hope in prelates
At courts abroad! Rags were your retribution,
Hedge schools, a visionary knowledge in verse
That hid itself. The rain-drip cabin'd the dream
Of foreign aid... Democracy at last.
White horses running through the European mind
Of the First Consul. Our heads were cropped like his.
New brow; old imagery. A Gaelic poet,
Pitch-capped in the Rebellion of '98,
Called this Republic in an allegory
The Slight Red Steed.
                  Word-loss is now our gain:
Put mare to stud. Is Ireland any worse
Than countries that fly-blow the map, rattle the sky,
Drop down from it? Tipsters respect our grand sires,
Thorough-breds, jumpers o' the best.
Our grass still makes a noble show, and the roar
Of money cheers us at the winning post.
So pack tradition in the meat-sack, Boys,
Write off the epitaph of Yeats.
                     I'll turn
To jogtrot, pony bell, say my first lesson:

Up the hill,
Hurry me not;
Down the hill,
Worry me not;
On the level,
Spare me not,
In the stable,
Forget me not.

Forget me not.

Flight to Africa and Other Poems

(1963)

Mount Parnassus

Never have I been in the south
So far from self and yet I must
Learn, straight from the horse's mouth,
To kick up my own dust.
Here is the source. Here was our must
I see no flowers to grass us,
Only the scale of Mount Parnassus:
Simplicity of snow
Above, the pillared drouth,
The worn-out, below,
I stray from American, German, tourists,
Greek guide, feel in my two wrists
Answer for which I have come,
The Oracle, not yet dumb.

Over Wales

Our aeroplanes fly quicker now. They go
To nineteen thousand feet or more; below,
The whiteness of cloud, cloudlet, unseen.
The upper world seems motionless: machine
Is poised in noise. Pearly, vert, blue, paler hues,
Horizoning. Passengers read the news:
Singer, the Common Market – turn the pages –
Hire purchase. Shipping. Ford strike for better wages.
Not long ago, I stooped from heaven to peer
Down rifts of tumbly rain, watching the drear
Glimmer of fens below in ancient Wales,
From a couple of thousand feet, woods, shadowy vales,
Thinking how Pyll or Gereint had pursued
Big game through forests with pike and gauntlet. Mewed
Among his rocks, a hideous dragon turned
His food to ashes, as digestion burned.
They spied him letting off his smoke. One day

Propelled beyond the map of Morecambe Bay,
Outside a hundred miles of hurricane,
I stared at the darkening rollers of thunder-plain,
Flawing, up-snowing, heard the engines thrum
Like hail on the wings of aluminium,
Then, of a sudden, far across the unsaily
Wave-tops, I saw the twinkle of the Baily.
The Airport measured gale force, grounded all flights,
And Ireland came up with its fairy lights.

The Stadium

(Hexad written in 1961 on hearing that the Stadium at Santry, Co. Dublin, was to be re-named after the new President of the United States of America.)

Do think of the Eumenides,
When Gael meets Greek. Three ancient cheers:
Deadheat of our last Olympic game,
Flashlight, cloud-negative, of Fame.
Millennium hush of hemispheres.
The stop-watch may be Kennedy's.

Ecumenical Council

What Bishop, Cardinal,
Will come back the same from Rome?
Good habit should never roam.
Aeroplane, car, din, all
Unbutton ageing men.
They fall without *Amen,*
Unpalaced by a pen stroke,
Brain-lightning or devil-stroke:
Choleric, uncontradicted.

Before. Such death is predicted.
No pill in hat or mitre.
The Church gets on. O might her
Words have been brief, though grave,
Whose conclave is the grave.

The Common Market, 1962

Why do you bog-trot from the wind
And damp, hee-hawing into Europe,
The latest cross upon your back,
To join that unholy family,
Forgetting all the patience, your rope
And straw? To every star you see,
Add stripe. The lion has been skinned:
War has a new whip for tradelets. Come back
Poor Twenty-Sixer. Live on lack.

The Abbey Theatre Fire

One of our verse-speakers, driving
His car at dusk to Alexander
Dock, saw a fine ship on fire, loitered
Among the idlers, urchins, at the gateway,
Came back by crane, warehouse, bollard,
The Custom House, corniced with godlings –
Nilus, Euphrates, detected a smell
Of burning again and in alarm,
Jumped out, to poke the bonnet, turned, noticed
Smoke piling up near Liberty Hall,
Smoulder of clothes. Suddenly, ghosts
In homespun, peasants from the West,
Hurrying out of the past, went by unheard,
Pegeen, her playboy, tramps, cloaked women,

Young girls in nothing but their shifts.
Glimmerers stalked, tall, mournful eyed,
In robes, with playing instruments,
By shadowy waters of the Liffey.
He drove around the corner, guessing
That flames were busier than their smoke
In the Abbey Theatre. Civic Guards
Shouldered, broke down the door-glass, carried
Out portraits in their gilded frames,
Yeats, Lady Gregory, Synge, Máire
O'Neill, Fay, F.R. Higgins, blindly
Staring in disapproval. Gong
And clatter. Firemen booting down
From darkness in their warlike helmets,
While flames were taking a first bow
And flickers in the Greenroom unlocked
The bookcase, turned the dusty pages
Of one-act comedies, cindered
Prompt copy. Noisier in the scene-dock,
Flats vanished, pallettted with paint,
The rostrums crackled, wooden harp
And flagon, mether, sword of lath,
Round shield, throne, three-legged stool,
All the dear mummocks out of Tara
That turned my head at seventeen.
The hydrants hissed against the mouthers,
Backing them from the stage and pitfall
Where in a gyre of smoke and coughing,
The plays of Yeats were re-enacted.
Our Lyric Company, verse-speakers,
Actors, had put them on without
A doit for eleven years. We hired
The theatre, profaned the Sabbath
With magic, speculation: *The Countess
Cathleen*, *The Only Jealousy
of Emer*, *Deirdre*, even *The Herne's Egg*,
Moon-mad as Boyne. *The Death of Cuchullin*:
We borrowed a big drum, clarionet, from
The Transport Workers' Union. Anne Yeats
Found in the Peacock cellar masks

Dulac had moulded.
                         So, I forgot
His enmity.
                    My own plays were seen there,
Ambiguous in the glow of battens,
Abbot, monk, sinner, black-out of Ireland.
Finis.
          Stage, auditorium, escaped
That fire but not from policy,
Planning new theatre, old mirth.
Yeats had not dreamed an unstubbed butt,
Ill match, would bring his curtain down.

Burial of an Irish President

(Dr Douglas Hyde)

The tolling from St Patrick's
Cathedral was brangled, repeating
Itself in top-back room
And alley of the Coombe,
Crowding the dirty streets,
Upbraiding all our pat tricks.
Tricoloured and beflowered,
Coffin of our President,
Where fifty mourners bowed,
Was trestled in the gloom
Of arch and monument,
Beyond the desperate tomb
Of Swift. Imperial flags,
Corunna, Quatre Bras,
Inkerman, Pretoria,
Their pride turning to rags,
Drooped, smoke-thin as the booming
Of cannon. The simple word
From heaven was vaulted, stirred
By candles. At the last bench

Two Catholics, the French
Ambassador and I, knelt down.
The vergers waited. Outside.
The hush of Dublin town,
Professors of cap and gown,
Costello, his Cabinet,
In Government cars, hiding
Around the corner, ready
Tall hat in hand dreading
Our Father in English. Better
Not hear that 'which' for 'who'
And risk eternal doom.

The Wounds of Fodhla

'We taught them a lesson at Killaloe
And serve them right.'
                                Evangelist,
Headlong, upset by farm-boot, fist,
Two teeth knocked out, a bit o' twist,
Bible kicked in the gutter but kissed
Next morning. Bench did not insist
Too much on detail:
                                'Case dismissed.'
Angelus rang.
                                'Next on the list.'
Should memory of the dead persist
In Protestant churchyards, old with mist,
Knowers might shrug:
                                'The same ado,'
Grim Ireton mock us:
                                'Pilallo!'

Flight to Africa

A bishop, one of our twenty-eight
Or so, walking his palace, pate
Alone, pondered the half-crack
In holy dado and addressed
His own.

         Too many are professed –
He argued – boys, girls, all in black,
Brown, white. The Church unbeds the State:
Charity taught to emigrate.
Farmyard and scythe gone. Grain unsacked or
Let down by rain for lack of hand.
Old times are off again. Great land
Is measured by a man on tractor.
What blank started this steeplechase?
Query is mine, but his the place,
Occasion, notable speech in Cork,
The Bishop, half freed from our constraint,
Indignant as a Celtic saint,
Beard plaited to fork or fiercer torque,
Within illuminated script
Or glimpsed, when Munster seems a crypt,
On corb disfigured in swirl of rain,
Became the lesson of our pain.
Unseen by all, air might have been sapphired,
A moment, and his ancient staff fired
With jewels, when the truth, somewhat
Confused, was heard and heeded not.
Lord, was it wise to disagree, shock
New seminaries, put in doubt
The good example of our Taoiseach
At Lagos, give him a culdee clout
Because the Nuncio upheld
His policy – where skin is black?
Sky-journey.
             Blueness about him:
                       delled
Whiteness below.

Seán left the wrack,
Appeared at Lourdes, pilgrim on knees,
Then up again from the Pyrenees,
Rome – Tunis – Tripoli – Qui-va-là:
Veiled faith, desert revolt, unseen.

Our Chief stood in Nigeria,
Hailing the flag of freedom, green
And white like ours – with the Six Counties
Cut off. Trade mission, helping most
Our Fathers of the Holy Ghost,
Grinned, nodded; hope of further bounties
From heathens. Once they rattled beads,
Were slaves of cotton, Protestant creeds:
Black brothers, now, whom diplomats
From Europe flatter with tall hats.
Carbon was sheeted. All seemed done
In piety. Our Merchant's Son
Flew nor'-nor'-east to pray at Rome
And gain, some say, more votes at home.

A poet, too, may ruminate
With guardian angels, forced to wait
On Irish bodies in South Korea
And Kenya, bandy the idea
Of Caritas to every land
Where trade put down a cloven hand,
Formosa, Burma, Africa:
I stop – so many end in 'a'.
Religion inspects us, takes the best:
Or is it only our unrest?
The dollaring of Dolourdom:
Bible or Stole in the world to come?
Does our Republic need old cause?
Exiles – in search of Penal Laws?
Or colleges abroad? Drum-roll
For our brave Sarsfields of the soul?
Celibacy in the Commonwealth:
School, hospital, church: more grants, less rates?
Armed escort in Protectorates?
Much good we do by loyal stealth.

Why should our politicians care,
If German, Dutch, Czech, Japanese,
Unpack their little factories,
Among our western legends, share
What goes?
                    'Your handsome Bishop Lucy,'
They sneer,
                    'forgets that farm-boot, fist,
Battered the mouth of evangelist,
Footballed the Bible from Killaloe. See
How, quickly stepping from a crowd,
Good priest assaulted gospeller
In Wexford town. Can tariffs err
When Irish missions are endowed,
Street-flagged? For Christ's sake, is he mad?'

Once they were heroes, each a lad
On his own. They fought the tammed
And shantered British, then they crammed
Machine-guns, shot at each other from tombs,
Old abbeys. Now in smoking-rooms
Hallowers sign, the half-lost drink:
Horse-killers, knights who of old salaamed
Mahoun. My rhyme answers their wink:
'Kiss the wrong ring and go be damned!'
Clappers may minstrel the Hierarchy,
Much thurifying unburn the darkie:
But will our North be *Notre Dame'd*?

Precautions

These scholars are modestly selective,
Who say our nuns in Africa,
Fearful of blackmen yelling 'Ya!,'
Tearing off starches, heavy drape,
Can take an oral contraceptive,
An hour or two before the rape.

How will they know dread time or place
That leaves the soul still full of grace?
Better to wear Dutch cap or wad
And after their debauching, use
Syringe or douche away abuse,
Without a sin, trusting in God.
Argument on the Seventh Hill
Compounds our doctrine for a pill.

The Last Republicans

Because their fathers had been drilled
Formed fours among the Dublin hills,
They marched together, countermarched
Along the Liffey valley, by larch-wood,
Spruce, pine road. Now, what living shout
Can halt them? Nothing of their faces
Is left, the breath has been blown out
Of them into far lonely places.
Seán Glynn pined sadly in prison. Seán
McNeela, Tony Darcy, John
McGaughey died on hunger-strike,
Wasting in the ribbed light of dawn.
They'd been on the run, but every dyke
Was spy. We shame them all. George Plant,
Quick fighter and a Protestant,
Patrick McGrath and Richard Goss,
Maurice O'Neill with Thomas Harte.
Were executed when Dev's party
Had won the county pitch-and-toss,
Pat Dermody, John Kavanagh
John Griffith, John Casey, black-and-tanned.
At Mountjoy Gaol, young Charlie Kerins
Was roped; we paid five pounds to Pierpont,
The Special Branch castled their plans,
Quicklimed the last Republicans.

Street Game

Unholy bits, ring, neck, of porter and Bass bottle
From the six public-houses at those four corners,
Nicholas St, Clanbrassil St, the Coombe
And Kevin St, shrine on high wall – fierce spot –
Protecting the Sisters of the Holy Faith, warning
By sun and moon the ruffians in top-back room
Or cellar. Last week I saw a marching band,
Small Protestants in grey clothes, well-fed pairs
Led by a Bible teacher, heard the noise
Of boot-heel metal by bread-shop, sweet-shop, dairy,
Scrap, turf, wood, coal-blocks. Suddenly Catholic joylets
Darted from alleys, raggedy cherubs that dared them:
'Luk, feckin' bastards, swaddlers, feckin' bastards!'
Too well they knew the words their mothers, fathers,
Used. Silent, the foundlings marched along the street-path
With click of boot-heel metal. We have cast
Them out. Devotion, come to the man-hole at last,
Bawls: 'Feckin' bastards, swaddlers, feckin' bastards!'

Four Letter Words

Let Greek or Latin burn the wick,
Inquisitive schoolboys learn to parse
Masculine, feminine gender. Back, front,
As noble stone, give no affront.
What classical word has bent to stick?
Did Aristophanes not farce?
Poor relatives, runting in slums,
Known to the police, down on their luck,
Fined forty shillings in the dock,
Filthy the joyful sign on walls
That Castor winged, egged on by Pollux,
Yet toss off rags when pleasure comes,
Surpass our polysyllables

Humiliation is *in situ*
And starts a problem that derides us.
Why should that mother have to sit,
If god had plucked her to his height?

A Simple Tale

A casual labourer, Pat Rourke,
Who hurried from bricking across the water
With wife and babes, could find no work here.
All slept in a coal-hole, heard
(When light, that dwindled through the grating,
Was Wicklowing from strand to hill)
The gulls, loop-lining near Dublin Bay,
Squabble for offal, rub of cur
Or cat around a dustbin, till
A-bang in breadshop, dairy. Brought
To Court, the little screaming boy
And girl were quickly, for the public good,
Committed to Industrial School.
The cost – three pound a week for each:
Both safely held beyond the reach
Of mother, father. We destroy
Families, bereave the unemployed.
Pity and love are beyond our buoys.

Medical Missionary of Mary

One blowy morning, Sister Michael,
A student of midwifery,
Fell, handlebarring from her cycle,
Her habit twisted around a pedal:
She suffered bruises on her riff,
Serious injury to the spine

And so, in hope of miracle,
Was brought, a stretcher case, to Lourdes
Out of the blue, above the shrining
Of snowy peaks: unchosen, uncured
Although she had made novena, kissed
The relics: worse than ever, came back
By London, lying on her back,
Saw there, thank Heaven, a specialist
And now is on the recovery list.

From a Diary of Dreams

Dreams wait around corners, linger in Jesus Lane
Under a gas-lamp, stand at urinals,
Purloin my blackthorn stick, shoes or new raincoat,
Give them back suddenly, are the sixth sin,
Strip me at night or in an afternoon nap,
Scatter my script beyond the microphone –
The red light on – then lure me to a lap.
Hurrying out of memory, impure things
Come back, the past, the present, intermixed.
I loiter in now-and-then, am bi-located
A saint, victim of diabolical tricks:
Dublin is London, elbowing rossie, bloke,
Chaff with me; the dead return, disturb my sleep,
Seeing them again, what can I do but weep?
Waking from dream into dream, all puzzledom,
I stray up stair beyond stair, fearful of hearting
Till darkness rooms my hand too near a fuzz.
The under-mind is our semi-private part:
Not senile lust but stirring of religion
Long since abused, below in the pit of us.
The goddess, striding naked, with prodigious
Limbs – worn-out image – thyrsis clad in ivy.
Satyrs in grove, back-gardening Priapus,
Pimp of the privet hedge, a watering-can spout,
Latin still blooms from clay. Our crookshank godlet

Shows what he has in store with nod and tod.
From temple steps, along a marble pavement,
Processions hymning under tilt of tower,
To forest worship, bear a gigantic dildo
Carven in ebony. Loins are the ages
Unknown to us. Lake-dwellings where women grilled
Middle-cut of salmon. Fire-brush cave
Where Long Legs, Big Head, the charger, have been pictured
With slot, kick-up, peazle. Catastrophe
Shook mighty carcases from the world, Sure Foot
Escaped the glacier and lava.
                                My youth
Comes back in lawless dream. Those hair restorers
Have dated Austin. I know their barber's pole.
Go, suck your sugarstick. Complaining with Luther,
I struggle in castles with the Devil, pitch
His fork to hell, yet sink, bubbling in pitch.
I hear the silly cry: 'Oedipus Rex!'
Silently masked, I stare into tragic speech
That shows the culprit below, perverts our sex.
Dreams of salt pillar, incest, pederasty.
Could I but use the ball-point nib – my rastrum,
Smooth flow, compose beyond your black and white.
Flying with Mr Morton, aeroplane banks,
The Phoenix Park aslant. Over the banks,
Wheels touch down, whirrers slow down, solid as sight
Again. Quickly he fixes metal weights
To steady the machine. Somebody waits
Beside the roadway. Cruise O'Brien, first wife
With him. He mounts, kick-starts his motor-cycle
And pillions me to the College, quick as mind
For early lecture.
                        White, shadowed by a Niké,
I am too old to memorise the rhyme-book
Gilded by Palgrave, study English metrics,
Bilging from isle to isle. The temple steps
Are hot. Far up a thymy slope, the skeps
Buzz, coloured in pale washes. All of Greece
Hid, feminine: I dream of the Golden Fleece.

At Radio Éireann, actors are in bed
Rehearsing. Pleased, I find myself with Dolly
'What does it matter?' She laughs as I touch her nose.
For hand has quickly found another dolly
With old-fashioned poke bonnet. Impudence knows
Of regular corrugations as in tyres.
Romans admired them, weighing much imprudence
On tiny scales before Vesuvius had fired
Stone shop and vapour-bath. No shame in smegma.
She holds me tightly and is much the stronger.
Soon, thinking of thrombosis again, I beg for
Mercy, but Slawkenbergious drones: 'What's wrong,
Old man?' So, mad as Turks, we pash. A main sheet
Goes knotting by Nelson Pillar. Clanbrassil Street
Is staring as I catch up, fumbally the blind.
Boys cycle past. We tiptoe around a blind
Corner.
       'Look, Dear, a policeman on his beat.'
'He turns.'
       Can heart forget that missing beat
Of mine? Two motors pass, more Civic Guards.
Mot jeers at us:
       'Give him your best regards!'
Canal lock is opening. Unprosecuted,
We lean against a door, New Ross bus due.
Must see her auntie, wax-work cousins…
               Red
Bulb on the indicator.
       Back in my bedroom,
I waken gaily, still dolled up.
       Shelbourne:
Last Saturday. Two nuns are at the PEN club
In blue-black hoods explaining holy cross-words.
'Girls in the Green,' I say, passing the palm-tubs,
Pleased by alliteration. Collecting Box
Goes by. Silver coin, nickel, drop in. Hubbub
Of drinking parties below, the click of lift-locks
From floor to floor. The blue-black hoods drift out.
Beloved ghost from Adelaide Hospital,
So grieved that she is paler than her spittle,

Is visiting us. Dorothy received
Eight pints of Dublin blood. Dogmatic faith
Flowing through English veins to every secret
Part, shamed her own. So she became a wraith.
'Take care! All Templeogue has been destroyed
By a whirlwind out of the west. A sudden void
Of mind. Families dead. Only one wall
Left standing.'
                    'No, no, not that. A criminal
Had set a time-bomb.'
                    'Was it erosion?'
                                        'Explosion?'
'Only this hush in which our fears are hiding.'

'Old houses are better,' I said, 'Gas-fitters idled,
Sent back for heavier kit, for sledge-and-wedge
To pipe our scullery wall.'
                    Hackney stable
Along King's Inns Street opposite the convent,
The archway, damp hiding in the cobbled yard,
Cab horses munching their hay. The kitchen table,
American oil-cloth on it. Aunt Ciss, still fond
Of me, sets down a plate of arrowroot,
I skim the cooling edge – the Redskin route –
The horses rear up. Mouth is eager to try
The slice of lemon cake. Open to far sky,
Demolished houses, scaffolding: the archway
Still there, the big black gate. No strawing sound
In manger. Uncle John is gone.
                    Rathgar,
North Circular Road are one. My mother has found
Another house and bought it. Timber, tarpaulin
Keep out the bad weather, the roof-tree sags
Side-door is knockered with brass, St George, the Dragon,
Red lacquer in beaded coil. Mother distressed.
My thousand pounds will pay for the new roof.
Too long her savings were mine.

                    In Bloomsbury,
Beneath a street-lamp are two prostitutes,

I stop to chat with them, aware of lewdness.
Neither has money. One of them smiles cutely:
'Did you try Mr Large?'
                              'Yes.'
'So did I,'
            The other winks her meaning.
                                        'Dot has nicknamed
That dirty trio, Mr Large, Mr Small
And Mr Horne.'
                  She pulls her knickers up
And says:
          'Bye-bye.'
                      Hurrying down the street,
We come to a cabman's shelter.
                                'Sausages
And mash for two.'
                    We take a corner seat.
I want to pay no more than one-and-ninepence,
Begin to argue with the aproned boss.
The girl pouts, lighting her cigarette from mine.
I wake confused, for Nora, coming in,
Unbars the shutter. I hear the nine-o'clock din
Of traffic.
            Down below, my twenty bobbers
Under the laurustinus. Blackbird hobnobs
With starling, chaffinch, blue tit. All of them waiting.
Then comes a young thrush, so virginal, she might
Have hurried out of the honeysuckle light,
Still variegated by the mottling shade,
Could I but count each brindle, spice-brown spot,
Or find, in cut-glass, the silver-topped pepper-pot,
That speckled her and daintified such white,
Castor of cinnamon.

                    The fir-tree rooks
Consider crusts that shine below, quick lookers
At open door and window that may shoot:
Cloud-droppers coming down by parachute,
Gun-metal-coloured, helmeted, goose-stepping,
Harmless HEIMWEHR.

Beyond the box-edge, rose-
Beds, currant, loganberry, raspberry rows:
Magpie, magnificence in black and white,
Disdains them all.

Quick shave reveals my plight,
Free-making with a poet's wife. Crafty,
I talk to keep his glance from us. She pulls
My hand away but shows me how her woollens
Part up the middles. Morality wakes me. No laughter
In courting slumber. Twice I have betrayed
My friend, marking the score, duet, big solo,
Finale, *con fuoco*, with Isolda,
Soon dream of Avril, lose her last address,
Go underground, come up at the West End:
Her carven brow on a commercial building
Near Aldwych and at Selfridge's. Figure
Her husband used for breasts had to be bigger.
I cannot find her body, always willing
To share the afternoon with mine. I miss
The train, the mail-boat, take a single ticket
By air. Too late. I weep for her. The kiss
Of steam, exiling coldness of the cross-tracks
At Euston. I hurry out into the hail,
Along the crowded streets. How can I hail
That injured driver when he has no taxi?
The Irish sea… our monoplane comes down
To an island. Waiter scribbles on his napkin.
I eat my lunch in haste, leave half-a-crown,
Run from the restaurant. Boys cycle, cap
By cap, along a causeway. Past old buildings,
I hurry over cobbles. Labourer
Points out the turn. Italian woman, filling
A bucket, takes me to the stairway, pier
Below, wave slaps the bladder weed. I peer
Below.
Hydroplane flown.
I am alone.

Dream scatters my script around the microphone.

Red light is on. I denture into talk.
Seaweed is idly slapping at ring and baulk,
Balance, control, are at the telephone...

Dream strip me at night or in my afternoon nap,
Purloin my blackthorn, shoes or new raincoat,
Give them back sometimes, lure me to lip, lap.
I stare from barred window at Ridley's, half sane.
Dreams breech me, nasty boy, are the sixth sin,
Stand under gas-lamp, leer from urinal,
Expose themselves, linger in Jesus Lane.

Martha Blake at Fifty-One

Early, each morning, Martha Blake
 Walked, angeling the road,
To Mass in the Church of the Three Patrons.
 Sanctuary lamp glowed
And the clerk halo'ed the candles
 On the High Altar. She knelt
Illumined. In gold-hemmed alb
 The priest intoned. Wax melted.

Waiting for daily Communion, bowed head
 At rail, she hears a murmur.
Latin is near. In a sweet cloud
 That cherub'd, all occurred.
The voice went by. To her pure thought,
 Body was a distress
And soul, a sigh. Behind her denture,
 Love lay, a helplessness.

Then, slowly walking after Mass
 Down Rathgar Road, she took out
Her Yale key, put a match to gas-ring,
 Half filled a saucepan, cooked

A fresh egg lightly, with tea, brown bread,
   Soon, taking off her blouse
And skirt, she rested, pressing the Crown
   Of Thorns until she drowsed.

In her black hat, stockings, she passed
   Nylons to a nearby shop
And purchased, daily with downcast eyes,
   Fillet of steak or a chop.
She simmered it on a low jet,
   Having a poor appetite,
Yet never for an hour felt better
   From dilatation, tightness.

She suffered from dropped stomach, heartburn
   Scalding, water-brash
And when she brought her wind up, turning
   Red with the weight of mashed
Potato, mint could not relieve her.
   In vain her many belches,
For all below was swelling, heaving
   Wamble, gurgle, squelch.

She lay on the sofa with legs up,
   A decade on her lip,
At four o'clock, taking a cup
   Of lukewarm water, sip
By sip, but still her daily food
   Repeated and the bile
Tormented her. In a blue hood,
   The Virgin sadly smiled.

When she looked up, the Saviour showed
   His Heart, daggered with flame
And, from the mantle-shelf, St Joseph
   Bent, disapproving. Vainly
She prayed, for in the whatnot corner
   The new Pope was frowning. Night
And day, dull pain, as in her corns,
   Recounted every bite.

She thought of St Teresa, floating
  On motes of a sunbeam,
Carmelite with scatterful robes,
  Surrounded by demons,
Small black boys in their skin. She gaped
  At Hell: a muddy passage
That led to nothing, queer in shape,
  A cupboard closely fastened.

Sometimes, the walls of the parlour
  Would fade away. No plod
Of feet, rattle of van, in Garville
  Road. Soul now gone abroad
Where saints, like medieval serfs,
  Had laboured. Great sun-flower shone.
Our Lady's Chapel was borne by seraphs,
  Three leagues beyond Ancona.

High towns of Italy, the plain
  Of France, were known to Martha
As she read in a holy book. The sky-blaze
  Nooned at Padua,
Marble grotto of Bernadette.
  Rose-scatterers. New saints
In tropical Africa where the tsetse
  Fly probes, the forest taints.

Teresa had heard the Lutherans
  Howling on red-hot spit,
And grill, men who had searched for truth
  Alone in Holy Writ.
So Martha, fearful of flame lashing
  Those heretics, each instant,
Never dealt in the haberdashery
  Shop, owned by two Protestants.

In ambush of night, an angel wounded
  The Spaniard to the heart
With iron tip on fire. Swooning
  With pain and bliss as a dart

Moved up and down within her bowels
    Quicker, quicker, each cell
Sweating as if rubbed up with towels,
    Her spirit rose and fell.

St John of the Cross, her friend, in prison
    Awaits the bridal night,
Paler than lilies, his wizened skin
    Flowers. In fifths of flight,
Senses beyond seraphic thought,
    In that divinest clasp,
Enfolding of kisses that cauterise,
    Yield to the soul-spasm.

Cunning in body had come to hate
    All this and stirred by mischief
Haled Martha from heaven. Heart palpitates
    And terror in her stiffens.
Heart misses one beat, two... flutters... stops.
    Her ears are full of sound.
Half fainting, she stares at the grandfather clock
    As if it were overwound

The fit had come. Ill-natured flesh
    Despised her soul. No bending
Could ease rib. Around her heart, pressure
    Of wind grew worse. Again,
Again, armchaired without relief,
    She eructated, phlegm
In mouth, forgot the woe, the grief,
    Foretold at Bethlehem.

Tired of the same faces, side-altars,
    She went to the Carmelite Church
At Johnson's Court, confessed her faults,
    There, once a week, purchased
Tea, butter in Chatham St. The pond
    In St Stephen's Green was grand.
She watched the seagulls, ducks, black swan,
    Went home by the 15 tram.

Her beads in hand, Martha became
    A member of the Third Order,
Saved from long purgatorial pain,
    Brown habit and white cord
Her own when cerges had been lit
    Around her coffin. She got
Ninety-five pounds on loan for her bit
    Of clay in the common plot.

Often she thought of a quiet sick-ward,
    Nuns, with delicious ways,
Consoling the miserable: quick
    Tea, toast on trays. Wishing
To rid themselves of her, kind neighbours
    Sent for the ambulance,
Before her brother and sister could hurry
    To help her. Big gate clanged.

No medical examination '
    For the new patient. Doctor
Had gone to Cork on holidays.
    Telephone sprang. Hall-clock
Proclaimed the quarters. Clatter of heels
    On tiles. Corridor, ward,
A-whirr with the electric cleaner,
    The creak of window cord.

She could not sleep at night. Feeble
    And old, two women raved
And cried to God. She held her beads.
    O how could she be saved?
The hospital had this and that rule.
    Day-chill unshuttered. Nun, with
Thermometer in reticule,
    Went by. The women mumbled.

Mother Superior believed
    That she was obstinate, self-willed
Sisters ignored her, hands-in-sleeve,
    Beside a pantry shelf

Or counting pillow-case, soiled sheet.
  They gave her purgatives.
Soul-less, she tottered to the toilet.
  Only her body lived.

Wasted by colitis, refused
  The daily sacrament
By regulations, forbidden use
  Of bed-pan, when meals were sent up,
Behind a screen, she lay, shivering,
  Unable to eat. The soup
Was greasy, mutton, beef or liver,
Cold. Kitchen has no scruples.

The Nuns had let the field in front
  As an Amusement Park,
Merry-go-round, a noisy month, all
  Heltering-skeltering at darkfall,
Mechanical music, dipper, hold-tights,
  Rifle-crack, crash of dodgems.
The wards, godless with shadow, lights,
  How could she pray to God?

Unpitied, wasting with diarrhea
  And the constant strain,
Poor Child of Mary with one idea,
  She ruptured a small vein,
Bled inwardly to jazz. No priest
  Came. She had been anointed
Two days before, yet knew no peace:
  Her last breath, disappointed.

Corporal Punishment

Earning their living with much pain,
Determined nun, priest, Christian Brother,
Bring down the stick or leather strap,
Let Queen Victoria still reign here.
Bad ones, who do not give a rap
For law, home-working father, mother,
In a state no piety can smother,
Thoughts pounding like a fireman's bell
To save the souls in them from hell,
Raise up a burning hand as ruler
For no retreat can make them cooler.
Old methods are impenitent.
The new complain. But all enquiry
Is boxed in office, filled with quires
Of notes on Corporal Punishment:
'The Minister for Education:
Cane-bottom chairs for deputation,'
Fidgety boy, struck on the head
In class at Glenageary, fell dead,
A smaller, kept behind locked door
In the new school at Inchicore,
Screamed, jumped from the first floor,
Breaking his thigh. No prosecution
Dare wall our young from persecution.

Living on Sin

The hasty sin of the young after a dance,
Awkward in clothes against a wall or crick-necked
In car, gives many a nun her tidy bed,
Full board and launderette. God-fearing State
Provides three pounds a week, our conscience money,
For every infant severed from the breast.

Unmarried Mothers

In the Convent of the Sacred Heart,
The Long Room has been decorated
Where a Bishop can dine off golden plate:
As Oriental Potentate.
Girls, who will never wheel a go-cart,
Cook, sew, wash, dig, milk cows, clean stables
And, twice a day, giving their babes
The teat, herdlike, yield milk that cost
Them dearly, when their skirts were tossed up
Above their haunches. Hook or zip
Has warded them at Castlepollard.
Luckier girls, on board a ship,
Watch new hope spraying from the bollard.

The Knock

One day in June as I was burking
A midnight thought, half-rhymes were scattered
By a soft knock and Father Bourke
Was smiling in the hallway, hat
In hand. A blackboard, desks and ink-wells,
Virgil, torn toga, little sinks
Of iniquity, were with him. Knees bare,
We studied, nicknamed, paper-chased
Beneath the Rock o' the Candle, fieldfaring
Together, saw the Shannon race
With us, bought sweets in Limerick
Or heard, on their pitch, the Apostolics
At practice.
          Eddie Bourke had sailed
On leave from Singapore, pale-faced
And handsome, a white-haired Jesuit,
Minding together tit and bit
Of this and that about me. Embarrassed,

Kid gloves in hand, he murmured:

                                   'Could we

Discuss religion?'

                     The baroque past

Restored, I ran from reredos, wood

Carvings, to see chapter in flames:

Cold fury of the Counter-Reformation,

And shook my head:

                        'I am contented'

'But Christianity?'

                   Head bent

Before a million altars.

                   'Look

At Templeogue,'

               I waxed,

                     'Demesne

After demesne is yours, life-savings

Bequests and temporalities,

This very house among the last trees,

My mother's gift at my decease,

Mission to China, Black, White Fathers

And Fathers of the Holy Ghost,

French Sisters of Education. Luther

Has fled among the burgraves. Hath

Is wrath and Least is Most.'

'Yes, yes,' he sighed,

                 'You speak the truth,'

'And what of you?'

               I thought,

                   'Obedient, dumb.

The gold of the ciborium

Reflects your watch'

               So, waving hand,

We said Goodbye.

             'I understand,'

He called back.

             'Write to me, in case, you...'

Collegians afraid of pandy-bat,

We need less pile on our praying mat.

Spoiling for faith, the Irish race

Had robed too late in Kenya, the Congo,
Japan, Formosa, Laos, Hong Kong.
Celestials with sunny cheekbone snipe at
Old Union Jack, new Stars-and-Stripes.
Yet I have learned, belief or doubt
Or both, a school-tie cannot wear out.

Richmond Hill

We lay on Richmond Hill
And the river below was still.
        People went by
        But the grass was high
Where my darling turned to bill
Her lipstick and my knees
Capped hers under the trees.
        Could I do less
        When her cotton dress
Was printed *Do as you please*?

Pleasure ran after us
As we hurried to the bus,
        Three looking down
        On London town.
Bed made all serious.
She mapped the mortal frame:
'This, that, those, need a name.
        Four-letter word
        Is too absurd.
Must there be smut with flame?'

Content, in a better world
Of love, her limbs were curled
        Closer to mine
        As if both spine
And spirit had been nurled.
Pleasure is in the round.

Soon with a double bound
    That could not last
    Being too fast,
Sense flew with the speed of sound.

'Now I must –' Smiling, she got
Up. Drowsing on her warm spot,
    I wanted, all haste,
    To clasp her waist,
Murmur in hottentot,
But dreamed my fable had carried
England to bed. Foe parried.
    Free State delayed,
    Then disobeyed
As though the pair were married.

Looking Back

I turn, forgetting good manners,
Look after them in the street,
Young girls, slim, rounded in slacks,
Leg-showing skirt or jeans,
For desire is polygamous
And what is shame but lust?

Gone is the ballet dress
That spread such a dainty frill,
Their hair is rolled up, tressed,
Into a conical hill.
They tint the eyelid, smear lip,
Red, orange, nail-tips, green.

Stiletto heels or flats,
Breast-cap or buckram falsies,
Kerchief, ridiculous hats.
See, how behinds are waltzing.
No man is monogamous
Darlings, come, take our dust.

Body has been corrupted:
Cesare, Darapti, Disamis.
True habit is voluptuous.
I'll study The Thousand Kisses,
Quarän, Old Testament,
Bow to the impudent.

Our Dumb Friends

With nothing to do, they run
Down lanes, in hope of a bite from
Dustbin, lost bone, sharing
Bad habit, sniffing, besniffed
At tail or stump, lifting
A leg every minute, sparing
A droplet, Sodomites
All, mounting each other for fun;
Most of them, celibate,
Victims of self-abuse,
Indecent exposure and nuisance.
Big, small, we cannot blame
Lickers we call by a pet name,
Kiss, fondle. Having no mate,
How can they sublimate
Their normal sex-life? Bitches
Are kept from roadway, ditches.

Guinness Was Bad for Me

Men elbow the counter in public-house, drink
Their pints of plain, their chaser, large or small one,
Talk in the snug, the lounge, nod gravely, wink fun
In meanings, argue, treat one another, swallow
The fume, the ferment. Joyful, self-important,
Soon all are glorious, all are immortal
Beings of greater day, hierophants;
Stately in white and gold-hemmed robes, dalmatics,
They celebrate the truth. Darkness is scattered.
Mazda no longer is to them a trick-cyclist,
Spokesman of epi-cycle. Nip, quarted liquor,
Gives them a universe that all can trust,
Cordial, benevolent, with anecdotes,
Star-finals, when they take off their Sunday coats.
At bolting time, each thirst becomes enormous,
Farewelling, farewelling, farewelling, because it must,
God-blessingers fumbling for the last warm bob,
Attendants in-and-out of the doorway. Lust
Beckons, a shaky hand still on the siphon.
Husbands remember, hurry home to wife on
Time:
      I could not drink their fill. Stomach
Would never bottle the joy in glass or tumbler.
Guinness was bad for me. I groped to Duke Street
By the back entrance at Davy Byrne's to puke
Down areas or, near the quayside, pallid
Beneath the barrel rows, undrunken gallons
That hid me. Bringer of rounds in Mabbot Street,
Our Double X.
          Soon, mackintoshed in London,
My body sank in torpor. I was undone
By mild-and-bitter. Escalator raced
Me, lock unwarded, hat fell off, shoe-laces
Knotted. I rode the bolster; picturing wall
Filmed upward, upward, to the ceiling: spool-fall
To nothingness.

In Chelsea, beer had coped
Chesteron, Belloc, lords of our misrule,
Fooling the World's End. O I could not learn
To drink like an Englishman.

                              John Power at thirty
Became my legend. Now and again he had toped
A province: Munster galloglass or kerne,
Spearing himself through forests in his shirt.
Dublin uncorked him. Cubed, oblonged, the abstracts
Went by. One night as he trousered home, plain facts
Were contradicted – body was bi-located.
Ballasting by Westland Row, the Montclare
Hotel, it waited for him in Merrion Square.
He heard hot-water tap among the leaves
Inside the railings. Suddenly in a maze
His wife was calling from moonlight, deaving
Ear:
       'John, whatever are you doing? John,
O John you're…'
                       Arc lamp, bed-side light, were one.
His hands forgot mahogany rails, quilt-edge,
Half-conscious.
                       My fellow-exile, he met the milkman,
The ten-ton lorries fruiting to Covent Garden.
Imperatives from his Junior Latin Grammar
Scrambled up empty bottles, exclamatory,
All shouting:
                  Frànge! Frànge!
                              In the West End,
He neoned from Square to Circus. Twice were broken
Near Regent Street, large windows of plate-glass
In fashion-shops with slashings of new sales.
Singled out as he doubled past, John woke
In Court, defendant known by cuts and wales.
Magistrate banished him for a year to Wales
Where panes are smaller.
                              But no promises
Could hold that Corkman from licensed premises
For long.

Street-lamping towards his home in drizzle,
One Sunday morning, dodman still a-fizz,
He drifted among shadows, hatted like people,
And moved with them in reverence, head bowed.
Befogged by pillars, the pious soon were kneeling
In prayer. A Chalice brimming with wine of Goodness
Came down to take his thirst from him. Hatred
Of Protestant service held him, splintering
Reason. His parents, pinched by a bad winter
Had been evicted. An urchin, near open fire,
He heard the story blaze. The Royal Irish
Constabulary had marched beyond the byre,
With baton, carbine. Seven shots were fired
At Heaven. Bailiffs with crowbar, battering ram,
Broke down the clay wall, tin-mended door, the jamb:
Unionist landlord watching from his lake-lodge.
John saw through fog a gold-ringed finger podge
A blessing. In his fury to break faith,
Despoil, he grabbed the astonished Graal, emptied
It: then, sack-clothed, devil-tailed, unkempt,
Tried to escape the smoke-coughs of his contempt,
Muffled by streets. But a young, boxing parson
Ran, left him with two Anglo-Catholic scars.
He wakened late in bed.
                              The day was dull.
No spirit or porter could hold him. Our Cuchullin,
His strength was not his own.

                              Feat must be epic.
Across the Irish sea, night-tumbling, trulled
By liquor when the bar was a-glim, he slept
Beside his baggage, wakened, breathing thickly,
Unsirened. Fishguard had become Rosslare.
Gulls dipped to slop and slob from the pure air,
Gangways were ready, hair-coil of rope tossed out,
Steerage, saloon in clatter, wharfmen shouting.
As bells ran: *Stop, Ahead, Astern.*

                              The steamer
Was backing seaward again. Cokers, shirt-sleeves,

Rushed down, saw by the ruds of the furnace flame,
Amidships, madman pulling at the levers
With many hands, coat off, sweaty, dirty,
Drawing a hundred pints that never came up.
Strength leaped beyond the metal, held down, clapped John
In rusty irons. Soon the demoniac,
Still shivering, all Guinness and Power, glum-eyed,
Was hurried by faraway voices into silence
By harrowed fields of Wexford, thirty miles,
And barbiturated in the big Asylum.

Midnight in Templeogue

Young wives unzipple near our Bridge,
Suburbed, soon to be bigger again.
Cork Kerry, gossip above their weanlings
With Moy, Claremorris. Little ones fidget,
Whimper at drop of skirt, slack, jean.
Villa by villa, condition makes friend.
All dress, remark that lunch is late, or
Tidy the pair in perambulator.

Here, after dark, is city-light,
Faint glow, advertisement in cloud,
Our frankincense, a grace reflected.
Forgetting their salaries at midnight,
Instalment, bank withdrawal, unreckoned,
Husbands enjoy what is allowed:
Obedience, unpyjama'd, receiving,
Receiving, quietly conceiving.

Templeogue House is without a lodge now.
Rooms have been blessed in which a pen scratched
Punch parties, elopement, chapterful
Diversion. Devil tries an old dodge
On Fathers O'Leary, O'Malley, wraps them
In warmer sleep. Hot jar is no match
For wily adept, young believer.
Few pledge the novels of Charles Lever.

Sky-light is bolted at Cypress Grove,
Where African students learn our meekness.
Beneath my window, garden is jungling.
Thrice, awful shriek of catkin or coven.
Tom-tomming in undergrowth has blundered.
I dream of Mumbo Jumbo seeking
His fled apostates, manhandling forest,
Wake, double. How can metaphor rest?

Japanese Print

Both skyed
In south-west wind beyond
Poplar and fir-tree, swallow,
Heron, almost collide,
Swerve
With a rapid
Dip of wing, flap,
Each in an opposite curve,
Fork-tail, long neck outstretched
And feet. All happened
Above my head. The pair
Was disappearing. Say I
Had seen, half hint, a sketch on
Rice-coloured air,
Sharako, Hokusai!

Right of Way

I cannot walk by the river now swishing
The grass, far as the dart of the kingfisher,
See cress, marsh-marigold, beyond the willow,
Hazel, wild privet, for the fields are villa'd.
Small owners have fenced the right of way, mere inches,
No wider than their graves. So, the green inches,
All tiny Irelands, are hidden around the bend
Of Summer-seen gravel. Walk has come to an end.
Outlawed by greed, I look down from the Bridge,
Remembering our covetous religion:
Held back, as when the sluices at Bohernabreena
Open and waters rush here through a mock ravine.

A Strong Wind

All day a strong wind blew
Across the green and brown from Kerry.
The leaves hurrying, two
By three, over the road, collected
In chattering groups. New berry
Dipped with old branch. Careful insects
Flew low behind their hedges.
Held back by her pretty petticoat,
Butterfly struggled. A bit of
Paper, on which a schoolgirl had written
'Máire loves Jimmy', jumped up
Into a tree. Tapping in haste,
The wind was telegraphing, hundreds
Of miles. All Ireland raced.

A Mile from Tallaght

Old Metal Polisher in the sky
Looked over valley, hill,
    On the sly
And gave the world another rub.
Car, wind-screen, wealthied by,
Silver-plated roof and hub.
     River, wet rock,
Were emeried. Derelict mill
Began to turn the water-wheel. Shock
Of ivy blossom spilled out
Gold. Fifty windows filled
And the new glass was spry.

Cypress Grove

I

'Grob! Grob!' goes the raven peering from his rift
Above Lough Bray, glimmer on eyelid, feather –
Shadow in water – sets out for Kippure
By upper Glencree, at morning, devil-dot
Above the last bog-cutting, hears the lark totting
And dips along gullies by the twig-drip of heather
Down to the pond-level, the steps of Bohernabreena,
Then winging over Seefin, takes the pure
Cold air – ravenous, searching – comes to that green
Bowl set among hills, Punchestown, its race-course
So often whiskeyed with the roar of crowd
Nearer, farther, as binoculars
Hastily swivel the Grand Strand, hoarser
Where black-red-violet-blue-white-yellow dots
Are hunched along the slope: backers from bars
And, shaded by huge umbrellas, bookmakers,
Are waving caps above the stalls. That hurly-burly
A mile away: he sees the pewter cloud

Above Church Mountain, past the double lake,
Flaps by the King's River, sandy spots:
Behind him the dairy farms – the acres tree'd,
Thin-streamed – then flies up where the gusts are blowing
Over the ceannavaun and nothing is showing,
Hidden awhile in vapouring of screes
'Ur! Ur!' he croaks to himself, a flying speck
And turning northward over Annalecky
Where a man by the Slaney might stoop to hook a
Trout, play it, looks down into Poulaphouca.

II

At daybreak, hurrying home too late, by peel
And pale, goes Jack o'Lantern, turning on heel,
Jumping the bog-drain, last Elizabethan.
The raven sees the doublet of that trickster
Darting, like his own flame-spot underneath,
While shadowkins play among themselves at nix
As early, the black fellow beaking along the Dodder,
Spies in a reedy pool the waterhen
Gliding behind the cress, a constant nodder,
Then mantles across the river to the fields,
The strippers half-asleep, where once the Spa
At Templeogue was fashionable, now wheel-less.
Hundreds of pigeons clap up from Cheeverstown,
Sink down again into the damp of the shaw.
He flies two miles by a gorse-budded glen
To a forgotten sandpit or a quarry
That leads the sheep to nowhere like a corrie,
Ironwork scraps, our twisted thoughts, unshacked,
Turns, seeing a single streak between the grass-mounds,
The paven conduit with an inch of ripple
That Normans drank in Dublin, centuries
Ago, provinces at their shaven lips.
It brims a stock-pond, hurries underground
Be cellarage of an eighteenth-century mansion.
The sewered city with a rump of suburbs
Has reached the pillared gate in its expansion,
Design of the daffodils, the urns, disturbed by

Air-scrooging builders, men who buy and sell fast.
One Gallagher bought the estate. Now concrete-mixers
Vomit new villas: builder, they say, from Belfast
With his surveyors turning down the oil-wicks.
The shadow is going out from Cypress Grove,
The solemn branches echoing our groan,
Where open carriages, barouches, drove:
Walnut, rare corktree, torn up by machine.
I hear the shrills of the electric saw
Lopping the shelter, unsapping the winter-green
For wood-yards, miss at breakfast time the cawing
Of local rooks. Many have moved to Fortrose.
They hear in my lifted hand a gun-report,
Scatter their peace in another volley.

I stare:

Elegant past blown out like a torchère.

On the Mountain Tops

Religion, shrining the country town,
The monthly fair, can now look down
On German settlers, half-empty village.
Beyond the last potato drill,
Where famine has never seen a stim
Because her hands are blind, with hymnal
And hold water sprinkled below,
The clergy bless another show
Of faith. On rock and mountain top,
Far South or West, contractors are popping
An iron cross in concrete, though gale force
Fork-lightning, hurled our hope from the grit
Of Carrantuohal, Galtymore.
The Devil cannot have his Bit now:
White dot in the Gap of Tipperary,
Look, statue to the Virgin Mary.
Only in Wicklow, railed-in fighters
With Father Murphy, withstand our mitres.

I Saw from Cashel

Wrinkling as Voltaire,
I saw from Cashel volt tear
Our silence, uncross the peak,
Hurl down iron, split block
Of concrete, shame the meek,
All might, reform the rock.

The Eighth Wonder of Ireland

I

Giraldus Cambrensis recounted the seven wonders
Of Ireland. Hot hedge, impenetrable pale
On fire, up, down, around, between and under,
Protecting the holy virgins from our male
Intrusion at Kildare. Bell, with a stoop,
Hobbling in round of mercy from the belfry
At Fore. Delight of priest and deacon, stoop
That brims with wine for daily Mass. Steep, self-
Descending, ten-mile-sounding, ship-devouring,
Green, glassy, walling Whirlpool. Bull-man
Mounting in turn twelve crummies, glowering
In field. Cross in the parish of Rathoath
That spoke against false witnesses on oath.
Tincture of island clay that cures the bite
Of reptile, adder, lessens ayen-bite.

II

To the seven wonders of Ireland, add an eighth.
Thrones and Dominions have changed our copybooks.
Crooked is straight, upside is down, pothooks
Are hangers, good is bad now, pity, cruel,

Free medicine, school-milk, contrary to Faith;
The old, the sick, cannot have soup or fuel,
Parents, who anguish vainly to support
Their infants, are robbed of them unhomed in Court,
Pelfing is grace, substance of self, a wraith.

Beyond the Pale

Pleasant, my Nora, on a May morning to drive
Along the roads of Ireland, going south,
See Wicklow hilling from car window, down
And pinewood, buttercupping grass, field-wire,
The shelves of hawthorn, konker bud on chestnut
Bulging with sun-shadowings, brook-lime,
The yellow iris-curl, flower o' the cress
And Slaney gliding around a sandy nook
Through flaggeries into the narrower falls,
Beyond the mills with rusty flange, cogwheel
And moss of the sluice, hear the jackdawing,
Yet sad to speed from the inn, along the bogland
Where State machines are cutting turf for miles
That furnaces may stop the centuries
Of turbary, put out an ancient fire.
Hardly a living soul upon these roads:
Both young and old hasten to quit the dung,
The chicken-run, lean-to, sty, thistle blow
Of fields once measured by buckshot, midnight bung.
Foreign factories in towns employ
Chattering girls: few levers for a boy.

Pleasant to climb the rock of Dunamace,
A goat upon a crag, a falcon swerving
Above heraldic shield of air, chevroned
With brown and or: later the rounded walls
And bastion were raised beside the squat
Keep: they could bounce away the cannon balls.
The culdees knew each drumlim, sun-thatched spot,

By rising road, fern-corner, come to Wolf Hill:
Men working underground, tap anthracite.
Stacks are shed-high. The heatherland is chill.
That earth is black except for a blue-white image
Seen far, a statue of the Blessed Virgin
Beside the road, a solitary hymn
To a great owner. Beneath the pious verge
Of the mine-hill is his public-house, his sign –
The Swan, beside a holy statuette:
Nearby his factory with store of drain-pipes,
Trim row by row, a Sacred Heart beset
By glass of shrine and on the outer wall
Behold a plaque in loving memory
Of Joseph Fleming, Irish patriot,
Industrialist and good employer. Night-stealing,
He fought the English, ready with rifle shot
To serve his country.
                              Higher still.
                                        Pleasant,
My love, upon Mount Leinster, passing the spruce,
Fir, pine plantations, as a red-brown pheasant
Comes bustling up from heather, bends the juicy
Grass-stalk, to scan the middle plain below,
A map of cloud, the fields of beetroot penned;
Dividing sea.

          Signpost to Kilkenny:
The Georgian almshouses, tree-pent, College
Where Congreve, Swift, had learned about addition,
The passage steps between the danks of wall,
Martins high up at the city bridge,
Swallows, their black-and-white playing at tig.
Along the River Nore, chasing the midgets
Where, biding in the sedge, the young trout nab
Their share. Behind the Thorsel, the Black Abbey,
A street of little shops, a painted set,
Drop-scene for Harlequin. Embattled might;
Norman Cathedral with its monuments,
Marble of tablet and recumbent knights
In effigy beside obedient wives, knees bent.
A black dog flamed, leg up. Dame Kyttler scoffed there

At Mass – her house is now a betting office.
Too long at night she had been irked by the Belt
Of Chastity. So, stripping to the pelt,
Leftwise, she wrote the Tetragrammaton.
The Devil came, volumed in smoke from a forge
Beyond the Caucasus, breakneck upon
Foul wind. She wanted topsy-turvy orgy
And, taking her by the loblongs, Fiery dawdled,
Un-padlocked her with ice-cold key. Melled, twisting
In exquisite pain, she lay with open wards
While her companion, Petronella, was kissed
Introrsely by Black Fitzjames, knighted in hell.
He picked her keyhole with his skeleton,
Fire-freezing through her pelvis, but she missed
The bliss, though he was cap-à-pie as Guelf.
Soon afterwards, they say, that demon sired
The black cats of Kilkenny. They fought for scales
Of market fish, left nothing but their own tails
And their descendants never sit by the fire-side.
Disedifying Latin, clerical tales
Corrupt us.

        Only one poet, Coventry
Patmore, who wived three times, has written of love
In matrimony, pulled the curtain back, showed
From post to post, the hush of featherbed,
Lace counterpane, mahogany commode;
And here from hoop and bustle, petticoats, pleating,
Long drawers, to eiderdown, our Fanny glowed;
Too cushiony, too gross, in such an abode
For Psyche.
        Our convert, right or wrong,
                        believed
That in the midnight transport, every spouse
Knew Heaven, like us, by the oriental spice.
So Virtue blushing at a little vice,
Turned down the incandescent mantle, unbloused
The globes of sin.

        'This, this, is telling secrets.
Burn every page,' wrote Gerard Manley Hopkins.

'Only upon that morning when the skin hops
To bone and sinew again, must Truth be published.
Then shall the Unmentionable be purified,
Pearl, ruby, amethyst, all grace inside.'

So, turning west, we drive to Borrisokane.
The Misses O'Leary own a small hotel
And shop there, have for pet, a middle-aged hen.
She clucks and picks all day, is never fluttered.
I see her twice a year, yes, know her well,
And spoon an egg of hers, boiled lightly, buttered,
At breakfast, scrape it to the very shell.

Delightful to be in Tipperary, greenest
Of all the counties, drive by coltsfoot stream
And spinney, gearing up to Silvermines
Forgetting that Europe closed the mountain till
Or hear the haggling at a monthly market,
Farmers go by and women with fat thighs,
The milk-cans clanking on their little carts, to
Co-operative creameries, light smoke,
Ruffle of separators: come to byways
Where sawmills whirr with easy belt, see glow
Of welding in forges, hurry to Lough Derg.
May-fly is nymphlike there, pearling her veils,
Soon is bewinged. The shadow of a berg
Is greening, paling. Dappers hear about them
The noise of carburettors, modern roar
Of water-skiing as the speedboats clap on
The spray. Young one, legs apart, toes out,
Classical in her scantlet of bright costume,
Our Naiad, offering wet little posy
To Nereus while summery splashes, tossed
By board or skip of rope, go bottoming,
Head over heels.

       Storm out of the South-West
From Banagher, Clonfert, across the flats,
Leaf-crushes of rain, the darkness coming faster.
The barges are rotting at wharves. Canal Hotel,

Where shivering children peep from broken panes,
At Shannon Harbour, now a tenement.
The lake-winds whistle, dip-dipping the slenderers.
In runs of air, the saltness is besprent.
At Gallerus, the pale Atlantic rages.
Bad weather, hard times, known to the Ancient Crow
Of Achill, flapping out of the earth-brown pages
Of manuscripts, the Stay of Leiterlone
Uncragging, Fintan, halfway from transmigration,
A roaming salmon, where billows dredge the shingle.

Now, after a century of rags, young girl
With skin the insolent have fondled, Earl
And settler in his turn, the Hag of Dingle
Is stretching. Eire, clamant with piety,
Remembering the old mythology.

Eighteenth Century Harp Songs

I
Mabel Kelly

Lucky the husband
Who puts his hand beneath her head.
They kiss without scandal
Happiest two near feather-bed.
He sees the tumble of brown hair
Unplait, the breasts, pointed and bare
When nightdress shows
From dimple to toe-nail,
All Mabel glowing in it, here, there, everywhere.

Music might listen
To her least whisper,
Learn every note, for all are true.
While she is speaking,
Her voice goes sweetly
To charm the herons in their musing.

Her eyes are modest, blue, their darkness
Small rooms of thought, but when they sparkle
    Upon a feast-day,
    Glasses are meeting,
Each raised to Mabel Kelly, our toast and darling.

Gone now are many Irish ladies
Who kissed and fondled, their very pet-names
Forgotten, their tibia degraded.
She takes their sky. Her smile is famed.
Her praise is scored by quill and pencil.
    Harp and spinet
    Are in her debt
And when she plays or sings, melody is content.

    No man who sees her
    Will feel uneasy.
He goes his way, head high, however tired.
    Lamp loses light
    When placed beside her.
She is the pearl and being of all Ireland
Foot, hand, eye, mouth, breast, thigh and instep, all that we desire.
Tresses that pass small curls as if to touch the ground;
    So many prizes
    Are not divided
Her beauty is her own and she is not proud.

II
Gracey Nugent

I drink, wherever I go, to the charms
Of Gracey Nugent in whose white arms
I dare not look for more. Enraptured
By a kiss or two, a little slap,
    Her virtue cannot harm me.

Delightful to share her company
Even with others. While she is speaking,
Music goes by and what she smiles at,
Would bring the swan back to the tide.
    Was ever plight so pleasing?

Her graceful walk, her pearly neck-lace,
And bosom so near, have made me reckless.
I want to sit, clasping her waist,
Upon her boudoir sofa, waste
    Hope. Days are only seconds.

Happy the young fellow, who wins
And can enjoy her without sinning.
Close in the darkness, they will rest
Together and when her fears are less
    She'll take his meaning in

And know at last why he is seeking
Shoulder and breast, her shapely cheeks,
All that I must not try to sing of.
The modest may not point a finger
    Or mention what is best.

And so I raise my glass, content
To drink a health to Gracey Nugent,
Her absence circles around the table.
Empty the rummer while you are able,
    Two Sundays before Lent.

III
Peggy Browne

The dark-haired girl, who holds my thought entirely
Yet keeps me from her arms and what I desire,
Will never take my word for she is proud
And none may have his way with Peggy Browne.

Often I dream that I am in the woods
At Westport House. She strays alone, blue-hooded,
Then lifts her flounces, hurries from a shower,
But sunlight stays all day with Peggy Browne.

Her voice is music, every little echo
My pleasure and O her shapely breasts, I know,
Are white as her own milk, when taffeta gown
Is let out, inch by inch, for Peggy Browne.

A lawless dream comes to me in the night-time,
That we are stretching together side by side,
Nothing I want to do can make her frown.
I wake alone, sighing for Peggy Browne.

IV
The Tantalus

In many a tree-hidden mansion,
Whiskey, ale, smuggled brandy
Are poured. From Castlebar
    To Westport,
I toast hospitable ladies,
Forget, at midnight, braided
Locks, pale skin under brocade,
Rogueries of persuasion
    And stumble to rest.

No Irishman would quarrel
With the clergy, who make war on
An act that is immoral –
    But better than Latin.
So let them have their claret,
Imbibe by the dozen or barrel.
I'll pledge them to the corridor,
The grounds, if I may borrow
    The Tantalus.

V
Breedeen

One day, as I went down a boreen,
When reeds by the lake were wheezing,
I spied, near a stone-wall, my own Breedeen
    In rain and sleet.

She waved a welcome to me, then ran
A throw beyond nettle, ragwort,
And her petticoat dyed with madder,
    Showed bare feet.

We struggled. I touched her funny bone.
Mouth yielded up a budding kiss
And I was lost in honeysuckle,
      Not rain or sleet.

A Vision of Mars

A vision of Mars, last night, has tired me, disheartened, numb, beguiled.
Great ships of the line, their wide sails tipped with ensigns, gold, white, blue:
No lantern shining from poop as the moon rose and cannon tided bumboats.
Rock frothed in lying ranks from Shannon to Slyne Head. The Northwest
                              blew.

Hope idled. In Europe, tossed waves crossed the Maes with spliced rope, log,
While sappers piled the earthworks at Namur, half-star, dyke, bastion.
Smoke heightened the towns with fire-fret spires where men devoured
                            horse, dog-flesh
To save our Catholic Majesty near Brest and nave him at High Mass.

Aisling

One day before Titan had lighted the way from his doorstep,
I climbed to a hilltop silled by mist and, wherever
I looked, were blue-hooded women who knew no envy;
They came from a mound without sound through the grey of heather.

As they moved, the light ran widely, hues in the south-east
Mapped harbours from Youghal to Galway. Spars were unshrouding.
Branches bore green foliage. Dangles bowed down
The leaves with acorns and Cornucopia spouted.

They lighted three candles, their hands white to the thumbnail
And I followed that band to the Shannon through pollen of Thomond.
Quickly they climbed Knock Firinne. Rock shaled and summered
As I asked Queen Eeval what task had summoned them.

That Queen, as she passed from the grass, eagerly told me
Why gladness had candled all Ireland – no sadness of story –
In the name of the King, who would bring us from shame to glory,
Holder of three Countries, undefeated, bold hero.

I started up from my dream, half seen, sad-hearted,
And thought of Tyrconnel dishonoured, quarrel in Eirinn,
The faith that has found and bound us, betrayed to foreigners,
One day before Titan had lighted the way from his doorstep.

O'Rourke's Feast

Let O'Rourke's great feast be remembered by those
Who were at it, are gone, or not yet begotten.
A hundred and forty hogs, heifers and ewes
Were basting each plentiful day and gallons of pot-still
Poured folderols into the mugs. Unmarried
And married were gathering early for pleasure and sport.
'Your clay pipe is broken.' 'My pocket picked.' 'Your hat
Has been stolen.' 'My breeches lost.' 'Look at my skirt torn,'
'And where are those fellows who went half under my mantle
And burst my two garters?' 'Sure, no one's the wiser.'
'Strike up the strings again,' 'Play us a planxty.'
'My snuff-box, Annie, and now a double sizer.'

Men, women, unmugged upon the featherbeds,
Snored until they heard the round clap, the step-dance,
Again, jumped up, forgot to bless their foreheads,
And jigging, cross-reeling from partner to partner, they trampled
With nail in brogue that cut the floor to shavings.
'A health, long life to you, Loughlin O'Hennigan.'
'Come, by my hand, I'll say it in your favour,
You're dancing well, Marcella Gridigan.'
'A bowl, Mother, and drink it to the last drop.'
Then came a big hole in the day. Light failed.
'Shake rushes for Annie and me, a blanket on top
And let us have a slap-and-nap of decent ale.'

Merciful Heaven, whoever saw such a big crowd
So drunk, the men with belt-knives at slashing, stabbing,
The women screaming, trying to hold up trousers
And others upon the table, twirling an oak-plant?
The Sons of O'Rourke came rolling from the doorway
In somersaults of glory. Bachelor boys
Were boasting, cudgelling more, more, more.
'My father built the monastery at Boyle...'
'The Earl of Kildare and Major Bellingham were
My...' 'Sligo harbour, Galway, Carrick-drum-rusk,'
'And I was fostered...' 'Pull the alarum bell.'
'A blow for your elbow grease,' 'A kick in the tump.'

'Who gave the alarm?' demanded one of the clergy
And swung his big oak stick – not as a censer.
Right, left, he plied it soundly to asperge them
In blood-drops, gave a dozen three more senses.
The friars got up with their cowhorn beads to haul him
Back, dust his habit. Three Reverences tumbled
Into the ashes; Father Superior bawling
Until that congregation went deaf and dumb:
'While I was studying with His Holiness
And taking Roman Orders by the score,
Yiz sat on a settle with an old story-book,
All chawing roast potatoes at Sheemore.'

Cock and Hen

A cock and hen strayed on their travels
From Birr to Navan, until one Thursday,
They dropped their tails in a prison-cell
At Sligo. Bar, bench, jurymen heard
That scandalous pair. Case was dismissed.
Struck from the list, so they went to the grazings
Of William MacShane. Near rock, cloud, mist,
They fed on fraughans, slept in a hayfield.

'You should have seen my cock as he reached
From his horse,' the Hen said, 'at the big fair
Of Galway, daring all, his breeches
So finely stitched, gold watch with figures,
Rapier hilt and spurs, new suit,
Gauntlets that fitted him, laced hat.
He rode, he dandied with polished top-boots
Of Spanish leather, crop in hand.

'I came to Tom Hood's,' the Cock said, 'hens picking,
No bantam or chick with them, I rustled
The straw and bustled beneath a half rick,
Then trod the layers quickly, hustling
Them off and lusted on the dung-hill,
Doors open. "Kill that new cock, Mary,
You've time to spare." She caught, wrung, weighed me,
Is it my fate to be plucked bare?'

'My grief,' the Hen sobbed at night on her roost,
'Bed-partner, who used to tread me gladly,
My children's father is boiled. His juices
Cling to the pot. Tail tingles, lonely, sad,
Feather and bone. A young Spring widow,
I snap my bill at those who shamed him,
Cursing the women at Ballinarobe,
For grain is chaff, without my game-cock.'

Rustic Match-Making

A lad, that I like, went to Michael in his best clothes
And bootwear to beg for his Peg. 'Well, I know it.
The girl that you fancy,' Mike answered, 'may soon be your own
For a pair of dairy cows and the little yellow pony.'

A neighbour ran quickly to Patrick James Maloney.
'My son can have Crumple and Dun with a new home
Of his own at Dereen with seventeen acres,' Pat told him,
'But I'll never bestow on Eoin the little yellow pony.

Praise of the people at local meeting,' he boasted,
'Were his, for at Mallow he won every run in the Spring Show,
At Youghal, he rallied the race. Tralee cheered his going.
No horse could compete in a heat with my little yellow pony.

At the Curragh, one time, he hurried a length beyond Whalebone,
Passed Waitawhile, Patient, Malvolio
And twice gained the Silver Plate, though Denis rode him
At Fairyhouse too rarely, my little yellow pony.

Mike has a fine farmstead, good head on his shoulders,
But to such a demand, out of hand, I say "no"
Let him part with his Peg or his Kathleen twice over.
I'll not give any man, as I live, my little yellow pony.

His pedigree, men agree, is a roll-call.
By Clinker out of Sidelong, Pride out of Bold Lass,
From Munster Lady, by Padereen, Moll foaled him.
He had the best sire in Ireland my little yellow pony.'

''Twould be a shame now to blame Big Patrick. He's older
Than I am and shambles with aches from the bedpost.
To the Chalybeate Spa at Tralee, all sprain and sore,
Let him ride with an old bridle his little yellow pony.'

The Adventures of the Great Fool

Over the hump and bump of Glen Bolcan
Where nothings talked, the Great Fool,
Far from an ale-house, plodded the road
And his face glowed in the blue moon.

He called, mile after mile, to late-goers,
Mortals afraid of him: 'Stop, have you
Heard of a sky-woman with crescented hair?'
They shook their pents at him, thick-dewed.

'The loveliest woman from mound or foreland.'
Glibs shook the more, turned back and scuttered
Away, unmarried mother and bachelor.
The Great Fool scratched his noddle, muttered.

Near dawn, he came to a hill fort.
Within the courtyard stood a Gruagach,
Eager for him. Silent, with twist
And hook, they wrestled until cock crow.

At the third round, the Gruagach fell back
Neck under elbow, at the eighth,
Lay dead. A pale girl in her night-dress,
Came out. Each breast was a May bud.

The Great Fool held her in his arms,
Kissed, carried her through fifty rooms
To her warm bed, unflapped the cod,
Fondled her body and pooh-poohed

Her fears. They splonked, week after week,
Until they were weak. She brought him soup,
Boiled fowl. They left on a fine day
When all the way was cock-a-hoop,

Ran down a valley where the water
Went in falls. She leafed a bothy.
She lay alone. She sang his strength back.
She gave him no lengthy kiss, but mothing

Of tongue tip. Mooning it out, there,
They guddled trout when the rains dimmed
Pools. She unbound her shame one night, obeyed
And took the weight of spunk from him.

Below the forest, they met a man
In iron panoply, 'A Gruagach,'
He said, 'has stolen my hound and speckled
Bitch.' Forest kecked. A giant hub-bubbed

To them. The splinters from his club
Flew round the lubber. The knight fell.
The girl, with a cry, stooped to his pangs,
But iron hinges rang his knell.

'Come to my fort, Great Fool, and guard
My wife, my courtyard and much gold,'
The Gruagach said. 'but keep your eye full,
While I am pulling down buck, boar.'

With hound and speckled bitch at heel,
He jumped from field to rock, uproared
Along a forest, while the Great Fool
Sat on a three-legged stool and snored.

'Wake up, wake up!' His dear one fuddled him.
'Take care, you must not take a nap.'
'No, no. I cannot hear the chevy.'
His head was heavy on her lap.

'Wake up, wake up!' She pulled at his lobe,
Nipped lug and probed. A young man stood
Before them with a smile. He sized up
The Gruagach's wife in air and rudely

Pinched her below. Quickly, the Great Fool
Got up and threw him, heard the thunder
Among the forests, rolled like an egg,
Groaned as a leg went under him.

He gripped the young man by the clothes,
But could not throw him in the dust.
'I serve the King of the Eastern world,'
He cried, 'and churled but never was I trussed.'

'They showed me in chains at a pavilion
But, one by one, I killed his champions.
I fought over Persia with nine phantoms
Voluming out of oil-jar, lampion.

'With tip of the whip in Turkish bath,
Girls raddled me. The eunuch daily
Barbered their base. I went on all fours.
Girls yipped me, rode me, played the male.

'But never was I billy-in-bowl
Legless, bowled over, till to-day.'
He gripped the young man by the smalls,
But could not sprawl him where he lay.

Then, in a puff, the stranger grew big...
The Gruagach stood there, red with laughter.
'I am your brother. You have proved
Your worth.' Great Fool was no longer daft.

The trouble in his brain had gone out
And reason shone from it. Elf-bolt
Was snapped by syllogism. Pot-hooks
Would open books upon his shelf.

He got up on his pins. Both hugged,
Shook hands and hurried to regale
Themselves, twice knew their wives, got blind
On the oldness of wine, newness of ale.

How Covetousness Came into the Church

Towards blueness of day, the Saviour
And Peter staved from hillock to hill
And, waiting near a hot boulder,
They saw an old man, shivery, chill.

His sleeves were tattered, his sandals broken,
He groaned and moaned by the last palm-tree;
Then hobbled two steps with his caubeen,
Stammered, beseeching them for alms.

Peter stood, fingering a copper,
But the Master stopped with a keen look
Then waved away the ragged spittle
And showed the spirit, unskinned, unclean.

The beggarman went with his groan and moan,
Old skin and bone. 'My simple Peter,
Look in the bowels of every man,
Not at the mantle or bare feet.'

They journeyed on. 'Soon you will see
Another meaning in My Word.'
An hour away, they met a bandit,
In his big hand was a sword.

He shouted for money, but the Master
Walked the faster and refused
An ear. The bandit followed, called
Up curses, bawled down Heaven, abused Him.

'He daren't fight or try to harm us
For we are armed with better than sword.'
His Teacher answered: 'You will learn
Soon, Peter, the sternness of My Word.'

So, in a week, they climbed two rounds
Of a pathless mountain, saw the greenness
Below, the greyness – rock and sun –
Above. Then thunder-rain and sleet

Came, black, brown, purple, hid the Truth
For Genii moved with yellowing hazes,
Indigo gloom. They heard two skies
Mingle, dash by. Nature was dazed,

Darkness, torn light. The mountain wheeled
Eastward. They reeled into a cave.
The bandit stood there, chaffed, allowed them
In. Peter bowed to their merry saver.

Badness brought comfort, royal robes
And hung their own near a ready fire,
Put down a wine-jar, rye bread, bunch
Of figs. They munched, drank, heard a choir

Of Seraphs. Judea came back with sun-spots.
Goodness poured money to help the pair
Upon their way. They staved in silence
And Peter smiled. Tongue did not dare

To speak. They came down to the greenness.
In a ravine. The beggar lay
There, 'Master, we are to blame. He died
From want.' 'He lied and now is clay.

Search in his pockets and coat-lining,'
The Master sighed, his face was stern.
Peter found silver and twenty gold coins
From Rome. But our first Pope must learn

His lesson. 'Go to the lake and throw such jingle
Beyond the shingle.' Doubtful, Peter
Stood near a boat-net, for he was tempted.
Fist slowly emptied the silver pieces.

He kept the Caesars. 'Small change is pelf,
But gold will help us to many a supper.
Who knows when purses will be stinted?'
'Bed at an inn, next day, a crupper?'

The Master gazed at him in sorrow,
'Put away morrow. Go back, purchase
Yourself from Caesar. Because you are greedy,
Must true believers despise My Church?'

Song of the Books

South-westerly gale fiddled in rigging;
Furled canvases in foam-clap, twigged
The pulley-blocks. Billows were bigger.
　　　The clouds fell out.
In Madmen's Glen, snipe hit the grasses,
Rains in Tralee had towned their phantoms
While rocks were thrumming in the passes.
　　　Below a shout
Was whisper and among the boulders
　　　The frightened trout
Were hiding from the beaten coldness.
　　　Soon every snout
Was gone. The noises of new shingle
Along the coast had swept the Kingdom
Of Kerry, league by league, from Dingle
　　　In whirlabout.

The tumult blew from Clear to Dursey
By mountain corners with its firstlings,
As though all Ireland were accursed.
　　　It blew from Cape Cod
Over the ocean from point and scraper
To Coomakista and escaped
Through gaps. Nothing could keep its shape.
　　　Grass knew it, tod
Unscrambled. Barley and oats were flattened
　　　In furlong, rod.
And in the cottage fire-light, shadows
　　　Put sod on sod.
Galloping on the skyline, Phaeton,
Had taken a short-cut of lightning, late on
His course; the horses in half traces
　　　Had been unshod.

The Skelligs hid again their stone-steps,
The hermit cells that had been skeps
Of Heaven's beeswax. Thunder slept

In a high coombe.
By Gallerus and Caherdaniel,
The torrents poured out. Barn, crab-tree wall
Sheltered the house at Derrynane:
    In lamp-lit room,
The Liberator marked a law page:
    Outside, green gloom,
Thick branches, glim of tideways raging
    With heels of spume.
A gust struck, snapping chain and rope-post,
Book-boxes of a Gaelic poet
On board a vessel sank with side-blow.
    A little doom.

Tomás Rua O'Sullivan,
Poet in bed, schoolteacher, postman
By day, counted the leap o' the coast
    From Port Magee,
Thinking of the new suit and trimmings
Daniel O'Connell had given him
And his boxful of books in a dim hold,
    Ready for sea.
Last of the race of the walking school-masters,
    In a century
Of Penal Laws, he watched the flood-gleams
    Yellow as pee;
Hurricane from America,
Bahamas, unslating, breaking ha-ha,
Swirling the hay-loft, rattling the paddocks,
    Walling the quay.

'If I walked,' he sang, 'through Ireland, Scotland,
France and the Spanish Netherlands,
Or was rowed to rope-ladder from a strand,
    Could I grip tight
A bundle of so many volumes,
Close-printed crams of knowledge,
To keep whole parishes from folly
    And speckle my sight?
Devil a one is left to hold

Near a tallow light.
Tramping the road, post-bag on shoulder,
    Such is my plight.
Curse of a poor man and the coxwain
On that treacherous crab-rock
That sank the gunwale and my boxful
    Of books in the white.'

'My manuscripts, that famous Psalter
Of Cashel, inked without fault;
Keating, who wrote among the Galtees
    In caves and fled
Through greenwood. Stories of Slieve Gowra,
Aughrim, Athlone, Gunpowder Plot,
The Siege of Troy, whiling the hours
    Away in a shed.
The Brown Bull, *Cattledrive at Cooley*,
    The Row in Royal Bed
I mentioned to my class in school-time.
    Much I read:
Tom Jones in his pelt, *The Vicar of Wakefield*,
Night Thoughts by Young; thunder-peal, graves,
The faeries, houses where key-hole raves.
    All's in my head.
Macpherson, Voster's *Arithmetic*,
Dowling's *Book-keeping*, Walter Binchie
On Mensuration, Patrick Lynch's
    Geography,
Another by Deignan, Comerford,
O'Halloran's *Ireland*, well-worded,
Compass and scale, right angle, surd,
    Every degree.
Virgil and Homer long I kept,
    De Catone,
Sermons, *The Pentaglot*, *Preceptor*
    Upon my knee,
With *Tristram Shandy* and *Don Quixote*,
Crook's Aesop's *Fables*, *Reynard the Fox*.
Our Rapparees behind their rocks,
    Drowned in the sea.'

That luckless poet, Macnamara,
Passenger to the Land of Fish,
Huddled upon the deck, suspicious
     Of all. He lay
Beside his crock of butter, smoked ham,
Nine stone of oatmeal and his sackful
Of new potatoes near the mast-head
     By night and day.
Phoebus shone on the curling crests:
     Winged fish at play.
Aeolus and Thetis sped the burly
     Ship. All were gay
Until a frigate hove in sight
Cannon-balls left their lightning,
The shouting, screeches of women, were frightful
     From scupper to stay.

But Macnamara soon came back,
Shipped his best poem, they say, from Hamburg,
Spoiled priest, teacher beneath a turfstack,
     All o's and a's:
A Protestant by day, shining
His top-boots, Catholic every night
Cross-legged behind a key, sky-headed
     With tra-la-la's
Of travel. Maybe he was shrived,
     Heard *Secula's*,
Blind wanderer at ninety-five
     In the Comeraghs.
Far different was Piaras FitzGerald,
Who fed his babes on Holy Writ.
He washed them, put them on the jerry,
     The best of da's.

Lightly, Red-head O'Sullivan
Who fought with Rodney, jolly jacktar
Too much at sea, thin as a marlin
     Spike, came and went,
Poet, schoolmaster, parish clerk.
He drank his Bible money at Mass-time,

A moll upon his knee, bare arsed.
    As impudent
As he, Magrath and O'Coileain,
    Both hated cant.
Each became to our annoyance
    A Protestant.
The priest denounced them from the altar.
They took their share of kisses, malt,
Religion with a peck of salt
    And were content.

At dawn, in a wood of sorrel, branchy
Dew-droppy, where sunlight gilded sapling
And silvered holly, or by the bank
    Of Brosna, Moy,
Our poets saw a woman smiling.
Her tresses, bright as celandine,
Could not conceal her pure white side,
    Was she from Troy?
Or was she Venus whose fondled breast
    Could never cloy?
Juno, half turning from her rest,
    To buss and toy?
That Queen of Carthage in hot haste –
Blue robe below her naked waist –
To make Aeneas in her embraces,
    Husband and roy?

She came at sunrise to our grass,
Irish or from a rocky land,
The gold-brown cliffs of Mount Parnassus,
    High-stepped by snow.
Cross-roads where Oedipus had killed
His father, hidden among the hills;
Honey and thyme; with tubas of silver,
    Processions go
Up winding paths to hollow Adelphi
    Where asphodels blow.
Rockage where the waters held
    In winter, throw

New light. Dark blue Aegean; pillars
In temples of Poseidon; downhill,
Circled with prayer, the pipes' shrill tune,
    That dolphins know.

Dreaming of Virgil and Blind Homer,
Schoolmasters cuffed behind a loaning
Or clamp, hearing the cowherds, dog-boys,
    Hurrying by.
Lurchers at heel, cold whistling fellows,
Giddy O'Hackett, Coxcomb O'Boland,
Buffoon O'Malachy, Pighead Moran
        Watched on the sly,
Irish and English words hobnobbing
        Where dealers buy,
In Castletown or striking the cobbles
        Of Athenry.
With sixpenny book in ragged pocket,
They climbed, bareheaded, to a Mass-rock,
Keeping poor soul within the body
        Cheating the sky.

Jacobus Egan of Killarney
And Peter Kenny, Kerryman
Who taught in cabin, leaky barn,
        From day to day,
Fitzgibbon, O'Connor, Gaelic scholars
Compiled their dictionaries, taught angles
The golden number, epact, scansion
        For little pay.
James Walshe and Peter Callaghan,
        After the hay
Was saved, told tales of the Fianna
        And drank stewed tay.
In Borris, Callan hedge-school
And Bantry, others showed the rule
Of three, the use of globes, spread news
        Upon its way.

Roll-call of nicknames: Christopher
MacHeavy Bum, O'Duffy the Tougher,
Belly McGuirk, Kelly the Buffer
        Lifting his can.
Wall-eyed O'Bryne, Belching O'Rourke,
Blear-eyed MacCullen, Game-leg O'Horan,
Farty MacGrane and the Tatter-coat
        O'Flanagan.
They taught geometry to laggards,
        Verses that scan,
Tagging good Latin in their rags,
        Knew priestly ban.
Talkative in his tavern at Croom
Among the poets, Sean O'Twoomey
Mocked each of them in the backroom
        With Merriman.

Men carried the first Earl of Lucan
Aboard a vessel, while his troopers
Staggered from missing step to poop-lamp,
        Most of them drunk.
Soldiers of fortune who fought in Flanders,
Austria and the Netherlands,
Deafened by Empires of cannonade.
        Hearing the honk
Of the wild geese, they drank at camp-fires,
        Snatching a chunk
Of bread or in a German tavern
        Joked with a punk.
They thinned the armies of Marlborough,
Earning good money with sword or musket,
Died, far from doorway of cathedral,
        Blessing of monk.

Archbishop Conry, learned prelate
And Jansenist, was spreading hell-fire
While Father Wadding plotted, when Charles fell,
        For years in Louvain.
There Brother Francis of Armagh
Was penning *De Prosodia*

Hibernica, short line and stanza,
　　Hard to explain.
MacAingil lanterned in a dark volume
　　The soul in pain:
All Belgium shone on Gothic column
　　Through leaded pane.
Monks laboured at printing press, selected
Type for a Gaelic or Latin text.
Our poets stumbled to the next
　　Mud cabin through rain.

We live again in a Penal Age
For teachers get unworthy wages
And clergy take their occupation,
　　Giving no lay
School benefit of weekly chaplain.
Pearse founded St Enda's, forbade
All punishment: pupils were happy
　　At task and play.
Our celibates raise cane and strap,
　　Smiling at May
Processions that hide their cruel slapping.
　　Children obey
In dread. Poor brats in smelly rags,
And boys, who wear a college cap,
Shuffle unwillingly to chapel,
　　Confess and pray.

South-westerly gales fiddled in rigging,
Furled canvases in foam-clap, twigged
The pulley-blocks. Billows were bigger,
　　The clouds fell out.
At Coomakista, grouse swam in grasses,
Hail hurled through Cumeen Duv. Phantoms
From Cahirciveen were in the passes.
　　Below a shout
Was whisper and behind a boulder,
　　A marabout
Could scarcely hide his bony shoulder.
　　Soon every snout

Was gone. A century of gods
And nymphs from Inch to Blacksod Bay:
Old knowledge scattered from the noddle
    In whirlabout.

The Thorn

In your decline, when truth is bare,
The thorn is seen without its crown.

The Jest

Half spirit, the older
I am, the bolder,
Yet add for a jest
That you may think,
Not beat your breast,
Invisible ink.

Every Fine Day

When I was taken out every fine day
Upon four wheels, we passed the Bluecoat School
Near Blackhall Place, stopped at St Mary's Abbey.
In winter time, my mother bought the best
Of Danish bacon, butter and eggs there; in summer,
The best of Irish bacon, butter and eggs.
But all was half abstract. Newness, I knew,
Crowed, cockhorsed, railed against life, was comforted
And wrapped again in nothingness. The Norman

Had clattered by. His plunder walled Grangegorman,
The grassy rides at Oxmantown. Orchards
Behind our house in Manor Street are built on,
Yet still I want for that Victorian fruit.

The Phoenix Park

So long ago
In a latrine,
Few hurriers know of,
Hid by a green
Tra-la in the Phoenix
Park, a wag,
With look of joy
On a notable deed
And final swish-up,
Remarked:
        'Last week,
Believe it, my boy,
Or not, I peed
With the Archbishop
Here,'
      How could I speak?
I turned away, meeking.
And yet that tag
Of getting even
Somehow in Heaven
Or upon *Der Tag*,
Though rather ribald,
May label the need
Of pride, when scribbled
For an old dog-lead,
Last travelling bag.

Fragaria

Nature
Remembering a young believer
And knowing his weakness
Could never stand
To reason,
Gave me from the lovely hand
Of my despairing mother,
A dish of strawberries,
To tempt
And humble the fast
That had laid me nearer than they were
Along her clay.

Jeanne d'Arc

Last night, souling the dark,
I dreamed once more of Jeanne d'Arc,
Burning to bowels. How soon
Did crackle of terror choke
Pommel, spur, demi–lune,
Throw off the goddam sticks?
Can the self, maddened or bold,
Outdo the bag of tricks?
Corpuscle is poltroon.
Always, poor ape, our coldness
That walks in heat without smoke.
Body is cunning. It sticks:
Unstupefied by Styx.

Following Darkness

Too old for spiritual sport,
Hospital sweepstake, charity pool,
Our daily whine of Mine is Thine,
With a few affairs to sort,
I emigrate to Liverpool
And possibly at a moment's notice
May have to hurry from our land
Before the aeroplane or boat is
Due, scarce a grip ready to hand.
Heavenly casket has been prised.
Sweet sense, so often, often, surprised
Be off, as clothes, you are too young still
And yet, and yet, I was so kissed,
Day, night had ached together. Glow turned
Around. The exquisite was stowed.
When words were changed, almost sung,
I saw Yeats shadowing from mist,
The Seven-Wooded, while A.E. on
His Sunday night ascended. Aeon
Was rolling from tobacco smoke.
Saved from our pit, awed by the play,
Not quite believing, I fell away.
And now, my thought half gone, I grope.
Blind beggarwoman, our fear unscaled,
May touch me; hem of chilling dress
Is more than eloquence. Failure
Will serve as dreams go Merseying
Again to a less expensive address
At Priory Road without bad hope,
Forgetting the cod-bewildered schoolboy,
Aunt, uncle, cousins, in Liverpool,
Fire, steel, slum, monarchy of smoke.

Rightful Rhymes

I
Irish–American Visitor

Up in the clouds, a blessed dot
Or down below counting each knot,
(Rome, Boston (Mass.) per kilowatt)
He labours, goes where time is not
Yet shared for a day our humble lot,
The half-door, hearth, three-legged pot –
And hearing chicks run, horses trot,
Put off the scarlet to come, forgot
The Capitol. A Marian grot,
A small green plot, now mark the spot
Where his poor father was begot.

II
Tale of a Tub

Dress with two studs
Or a back one: dirt
Of surplice, shirt,
Is brothered in suds.

III
The Plot

So, in accordance with the plot,
MacDonagh, Plunkett, Pearse, were shot.
Campbell dropped dead in a mountainy spot,
Stephens, lifting a chamber pot.
O Conaire went, a ragged sot.
Higgins was coffined in a clot.
Twice-warned, when must I join our lot?

Mnemosyne Lay in Dust

(1966)

Mnemosyne Lay in Dust

I

Past the house where he was got
In darkness, terrace, provision shop,
Wing-hidden convent opposite,
Past public-houses at lighting-up
Time, crowds outside them – Maurice Devane
Watched from the taxi window in vain
National stir and gaiety
Beyond himself: St Patrick's Day,
The spike-ends of the Blue Coat school,
Georgian houses, ribald gloom
Rag-shadowed by gaslight, quiet pavements
    Moon-waiting in Blackhall Place.

For six weeks Maurice had not slept,
Hours pillowed him from right to left side,
Unconsciousness became the pit
Of terror. Void would draw his spirit,
Unself him. Sometimes he fancied that music,
Soft lights in Surrey, Kent, could cure him,
Hypnotic touch, until, one evening,
The death-chill seemed to mount from feet
To shin, to thigh. Life burning in groin
And prostate ached for a distant joy.
But nerves need solitary confinement.
    Terror repeals the mind.

Cabs ranked at Kingsbridge Station, Guinness
Tugs moored at their wooden quay, glinting
Of Liffey mudbank; hidden vats
Brewing intoxication, potstill,
Laddering of distilleries
Ready to sell their jollities,
Delirium tremens. Dublin swayed,
Drenching, drowning the shamrock: unsaintly
Mirth. The high departments were filed,

Yard, store, unlit. Whiskey-all-round,
Beyond the wealth of that square mile,
    Was healthing every round.

The eighteenth century hospital
Established by the tears of Madam
Steevens, who gave birth, people said, to
A monster with a pig's snout, pot-head.
The Ford turned right, slowed down. Gates opened,
Closed with a clang; acetylene glow
Of headlights. How could Maurice Devane
Suspect from weeping-stone, porch, vane,
The classical rustle of the harpies,
Hopping in filth among the trees,
The Mansion of Forgetfulness
    Swift gave us for a jest?

II

Straight-jacketing sprang to every lock
And bolt, shadowy figures shocked,
Wall, ceiling; hat, coat, trousers flung
From him, vest, woollens, Maurice was plunged
Into a steaming bath; half suffocated,
He sank, his assailants gesticulating,
A Keystone reel gone crazier;
The terror-peeling celluloid,
Whirling the figures into vapour,
    Dissolved them. All was void.

Drugged in the dark, delirious,
In vision Maurice saw, heard, struggle
Of men and women, shouting, groans.
In an accident at Westland Row,
Two locomotives with mangle of wheel-spokes,
Colliding: up-scatter of smoke, steel,
Above: the gong of ambulances.
Below, the quietly boiling hiss
Of steam, the winter-sleet of glances,
    The quiet boiling of pistons.

The crowds were noisy. Sudden cries
Of 'Murder! Murder!' from a byway,
The shriek of women with upswollen
Bodies, held down in torment, rolling
And giving birth to foundlings, shriek
After shriek, the blanket lifting unspeakable
Protrusions. The crowds were stumbling backward,
Barefoot cry of 'Murder' scurried.
Police batoned eyesight into blackness.
      Bandages were blurred.

Maurice had wakened up. He saw a
Circular peep-hole rimmed with polished
Brass within the door. It gloomed.
A face was glaring into the bed-room
With bulging eyes and fierce moustache.
Quicker than thought, a torchlight flashed
From wall to pillow. Motionless,
It spied until the face had gone.
The sound of sleepers in unrest:
      Still watchful, the peep-hole shone.

What night was it, he heard the creaking
Of boots and tiptoed to the peep-hole?
Four men were carrying a coffin
Upon their shoulders. As they shuffled,
Far in his mind a hollaloo
Echoed: 'The Canon of Killaloe...'
Death-chill would mount from feet to limbs,
His loins, secretion no longer burn.
Those shoulderers would come for him with
      The shroud, spade, last thud.

Nightly he watched a masquerade
Go by his cell and was afraid
Of one – the stooping, bald-headed madman
Who muttered curse after curse, his hands
Busily knitting, twiddling white reeds:
So huge, he seemed to be the leader.
The others tormented by their folly,
The narrows of the moon, crowded

Together, gibboned his gestures, followed
    That madman knitting reed, brow.

Once, getting out of bed, he peeped
Into the dormitory. Sheet
And slip were laundry-white. Dazes
Of electric light came down. Patients
Stirred fitfully. Their fidgeting marred
With scrawls the whiteness of the ward,
Gift of the moon. He wondered who
He was, but memory had hidden
All. Someone sat beside him, drew
    Chair nearer, murmured: 'Think!'

One afternoon, he looked in dread
Into the ward outside. The beds
Were empty. Quiet sunshine glowed
On waxed floor and brass. He hurried
Across to the high window, stood
On the hot pipes to see the view.
Below there was a widespread garden,
With shrubberies, walks, summerhouses.
He stared in wonder from his bars,
    Saddened by the boughs.

III

Men were looking up
    At the sky
As if they had lost something,
    They could not find.

Gesticulating by summerhouse,
    Shrubbery, side-path,
They wandered slowly, pallid dots,
    Faces gone blind.

Looking down from the bars
    With mournful eye
Maurice could see them beckoning,
    Some pointed, signed.

Waving their arms and hands,
    They wandered. Why
Should they pretend they did not see him,
    Lost to mind?

They walked to and fro
    By shrubbery, side-path,
Gesticulating like foreigners
    Or loitering behind.

But all were looking up
    At the sky
As if they had lost something,
    They could not find.

IV

Tall, handsome, tweeded Dr Leeper
Inspecting the mindless at a glance
Quick-striding, always ready to leap,
A duffering Victorian;
The mad-eyed Dr Rutherford,
    Agreeable in word
And the Superintendent, Mr Rhys,
That burly Welshman ready to pounce
From everywhere with his band of seizers,
    Drag maniacs as they bounce.

One morning as he washed his face
And hands, he noticed that the basin
Was different: the soap-dish had
Been moved an inch. Was it a trap
To test his observation? Cuting,
He put it back for he was sure
It was a spy. Yes, his suspicions
Were right. But would he not forget
Next day where he had moved the soap-dish,
What other trap his foes would set?

Often he stared into the mirror
Beside the window, hand-drawn by fear.
He seemed to know that bearded face
In it, the young man, tired and pale,
Half smiling. Gold-capped tooth in front
Vaguely reminded him of someone.
Who was it? Nothing came to him.
He saw that smile again. Gold dot
Still gleamed. The bearded face was drawn
With sufferings he had forgotten.

Sunlight was time. All day in a dream
He heard the quiet voice of steam,
Drowsy machinery, hurried
A student again. Class-books were stirring,
His footstep echoed by Grangegorman
Beneath the granite wall, enormous
Gate. Was it the Richmond Asylum? He pondered
Beneath the wall, still heard the hissing
And lisp of steam in the laundry
There, memory afoot, he listened.

Out of the morning came the buzzing
Of forest bees. The tiger muzzle
Gnarled as myriads of them bumbled
Heavily towards the jungle honey.
A sound of oriental greeting;
Ramàyana, Bhagavad-gita,
Hymnal of Brahma, Shiva, Vishnu.
'The temple is gone. Where is the pather?'
A foolish voice in English said:
'He's praying to his little Father.'

Weakening, he lay flat. Appetite
Had gone. The beef or mutton, potatoes
And cabbage – he turned from the thick slices
Of meat, the greasy rings of gravy.
Knife had been blunted, fork was thick
And every plate was getting bigger.
His stomach closed: He eyed the food,

Disgusted: always beef or mutton,
Potatoes, cabbage, turnips. Mind spewed,
Only in dreams was gluttonous.

V

Maurice was in an Exhibition Hall
Where crowds of men and fashionable women
In bosoming dresses, embroidered shawl,
      Were moving. But a silent form
Was waiting in a corner. Up marble stairs,
He hurries from mirrored hall to hall, by glimmer
Of statues in niches. The Watcher stares,
      Red tabs upon his uniform.

Again he mounts the steps, alone,
Self-followed from mirrors to hall, the crowd
Of visitors waltzing below,
And looking from the bannisters
Upon the billiard tables, playerless,
Green-shaded, saw the Watcher with a frown
Behind a pillar, standing motionless
      Casting the shadow of a policeman.

Once, wandering from a hollow of asphodel,
Still flowering at mid-night, he saw the glint of
Gigantic row of columns beyond the dell,
      Templed, conical, unbedecked
And knew they were the holy ichthyphalli
Curled hair for bushwood, bark or skin
Heavily veined. He worshipped, a tiny satyr,
      Mere prick beneath those vast erections.

Joyously through a gateway, came a running
Of little Jewish boys, their faces pale
As ivory or jasmine, from Lebanon
      To Eden. Garlanded, caressing,
Little girls ran with skip and leap. They hurried,
Moon-pointing, beyond the gate. They passed a pale

Of sacred laurel, flowers of the future. Love
    Fathered him with their happiness.

Always in terror of Olympic doom,
He climbed, despite his will, the spiral steps
Outside a building to a cobwebbed top-room.
    There bric-à-brac was in a jumble,
His forehead was distending, ears were drumming
As in the gastric fever of his childhood.
Despite his will, he climbed the steps, stumbling
    Where Mnemosyne lay in dust.

Dreaming, as sunlight idled, Maurice believed
He darted by with sticks of gelignite,
Unbarracked County Limerick, relieved
    His fellows, fought to the last bullet.
Daring Republican of hillside farm-yards,
Leader of raiding parties, digging at night,
He blew up lorries, captured British arms.
    Rain-hid, he cycled to Belmullet.

Drowsily Maurice was aware
Of someone by his bed. A melancholy
Man, sallow, with black moustache, sat there.
    'Where am I?' Voice was hollow.
The other brooded: 'Think.' His gaze
Was so reproachful, what was his guilt?
Could it be parricide? The stranger
    Still murmured: 'Think… Think.'

VI

One night he heard heart-breaking sound.
It was a sigh unworlding its sorrow.
Another followed. Slowly he counted
Four different sighs, one after another.
'My mother,' he anguished, 'and my sisters
Have passed away. I am alone, now,
Lost in myself in a mysterious

Darkness, the victim in a story.'
Far whistle of a train, the voice of steam.
Evil was peering through the peep-hole.

Suddenly heart began to beat
Too quickly, too loudly. It clamoured
As if it were stopping. He left the heat
And stumbled forward, hammered
The door, called out that he was dying.
Key turned. Body was picked up, carried
Beyond the ward, the bedwhite row
Of faces, into a private darkness.
Lock turned. He cried out. All was still.
He stood, limbs shivering in the chill.

He tumbled into half the truth:
Burial alive. His breath was shouting:
'Let, let me out.' But words were puny.
Fists hushed on a wall of inward-outness.
Knees crept along a floor that stirred
As softly. All was the same chill.
He knew the wall was circular
And air was catchcry in the stillness
For reason had returned to tell him
That he was in a padded cell.

The key had turned again. Blankets
Were flung into blackness as if to mock
The cringer on the floor. He wrapped
The bedclothes around his limbs, shocked back
To sanity. Lo! in memory yet,
Margaret came in a frail night-dress,
Feet bare, her heavy plaits let down
Between her knees, his pale protectress.
Nightly restraint, unwanted semen
Had ended their romantic dream.

Early next morning, he awakened,
Saw only greyness shining down
From a skylight on the grey walls

Of leather, knew, in anguish, his bowels
Had opened. He turned, shivering, all shent.
Wrapping himself in the filthied blankets,
Fearful of dire punishment,
He waited there until a blankness
Enveloped him... When he raised his head up,
Noon-light was gentle in the bedroom.

VII

Beyond the rack of thought, he passed
From sleep to sleep. He was unbroken
Yet. Religion could not cast
Its multitudinous torn cloak
About him. Somewhere there was peace
That drew him towards the nothingness
Of all. He gave up, tried to cease
Himself, but delicately clinging
To this and that, life drew him back
To drip of water-torment, rack.

Weaker, he sank from sleep to sleep, inward,
Then Dr Leeper sprang at him. Four men
Covered him, bore him into the ward.
The Doctor bared his sleeve to the forearm.
What was he trying to do? Arms rounding,
Held down the hunger-striker, falling
To terror, a tube forced halfway down
His throat, his mind beyond recall.
Choking, he saw a sudden rill
Dazzling as baby-seed. It spilled

In air. Annoyed, the Doctor drew
Back, glucosed milk upon his shoulder
And overall. The rubber spewed
As Maurice feebled against his holders
The noise and fear of death, the throttling.
Soon he lost all consciousness
And lay there, all the struggle forgotten,

The torture chamber and the pressure.
He woke in bed. The counterpane
Gentle with noon and rid of pain.

Weaker, he crawled from sleep to sleep.
For Dr Leeper sprang, incensed,
At him with many hands, keeping
Him down, but it was someone else
The men were trying to suffocate.
He saw the patient on a bier,
Submissive to his fate,
Young Englishman, brown-bearded.
Engine uncoiled, the measure tilted.
Dazzlement of the sudden rills.

Midnight follies. Shriek after shriek
From the female ward. No terror
Of clanking chains, poor ghost in sheet,
Vampire of bloodless corpse, unearthed,
In Gothic tale but only blankness.
Storm flashed. Dr Rutherford spoke.
Maurice whispered from the blanket
The one word: 'Claustrophobia.'
That remnant of his memory
Carried him to the dormitory.

VIII

The heavens opened. With a scream
The blackman at his night-prayers
Had disappeared in blasphemy,
And iron beds were bared;
Day was unshuttered again,
The elements had lied,
Ashing the faces of madmen
Until God's likeness died.

Napoleon took his glittering vault
To be a looking-glass.

Lord Mitchell, pale and suffering,
Fell to the ground in halves.
The cells were filling. Christopher
O'Brien, strapped in pain,
For all the rage of syphilis,
Had millions in his brain.

James Dunn leaped down the dormitory,
Thought has no stopping-place,
His bright bed was a corner shop,
Opening, closing, late.
Behind a grille, the unfrocked priest
Had told his own confession:
Accidents in every street
Rang the Angelus.

Flight beyond flight, new stories flashed
Or darkened with affliction
Until the sweet choir of Mount Argus
Was heard at every window,
Was seen in every wing. The blackman
Kept laughing at his night-prayers
For somebody in white had taken
His photograph downstairs.

When sleep has shot the bolt and bar,
And reason fails at midnight,
Dreading that every thought at last
Must stand in our own light
Forever, sinning without end:
O pity in their pride
And agony of wrong, the men
In whom God's image died.

IX

Timor Mortis was beside him.
In the next bed lolled an old man
Called Mr Prunty, smallish, white-haired
Respectable. If any one went past,

He sat up, rigid, with pointed finger
And shrieked: 'Stop, Captain, don't pass
The dead body!' All day, eyes starting,
Spectral, he shrieked, his finger darting.

Poor Mr Prunty had one fault
In bed. Nightly he defecated.
Warder, great-handed, unbolted his vault,
Swept sheet and blanket off in a rage
At 'Murder! Murder!' dragged the body
Naked along the corridor.
Trembling beneath the piled-up bedclothes,
Maurice could hear bath-water pouring.

Far doors were opening, closing
Again. The corpse was clumping back.
The warder stuck it on the close-stool,
Laid out clean pair of sheets and blanket.
Soon Maurice waited for his turn,
Whenever he wet the bed; sodden
Sheets pulled off. The warder called him 'Dogsbody',
Christened his ankles with the key-bunch.

On winter evenings, Dublin guff,
Warm glow, world-shadows as the warders
Chatted together; rustle of *Late Buff*
Or *Final Herald* by the fire-guard.
The Liberties were rainy, sleeting.
Stop-press, exciting story, 'Hawker's
Flown the Atlantic.' Shouting hawkers,
Stall-owners, bargains, in Thomas Street.

Maurice lay listening to their talk of sport.
One night they climbed to the Robbers' Cave
Beyond Kilmainham, above the coach-road.
Often he heard them repeating a tale
Of the Gate, the Garden and the Fountain:
Three words that lulled him as he fell
Asleep: Mesopotamian sound
Of a claustral stream that stelled him.

The words became mysterious
With balsam, fragrance, banyan trees,
Forgetting the ancient law of tears,
He dreamed in the desert, a league from Eden.
How could he pass the Gate, the sworded
Seraphim, find the primal Garden,
The Fountain? He had but three words
And all the summer maze was guarded.

All through the night the warder sat,
Chair tilted back, beside the fire;
Reason, the master of ancient madness.
He read a novel by shaded light.
Wakefully, Maurice watched his shoulder
Wrapped in a travelling rug, eye busy,
His great arm raised to unscuttle coal:
Cowl-like, monk of the Inquisition.

Tall, handsome, tweeded Dr Leeper,
Inspecting the mindless at a glance,
Quick-strider, always ready to leap,
The mad-eyed Dr Rutherford,
    Agreeable in word,
And the Superintendent, Mr Rhys,
A burly Welshman, ready to pounce
From everywhere with his band of seizers,
    Drag maniacs that bounce.

X

In winter around the fire,
Soldiers at a camp
After the long rout.
Brass helmet tipped with coal
By the fender and fire-guard.
A history-book lying on the floor.

In the dark, secured,
They lie. Every night
The news is going into the past:
The airman lost in Mozambique,
Far shouting at the General Election
And the Great War ending
In drums, processions
And a hooded Preacher
At the Pro-Cathedral.

They lie, in the dark,
Watching the fire, on the edge
Of a storybook jungle: they watch
The high boots of the colonists.

The scales are broken.
Justice cannot reach them:
All the uproar of the senses,
All the torment of conscience,
All that twists and breaks.
Without memory or insight,
The soul is out of sight
And all things out of sight
And being half gone they are happy.

They lie in bed, listening
To the sleet against the bars, train
That whistles from the country. A horse-car
Waits under the oil-lamp at the station
And turns into a drosky.

On a sun-free day, his senses lied, for
They showed him a man that had been killed.
His severed head lay on the pillow
Beside him, grey-bearded, with lidded eyes.
No axe… no blood. How did it happen?
He looked again. Slim palms had placed it
Nearer the window: hallucinatory
Head of an aged John the Baptist.

Soon Mnemosyne made him smaller,
A child of seven, half gone to sleep.
His mother was at her sewing machine,
The shuttle clicking as she followed
A hem. Outside, the praying garden,
Late blossom of the elder-trees:
Twilight was hiding from his elders,
The toolshed, barrel, secret den.

Suddenly over the lower wall,
Madmen were leaping into the yard
With howls of 'Murder!' scarcely a yard
From him. He jumped out of the darkfall,
Awake, chill, trembling at the din.
There on his bed, a terrible Twangman
Was sitting. He muttered 'Hang him! Hang him!'
As he nodded, twiddling paper spills.

Maurice would stray through the back streets
By shuttered windows, shadowy Railway
Station, by gas-lamps, iron railings,
Down Constitution Hill. Discreetly
Concealed in every cornerstone
Under the arches, Echo resided,
Ready to answer him. Side by side,
Stepping together, the pair roamed.

Often in priestly robe on a
Night of full moon, out of the waste,
A solitary figure, self-wasted,
Stole from the encampments – Onan,
Consoler of the young, the timid,
The captive. Administering, he passed down,
The ward. Balsam was in his hand.
The self-sufficer, the anonym.

XI

Maurice lay quiet. A summer month
Was at the window. He eyed the plateful
Of tea-time cakes that Mr Prunty
Was gobbling up, saw in dismay
Pinking icing disappear in grunts,
    Hearing below,
Far-away voices of the May
    Leaf – thin and low.

In June, upon the little table
Between the beds, he saw a dish
Of strawberries. As they lay
There, so ripe, ruddy, delicious,
For an hour he played with his delay
    Then in delight
Put out two fingers towards the wished-for,
    Ate for the first time.

XII

Nature
Remembering a young believer
And knowing his weakness
Could never stand to reason
Gave him from the lovely hand
Of his despairing mother,
A dish of strawberries
To tempt
And humble the fast
That had laid him nearer than they were
Along her clay.

XIII

Summer was shining through the bars.
He lay there hourly, puzzled by voices

Below in the forbidden Garden
Beyond the Gate, from his own void.
But all the summer maze was guarded.
  He dreamed of the Fountain
Glistening to the breeze, self-poised,
  Lulled by the sound.

Often he touched the hardened cage
Around him with its band of steel-hoops.
His ribs were bulging out. He weighed
No more than seven stone. Unwieldy,
He wondered why he had been straight-laced
  Straight-jacketed.
But soon his suture would unseam,
  His soul be rapt.

XIV

Maurice went with the crowd of patients
Slowly down the winding stone-steps
Within a fortress where the daylight,
Arquebus'd in cobwebby corners, slept,
Down step by step until he came
  To a concrete yard.
He hurried forward, was kept back.
  The way was barred.

Thickly clad like an imbecile,
No buttons to open in front – safe wear –
He met in the like dungarees,
A grandson of the astronomer,
John Ball, with flippers to his knees,
  A haberdasher's
Dwarf, mumbling Joseph Dunn, the three
  Of them, churn-dashers.

Quicker and quicker as they walked
Together, arm in arm, John Ball
Panting hard with squeak or squawk

Or letting out a mighty bawl
When Maurice pinched him slyly, three gawking
    Round and round,
Bouncing to an invisible ball
    Over the ground.

Round and round for exercise,
The trio pranced upon the concrete,
Each of them a different size,
Madder than athletes trained in Crete
Maurice forgot his ancient sighs,
    Round and around
Escaping out of the Asylum,
    With leap and bound.

They squawked and muttered. Maurice laughed
To find he was an imbecile,
The quickest of them and the daftest.
Faster and faster the trio reeled
    In-loony-go-round
John Ball snatched dirt and tried to eat it,
    Stamping the ground.

XV

Among the imbeciles was Mister Radcliffe
Mahogany skulled, molarless, with two paws,
Spoonfed on pap. When he was teased or slapped,
He howled: 'Holy St Francis, stawp it, stawp it.'
And Mr Thornton, light-footed as the waves.
'Cresh o' the waves,' he sings, 'cresh o' the waves.'

That dangerous lunatic called Bobby Walpole,
Machine in need of constant supervision.
Nightly he knocked his head against the wall,
'The same little man,' he cried, 'It's a der...is...ion.'
Often he darted past, pulled out his yard,
Pissed through the fire-guard, yelled from the yard.

Below, Tom Dunphy, tall, milk-blue-eyed, black
Moustache and sweet expression. He would rage,
Calling down curses on the hellish pack
Who wronged him once. Remembering that outrage,
He stood and trembled – he could scarcely breathe –
A farmstead shook with him in County Meath.

Mr Crosthwaite had fought in the Boer War:
They said it for a jest. His tongue sprang up
To lick the dribble from his nose. 'How are
You, Mr Crosthwaite?' 'Very well, I thank you.'
But Maurice had other friends to nod to, talk to.
Down Grafton Street, they gossiped as they walked.

Sandow A. Jackson, powerful fellow, half-caste
With rolling eyes, whose tigering was heard
In jungle storm, but often he was downcast.
Lord Mitchell, handsome, haughty, auburn-haired,
'Curs, villains, scoundrels, ruffians, I know your bluff.'
He leaped in rage. 'Curs, villains, scoundrels, ruffians.'

One day when all were splashing in the wash-room,
Taps loud and soap-suds gleamy, he drew back
His foreskin, pulled out something pink and posh
And dipped it in the flowing basin. 'Look at
The dirty fellow washing his cock!' a new warder
Said. Maurice sniggered at his purity.

Mr McLoughlin, northerner, with a red beard,
Tall, homicidal but a good companion.
Maurice was always friendly, though he feared
Him. Daily they talked in French for practice.
One day he blew his noddle off. Maurice yelled.
Four warders bore the madman to his cell.

The King, white-haired, apopleptic, paunched
Old gentleman, was often in a passion.
He jumped and stamped upon the floor, haunching
His frockcoat tails up, claimed he was the bastard
Of George the Third. The King sat in the parlour
As if it were the House of Parliament.

Then Master Hayes, the Fat Boy on a school-bench,
A Doctor's son in snakes-and-ladders suit,
Writhing, tortured with pain that hid his moon-cheek.
Farrell, the undertaker, ghostly suitor,
Gliding to death in patent leather slippers.
His coffin was already on the slip.

Christopher O'Brien, white-haired, portly,
Megalomaniac, a buyer from Clery's.
He wept at night, knew the enduring cold:
And Mr Smythe who read the *Times*, a queer
Parcel tucked under his arm; that London journal
Had scraps and pieces for his hungry cats.

Mr Kinehan, a wealthy distiller,
Smiling: 'The Osbornes... those ridiculous people.'
He cluttered up his collar with little bits
Of wire, conducted lightning from his steeple:
'Crude paraffin is excellent for hair,
But much too strong for the drawing-room. O not there!'

Mr Cooper, huge, bald-headed madman,
Building contractor, busily twisting pipe-spills,
Who raged around himself until he was padded.
Maurice once saw him chalking on the billiard
Table: 'Oul shitin' Jases.' Guilty, he ran,
Last of the stercorarians.

Skipping along came youthful Sainsbury
In pea-green jacket, trousers, cardigan.
His cheeks were tinted as the wild rose-berry.
He cracked his fingers, called out 'Caesar... Caesar.'
The Captain strode in military coat
With pointed beard, Elizabethan cut-throat.

But best was nonchalant Ben Kane
Eager, active, reading the daily newspaper,
Helping the warders, carrying a rattan cane
Or tennis racquet every day.
Maurice had thought he was a medical student,
So nonchalantly, so happily, he went.

Ben told him of his one romance, a smiling
Girl, peeping from the lavatory pane
At eleven o'clock. They beckoned, made little signs,
One to the other, as they pulled the chain.
But she was sent to the Asylum at Ennis
Or Ballinasloe. Ben laughed, sighed, played lawn tennis.

XVI

Mr Cooper lifted his mortar hod.
A tree dropped Dr Rutherford, he
Stopped Maurice with a passing word,
Whispered him: 'Do you believe in God?'
He answered 'Yes.' The little Hindu
Hissed like a cobra. Mr Spender
Blasphemed and broke his only suspender,
Dancing with Gupta in his skin.

Maurice was drowsing. Telephone rang.
He heard a voice... long distance call...
Buzzing of words beyond recall.
'Mr Devane, Mr Devane,' it sang.
He turned around, held the receiver.
The voice was indistinct. It faded
Out. Negroes chattered in tropic shade.
Was it a trick of the Deceiver?

His Uncle George with twirl of bowler,
Gold chain and fob, was in the common
Room. Maurice thought his accent common
But tried to smile. Was he a bowler?
Then Dr Rutherford, the mad-eyed,
Questioned him. 'Is he well-to-do?'
As Maurice hesitated, the Hindu
Monocled him. Quickly, he lied.

One afternoon he opened the bookcase
Found *The Black Monk and Other Stories*
By Anton Chekov. Nothing could hold his

Attention. The words had changed to pothooks,
Hangers. Words hid their meaning from him.
They turned to Russian again. His steps
Faltered. Lear roamed across the Steppes.
The jester disappeared in dimness.

XVII

Summer was sauntering by,
Beyond the city spires,
As Maurice went a-walking
With Mr Rhys by white-and-
Blue trams and jaunting cars,
Into a Picture Postcard
Of the Phoenix Park,
Along the People's Garden,
The railed-in chestnut trees,
Borders of marigold,
Clarkia and rose-beds,
Sunflower, blow-as-you-please.
The Wellington Monument;
Iron reliefs, old gunnage –
He wondered what they meant –
The Fifteen Acres, the Dog Pond.
But there was nothing beyond,
Only the Other Side.
His family lived there.
Thinking of them, he sighed.
As they turned back, he stared
Into the camera
Of mind, the double lens
Was darker. *Mensa*
Mensae. The passers-by
Kept off forbidden grass,
Stopped at the gay kiosk
For real Picture Postcards.
Slowly he counted the lamp-posts
And all the city spires,
Counted the blue-and-white

Trams and the outside cars.
He saw Columba O'Carroll
Who smiled as he raised his hat
Behind invisible bars,
Soon recognised the barracks,
The plane-trees, cannon balls,
Remembered aniseed balls
And Peggy's Leg, luck-bag.
A small boy must not lag.
They crossed over Kingsbridge.
The Guinness tugs were roped
Along the quay, cabs ranked
Outside the Railway Station:
Couplings of carriages.
A gig went spanking by.
He heard an engine whistle,
Piffle away in the distance.
Poetic Personification:
Hope frowned. Up Steeven's Lane,
He walked into his darkness.
Classical rustle of Harpies,
Their ordure at Swift's Gate.

XVIII

Rememorised, Maurice Devane
Went out, his future in every vein,
The Gate had opened. Down Steeven's Lane
The high wall of the Garden, to right
Of him, the Fountain with a horse-trough,
Illusions had become a story.
There was the departmental storey
Of Guinness's, God-given right
Of goodness in every barrel, tun,
They averaged. Upon that site
Of shares and dividends in sight
Of Watling Street and the Cornmarket,
At Number One in Thomas Street
Shone in the days of the ballad-sheet,
The house in which his mother was born.

Old-Fashioned Pilgrimage
and Other Poems

(1967)

Old-Fashioned Pilgrimage

I

The New World was before us. Quick-eyed, as invisible
Search-lighting, black triangles came, three of them, darting
Around the *Sylvania*, the inky nibs of war,
Then disappeared into their own dangerous blue-prints:
'The finest navy in the world,' a tall American
Remarked, as he leaned on the taffrail. To the larboard,
The promenades were glassing, level above level,
And passengers gathered to greet the Statue of Liberty,
So prim, Victorian on her plinth, spike-headed as the future.
Then, out of the blurs of the Gulf Stream, to measurements
Of sun, white rhomboids, of a sudden, the cubical
City, New York, dollared the sky.
                                            No muscular tug-boat
Hoarsened: stateliness gliding surely. Dock by dock
Were liner'd. The rope was cast. The gangways rattled down
Above the motionless funnel the air was in a sizzle.
Soon in the spacious waiting-hall, baggaged, dumping,
Chalked, Padraic Colum saluted, welcomed two voyagers.
Our words clasped hands.
                                    The night illuminated Broadway
With fire-red fluor, square, zig-zag: advertisements scaled
Up, down, their letters. Pale-green and ivory, the lights
On Hudson Bridge were prinked. Below, the traffic speeded:
White, ruby, lavish pinchbeck of commerce, noisy pleasure.
The narrow streets were brilliant: perpendicular
Buildings above them, shadowy, locked. Along the Elevated
Railway, rumble of vanished trains: the cops and crooks
Leaped on to the tracks, aimed at the past and sent my boyhead
To the Rotunda, the Volta in Dublin, bespectacled
James Joyce, half peering from the pay-desk into
The web of Penelope. Soon, carcanated,
We metre'd along Eighth Avenue to Central Park.
Death-shriek of police-car wakened me up at two o'clock
That morning. Cautious as pigeon or criminal, from the fourteenth
Storey, I watched the silent bulleting below, the police-car

Still shrieking in the vacant light. Wealth – as
In ancient Rome – at war, nightly, with black, poor white.

II

Big city where the advertising sky is hot and hurried,
No street-bench for the back or public lavatories.
Black drivers of street-cars pulling their lever awkwardly
At red-eyed traffic stare, counting out cents; the dirty
Subway, the turn-stile, down steps to the empty platform
The dumbling trains, conductorless, no human form,
The stations flippering by us – Fiftieth, Eighty-Fourth
Street – One Hundred and Third Street – Madison Avenue,
Newspaper stalls, candy machines, everything new,
Upstairs again to the sudden nonce and noon of Fordham,
The crowded Broadway, Cadillacs and brisking Ford vans.
Here, there, we strayed, asking wearily for the small white cottage
Of Edgar Allan Poe from mothers in gay short cottons,
Men out for lunch. A policeman knew the locality:
'You mean Poe Park. Turn left. You'll see it there before you.'
We came to the Poe Tavern, Poe Café, Poe Launderette,
Poe Park, the bandstand, benches – neatly inset
Against the bushes, park trees, I saw, still legendary,
Small, white, one-storied, the cottage of eighteen-thirty-seven.
There was the old engraving that I recollected
So well, the frontispiece to the *Collected Works*
Of Edgar Allan Poe. In that old-fashioned volume
Remained the pale consumptive girls whose glance illumed
The midnight, fearful of the vault, damp, cerements,
The house of Ussher, mouldering, the woodland scent
Of leaf-decay, poor wet-their-drawers, not one robust:
The poet was frenzied by them in his thoughts, the bust
Of Pallas in the shadow: Ligia, Eleonore,
Morella, Berenice, phantoming his stories,
The stir of Gothic tapestries, the Saracenic
Lampion, cold glow of antique jewel, the scenic
Background always the same. What tropical terror had Poe
Sucked from the milk of his black nurse, what poems
Of African forest, slave-ship, devil-masking rites

From the Dark Continent had buried all his writings
Under imagination?
                    I dreamed in Baltimore:
My sixty-five years went by, whispering *Nevermore*.
I heard a rustle in the dark, a hand on comb,
Was I the last young poet to lie within a woman's
Black hair, so monstrous it seemed to drag backward
Her naked body, hiding the white of knee-caps, vulvine
Dwale betwixt as I fingered the downfall of a vine
That trellised the casement of the castle-room where Ligia
Was lying? Cornelia, in the candlelight, uneasy
With love, thin pallor and gloom under her nightgown, half seen.
How often I breathed within that heaviness in candle-lit-flat,
Tempted into her opening mouth as she lay flat
Beneath me, refusing to give all, fearing the pain,
Long hours withholding her womb until the window-pane
Unlidded us; dairy cart rattled down Pembroke Street.
Half crazy with that nightly taste of her, unbroken
Fast, quickly I echoed the emptiness outside;
Or stopped by the kerb, front brake of my cycle, frictioned, on fire,
Hearing from a midnight street the crackle of British bullets,
Stared at the blind where her half virtue satisfied
Itself in sleep. I gathered again in romantic desire,
A rustle in the dark, that heaviness, pell-mell,
Around my face and arms; her boy-like breast and pelvis:
O could the Church have allowed us pessary, thin cover,
I would not so abuse what others coveted.

Custodian was at lunch. We legged over a wire-post.
The door of parlour was open, coloured postcards
On show. We hesistated in that meagre boxroom,
Where his young wife had lain, hearing a far rumour,
Hugging the warmth of her Persian cat until she coughed
Her life away, a room scarce bigger than a coffin,
Dark, windowless. Drink, poverty, demon'd his pen.
Outside in Poe Park, beneath the sun-trees, old people bent.

III

Driving along the speedway, parklike with new green trees,
For miles, we talked with Vivian Mercier, came at last
To country shout of advertisements, the Whitman Tavern,
The Whitman Café, Whitman Launderette, turned to the left,
Into a tree-topped lane. There in an open field, the farmhouse
Where the poet had been born: the English, red-hooded
Well. Beside the door, good thought had planted a lilac:
But we saw no elegiac bloom upon it.
                                        Within,
The kitchen, bare scrubbed table, dishes, churn-dash, copper
Vessels, the faggot pile on the wide hearth: Dutch neatness
Ready with sweeping-brush, the cooking pans a-shine
From floor to low ceiling; upstairs, the Bible in bedrooms.
Quietly picking a postcard, I heard his free-verse come,
In a rhythmic run of syllables that spread around me, loud
And soft, until I recalled the Springtime combers rolling
Along the leagues of wild shore, spray-light of Paumonok,
The Fifth Month grass, the briars and, somewhere beyond the sandhills,
The bird from Alabama sang again. I was a
Boy turning that once forbidden book, *The Leaves
Of Grass*, word-showered, until my body was naked and self-proud
As I looked it boldly up and down, vein-ready, well-stocked;
Joy rising. Ever the trust of loving comradeship,
Europe, America, Asia, Africa, together.
I opened my collar, ruffled my hair and my body ran
By the leagues of wild shore, spray-lift of Paumonok.

IV

Clothed in noonlight we crossed at last the Delaware
Into that other age of cuspidors, aware
Of higher industry, factories, warehouses,
Steel-rolling mills near the bridge. Could I foretell
That sign of his neglected fame, the Whitman Hotel,
Old-fashioned, ample, against the Pennsylvanian sunlight,
World prophecies that the Civil War had shot asunder,
The punching, pounding din of engine shaft, belt, cam?

We went through streets ray-ways of a slum in Camden
Town, frame-houses, stores, heaping of metal scrap and tyre,
Wandering, confused, until my back begin to tire,
Then suddenly, my hand was steadied by the Muse
And across the grime of a by-street we glimpsed the small Museum.
Two-storied frame-house, sky-stained, but very comfortable
Within. I saw his leather-worn armchair, and his round table,
His grey sombrero hat, stout walking-stick, upstairs,
The bed and hipbath. We added to the dusty stares
Our mote and beam. In reverence, I touched the bedpost,
Then lingered awhile among the picture postcards
And dallied with the janitress, a black girl, tall and handsome;
We talked of Whitman, Wordsworth, while in secret my hand
Pilgrimed among his manuscripts. Too soon we left
The house, clothed again with afternoon, turned left,
Still thinking of his scant possessions, his rocking-chair,
Found in the cemetery a massive vault under a rock,
His name above the gate. I grasped the chilly railing
And stared into that hollowness. Why should I rail
Against him – a shaggy, bearded Victorian
Sharing the optimism of statesmen, historians?
He paid for the bluff chiselling: Walt Whitman
Awaiting the resurrection. Why should you care a whit, man?

V

I heard far soldiers, tramping behind horse-batteries,
Whistling cheerily at daybreak the tune of *Maryland,*
My Maryland. What local scribbler had borrowed that refrain from
One of the Oriental poems of Clarence Mangan?
Pot-happy in a noisy Dublin tap-room, he heard the words
Come singing: *Karaman, O Karaman.* In a mild land,
Of green glades, staying with Sylvia and Bernard Haviland,
I sauntered at early morning under the tall trees
Of a roadside wood, so cool it seemed to be a reflection
In shadowy skies, leaf-waters. Echoes were hidden in it,
Red Indians, as silent as their camp-smoke or Quakers
In the new settlements. At night, I pushed aside
The tropical noise-curtain of the katydids,

Blinked into light. In that mild greenness of a shire we saw
The eighteenth-century meeting-houses, simple
As prayer. We knelt on a Sunday morn waiting for the
Spirit to come to us from Antioch.
                                        A motoring map
Showed Baltimore: I heard the shouts of the elections –
Men crowded in gas-lit taverns – and thought of Edgar Allen
Poe reeling from horrors of his imagination, falling
From gutters into delirium. At noon, we drove
For a hundred miles along a great speedway, past the
Cashing of supermarkets, cafés, restaurants,
Motels, garages and small factories. Here, there,
On gateway, notice-board, roll-call of Irish names,
O'Sullivan, MacNamara, Cassidy, Malone,
Molloy, Lavelle, O'Herlihy, O'Driscoll, Carroll,
Our emigrants, uncoffined on a huge shore, their ragged
Holes, empty pockets, the size of dollars. A hundred miles
To Washington. We drove, of a sudden, into the future;
A poster with large letters: NO PEDESTRIANS.
There in the capital, shone white the Government
Palaces, Equestrian statues of Generals
Reared in avenues and parks. Trim, Georgian,
The White House: President Kennedy, head-struck already,
Worked, state-surrounded, among his secretaries and typists.
Goose Creek which Thomas Moore had satirised was now become
The Tiber: woods and lumber camps, long since were changed
To marble. Back, for a hundred miles, to Maryland,
By cashing of supermarkets, cafés, restaurants,
Motels, garages and small factories, by dazzle-dip
Of head lights. In bungalow, expensive mansion,
The Irish names slept. Beyond the corncobbed fields, the ridges
Of the Welsh Hills, we turned into a side-road, moon-stemmed
By woods, then stopped. Wearily, with bare arms, I pulled
Aside the tropical noise-curtain of the katydids.

VI

Charles Dickens bustled with baggage, travelling rugs, shawl
From the old railway station at Boston, lecture-touring

In the late eighteen-thirties, brandying himself from the wing,
Pickwicking, Little Nelling, Oliver Twisting, his wonderful
Pages in overheated halls, in theatres.
We stayed in Cambridge with Mary Howe and her husband.
    Around
The corner, I found, to my surprise, the stately home
Of Longfellow, the drawing-room, all mahogany and silver,
The library, still shelved with books, and passed nearby,
Pleasant among the flowering shrubs, the house of Lowell.
How could I tell without being told, that underneath
The rosebuds in the city park the automobiles
Of businessmen were garaged, bumpered, ready to
Emerge at evening time, the scrabble of a thousand
Grubs, wing-growing, day-blind, through the narrow streets and squares?
I crossed a Harvard Lawn, red squirrel before me, entered
The Poetry Room. Somewhere among the file there of records
My voice was waiting for a much-confused young man.
One day, I drove with Horace Gregory by the red flowers
Of Lexington up, down, the shaded inclines
To Concord, quiet as an English Thorpe, and saw
The large white house of Emerson, as if rebuilt, for
In that eternal present all was the same, the study
He thought in, the furniture, bookcases, sofa.
Opposite among the trees, I glimpsed the lofty manse
Where Hawthorne had lived: at Walden Pond, I looked over
The water towards the Indian woods, dark now unpathed: somewhere
Among them, the threshold of Thoreau's hut was found, sunken
In clay. Gladly into the Oversoul – all light
And glory – that Emerson wrote of – I groped when I was young
Out of the medieval Undersoul, the gloom of our
Religion. That transcendental vision had inspired
A.E. and Yeats: suddenly Walden Pond was hidden
By drizzle: the sedges were murmuring around the lake-isle
Of Inishfree. On a Winter day, deep silenced by the snow,
The poet, F.R. Higgins, had stood here, a pilgrim
As I was. Yeats sent him to drum-stick the Abbey Players
Farcing from State to State. Too bulky for berth, love-songs,
Higgins came back to death in Dublin, carrying stage
And drop-scene as a saint his church. We passed the battlefield
Again, the city park where roses have their roots in cars.

Napalm

Cloud-coming-down, American air-pilots
Tumble to risks. Trickle and rill
Are rivered again as, flying low,
Foresting propaganda, they pile
Revolt where ground-leaves are guerrillas,
Branding the water-buffalo,
Unjungling tiger and elephant
With toss of napalm bombs that peel off
The shrieking skin of mother, infant,
While Bishop of Koutum appeals
For funds, though conscripts pray that soon
The big dropper, the dark one, the monsoon,
Will tent them. United Nations are mum
And Johnson lariats with the dollar.
Our clergy, faceless as mummers
Of darkness, have dressed up a rag doll
That must be nourished on paper money,
On public smother of their late victims,
Saffron to soot of Buddhist monks
Still petrol-stained. See the brown face,
Those slanting lids, the thin eye-brows:
Ambiguous Madonna of Victories.

Robert Frost

After the Honorary Degree,
He sat there in his borrowed robes.
I thought of him farming in Vermont,
Composing that plain, wiseacre verse
Of his: all summer, one degree,
Between the lines, of hidden frost –
When, lo! a whirlwind snatched the sofa
From under us and Robert Frost
Was flung upon the ground, a Job

Of eighty-two, suddenly stricken
By family woes, the heavy stick
Above, shaking his body. He spoke
Of debts, ingratitude. Embarrassed,
I bowed with him. Was I the last
Poor comforter to listen? Must
We rend together the unholy mantle
Of poetry; half naked, scant,
Yet full of days, encounter dust?

Ezra Pound

I

Too often I pooh-poohed his poems
Surveying the inkiness of the globe,
Missouri, London, Paris, Po.
Why should my pen, I thought, dip pity
In praise for another American poking
At European curios
In the backroom of our Serendipity
Shop, gawky stranger from Idaho,
Rough rider with Stetson, jaunty pose,
Browning in holster, nudging the elbow
Of Yeats and T.S. Eliot:
Then, slipshod, pushing a Chinese cart
Loot-laden with Oriental art;
Discovering in Provence that Ver
Had shown her greenness to young trouvère
And troubadour? Each poly-canto
Lengthened for ragers who can't toe
The literary line. Impatient
Reformer – public account marked paid –
Behind barbed wire and in asylum,
Still he wrote on, louder in silence,
For how can frankness show the traits
Imperialists denounce in traitors?

Debunker of Swiss bank, usurers,
He counselled poets: 'Use your errors
Wisely, forget the democratic
Let down, the academic tie.'
Saftey of the world go bare,
While Spender wrestles with his fire-hose,
In vain, Auden becomes a choir-boy.

II

Rhyme, echo the name of Ezra Pound
Whom the war capitalists impounded.
For miserable years he pounded
The wall of modern verse, expounded
The madness of dollar, franc and pound.
Forget the theories he propounded,
But praise the language he compounded.
The centuries are in that pound.

Fiesta in Spain

Gaity of religion chased us
Away from Andalusia,
Shrines in a cathedral, enchased
Screenwork of silver, gold,
Passed by. We could not linger in cities
Of Spain, more than a day or lose
Ourselves, in, out, of plaza, sit
    In cafés. We had to go.

No room in lodging or hotel
From Algeciras to Madrid.
So we must drink up our Martel,
Tip, hurry from the Fiesta.
The flags were out, the sun in Cancer
The population glad to be rid

Of tourists, French, American,
        However profitable.

We flowered again in the Alhambra,
Fountained in court garden, arabesqued,
As we were eating sausage, ham-roll,
        Mile-speeding in a train
Far from Granada, to spend a day in
Lofty Madrid, seeing the best at
Museum, Art Gallery, sun-dazed:
        Faith still upon our trail.

Crowds at a pedestrian crossing,
Watched figures in white or black, peaked hoods,
Sufferers bearing wooden crosses,
        Jewelled shrines of the Madonna:
Torchlight of shadowy Inquisitors
Whom time has turned to peekaboo,
No longer burning the inquisitive
        In batches at Madrid.

A day and night at Cordoba:
Tooled volumes, handbags, leather cases
In the small shops of the cordwainers,
        Then westward to Seville:
Cathedral, art galleries, museums,
Shutters of sixteenth-century casements:
Guitar unstrung: Religion amused
        To see us hurry past villas.

Each day we saw the windowing plain,
A greenness lined with red-brown tilth,
Suddenly in his dust-cloud, plain
        To be seen, Don Quixote
With Sancho Panza, ever riding
By windmill, cornfield, lance a-tilt:
Cervantes with merry scratch deriding
        Romances that had quickened.

Bosoms of ladies whose Launcelot
Tumbled knights headlong out of casque:
A tournament of broken lances.
      Jerez de la Frontera:
We saw in ancient store and cellar
Wine-stain of might, tonneau, cask,
Gonzalez, Pedro Domecq, selected
      The choicest in bodega.

We noticed only one man salute
A priest or chapel: hatred, mirth,
Of religion too certain for salvation.
      Beggars thrust out their corns.
Blindmen were calling out Lottery draw;
Liberty gaoled. American
Revolver at belt, monied to draw,
      Police stood at every corner.

Palaced at night, the Dictator
Smiles in his sleep. Semblances
Of stooping angels ridicule
      That face on a holy pillow.
Grey uniform of frankincense
Is dimmer. Vatican Council assembles
A second time. General Franco
      At last must swallow the pill.

Remembering churches with bedizened
Madonnas dressed in stately velvet,
We dined one evening at Cadiz
      On soup, fish, fricassé,
Then, thinking Spain was too peculiar,
We fled into velocity
Beyond the pillars of Hercules,
      Rested in Africa.

García Lorca

García Lorca pursuing in ballad
Capricorn lads of Gypsy lore on
Plains of Andalusia
Till all was lucid, image-plain:

Unseen upon the granite peaks
Above Granada, the Sierra
Nevada hid from him blood-feud,
Shapes of the future. Poetry never

The like. Tales of the Civil Guards,
Mouth-rose and garter, love most likely,
Leg whiter in dance, cave-hid flamenco,
Flaring of men and Papal Legate.

Cruelty of medieval
Spain, heavy valance hemmed with cruor,
Incense, church martyrs and Moriscoes,
His words could risk the scream of sense.

He knew the purlieu of skyscrapers,
Lyrical skryer in New York,
Negro, poor white, the tall apartments.
Brazil and Paris made him groan.

Bull let out in the arena
Would gore his renes, that day the bullet
Spattered his songs so near to home,
Called homosexual, spat on.

Pablo Neruda

So many bald-headed,
Fat little men
Were at the Congress
Of International PEN
That I was wrong
Nine times in ten.
I searched and days
Went by, for how could I know him
If not by song?
It chanced of a sudden
Under the Andes,
The ancient forests
Of his metaphors,
Creeping soap-tree,
Honey palm,
Swan with black poll,
Dire anaconda
In water-hole,
Near Aconcagua,
Consulting a lady palmist
Who spangled a piece
Of cocoa matting.
With panama hat
And neat valise,
All in a doo-da,
I met him – Pablo
Neruda.

The Paper Curtain

Brandy bottle uncorked. Byronic verse,
Rhyme after rhyme, was echoing near the snow-peaks,
Heroic couplets lost in the great averse,
Anacoluthons flying from every ravine.

Sashes blew in, uncanvassing the easels
In the Parisian studios: thick oils,
Indigo, white, black, smearing the turpentine,
For storm had broken among the Austrian
Alps: Nature still daubing her old romantic drop-scene,
Gusts baffled down from ridge to ridge by pine-woods,
Turning the valley foliage into turmoil.
Torrential rain had hydra'd the river below
The narrow bridges, cloud hid the upper snows
Of Himmelberg. The thunder-claps were cannon
Balls, rolling in a mighty canister.
We heard gigantic foot-steps that seemed to drag on
From gorge to vapourish gorge, by Klagenfurt,
Kaus, Worthersee. The medieval dragon
Was out again. Rock-castle, citadel,
Were taper-lit. Pages of Delacroix
Blotted with ink and sandy spots. The future
Suddenly intervened with catalogue, list.
The lightning legs of Signor Marinetti
Kicked literary dishes of spaghetti
Into the courtyard below. The orange-trees
Were bobbing in their tubs. The European
Scene was changed by onomatopoeia,
Staccato, dentals, high explosive syllables,
Our mail-coach that was rattling through the storm,
Ground-base of clattersome hooves to harness bells,
Lumbering on rainswept roads, had been transformed
Into a luxury coach veeing brown-spray,
All windows shut, gears grinding, the screen wipers
Unable to wash the darkness out of daylight.
Then came the Snicker-Snee. All heard the swipe,
Tearing of sky apart, a mighty rent
As Summer came back to us with new displays
Of hill-wood, peak. To our astonishment,
We had passed what a Bank Manager, forgetting
Accounts, had called the Paper Curtain. Lies
Stormed far away, politics raged. The wet bus
Flashed with new glass. We entered a road-tunnel,
Sun-mirrored again as we crossed the Frontier.

So we came to Yugoslavia.

Late brown was greening in the communal fields
Where men and women worked together. No tractor
As yet had driven them from that fertile tract,
Far off, red globular spires of little churches,
Each on its hill, farm-houses, wooden frames
On which the hay was drying. Horses and carts
Went by. A backward journey into childhood.
A woman beside me daintied with powder puff.
Along the railway line contented puff-puff
Was speeding by. Soon in a far town
I would see again the little trams, sit down
In them. This was at last the happy land
Which Blake and William Morris saw in visions,
Here angels of dissent might make a safe landing,
For Roman Catholic, Moslem, Orthodox
Soon had to end their theological divisions,
No longer squabble over doxologies
And dogma.

          In the old-fashioned Grand Hotel
At Bled, I looked into the family albums.
Victorian spinsters with sketch-books, parasols
Had dreamed here of a pastoral solitude
Among the Alps, admiring the water-colour
Of lake, church-island, wooded slope, the skiff
Below the Bishop's Palace, arrogant, cliffed.
I asked a poet in the lounge:
                    'Tell me,
What happens to the profits of the Tourist
Trade?'
        'They are shared by us.'
                    Portrait of Tito
Above us. Was my question indiscreet?
Our dream of a co-operative state has yielded
To private enterprise, our smaller fields
Divided again. The labours of Horace Plunkett,
A.E., have been forgotten.
              Here no slums,

No beggars, unemployed or wretched poor,
A happy land. I thought of our ill-fare state,
New rich against the poor, the Corporation
Officials of Dublin evicting the infirm
From feeble rooms, the bribes of building firms,
Our old age pensioners, newspaper boys
In bits of unholy sackcloth, bad boots, on winter
Nights. Revolution still in dirty splints,
Eyes bandaged.
                        White steamer on the Adriatic:
We saw by shore, on islands, trees come down
To wade, stopped at a medieval town,
Dubrovnik, fortified with towers, steep rampart:
Wine-shops, jewellers, in the older part:
No traffic, narrow steps I dare not climb,
Cool passage-ways hid from the glowing climate,
No corbel later than the Renaissance.
On Sunday, stately peasant women in splendour
Of pleated linen, costly head-dress, bodice,
Embroidered apron, long white flowing skirt.
Part nakedness not seen in Spain, the pert
Girls in bikinis at the sea-side resorts,
Indecorous dots of yellow-white, red-blue,
Or multi-striped, like liquorice all-sorts,
Bobbing themselves up, down, non-stop revue.
Sea-urchining, I followed their starfish bodies.

At Postoynska where great stalagmite
Met stalactite, we trucked on tiny train
Three miles, then turn about and out again.
Here partisans had hidden gelignite
And Tito planned the future in the night,
Guerrilla tactics thinned the German horde.
Here fighters kept their ammunition, hoard
Of arms. Sun-glad, we hurried to unfreeze
Ourselves.
                        In every town and market place,
Statues designed by sculptors with a free hand.
Ashamed of our own stuggle when all Europe
Became a battle-field and aeroplanes

Unwombed the frightened cities beneath, we buy
Our cheaper cuts from monumental masons.
Sightseers in embarrassment pass by,
Not so the united Croat, Serbian,
Putting away old enmity, to save
The State.
           One day at Zagreb my wife and I
Lay under a tree near flowers in a park, shelter
From hot dictatorship of the sky,
And soon passed from imported noise of Shell
And Mobiloil until a policeman woke us,
Neat automatic in his holster. Obedient,
Some workmen sprawling on the grass, got up.
'Police State!' I hissed. But it was only a joke.
The men laughed, hurried back to factories
And engineering plants, while at our ease,
We sauntered to a nearby café, sagged
Into our basket chairs, and drank iced lager.
How can our vanity eliminate
The Border, make all sing *God Bless the Pope*,
While our investors double what they have?
Often I think of that Utopia
For so it seemed: but I remember most
The lovely children of Yugoslavia
At play in public park with sun-gold limbs.

Letter to a Friend

All day I have a mock fire on or
Off. Nightly we have a real one.
No Admirals, no Tigers, honour
Our garden. So chill the month of August,
While you, hotheaded on the Rialto,
Have stopped to wonder at august
Palaces, churches near gondola posts
And tease me with a picture-postcard –
Carpaccio. What can I say?

Local affairs are much the same.
Swallows are railing and our robin
Thinks we'll have snow. Hotels still rob
Our visitors. Grave-diggers are
On strike. Death loses dignity:
Priest mumbles, relatives must scab,
Pass picket, shovel in their dead
With tears, pass picket again. Headstone
In yard is waiting to be scabbled
And lettered for all time. Printers
Are out, this time on principle:
Newspaper offices closed down.

The Government is pulling down
Georgian houses before the strike
Is over lest the lightning strike
Them. Many advertising agents,
Shopkeepers, vanmen, newsboys, deprived
Of work, have retired into private life.
I am consoled despite old age
And pen in need of book-reviews,
While you are changing all your views,
For something has happened to this eye,
Since it discovered homonyms.
All things shine now, all have nimbus,
Nature displays nimiety;
Though dampness lodge the grain,
Vague shadows move around in greyness,
A cloudy lid hid Ireland's Eye.

The Penitent

A Deputy, frightened by age, yet loath
To fumble in his own despatch case,
Examine our way of life on oath,
Had need of sinlets to confess;
Old boy, past pupil with a torn satchel,
Knee-cap he found too simple.
                              'Bless me,
Father, for I have sinned... twice, no,
On three occasions have erred, spoken
Uncharitably.'
                    'Were you provoked?'
'Provoked!'
                Forgetting the sacrament,
Moustached by indignation, head grey
Again, he muttered our highest name
Half in the dark before mind meant it.

'But he's a saint...!'
                        the priest exclaimed,
Unghosted by astonishment.
All had become irregular.
Elderly sinner jumped up, slamming
The hush in answer as he went,
Mouth, ear, street-wording our Civil War.

'So, national sacrifice is lambed.
But tell me, now, who was at fault?
Who shed that double document,
Defied the lording from pulpit, altar?
What cuffs in ballot box exalted
Him?'
        Traffic diverted argument.
Why should the Devil leer, assault
His decency in sight of palm-tree,
Lasting reward? He envied the foe,
Waited on, plauded by the holy:
Statesman or spirit, remote and calm.

A Young Member of the Party

He never aimed at a window pane
But talked in the election campaign,
Then sold his four-roomed bungalow,
For ceiling, thin wall, taxes were all low,
Bought a great house with illuminated
Fountains
Plashing at night to please late-goers
In cars. But how did this young lad,
Who came from a hayloft, get by ladder,
Not carpeted stairs, to the third storey?
Old folk in Kerry had told him a story
Half lost: 'The Naked Man of the Riff
Mountains'.
And a secret hint of the new tariff
On legs in need of rayon stockings,
Had filled his shelves with their imported stock.

At Middle Abbey Street Corner

Street preachers who have a boiling pitch
Here, do not need to shout or pitch
Their voices higher. Microphone
Can burn or save Pat, Tom, Mike.
With hymning hand, they sing to us.

Harmonium wheezes: 'Jesus! Jesus!'

At the Opposite Corner

History winks at us for Roman
Catholic, Protestant, love mankind now,
And hide the charlock in the cornfield.
But the Legion of Mary keeps a stall
For purchasers around the corner
Of Middle Abbey Street, forestalling
Question with booklets, gay in hue,
On dogma, thaumaturgy, hue
And cry against the Huguenots.
So, when the Band of Hope has raised
White faces to the electric rays
Above, hymning a Halleluiah,
Catholic pamphlets echo: 'Yah!'

Nova et Vetera

Modernism has been silenced,
Theories and latest facts of science
Disputed while the Holy See
Evades all need for synthesis,
Unmoved by the writings of Loisy,
Le Roy, Murri, Père Hyacinthe
And Schnitzer, Fracassini, Baron
Von Hügel, who shook the rusty bar on
What man must think. Among those few,
George Tyrrell of Dublin, whose books were banned,
A Jesuit, then loving husband.
Maid of the unexampled Future,
Descend now. Is it premature
To ask one question? Will they be raised,
When cruel centuries are old,
To shrines, with ring of pointed rays,
Glorified, ensainted, aureoled?

The Pill

Must delicate women die in vain
While age confabulates? Not long
Ago, I knew and wept such wrong.
My favourite cousin, Ethelind,
Bewildered, shaking a head of curls,
Was gone at twenty-two, her babe
Unmothered – she had so little breath.
Now prelates in the Vatican
Are whispering from pillar to pillar
Examining in Latin the pill,
Pessary, letter, cap. What can
We do until they have decreed
Their will, changing the ancient creed,
But lie awake on a separate pillow?
Now in a sky-tormented world,
These nightly watchers of the womb,
May bind archangels by the pinion,
As though they had dragged them down to marble
And bronze, dire figures of the past
That veil a young girl in her tomb.

Our Love Was Incorruptible

Our love was incorruptible,
And she would never frown, say 'No,'
For we had read sex manuals,
So there was nothing else to know.
Sometimes, for sport, we'd interrupt
Coitus, warmth of legs and arms
Held firm as in a gentle vice
Till suddenly the bliss let go.
Women, avoid the bed advice
Of priests, who tell you to add sum
To monthly sum, avoid the foetus

That shouts to everyone 'Adsum!'
The rhythmic method can defeat us.
Now that the Cardinals are rubbing
Hands, will they permit us to be rubbered?
Let postman bring us birth-control,
For English stamps look innocent.
Hidden where not a soul can see, men
Open with caution what is sent
To lessen joy but keep back semen:
Plain envelope without a letter.
With careful fingers they unroll
The teated, pearly, glistening letter:
And women, too are rightly armed
To meet them on that battlefield
Where in the dark tent they can feel
The foeman creep on knee and elbow.
No longer do they fear the ell.
It's but a yard that they can capture,
All pessaried, syringed, war-capped.

The Redemptorist

'How many children have you?' asked
The big Redemptorist.
                              'Six, Father,'
                                        'The last,
When was it born?'
                          'Ten months ago.'
'I cannot absolve your mortal sin
Until you conceive again. Go home,
Obey your husband.'
                          She whimpered:
                                              'But
The doctor warned me…'
                                    Shutter became
Her coffin lid. She twisted her thin hands
And left the box.

The missioner,
Red-bearded saint, had brought hell's flame
To frighten women on retreat:
Sent on his spiritual errand,
It rolled along the village street
Until Rathfarnham was housing smoke

That sooted the Jesuits in their Castle.
'No pregnancy. You'll die the next time,'
The Doctor had said.
                              Her tiredness obeyed
That Saturday night: her husband's weight
Digging her grave. So, in nine months, she
Sank in great agony on a Monday.
Her children wept in the Orphanage,
Huddled together in the annexe,
While, proud of the Black Cross on his badge,
The Liguorian, at Adam and Eve's,
Ascended the pulpit, sulphuring his sleeves
And setting fire to the holy text.

Catechism Lesson

The coldness of the Holy Spirit
Breathes on the North. The Gulf Stream
Is berging. To-day a Jesuit,
Half nodding in the classroom,
Droops with the wings of his soutane
And in the fourpenny school
The Christian Brothers ply the rod.
                              Too late,
For, arrogant, as the ages
Of persecution, greeted,
Escorted by Ecumenical Councils,
Heresy walks the street.

Pigeon Pie

Many the joys of a religious
Vocation both for scholar and dunce,
But best of all was pigeon
Pie, thymed for cooking, saged, parsley'd, potherbed,
Blessed. Every Benedictine brother
In the big monastery at Dunster,
Except in Lent, was much addicted
To mighty wallops of that pie
Which much increased his piety,
For it was tabled twice a week,
Fit nourishment for strong and weak –
And twice a day at Carnival time.
The Norman masons had built a round tower
Of cyclopean thickness, a dove-cote
For the Community of Grey Coats:
A married order. Flying around
The farmyard, hunting-stable, barn,
Five hundred pigeons sported, Carneaux,
Mondain. Pleasant the murmuring, cooing,
Beak-kisses, treading in the coops
And pleasant, too, the billy squabbles
All day in hunger of the squabs.
A well-oiled mechanism – the Potence –
An iron pivot, revolving post –
Turned at light touch with a fat monk
Upon a ladder. He could reach
And grasp the plumpest without a screech,
But when the narrow loft had stunk
Too much coof came with bucket, mop.
Out of the apertures, the flock
Flew, scattering feathers, like flocculi,
To feed on vegetables, crops,
Pick, peck, the countryside. Poor villeins
Muttered against the holy villains
With half a harvest in their crops.

Custom House Official

Idly I watched a youngster firing volleys
Of laneway stones at a broken bucket, plate,
Thought of Ignatius at his daily toil,
Tearing out coloured illustration, plate
And photograph from large expensive volumes
Art books displaying the lines of life, exposing
Our allotted shame – in marble, bronze, grain oil.
He hated, rejected, much of classical sculpture,
Gods, goddesses, in all their naked poses,
And, in particular, two slender figures
The Apollo Belvedere and Mercury,
Who had no decent cockleshell or fig-leaf,
To him the female was a meretrix.
Let Michelangelo undo his painting,
Expulsion from Eden, fresco of our First Parents,
Multiple in the Sistine Chapel, a pair
Without a leaf between them; the huge statue
At which so many visitors have stared:
His David, first to show, in bronze or marble,
Thick ring of circumcision and the glans.
The brown and gold of Titian's *Pastoral*
Courtier, peasant, lady playing on her lute.
Tiepolo's gay, blue and crimson tints
On ivoried ceilings. The *Venus Triumphant*:
Cupids with petal-winglet, rosy infants.
Venetian canvasses of Tintoretto,
The same religious pictures of Guido Reni,
The Crucified without a single scrap
Of loin-cloth. These, indignantly, he scrapped.
Great-bosomed bourgeois wives, nippled by Rubens,
Round-bellied as their husbands or Dutch cheeses
Tumbled in noonlight on a bed. Bending
To see the crack of paint between their cheeks,
Ignatius hid them. Later delights of Paris,
Spring days of hoop-là, yellow parasols,
The Champs Elysées, riders, carriage row,
The trees that pry in *The Picnic* of Corot:

Men sitting in shades of green, a naked model,
Flesh tones that startled all. Modigliani:
Black torsos, stone, paint, taken by surprise:
Gauguin beneath a palm-tree with rakish beret,
Papuan women, coffee-brown breast, red berry.
Ignatius turned his glance from drawing, plate,
In wicked works of anthropology:
The jungle savages of the River Plate,
The Dyaks carrying Grand-dad's empty skull
To aggrandise their loins. Poor Ichthyphalli:
Faith of their fathers, all that we abhor:
The anatomical: Fallopian
Tubes, body dissected, viscera examined.
This conscientious Civil Servant had ample
Excuse. Gloving the privy paw, he cites
For all who remonstrate, one example:
Modest Director of the National Gallery,
Who, setting fire one day to his moustache,
Had hidden *The Sleeping Venus* out of sight:
One hand fondling in noon-dream the golden tache.

A Student in Paris

He dreamed of pure romance, *gestes*
D'amour, ladies with graceful gestures,
At night in the arms of a new surprise,
Became as amorous as Paris
When he was turning the goddesses –
Dummies undressed in a window – deciding
Which one should have the Beauty Prize
For her white apples, hurried to Paris
Faster than piston of mail-boat, night-train,
To rid himself of a celibate training.
On his first morning, he crossed the road
To a cheap wine-shop. Was the uncovered
Waiting for him? Soon he discovered.
The patron brought him behind a row

Of monastic bedrooms. Her hair not up
As yet, a girl of seventeen
Ran to him gaily, slender, supple.
Laughing and shameless, she took him in teeny
Hand, stooped to fondle, kiss new poppet,
Practise the naughty *fellatio.*
Then after love-preliminaries,
So unexpected, caught him, fell
Upon the bed, dangle of limbs.
Two minutes later, he thought, 'I'll pop in
Again this afternoon,' came back,
A new man, saw to his disappointment
A fat one rolling on her back.
She smiled, pulled up her vest and pointed
Below. So while she romped, he ramped.

Maurice became an earnest student
Of venery, hieing to the stews
At darkfall, roaming about the red light
Quarter, impatient, always ready
In café, at kerb, to stop a likely
Girl:
             'Voulez vous faire l'amour?… You like
Zig-zag?'
             'Mais, oui.'
                         Then:
                                   'Combien?'
'Vingt francs.'
                   He wondered would her comb be an
Ivory one; safe in a small hotel
Where none would recognise him, tell
What he was up to.
                         'Excusez moi.'
Hospital nurse stooped to inspect
His part first, made him wash and dry it,
Sometimes hand-towelled him with a dry
Or business smile.

                   He lay expectant
At night, dreaming of different ways.

Often he pondered on Messalina,
Empress of Rome, whom Juvenal
Denounced, though she was never venal.
He saw her in a brothel, leaning
Against the wall with gilded paps,
Long body whiter than papyrus.
Knees up, she bore assault of privates,
And, quickly, warrior-like, deprived them
Of their advantage. Head down, gladdened
In her arena, gladiator
Would crouch: her legs went round his waist;
Next, pumiced athlete or wealthy wastrel,
Son of a Senator, wine-bibber
Spilling fiasco too soon on her bib.
Often she prayed that Jupiter
Would come down, having pitied her,
Reveal himself as bull, swan, eagle,
She would be fierce as him, as eager,
As uncelestial, jubilant.
Unsatiated by the organ
At midnight, no longer orgulous,
She had sought in vain for the Divine
To pluck and tread her, turned to vine.

Autumnward, Maurice slowly wandered
By palaces along the Seine
Where pride had eagled plinth and wall.
The law of natural pleasure saned him.
Joyful, he lingered by gold-brown trees,
Paths of dark topia, green box
Beyond the Petit Trianon,
Or on the quays, looking in book-box
For more Erotica, Louys,
Crebillon, the enchanted sofa
That thrilled a Do-re-me-so-fa
Under the farthingales of ladies
Whose gallants whispered indecencies.
Often he read Catulle Mendès:
Impudent stories that shuttered day.
So Maurice worshipped, early and late,

Imagining all to be priestesses
Kindling the tripod on tessellated
Pavement: his favourite, stray vestal
From Rome, who wore so short a vest,
It showed her dark-curled V-sign. How many
Such women had he known in turn,
Lucullus finding on the menu
One dish? He left the Hotel Jules
Caesar with only his return
Ticket, five francs, a Juvenal;
Too young to weigh the mediaeval
Degrading of Phallomeda,
Whose votaries take off fallals
To earn their living, pay their homage,
By night to what is called unholy:
The street a temple, bidet a throne.

More Extracts from a Diary of Dreams

I sat in a comfortable lounge in Dunleary
Puffing tobacco smoke, talking with learned
Companions about statistics, Mervyn Wall
Beside me at a small table and near the wall,
His back to us, the bold Sir Myles na gGopaleen.
He turned to order another round and leaning
Across the counter, remarked: 'We'll go on a skyte.'
Then we were belting up into the sky,
Fast in his stationary monoplane,
Anxiously looking down at the map-rolling plain
Of Leinster. Myles, being a cracked pilot,
Had jerked the joystick, avoided eleven pylons:
Soon he was running the light machine along
A road between stubble-fields. Light was longer.
Why were we all in a motor car: the miles
Chasing us on with hill and thicket? Myles
Turned at the wheel, our Gaelic satirist,
To glance at the tiny dial on his wrong wrist,

Luminous as a miniature city;
He stopped where a mad tree flourished the signature
Of lightning.
　　　　　　'We'll take a byroad, avoid the sentries' —
And through the coming twilight, hawthorn scent
Wafted a secret menace. We had no passports,
Identification papers. How could we pass
The German Frontier? At dawn, we saw
Young Austrians hurry by tavern, workshop, saw-mill,
And outdoor café, feather in cap, green clothes,
Although the nearby factories were still closed
And girls with yellow toques like beehives, gay,
Abuzz with mischief, showing their engagement
Ring. Soon we were in the city. Traffic slowed
At corners. We read the Anti-British slogans.
Outside a public lavatory, a queue
Of people hitlered at me, suspicious, curious,
I footed impatiently. Myles disappeared,
Then Mervyn. I wandered along a side-street, peered
For an alley or convenient by-way;
With Travellers' Cheques or marks to buy
A meal. Fear overtook me. I dodged it, half ran
From the great square down an avenue at random.
Then, suddenly, I was at home in the past,
But what had happened to my mind? I passed
My father and mother entertaining friends,
Too busy to recognise me: in a frenzy,
Turned to a strange doorway, under a weight
Of woe. Mervyn and Myles came in. 'Tell me,
What is the matter?' Voices were telephonic.
I had been vague at Dunleary. Later, they tied
And locked me in a Round Tower beneath the cross-ties,
The cobwebs, in case of an emergency,
While I was hopping mad for the 'Gents'.
They heard my heavy breathing in sleep, then left me.
That afternoon a tall German lieutenant
Gave us safe conduct. Time and again, these lapses
Of Memory. I tore the perfume from my lapel,
Unbuttoned my collar. Why must I analyse
Myself in dreams, try to escape the lies?

The local farmers and their big wives hobnobbed
As porter stank around the kitchen. Bulmer Hobson
Opened a heavy tome, *Apples and Cherries*,
With handsome primer type upon a chair.
He bent, short-sighted, read an allegory
Of Ireland to us. Heavier foot and leg
Stirred on the floor or against the settles, for the people
Were puzzled by that historic fable. I peeped
At red, green, illustrations. All shambled out.
The play had just begun. Nearby the outhouse
An old grey and his wife, a middle-aged,
Respectable woman, were acting near the midden.
I thought uneasily of their clumsy coupling,
After she loosened his haybag, washed her tea-cup,
Lying beside him at midnight, hand in his mane.
For centuries since they had crossed the main,
He had been overburdened, whipped, oppressed
By renegade and landlord. Dearly she pressed
His muzzle to her. He had known the Dane
And now she warns him, tearfully, of danger
To-day in the market-place. His eyes are worried
And sad as he blinks at her, puts by her word.
At a gallop, jumping the hedges, come the sons
And daughters of the gentry, cloud-borne sunlight
Flashes on fair head, fawn jacket, spur;
Vindictive, they canter from the dust they spurn
Until they seem a company of the Sidhe
Riding across the reed-tops of Lough Sheelin.
The horse had been struck dead, his rider tumbled.
She got up – Revolution on a tumbril:
There on the road, blood of our country trickled.
That girl stood naked but for the tricolour
That hid her pelvis and the gold brassiere,
Emblem, I thought, of our Literary
Revival.

    Another volume by James Stephens,
Stories among Women. He had unjapered
Our literature. Middle-aged women pursued
Beauty. With taunting words, insults, they shooed

Her. Then, out of a silence came the murmur
Of approaching horror: 'They have murdered her.'
A dying girl sat up in the hospital
Ward, suddenly gay. She coughed, brought up her spit,
Blood-phlegm, boasted she was promiscuous,
Telling the nuns of pleasure they had missed.
'Better,' she laughed, 'to fornicate than burn.'
She vanished from the theatre. An auburn
Wig lay near the footlights, torn from the dissevered
Head, papier mâché, a string-ball, several
Props.
      Had I remembered that lyric inspired by Mabel
Beardsley, the head-long dance of Salomé?

Day-dreaming still.

      Before the hearse
Had come for my saint after the dress-rehearsal
On the Abbey stage of *Sister Eucharia*,
Thinking how much I had admired and cared
For her, I sat in the stalls with Eithne,
Hearing my words still mingle with her breath,
Then, glancing down, I saw her holy garment
Part and reveal a naked thigh. Regardless,
I pushed through blueness of passion-flower, senses
Glowed, thuribled under a cloud of incense.
I whispered my condition. Had I incensed her?
She smiled to see my clothes were disarranged
Like hers, murmured: 'The matter can be arranged.'
I laughed because her voice was so sedate, yet
Improper. 'Darling, can we make a date now?'
But in an overjoy I wakened, just
Too soon for her at six o'clock.
      Justin
Martyr had dreamed unchastely of Diana
Beneath the statue of Ephesus. Answer
Sea-rang from a future shrine in Asia Minor
Narrow within a wall of gold and azures.
The pagen philosopher cried out, 'I confess
That sin,' beneath the sternly gentle icon.

Day-dreaming still.

                I gazed at palaces,
Administrative buildings, Palladian
In architecture, noon-glitter on the car-parks,
Flowers, cooled by rose of fountains, in small parks
In front of the museums, art galleries,
Wide steps, equestrian statues in bronze of gallant
National leaders. By a marble balustrade
I crossed, re-crossed a river three times, strayed
By astragals. Where is it situated,
That capital too large to be the City of
Three Bridges?
                Turning to the right, misled
Again by Lemprière, under the ledge
Of a long wall, I saw, undesecrated,
The naked statues of five goddesses.
Their eyes were china-blue, their lips envermeiled:
Zones of delight, scatterers of virtue.
I peered through the shadowiness at each vulva,
Ready for Jupiter on a cloud or Vulcan
Who works below. So quick the hypertaxis
Of divinity that I ran where yellow taxis
Were speeding by, the flag down, to a railway
Station and idly, for half an hour, I waited
Beside the kerb, hearing the duller churr
Of factory belting. Then, I was in a church
Crowded with people, banners. *Dominus
Vobiscum.* I could feel from the terminus
The heat of steam.

                Over a glass of claret
I turned to make my intemperate declaration
For I was thinking of a delicious first act
With her. Quickly that cool, so charming, actress
Said, 'Oh, do let me make you a cup of tea':
Afternoon cure for male unchastity.
And so in dreams I have never upstaged Sheila.
Often I smile and wonder what she'll do
When someone comes along who is better endowed.
Make tea for him? Or take it lying down?

At a meeting of share-holders and customers,
All was uncarried. In vain, the Chairman, Sir Thomas,
Called speakers to order. A man held up his dentures,
Pink plastic in bits. Another showed a dent.
A third had stuck his set with Seccotine.
After the uproar, I left with the Secretary
In haste.
            'At five,' she said, 'I always get restless,
Have tea, poached egg on toast, at a restaurant,
Then go to the Dullies. To-day, we'll watch the News
In my bed-sitter.'
                    She talked about debentures.
'Mine is all right,' she whispered, 'Have I bent yours?'

I woke that afternoon with a new word.

Those voices again.
                    'Why do you want to go to
New York?'
            'If you were living long ago,
Wouldn't you like to visit Babylon?'

Half waking, I heard those voices babble on.

I met them in a Café: Donagh MacDonagh,
His wife in a mantilla, eyesome donna.
'Why have you come to Rome?'
                            'To kiss Big Toe.'
'You've changed. You used to be ambiguous.'
'Look closer at me. I'm not here in the body.'
'Where are you?'
                'In Dublin, drinking at the Bodega
With Seumas O'Sullivan.'
                        Under a street-lamp,
The close in-searching kisses that Shulamite
Gave me so long ago, unvirgining
Herself after too many spots of gin,
Within my Gentile arms. Her lips were full
Of me. Slim shoe, ankle so beautiful
She might have danced before the unveiling Ark

Or been the desert-slave of a Patriarch,
Each kiss – that of a different wife or mistress:
The tent-fold joys of a polygamist.

It was in Belfast after a cocktail party:
She kissed me passionately; her lips were parted
As if she were still murmuring: 'Ju-jube.'
And mine, surprised, became as jubilant
Then suddenly she pushed me out of the taxi:
'You're dirty. Take a bath.'
                     Why should she tax
Me with uncleanliness? I ran upstairs.
A woman stood up in the bath. My stares
Were in her smile. She handed me the loofa
And the soap, so English, so aloof,
That I woke up.

          A girl tickled my ribs
Until I was blousing between her curls, her ribbons:
An unvictorian picnic in a knolled,
Beechwooded shire. I think of Matthew Arnold
And Marguerita, for a Swiss girl on impulse
Stooped down and kissed me full on the mouth. My pulse
Went frou-frou as the streamers of her bonnet
Above me. Lozenges of affection, bon-bon
Of memory.
         Last night, flirting with Susie,
I emptied out a pocketful of sous
To buy another round of darkness. She kissed
Again and again but kept to herself the kist
Of ripening apples she brought from Scotland.
                          Dora
Must have an open vowel-rhyme. Adorable,
Milk-soft her kiss as though she had just suckled
Her babe and wanted, for gentleness, to succour
Me.
      Who were those girls in the smart uniform
Drinking large gins-and-tonics, come from the formless
To a Continental bar festive with bunting?
Only their kisses, Rosae Floribundae,

Remain. As I grew bolder, each resisted
With kisses, kisses. Their lips were so persistent,
So near, that mine were soon competitors.
Sweet nothings of night. Dear nothings. The last of petting
Parties.

   Left Nora, strolled into Regent's Park
And found myself in the twilight of Genesis,
For the branches were closer, the prim shrubberies
Waving their gamps in fear as if primitive
Monsters were roaming behind them through miles of cane.
The clouds were gone from the sky for a hurricane –
Matilda or Deborah – was near. I hurried
To the main gate. The shops were lit up, a car, a van,
Went by, a white expensive caravan
Came, swerving. I turned back at an electric post
To ask a lad dressed like a little post-
Man:
   'Where is Regent's Terrace?'
         'You pass the cowboys
Riding to Sacramento – no country for cowards –
Shots empty a saloon: Gentleman Dan
Gets off his broncho – he's the famous dandy –
And Redskins ride around a covered wagon:
I mean three cinemas.'
      He winked, was gone
Forever, poor child. I went into a garden
With tables; vague men were in a smoking den;
A Georgian Mansion with shabby yellow paint
And stucco. Again that sudden fear and pain,
The loss of memory. Into the new,
I strayed by crescent, drive, grove, avenue.

That dream again.

     I stumble from kerb to dub,
Weak-knee'd, alone, into a Greater Dublin,
New crescent, avenue, small gardens, villas,
And bungalows. Below me was a village
In ruins, a hollow, old cars in a quarry.

Still miserable. Yet we had never quarrelled.
But where was Nora? The police would help to find her,
Broadcast an urgent message. Was it the final
Moment of separation? Solicitor
Had given her money. What is her address?
At morning, I stare in vain at an empty dress,
Half hidden by my tears. Then I woke up
And knew she was asleep nearby: our woe
Postponed.
         Why should the aged be unhappy,
Mope in the dark, when the unhappenable
Is theirs and they can glide between the shades
Of meaning in a dream, talk to the shades,
Unchaperoned, watch every job of nature
That proves the midnight merriment innate –
Fire in the great vein – and when desire has chased
After high boot and bulging stays, be chaste?

The Echo at Coole and Other Poems

(1968)

The Labours of Idleness

Beddoes had met him, slender, tallish,
A bald-pate in a brown surtout
Leaning, one evening, against a tallboy,
Handling a duodecimo,
Mathematician, stammerer,
And poet, master of decimals,
Odd character at forty-two.
Somewhat lacking in stamina.
How often he had dipped his pen
In tear-drops, writing another letter
Of misery to dear Miss Mitford,
Whenever she would let him,
Trying to explain his long *Nepenthe*,
In which the sense was sometimes missing
From rapid octosyllabic lines:
Then off with her bonnet, woolly mittens
To praise the badly printed pamphlets
So worthy of gilt edge and octavo,
Or hurrying the ink to scold him
For perilous ode or skolism!
Too many seasons he had dreed
Endless sadness in sadder dreams,
Thinking of childhood days at Springfield
In County Dublin, impatient, waiting
For the first budlets of the Spring.
That night he had heard Kiltiernan waites,
His grandfather gave him a Christmas box
To bulge his stocking, a little pony
That he could ride from hedge, clipped box
A living present costing a pony.
He soon forsook garden and grot
That he would pearl with a graceful nymph
From Penneus, afraid of the nimble
Satyrs, a little too grotesque.

Mooning at day in the night-shadowed Dargle,
I see him later, young George Darley,
Heliconned graduate from Trinity
College already lightly tringling
His rhymes: bird-pen to fern-drip, cascade
Where very morning ray was downcast,
Paler in leaf-gleam than the beeswax.
He fled when brake or wagonette
Came on Bank Holiday with the Waxies
From Dublin to disturb the wagtails,
Sporting with wives, sweetheart, their coat-tails
Whirl on the green, forgetful of last
And upper. They went, leaving the last
Echo still reeling. He would loaf,
Gorsing beneath the Sugarloaf
Down by the Rocky Valley: foxglove,
Stone-wall, no higher than a fox
The bracken hides.
                    He took no part in
Dublin Festivities, parties
Where, in their blood-red jackets, Lancers
Were moving gaily in the Lancers
Or ever ready for the quadrille
Stood to attention, social drill;
Advancing soon, from right to left,
Or bowing in ladies with a fan,
Who curtseyed when the Lord Lieutenant
Held Court. Georgian houses, fanlights,
Black lion-knockers: city of Lover
And Lever.
                Hurried on by fancy,
He climbed the path to Lover's Leap,
Went by the cloud-visited woods,
Rivering gleams, at Woodenbridge.
Or saw reflected in the Avoca
Flowering laurel as he invoked
The Muse.
                Unhappy poet in London,
With pen that kept away the dawn,

He heard at night quick step on grating,
Carriages going by with peers.
Mirrored in manuscript, he peered
Into the misty Garden of Wicklow
Unweeded, sad, until the grate
Was chill as misery, the wick low.

A Centenary Tribute

I
W.B. Yeats

Often I thought, only a stone's throw
From him at Riversdale, of that old man
Still seeking his perfection, still in the throes
Of verse, yet every word at his command,
Or wheeled along the garden in a bathchair,
Wild with impatience for a better couplet
To link divided rhyme. But I was chary
Of seeing that house, his study, the bedroom wall
On which he knocked at morning for his cup
Of tea — hedge-walking tramp with empty wallet,
Stories of the great Cholera, bedraggled,
Woeful as Raftery beneath the ragged
Thorn. Donkeying the little roads of Sligo,
Had he not seen them in childhood, the wrynecked, the sly go
Past, later heard in the sitting-room at Coole
Of spells that twitched the muslin from the cooler,
Bewitched the cream? He told us of rapscallions
Who had swiven too quickly, never given a rap,
When Crazy Jane dirtied her petticoat,
Respectable journeymen who bedded a coat
Beneath her in a dyke, poor Tom at Cruahane
Dancing in glee when miles of daylight crew
With genderings, best in the open air
As Wordsworth said.
                    Last ruffle in what eyrie?

The asters by the drive were not as gay
As when I saw them, a stranger passing his gate.
The apple trees that had topped the orchard wall
Were gone save two, sweet wood cut down and charred.
More grass unmarked the croquet lawn: the mower
Unused. The twilight seemed to mock and moe
At me. Bewildered, I tried to find the hall door.
All had been changed: the stone-steps, railings hauled
Away: new side-porch to that Victorian
House; memory of the past evicted.
Contemporary fashion was villafied
Inside. All that the poet had defied
And raged against seemed to be on its guard.
He would have thought the furniture, carpets, garish,
Expensive.
                Some night, perhaps, the Great Mood
Will change all in a dream: the house restored,
Old mortar used again by it as in a story
That Sato's sword may glitter at the moon.

In the Savile Club

I met him at four o'clock in the Savile Club
Within the Lounge, chairs waiting for artist, savant,
Bohemian. Smiling, all savoir-faire,
Yeats rose to greet me, stately, cloud-grey-tweeded,
White-haired.
                'I am in London about my book,
A Vision.'
                Holyheading back to Dublin,
Nine years before, I saw the shadowy poet
Stoop in a drawing-room in Kenilworth Square, women
Around him, explaining the Phases of the Moon,
Cube, mystical circle, black disc, white dot, the Wheel
Of Fortune, diagram of past in future,

While, geometrically, all the Heavens
About him, mapped the darkened walls with starlit
Points. Week after week, I heard his astrologising
Until a hand got up, switched on the light.

Then I was listening in London.
                                    'Many
Will disagree with much I have written. But
I think I have solved the Arcane Problem.'
                                        Head
Bowed low, he stood, respectful, for a few
Moments before himself.
                            Incredulous,
A son of Nox, I waited.
                        We sat down
At a small table. The waiter brought us tea.
Then Squire came in: Sir John becoming Jack-
A-napes, shook hands, then whiskeyed under the table.
We stared. He climbed over the bar.
                                    We talked
Of poetry. I turned the unwritten pages
Of my new book, *A Critical Study
Of William Butler Yeats*, chapter eleven.
He interrupted. 'There are portraits of me
In Liverpool, Birmingham, Edinburgh,
And other Galleries.'
                        The pages eared
Each other.
                'Do you agree with Forest Reid,
He writes…'
                'I have forgotten his book.'
                                        My own
Remaindered, head was tumbling after it.
Soon, speaking of his plays, we leaned so close
That I could see a tiny brown eye peeping
Behind his left lens cutely from the Celtic
Twilight at mine. I tried to stop the moment
I dreaded so much. Had I not promised the young
Director of the firm that I would ask him
The truth about his lyrical love affair?

I groped around the Nineties.
                                    'Mr Yeats,
In order – as it were – to understand
The Wind among the Reeds, those exquisite
Love lyrics, can I venture to ask what is –
If I may say so – their actual basis in
Reality?'
                        How could I know a married
Woman had loosened her cadent hair, taken him,
All candlestick, into her arms?
                                    A stern
Victorian replied:
                        'Sir, do you seek
To pry into my private affairs?'
                                    I paled.
The poet returned. His smile kept at a distance.
'Of course you could suggest – without offence
To any person living – that...'
                                    I lost
His words. Maud Gonne was talking to me in that cottage,
At Glenmalure. The parrot squawked: canaries
Twittered: the wolfhound yawned. Her golden eyes
Were open to mysteries.
                                    I took my hat,
Leaped square and crescent at a bound,
Confused by all his gyres – and I am bound
To say I left that book, unchaptered, unbound.

The Echo at Coole

I stood one day in the great Pleasure Garden
At Coole, where the catalpa blossoms – handing
Out pods in Autumn, long as cigars that George Moore
And Edward Martyn smoked after their dinner
At Tulira. Sad wilderness of panicles,
Roses gone thorning, seven leaves instead
Of five, gay, sportive blooms that had lost their seed

And names in lengthy Latin. I stared awhile
Beneath the copper beech where a railing guarded
Initials, wintered in the bark deep-cut,
Of W.B. and Y., A.G., A.J.,
A.E., and S.O'C.: thinking again
How Lady Gregory would drive twelve miles
Day after day, sun-reining in a phaeton, along
Her avenues – with Phaeton – through the Seven Woods,
By alleys of wild privet, lake-lingering,
To count the Swans for Willie.
                                        I came to the bust:
Maecenas crumbling on his pedestal,
Obeyed the clear instructions in that unfinished
Poem of Yeats, calling to find the Echo
That lives by the high wall at the left-hand corner
In private:
                    'Echo, whereabouts can you hear
From?'
            Here.
                        'My task in the future, can I know?'
            No.
                    'Must I still hope, still body on?'
                                                    On.
'Yet how can I be certain my way is right?'
Write.
                'Tell me what thoughts had Carroll O'Daly, Swift,
Who called on other echoes, lonely as you?'
                                                    Yew.

A.E.

A.E., taking the pipe from his mouth again, like
A stout Faun or rather a big-bearded Pan,
Remarked as he pondered in his chair:
                                            'The old man
Is talking to himself.'
                        I saw behind him,

Gold-leafed, with their dark blue or olive bindings,
The Collected Poems of William Butler Yeats,
Macmillan'd in a row.
                              I wondered were they
A purgatory the poet had ghosted from hatred,
Incessant, inner circles, of repetition
Systematised by metaphysics, late
Excuse for fantasies, that never let him
Be still when he became a man of letters,
Discovered in old age the physical.
'His lyrics are Saturnian rings illumined
By colder fire.'
                              'What of our common ill?
Do they explain it?'
                              'If rhetoric can last,
Then all that lonely, premeditated art must.'
Scene-shifting, Joyce hurried from Night-town, tired, half-blind,
Black spectacles became a grin:
                              'Who's spending?'
'You chaps are too expansive. I'm expensive.'
He pushed away the cockles and mussels,
Ordered himself a bottle of cheap white wine.

James Stephens

Up, down,
Hilly road,
I rode
From Dublin Town.

Whirr of ball bearings
Seemed to be bearing
My body aloft,
Higher than hay loft,
Hedge where a tinker
Bottomed a pan:
At a turn, I tinkled

The bell. Near daisies,
Boy scout with pannikin,
Stared at the day.
Passing a horse-box
At the Jolly Topers,
Fat man in gaiters;
Tall, iron gates,
Flowers, topiary
Yews, prim box,
I belled at a corner
Beyond a cornfield,
Came to my elm tree.

Soon with my elbows
In leaves, I loosened
My fluttering bow,
Undid front stud,
Forgetting my studies,
Attempts at doggerel,
Mind on the loose.
I opened a dog-eared
Book under the jade
Buds: James Stephens.

Big, little, words,
Were hopping on twigs,
As though they were birds,
But how could I twig them?
With chirp and twitter,
They teased and twitted me.
Each cloud was white,
Lark sang, the sun
Was steady and bright,
Grass, green, sky, blue,
The breezes blew
And were full of fun:
Half abstract, essence,
The songs of James Esse.
And I joyed in his joy
As if his enjoyment

Had all been meant
For me on young elbows,
In the greenest of elms.

Then I thought of the slums
And my spirit slumped
Into the tenements
He came from, back-rooms
With ten, twelve, bare-footed
Children, wives bearing
The next one, gutters
With tin cans, straw, fishguts,
Men with torn cuffs
In the Coombe, or Cuffe Street,
The homeless arrested,
No stone to rest on,
The Mendicity Hall
At night, our city
Of broken windows
And Penal Law.

The elm had wintered,
One leaf left. Saddened,
I saw the saddle
Below.
      Velocipede
Got up and peed
On the piss-a-beds
Left then bedabbled,
I crushed the green leaf,
Saw all in relief.
Up, down,
Hilly road,
I rode
To Dublin Town.

F.R. Higgins

Telegram picked up my clothes that afternoon
Near her divan – and I was driving, wan-looking
From London streets to half-light, hint, nuance.
I heard his song praising the County of Mayo,
My map to the smaller roads around Brackwansha;
White miles of Springtime hedge, the blossoming sloe,
Japanese lacquer, I thought, and driving slowly,
Saw Fuji-ama in the distance, gay
Peak, delicate blue lake, a tale of Geishas
Dragonfly brooch, hot-springs, the reed-thin mats.
Behind the paper pavilion a light fan toyed.
I was a child buying an ounce of san-toy
In the corner shop when nothing else could matter.

Beyond a little dampness of ragwort, flagger,
The car stopped. I was at the cottage gate.
The poet came out with lumbering gait,
His wife behind him: teapot on the warm flag
Inside, the turf aglow.
                  At twilight, we wandered
From a stir of bushes to an old story
Restrung by Ferguson, the stepping-stones
Where long ago the Welshmen of Tirawley
Had chosen loss of their sight by red-hot awl
Rather than gelding. Bloodred, eyes burst, unsteady,
The blindmen crossed, all fingers, in haste to get
And train new sturdy sons who would not forget
The night of vengeance. Beyond the lake
Mount Nephin dimmed, its ghost-head lay
In reeds. The west had vanished. Venusberg
Called seventeenth-century lovers to convenient
Retiring places. There the young fled up,
Free-making together; big, little, sins in the flesh,
Forgiven. The Wife of the Red-headed man who feared
After the Day on the Mountain, the freezing pits
Below her, saw a mist-big youth draw near.
She liked those cloud-come fellows with a wild flow of

Locks, chancy kissers before delight has flown,
And so on a night of frost their strength was pitted.
Girls, without dowry, wedded to old men
Who sat up nightly in bed with wheeze and croup
Or, blankets around them, tried at cropper and croup,
In vain though priest had blessed them with Amen.
These came in pairs to the Well of Knowledge, learned faster
Than bucketing, and gathered in hazel nuts.
How could I know my hands would be held fast
By twisted ropes of straw so soon?
                                        For breakfast –
Alarum clock at twelve – pot-oven bread
And slices, thicker than pancake, of a goose egg
King Guaire would have relished. Postman gossiped.
Gorse-bright beyond the ridge a goshawk went.
The kettle steamed below the hook. We sipped
Hot tea. Whiteness of sloe was there outside
And from the Moy an air made little signs
In the road dust.
                        At darkfall, we dropped in
To a clay cottage where an elderly couple,
Poor, belaboured by the monthly rent, were raffling
Their donkey, to talk awhile and take a drop. In
The bedroom the woman poured out for me a cupful
Of poteen. In the kitchen the low rafters
Were merry. Like a man, I gulped it down.
Sex-fire of potato made me feel so doughty,
I leaped into the kitchen, grabbed the plumpest
Girl, whirled with her into a jig that plucked
The fiddle-string, jumped, hit the paraffin-oil
Lamp overhead, immodest, in a moil,
Clapping her bigger rounds, then suddenly sober,
Sat on the table above the benchers. So
I learned my lesson.
                        Sometimes through mist we rowed
For miles along the lake to a white-washed row
Of island cottages, drank tea while a man got
A bottle of poteen – six shillings – from rock
Or rusty islet by the mercy of God,
For Civic Guards lay in a little creek

Watching the come-and-go of island Larry,
Tim, Mickie, bigger in German bionoculars,
Or stopped to inspect and fine the donkey creels
Upon the road, taking away the medicine
And merriment that lead a man to wed sin
At any hour.
                    Fred drove his scarlet car
So fast the radiator bubbled over,
Stirabout dancing from supper with the pot-lid,
Along the unbending road to Castlebar.
We shook the whiteness of sloe, unseen
On Pegasus, dusting along boreen;
Pursued by every risk, we came to little
Towns, Raftery had known so well, Claremorris
To Carra, Gullen to Mile-bush, to Killeaden,
The best of all for had he not declared
In drink that he would bear the Branch to it?
All manner of things grew there as they thought fit,
Barley and wheat, the oats, rye, close as handgrip,
Gilding as griddlebread and he would be
A month there at the very least, lying
In bed and making poems. The blackberries,
Raspberries, strawberries, weighed down the basket
With thumping. Poteen was sold without a licence.
Varieties of wood were carpentered, handsome
Mahogany, green-oak and beech. Scholars
Behind a hedge were learning Greek, Latin, sums.
At morning chimneys had a quiet smoke
Together. Birds, that gave a foreign cry
To smaller fields and the cuckoo before his voice broke,
The thrush, the goldfinch, were busy answering
Each other. Soon the beagles were in full cry.
Gentlemen riders took stone wall, the fox
Was seen, a brush beyond the river-gardens
Along the Moy. Mail coach went by. The Guard
Lanterned. Inn faces were a-glow at Foxford
And in his big house, Frank Taafe was keeping
The table in a roar.
                    The Norman keep
In which, with nineteen sons or more, a farmer

Was living at Ballylee had seemed too far
For us; its future hidden.
                    There Raftery
Sang twice of that sky-woman, Mary Hynes,
On Sunday in her simple finery,
So fair that all might think Low Mass was High Mass
And when she bowed, going on one knee,
O, then, the solemn congregation rose
And went, praising at every door, the Rose
Of Ballylee.
            The poet was among
His people, true to the little river-gardens
Beside the Moy where hae' pennies and farthings
Were more than pennies when he played at Hide-
And-seek, or Sally Water, before words sung
To him or he had heard of the Love-songs Hyde
Collected. Half awake, he made his lyrics
In bed, in mountain mist, under a hayrick,
Drowned bush, like Raftery, fitting the words
To the wandering tunes he hummed, the quarter-tones
All going their own way as he intoned them.
He sang of fairs at Maam-turk, western towns
Grass-grown, so quiet, they seemed to have lost their names,
Matchmakers who buckled girls without a dowry
To aged wickedness that tried to shame them
With show of wrinkles, lovers on their own
Upon Mount Nephin in sloe-time. What could they own
But ill-luck and all their kisses, a ballad sheet
Or song, white as the pillow slip and sheet
Merrily spread on hedges below, smaller
Than the last dip of handkerchief seen by exiles?
Often he rowed out to the hazel-isles
At twlight, drifting beneath an abbey wall
Or paid the rounds in Galway with O Conaire
In a wine-tavern, thinking of that slip
Of a girl, the Queen of Sheba, arm
In arm with a randy sailorman, whose ship
Had put to sea. Often he made no bones
Of it, but sang his *Song for the Clatter Bones*,
Paid on the dot. There was a whispered cottage

Nearby that had for its invisible sign-board
Or merry bush, a ragged pair of knickers.
Gamey young fellows and girls came in. Old Nick
Was there. Most nights we hurried to the petting
Party despite the spiritual peril,
To talk or dance until the midnight lamp
Had been extinguished. Hidden girls and lads
Kissed, cuddled closer. Those upon my lap
In turn weighed different in the dark. My knees
Felt the warm lightness, warmer heaviness
So near and yet so hostile to what I needed:
The gift that nobody dare ask from Heaven.
Mouth upon mouth, the holding back of breath:
Hand moving down from scapulars to breasts,
That must have been milk-white. It stole
Halfway in sinfulness until the iron
Chastity Belt was cross-barred: Holy Ireland
Defending virtue. No need for priestly stole,
Half-open Catechism. How could I bear
Those nights, caressing too much that was bare?

Car-driven by the Erinnys, I fled
To a hotel, pursued by all the fledglings
Of Coelus, to listen among the damp anglers,
Their waders off, discussing every angle
Of sport. There on a ridge between Lough Conn,
Lough Cullen, reading *Silva Gaedelica*,
I hurried from shower to shine with wild goat, gad,
Thinking of Maravaun, that royal hermit,
Who wakened himself at night lest he emit
What spirit dreaded.
                            Faithful, yet half undone,
I was hurried by swish and rattle again to London,
Rocked, light-housed in slumber. I had met a force
In ancient Connaught, shape-changing with the dark,
That put away Love's little metaphors,
Hoop-la, quoit, eyelash kiss, quivering dart.
Rhyme-catching as Owen Ruadh O'Sullivan,
Hedge-poet construing more than Latin grammar,
I stepped out fully stripped from a telegram,
Wakened the Muse that afternoon on her divan.

Paupers

I duffered along the main street of Gort,
Pricing the hardware, cartons, tin cans,
Came to a laneway and saw the County
Workhouse, peak-roofed, the lattice windows
Broken, then stopped awhile in a sort
Of dream. Here, paupers beyond my counting,
Rain-driven, trudged to their last resort.

They got up when the harsh bell rang,
Huddled on yard-bench or in ward,
Inmates, whose clothes were grey as snuff,
Talking of airy holidays among
The hills. Once men had been rewarded
For song. Now at Christmas they got plumduff.
Speeches were made and ballads sung.

They gossiped together in English or Irish
Of ancient cures for every illness,
Lussmore, wild camomile, knapweed,
Parsley for gravel and the fireish
Ache, much better than any pills;
Of water-buttercup and tansy,
The Journey to the Well of Wishing.

They told queer stories. At Ballytomane
Castle, a man who had bought a pigling
In Galway, roasted it on a black night:
Soon, an enchanted cat with smig
Nine inches long, clawed at him. Trigger
Of shot-gun clicked, then gelignite
Blew out a phantom with reddish mane.

Poor Johnny Moon was tickled by angels
Laughing like geese, they tweaked the bedclothes,
Poured moonlight into the chamber pot.
His mother collected silver change
And when she wished it, none could close
The door. Her kitchen was a pothouse
With whiskey for the credulous stranger.

Whaney, the miller, dug for a crock
Of gold. The millstone fell on him.
They say there was treasure at Fidoon,
At Kilmacdaugh, the sound of hymning
Inside the Abbey, music of sod
From fairy rath and grassy dun,
A corpse flung out in mockery.

At Ballybriste, a car with headless
Driver rolled by. At Coole, a servant
Had seen a coachful of ladies, their hats
Dotty with feathers. The red, red woman
Of Feackle heard punishment, deserved,
In Kilbecanty cave, clutter of planks
Hurled into the water upon a head.

John Curley, the cartwright, was away
For seven years. A Scripture Reader
Found him on a stone-heap. John showed him
The hawthorn – fragrance weighed it down –
Where music beguiled him to water, reed-grass.
James Saggerton had met the poet,
Dark Raftery, helped him on his way.

John Kieran found a bottle and a rack-comb
That turned him young. His hair was black
Again. A Flannel-seller at Drumcoo
Saw twenty jockeys, all capped, ride fast.
Leaves shook: the pigeons were afraid to coo.
A fog went round and held him fast
Although he could hear the tea-cups in his home.

Men talked of the stuttering Amadaun,
A staring youth, who gives the stroke
That paralyses. At Ryanrush
A woman, dew-faced, in the dawnlight,
Had heard the invisible go by.
'God bless you!' she cried, plucking a rush
For safety as they tallied her shawl.

Women told stories of Biddy Early,
The witch of Feackle, who had a bottle,
In which she spied the comers from the fairs,
The local market-sellers, late and early,
The priest upon his pony at a jog-trot
Preparing to rout her. The troubled brought fairings
And she bespoke both the poor and the great Earl.

The last of her five husbands lay
Abed, drunk all the time, a weakling,
His spat long spent. Whiskey and claret
Were stored there. Heaven-struck laity
Were healed by her on Sundays and week-days.
The oyster sellers limped from Clarenbridge.
Eel-fishers coughed from road to her laneway.

A lady came from seven woods, a lake,
Bringing the inmates twist, snuff, apples,
She took their minds away in a basket,
Left them on feast-days a curranty cake.
Often she came with her poke and sat
On a bench in the yard with them, asking
Questions, hearing story and lay.

Paupers who knew traditional tales
That bulged the pocket of time, grumbled
And groaned over skillet, mug, hoarded
The secret of caves, of sea-woman unscaled,
Merriment of the wake-house, rumble
Of death-coach, forgot their sorrow
In ruins where the banshee wailed.

The House-Breakers

As I was trespassing among the Seven
Woods — sun-beamed gloom and greener shadowings — I
Met with a western wonder. Blue ray severed
The stillness twice. Was it a spirit that eyed me
Or the great Peacock that Yeats made out of pride?
Leaf-hidden. I saw him in sky-blue waterproof
Flash as he crossed a lawn with rod, gaff, basket:
Around wide steps the marigolds were basking.

Later in a small house across the road,
He talked to me of Walter Savage Landor
And, then, of the Jacobeans. Upright, he rode
The classical mount, though portly as a landlord,
Brown shooting-jacket unbuttoned, waved his hand.
The board was set, the dishes in a row
And I sat down to lunch. His young wife, George,
Left us together. Still in that Georgian mansion,

Chimneyed in woods across the way, he spoke
Of Japanese processions, medieval
Costume and masks. I saw a dazzling spoke
Of the Great Wheel. A mile off, cottage eaves
Were ready for nesting. Rafters were evened.
The local carpenter worked with gimlet, spokeshave.
At fifty the poet had married Miss Hyde-Lees
And bought that Norman Tower at Ballylee.

Woods, that had scattered leaves, Protestant tracts,
Cut down, big house thrown out on the roadside.
Hatred's, that well-known Irish firm of Contractors,
Counted the lumbering lorries with their load.
Darkening skies were Michelangelo'd
With muscular cloud. Blake prophesied. Chain, tractor,
Left the Unburnable Wood. Bird-flocks were plaintive
That year. Ann Gregory made no complaint.

One David Frame, adventurer from Scotland,
Came over, bought up many mansions, ransacked them,
Stripped roofs of valuable lead. Scotfree,
Through all the land the quick-bid rascal ran:
More ruins bowing to that cateran
Who took brass knocker, marble, flooring, wainscot
From Henry Grattan's house in Enniskerry,
A nation's gift, despoiled Meath, Cork, Clare, Kerry.

There is a weedy plot at Laracor:
Once cottage, where Stella resided with Mrs Dingley,
Busy with dairy, preserves and cordials,
Listening on Sabbath morn to the ding-dong
Over the hush of pasture, birding dingle:
Decanus putting on gown and surplice. Accordion
Is merry in the twilight there. The County
Council of Meath has closed the long account.

At evening in her villa, Mrs Delaney
Would entertain her guests, fill tea-cup, wine-glass,
And hear the Dublin gossip, dressed in delaine,
Gay as her paper-flowers, in Glasnevin,
There Swift and the Doctor riddled. (That glasshouse
Was shattered by our nuns, though Time delayed.)
Swift grumbled a lot about his servant, Patrick,
Helping himself from the side-board in St Patrick's.

Shadowy things are rubbled in Hoey's Court
Where the Dean was born. Indigent as an usher,
The great man rose. Cabinet, courtiers,
Were in his ink-well. Greatness is ushered out:
Birthplace of Clarence Mangan. Ussher's house has
Three storeys down. Sky shows more courtesy.
Of Thomas Moore, no longer any sign:
Only a public-house with a new sign.

What of John Philpot Curran, orator,
Patriot, wit; his daughter, Sarah, writing
Lover-letters to Robert Emmet? House and orchard
Are low, her grave once blessed by Protestant rites.

Loreto nuns, believing we are right,
Proud of bad buildings, chapel, oratory,
That shame-cut stone in Celtic-Romanesque,
Bought up the land and let their cattle roam there.

Mayor, Aldermen and councillors detect
Georgian crack and strain in Merrion Square;
Before they can be found. Young architects
Copy out modern plans with ruler, square.
Contractors nod. Has anyone been squared?
Official, night-student from our Technical
School? Iron balustrade, high fanlight, storey,
Are gone. New glass and concrete end their story.

The Uncommissioned

We, who are old in craft, look down
Over an unredeeming shoulder –
Our hope long past – as Orpheus
Into the distant abstract where song,
Still daylit, endears the arms of Dis,
Forgetful of the exterior cold,
Meridean mouth too often kissed.
If notes of the lyre draw a withered sound
From the evergreen, who will inspire
The mind, what patron commission or fee us?

Gerard Manley Hopkins

Glasnevin has a neglected grave:
An English poet, who was converted, ordained,
Lies there; no laurifer, no graven
Angel above a name disdained
For years. The weeds sprung up, few pensive.
Tell me, Loyolans, what recompense
Had Manley Hopkins? Who took the measure
Of his extraordinary measure?
What compound helped him to escape –
Christ-you-knocked – from our Land-war-inscape?

Song for Cecilia

Before I touch those young lips
And our goodbye was sealed,
Then lightly franked by their lipstick
Within the lift, Cecilia
Half-smiled, pressed Button G
And switched the current on.
No ordinary occurrence:
That kiss without a sound
Became an apogee
Just as we reached the ground.
In kindness to an elder,
So much must be withheld,
I'll think of a little story.
One night at Liberty Hall,
A lift no finger may halt,
Descends from the fifteenth storey
And keeps our kiss so long,
We part with a shy 'So long!'

Afterthought

As I went down by the Custom House,
I thought of the duties on make-up
Young women are accustomed to.
Happy that day, I tried to make up
A parcel for Cecilia,
Then swore at every lip-tint, new shade.
What lovelier crimsons does she conceal
That put all lipstick in the shade?

Nunc Dimittis

It is her lovely voice, I
Hold, whenever we part,
Sharing one breath, silenced
By lips that dare not part.
Suppose in that sweet confusion,
They opened unashamed
And mine did just the same,
Touching moist syllable
On her tongue-tip
Lightly, would she refuse
What others have permitted,
Run from the purlieus
Of her alarm, church-shadowed,
Whispering: 'Nunc dimittis'?

The Knot

No, surgeon, not
The genital knot.
When rubber glove
Has twisted love,
Wives are a week-end;
Body is weakened.
Soon age will ape
The branches, jape
Land-girls below.
Better lie low!

At the Dáil

In a reply to Mr Haughey
Echo confused hee-haw with haw-hee,
Bold cry that brings down rain on crop,
Muddies the latest hunting-crop.
What Minister for Agriculture
Has ever donkey'd such difficulty?
He will not meet those ageing farmers
Because he thinks they have walked too far,
Ignores the fists that dig, sow, thresh.
They sleep and wake upon his threshold,
Exposed to uncivil cuffs of Winter.
He looks, heat on, from a Government window.
Above, a tattered Union Jack
Proclaims the haughty rule of Jack-boot.

Above Party

(At the opening of the new Abbey Theatre, 1966)

'I am a stayer,' declared
Our Chief, in drolling aside
That bonfired the hills of Clare.
Stalls cheered. History sighed.
But Gallery had won:
'You're not the only one!'
How often he has stayed
Where every soul is staid,
Talking with Bishop, Head
Of Missionary Order:
High up with lowered head,
Pleasantly peering down
At Mother Superior.
He was our Liberator
Once, sternly disobeyed
What Hierarchy bade.
Bell threatened, did not dare
To ding-dong in Kildare
And excommunicate
The man who loved our Kate.
Candle went out. His Party
Boggled on platforms, parted
From principle, forgot
His words. They persecuted
Irregulars who had fought
For him, put down revolt
Showed up their volte-face,
Untroubled by a thought
Of Eamonn-an-Cnuic.
Few heard the rifles click:
Twelve men were executed,
A boy was hanged. Secret
Newspaper Censorship
Unarmed all. Do not seek
Lime on their riddled bodies,
Torn pamphlets. Lifting censers,

Mount with our Man of God;
After their smoke has blown
His soul up and no one prays
For it, columns will praise
His courage. When European
Cities were scattered to blazes
And skies gave blow for blow
As hate of the Great Powers
Changed banknotes into gunpowder,
He kept our country at peace,
Despite the lies and blame.
In age he bowed to the Church –
Not to the threats of Churchill.

Black, White and Yellow

Let Asia rattle with monstrous arms,
Democrats kiss baby-in-arms,
Pull pigtail, ribbon, pinch cheek without down,
Scattering torture, napalm in downpour,
Only when skinning a small nation
From safeties air-granted by its neighbour.
Why should good conscience be ashamed
Of scorching bunker, sky-raked, ash-aimed?
Liberty, booked up on campus, burns, too.
Young conscript stares at his burial
Number. Look, Peace, red map in fist,
Calls up its ghost, the pacifist!
Big Chief, Ku-Kluxed by his doughty gunmen,
Plays peekabooo, back-door bogey, doubtful
Of hymnal guitar, southern riot,
Horse-trampled student, Lutheran writher.
He fears a minor operation –
Junk smithereened by our naval ratings,
Reed-village, rice-crop, forestry, gutted –
Lest scalpel show his lack of guts.
Spring-heeled, our hate with a single vault

Has hitlered the isolating vault
For anxious satellites to copy
Down there, in desert, bush: while cops,
Concealed by our planetary black-in,
Discount reports of white men, black men
Shot dead in our streets; corporals
Roster the thousands of yellow corpses
Far jungles bring back to life; victims
Who boast La Belle France was bamboozled
By lob-fire cunningly bamboo-celled –
And claim unnatural victory.

The Council of Churches

(A serious trifle)

Now skirts are up
And girls are bare-kneed,
Gladness is meant.
Let foul Iago
Whisper of tupping,
Unturban a Moor;
Elderly men
Who can no longer
Faire l'amour
Or have a go
As years ago,
Despite their need to,
Only succeeding
In dreams, when wrongly
Caressed, lip-tempted
By succuba, waken,
Weak, ashamed
Until they remember
The faithless member
And bless the naked,
Adorable act,
Sigh for lack of

It. Humour is coarse
Because the duct
Has a double use,
Yet joy at its source
Was never deuced.
So let them tell
Anglican youngsters,
Waiting for Tele,
That all besung,
Carven in temples
Of India, Greece,
Rome – ambering ember,
Tapering grease –
However ancient,
Cannot be shent.

Love, Joy, Peace

Unseen evangel
Who kept on writing
His *Love, Joy, Peace*
Along our pavements
With only a piece
Of common chalk
In an ageing hand,
Was surely right
By a long chalk
Whenever he bent
From darkness, wrote
Each word by rote.

Rousseau

I

How soon would that awkward boy
Forget the decrees of Calvin,
Take to the roads of Savoy,
Meadowing ways, vineyards?
Romantic scenery
Had opened the Alpine book
For the first time. He looked,
Read much, came to a courtyard
At dark-fall; a winged mansion.
Knock dished him a kitchen supper.
Genius, not yet a footman.
Winter velured the curtains:
Madame de Warren taught him
A measured prose, good manners,
Correctness when he waited
Upon her. Folios sought
Him, music. Late on a November
Night, Madame, lifting a skirt-hem,
Smiled, beckoned him upstairs
To her bed and with much patience
Gave ignorance a lesson.
He would improve, lean less on
Her. Nature was relieved.
The classical would yield
To the new, the romantic idea:
Irregular verb, sweet noun.
Another Heloise
Would lie at length beneath
Him, hear the forest sound
For miles, before the wreath
Had withered his renown.

II

Pale, lank, in bottomed wig,
Lover at night, lackey
By day, how could he tell
Madame, without a wigging,
That he was discontented?
Natural innocence
Could bless – and yet he lacked
Pickle of kindness kept
By morning pang. Schoolmistress
In search of riggishness
Had often let down his breeches,
Put him across her knee,
Pulled shirt-tail up and caned
Him into puberty,
Sharing the pleasure, the pain,
That squirmed beneath her switching
Until the momentary
Flow of the last stroke
Made both of them ashamed
Again.
　　　　　What women would rue so
Dearly the pen of Rousseau:
Poor orphan of Urorrhea
Whose fame was European?

In the Rocky Glen

Rakishly in her sports-car,
Miss Mollie Garrigan
　　　Came round the bend
　　　Of the Rocky Glen,
Clapped brake on, lingered, crossed
Her legs, then lightly tossed
　　　A curl at us. Startled
　　　We saw one garter

On a thigh so radiant,
We warmed to the radiator.

Two poets, young, unwary,
What could we do but stare,
    Secretly eye it,
    Pretend the sky was
Her garage? We kept to the left
And there, with a smile, she left us,
    Drawn bow took aim
    And pinked our shame.
O was it the brat with the quiver
Who made our senses quiver?

We felt the prick, a limpid
Gaze mocking our double limp.
    How could I have guessed
    I would be the guest
Of the god, that his missile would glow
Once more in the County of Wickow
    As I lay in bed,
    Bow-twangled, ready,
That soon with Mollie beside
Me, ache would be mollified?

I heard her wash and prepare:
No need, for she was as bare
    As I was, to bolt
    The door. Bolster
Had hidden her crêpe-de-chine nightdress
Displeased by so much whiteness,
    Because in our contest
    There was nothing at all on
My handsome, my black-haired darling
Except a new pair of garters.

The Bolshoi Ballet

Romantic divertissement, ballets
Bring verse old-fashioned as swan, cygnet,
Powder-pale brides that Gautier
Imagined. Baton lifts. At a signal,
Silent dancers obey the composer:
      Pirouette, on the points, pose.

Gliding from sylvan shade come swans for
The stage ripples its waters. Lightly
The corps-de-ballet in a white waltz,
Hover of gauze and feather, alights
So delicately, all seem made
      Of air in the shape of maidens.

The puppets of Coppelia
Wound up to click of clock-work,
Are footing in cloak and copatain
Moujik in high boots, wife with gay clocks,
Must squat to show her drawers. Fokine
      Put turns into their folk-dance.

Ethereal in bridal veil
The wilis glimmer from the graveyard,
Their fatal love of no avail.
Luring young men, they keep a yard
Of silk from them, sink into clay
      As though the trap-door claimed them.

The fantoccini in *The Toyshop*
With prices on them, tomboy, urchin,
Tumble from shelf. They flirt. They toy.
Shopkeeper ogles, gigantic chop
On knuckles, extinguishes the candles
      That mock their knees in the can-can.

At Covent Garden, I watched Massine
Leap from the barber's shop. Razor
Could flash no quicker. I had seen
Those thirty seconds of ballet raise
To greatness the lather of daily task
    In *La Boutique Fantasque.*

Love went out of the window, clad
In pink, Nijinsky sprang to nothing,
Stalls, gallery, they say, were mad
As he was later, a broken thing.
Applauding audiences rose:
    La Spectre de la Rose!

What of Alicia Markova
In entrechat, glissade, fouette:
The ever-slowly-swanning Pavlova,
Black drapes, a spot, her only set?
Those Russian dancers never slipped
    However quick the slipper.

Red gelatine cragging the Bröcken,
Young witches kicking up their sabots,
Showing white fork to buck-goat, brock,
Greasing the broomstick for the Sabbath
Bundled in rage, borne off by demons;
    Dance of the unredeemed.

Romantic divertissement, ballet.
The stalls, are vacant, gilded boxes;
Audiences, dancers, gone away.
The dolls are lifeless in their boxes
The iron lid has been clapped down
    And only darkness is clapping.

New Liberty Hall

Higher than county lark
Can fly, a speck that sings,
Sixteen-floored Liberty Hall
Goes up through scaffoldings
In memory of Larkin,
Shot Connolly. With cap
On simple head, hallmark
Of sweat, new capitalists
Rent out expensives suites
Of glassier offices,
Babel'd above our streets,
The unemployed may scoff, but
Workers must skimp and scrape
To own so fine a skyscraper,
Beyond the dream of Gandon,
Shaming the Custom House
The giant crane, the gantries.
Labour is now accustomed
To higher living. Railing
Is gone that I leaned against
To watch that figure, tall and lean,
Jim Larkin, shouting, railing.
Why should he give a damn
That day for English grammar,
Arm-waving, eloquent?
On top, a green pagoda
Has glorified cement,
Umbrella'd the sun. Go, da,
And shiver in your tenement.

In O'Connell Street

One night when the east wind had sharpened
New lights in the fifth and eleventh storeys
Of Liberty Hall, I glimpsed the liftmen
Not yet in uniform. The Liffey
Frothed and Guinnessed as I came from Store Street.
Coldness kept thinly to the one key
Of wintriness that was all sharps.
Cornered by a gust at O'Connell Street,
Past the Four Angels, where bus conductors
Leaned against a bank-door near Forté's
Saloon, I saw a procession of forty
Or more poor people, shabby, ill-fed,
Struggling along with hope, unfed up,
In the middle of the street, some holding
Torn bits of paper and old cardboard;
Few on the pavement, hardly a car.
'Our babies die!' 'We have no homes.'
I read their grief. They had been put out
(But politicians are never put out)
And housed in an old British barracks,
Chill dormitory, one gas-stove, WC.
Men, women, apart: the big door barred
At ten o'clock. Where all could see,
How might young couples go to bed?
Their children were sent to Industrial
Schools, paid for by the State, our Bedlam
Of faith and charity. The dust,
The mucus, of Empire that cries 'Atishoo!'
Has blanketed our Politicians.
Displeased by those who have made a stir,
Mr O'Malley, Minister
For Health, defends our Ill-fare State.
I read in a cloud his public statement,
Stare at my hand which had shaken his
At Gort. He glibs our hysteria,
Denounces the marchers as malcontents
And now they shiver, protest from tents

On a waste of rubble near Mountjoy
Square, with a fine view of the mountains
Like J.M. Synge. Once a hard chaw
In his despair of truth had chalked
On a long wall near the workhouse
At Loughinstown in letters so large
They might have been scrawled by a seer at large,
Or manifested in God's own writing,
Quotation from His Book of Words:
The Poor have no Friends, only their Rights.
I saw in the gleam that comes from a poem,
Dublin, Calcutta, Singapore.
Still in that cloud I held my hand out,
Thought of our Minister and his hand-out.

The New Tolerance

Now that ecumenical pates
Are suffering from modern knocks
And much that was anticipated
By our Erasmus and John Knox,
We cannot keep at a sniffy distance
From one another. Methodist,
High Anglican have got to exchanging
Church, hall and smiles, discussion of change,
For the True Church, it seems, is one
Of many. Brother Augustine has won
And so we may become observers
Of different sects and services:
Lutherans, Presbyterians,
The Holy Rollers, Wesleyans,
Low Church, Episcopalians,
Dissenters, Unitarians,
Likewise the Sabbatharians,
Wee Frees and Congregationalists,
Genevan creeds of Non-Conformists
And the odd ones time will unlist:

The Nazarenes, the Irvingites,
The Brownites, the Paisleyites,
Moravians and Mennonites,
The Plymouth Brethren, Latter Day
Saints, Latitudinarians,
Mormons, who had a choice like Shem
Of several wives in their chemises,
The Second Comers, Seventh Day Adventists,
Faith Healers or Christian Scientists,
Those who believe in a new Pentecost,
Aimée Macpherson, whose Temple cost all
Those dollars, the Salvation Army
Calling street-sinners to the arms
Of Jesus, poor Johanna Southcott,
Who prophesied that she would drop
The Holy Infant but died of dropsy,
Leaving an empty box and cot,
Jehovah Witness, in his watch-tower,
Each man, winder of his own wrist-watch,
All other evangelical sects
That have no clock-house, bell or sexton:
Our older Churches, Coptic, Syriac,
Disputing over verb or accent,
The gold-voiced Greek Orthodox,
The Russian, the Armenian.
All those who have found so many meanings
In Gospel, rite, doxology,
The Bible in a public frenzy.
I went on a Sunday with the Friends
To an old Meeting House; sunshine
Of Maryland windowed there. Shyly
I heard the words of Holy Writ,
Sat on a plain bench, void in spirit.

A Statue for Dublin Bay

Led heavenward by a big ganger
Or legionary, Dublin dockers
Have saved each week from their pay-dockets
And overtime until they have got
A sum of twenty thousand pounds,
Copper and silver turned to ingot,
Daily unloading or holding cargoes,
Handling ton, hundredweight and poundage,
While heavy lorry, or car goes
Laden with merchandise
And sailors whittle the distance, splicing
Their ropes. With crane and mighty knocking,
Faith will erect on cockleshell rock
A statue of the Virgin Mary
With solemn Latin, customary
Hymn: glorious, tall, in blue-and-white,
Skylit by day, illumined at night-time,
Whether billows are rising, falling:
Piety manifest to all
Within the tideway.
                          But now the crux.
Our hyperdulia is mundane.
The Mother of God will have a lower
Place, for the Cardinals below
On earth have remembered the Lux Mundi
And so our idol will look to seaward,
Proclaiming nothing but heresy.

The Subjection of Women

Over the hills the loose clouds rambled
From rock to gully where goat or ram
Might shelter. Below, the battering-ram
Broke in more cottages. Hope was gone
Under the legendary Maud Gonne,
For whom a poet lingered, sighed
Drove out of mist upon a side-car,
Led back the homeless to broken fence,
Potato pot, their one defence,
And, there, despite the threat of Peelers,
With risky shovel, barrow, peeling
Their coats off, eager young men
Jumped over bog-drain, stone, to mend or
Restore the walls of clay; the police
Taking down names without a lease.
O she confronted the evictors
In Donegal, our victory.
When she was old and I was quickened
By syllables, I met her. Quickens
Stirred leafily in Glenmalure
Where story of Tudor battle had lured me.
I looked with wonder at the sheen
Of her golden eyes as though the Sidhe
Had sent a flame-woman up from ground
Where danger went, carbines were grounded.

Old now by luck, I try to count
Those years. I never saw the Countess
Markievicz in her green uniform,
Cock-feathered slouch hat, her Fianna form
Fours. From the railings of Dublin slums,
On the rickety stairs the ragged slumped
At night. She knew what their poverty meant
In dirty laneway, tenement,
And fought for new conditions, welfare
When all was cruel, all unfair.
With speeches, raging as strong liquor,
Our big employers, bad Catholics,

Incited by Martin Murphy, waged
War on the poorest and unwaged them.
Hundreds of earners were batoned, benighted,
When power and capital united.
Soon Connolly founded the Citizen Army
And taught the workers to drill, to arm.
Half-starving children were brought by ship
To Liverpool from lock-out, hardship.
'Innocent souls are seized by kidnappers,
And proselytisers. Send back our kids!'
Religion guffed.
                    The Countess colled
With death at sandbags in the College
Of Surgeons. How many did she shoot
When she kicked off her satin shoes?

Women rose out after the Rebellion
When smoke of buildings hid the churchbells,
Helena Moloney, Louie Bennett
Unioned the women workers bent
At sewing machines in the by-rooms
Of Dublin, with little money to buy
A meal, dress-makers, milliners,
Tired hands in factories.

                    Mill-girls
In Lancashire were organised,
Employers forced to recognise them:
There was the cause of Eva Gore-Booth,
Who spoke on platform, at polling-booth,
In the campaign for Women's Suffrage,
That put our double beds in a rage,
Disturbed the candle-lighted tonsure.
Here Mrs Sheehy-Skeffington
And others marched. On a May day
In the Phoenix Park, I watched, amazed,
A lovely woman speak in public
While crowding fellows from office, public
House, jeered. I heard that sweet voice ring
And saw the gleam of wedding ring

As she denounced political craft,
Tall, proud as Mary Wollstonecraft.
Still discontented, our country prays
To private enterprise. Few praise
Now Dr Kathleen Lynn, who founded
A hospital for sick babes, foundlings,
Saved them with lay hands. How could we
Look down on infants, prattling, cooing,
When wealth had emptied so many cradles?
Better than ours, her simple Credo.

Women, who cast off all we want,
Are now despised, their names unwanted,
For patriots in party statement
And act make worse our Ill-fare State.
The soul is profit. Money claims us.
Heroes are valuable clay.

Miss Rosanna Ford

On the third day, a lodger broke in the door
Of the bed-sitting-room. He stopped, aghast:
Half dressed, almost deceased on the floor,
Because she had no shilling for the gas,
Blue-handed, freezing, Miss Rosanna Ford lay.
There in that room, to let now, the cold
Stared at the intruder, kept its hold.
Spinster of 37 Wexford Street,
She lived alone, aloof at eighty-four,
So indigent she seldom could afford
Sufficent warmth or food for the cupboard shelf.
Furniture auctioned, inarticulate;
The window whitely fronded by Arctic wind:
Outside the passing motor cars, the Ford vans,
Were hushed by the funeral of the late snow.
A church-bell, tongue in cheek, remarked the date
And Christmas presents in fashionable stores,
Dropping their pretty veils of crêpe, vanished.

The New Cathedral in Galway

Here is the very spirit
Of hard-drinking, sea-mouldering Galway:
A building ugly as sin
To prove the Boys sincere
And still a decent crowd:
Another thorn for the Crown
Of Thorns, a large gall
In the Sponge on Spear.

A Reply

Don Quixote, if I
Remember rightly,
After he rode from
The dust of roads
Along the plain,
Ignored the millers
Unbagging grain,
But attacked the mills
That had become
Their feudal lords
Confounding all comers
With horde'd blows.

In Kildare Street

On a spring day as I stepped along Kildare Street
To the National Library, eager once more
For sunshine of the octosyllabic measure,
Arcaded with graceful pillars, sounded for use
By Calderón in one of his sacred dramas,

El Magico Prodigioso, which tells
How Cyprian, a young philosopher,
Went out from Antioch when the pious crowds
Were trumpeted to the new expensive Temple
Of Jupiter, and thinking of the new faith
In a small wood near the sky-visited grove
Of Daphne, despising the trumpery, the garlands,
Met by a tree the Spirit of Evil in short
Festival busking, disputant, wit:
Suddenly I saw him approaching me, a hated
Man, elderly, stout. Somehow, I thought at once
Of Genevan black and white, took his clear glance
In mine so troubled with youth, knowing he was
Sir John Mahaffy, Provost of Trinity
College; still in that academic wood, reflected:
'He walks too certainly. How can he put
Away the pagan stroke, the seizure, clot,
That lurks by lamp-post or near four-poster?'
                                                    I stopped

To stare after him, admire. My wrist
Held centuries of reform. The glow of
High grammar – for how else can I find a name
For it – had purified my mind. Astonished
In all that moment, quite gone from traditional hatred,
I had become one of our minority.

At the House of Commons

Foot-handed, I waited in the Lobby,
Poor relative from Athlone or lob
In boots, for the Father of the House.
Too soon I would hear his greeting: 'How do
You do?' and ask him weakly:
'Sir, can I write for your new Weekly?'
Quickly I saw him talling before me
With a smile, then, frown: T.P. O'Connor
In summer-grey frockcoat. Three, four,

Members came out. One glanced from the conning
Tower of a submarine in the foam-race,
Marked me; a small man, determined, chubbed.
I recognised him – Mr Churchill,
And drew back servile as our race.
Darkly, that young-man-killing Warlock,
Lord Kitchener who had no Last Post –
Drowned finger pointing from a ripped poster –
Asked: 'What did *you* do in the Great War?'

The Vocation

On the grass near the old sluice-gate
She sat and watched the water slew
Below, excited, happy. 'I've
Only a day left now. Indeed,
Scarce time,' she smiled, 'for a good deed.'
She heard far down the quiet tinkle
Of a pool, and then, behind the ivied
Wall of the mill, a drunken tinker
And his trull squabbling, got up, ran
To plead with them, all little random
Words.
      Religion, cold, unfeeling
Came nearer, darkening the fields.
The man muttered, the woman wailed
Into her shawl. Both shambled away.

Angelica was not robust
Enough to scrub the convent floors,
That ritual of humble pride.
An old nun handed her a duster
Or pushed her a tin of polish, pried:
And still her visions were sweetly floral
As she drifted towards the altar scent.
But in a year she was sent away.
Sometimes I see her in a car,

Ashamed to meet acquaintances,
Unhappy, her prayers of no avail,
Beyond the reach of her dear saints.
No longer is her young soul carried
To joy. The Mass bell will not ring
For her. She must not see through the veil,
Wear for the first time a marriage ring.

No Keepsake

Strip off that lovely wedding gown
Worn only once, give it to them.
Sisters will cut, unpleat, re-hem
Satin or silk in sewing-school,
Making it into surplice, alb
Or chasuble for missioners,
Who bring the native to Calvary.
Impatient husband, do not frown
On such a gift. Respect the veil.
Stop, do not lift that fearful tulle
So quickly! No white Father errs
Though tempted by all that is forbidden,
In tropic heat, on runners' trail,
Or dreams of nuptial pleasures hidden
Under long skirt, retiring train.

On a Bright Morning

A blackbird sat on a sun-spot
Warming his wings. Down by the bridge,
Flying from our elm, fat pigeon
                Had slowly got
                Himself into hot
Water. Along the garden walk

The scattered crumbs still lay.
Up in a pine, magpie was talking
Too much. I whistled in vain, for the sparrows,
After a dust-bath under the rose-buds,
Had gone on a holiday
To the river bend. I saw them play
  A game of 'Shall we?'
   'Yes, Let's,' beside the shallows,
Then feather the drops to spray.

The Last Ditch

Was it an engineer
Busy over a plan
To bring the city nearer,
Who tore up aquatic plants
With fountain pen, would not let
Inches of rivulet run
Where Spring had set a sill
Of flowerets? I could name
Among those little neighbours
Of mine only a few
Of what our County Council
Considers to be refuse;
Mare's tail that must have pined
A million years to be pine
Or spruce, young reed and flag
That helped me when spirit flagged.
Duckweed, sagittaria,
Might have spread there by road-tar.
They would have been known to Wordsworth
But what are my words worth now?
I jingle while men pipe down
Delight and look at the mist in
The southwest, think of the missing.
Beyond the pneumatic drill,
Small things uncurl a damp tendril,
Up there at Piperstown.

The Knuckleduster

Blackthorn was pinking, the sloe
Ripening slowly
As I came to the Hill of Slane,
Thought of the nearby slain.

Ink-horned by religion,
We fled at Boyne and Oldbridge,
With an English king,
Exiled our own kindred.

On Sunday in chapel
I read a black chapter,
Smoke column, massacre:
The Protestant Bible
In Irish at Masstime.
See how our massive walls
Crack! Modernist Bishops
Blame Faith in its dotage.
Better to imbibe
Pints in the boozing shop;
For Percy Bysshe Shelley,
Who lay among shells,
Prophesied the New Age.

Angels knocked angels
Down. The *Knuckleduster*
In Aungier Street
Knows 'hath' from 'dost'.

Lactuca Prodigiosa

The Wise Woman, who lived beside the mill-pond
In the small cottage, had stolen the delf-egg
From their one hen and hid it on a shelf
Between the tea-caddy and the box of Beecham's Pills.
Often John met her wisdom as he pondered
Where crested grebe swam into the beyond.
One day she told his wife of a secret salad
So crisp – he might have got another lad,
Clovering in a field near that English wood,
Gone home beside the garden plums to lie on
The bed: a dish of lettuce with dandelion,
Sage, mint and tansy, endive, chervil, nasturtium
Leaf, hard-boiled egg, thin chives, parsley, cucumber
Tipping of thyme, sliced carrot, beetroot, onion,
Tomato, sorrel, rue, and early scallions,
Mustard-and-cress, banana, apple, orange,
Pale chicory, rosemary and potherbs,
In a great beechen bowl, so chilly, hot,
It made their appetite the greedier:
Ashine with olive oil, with vinegar,
Over ground nuts, Jane grated Parmesan.
John thought of a Middle Irish tale the scribe
Had kept in Latin because it was too ribald,
The first account in our country of artificial
Insemination; but not by cattle officials.
A tale of Monasterboice.
                            There was a king's
Daughter who came to wash her face, neck, shoulders
One morning in July beside a pure cold spring.
Hidden within an oak-tree, a spry robber
Was peeping at her modesties that bobbed
Up, down. He almost jumped on wild violets
To rape her, feared to lose his head. Elated
By lust, he closed his eyes and violated
The princess in his mind. *Dum masturbavit
Et, subito, ejecit. Semenis gutta
Cadit ad holum.* That drop slid by ill-luck

Into a lettuce and lay within a ruck
Of leaves as she was stooping sweetly to pluck
The dewy head. At evening she ate the salad
And never was simple supper so delicious,
For she was innocent and unsuspicious
Until her morning sickness came. She bore
Boldly in her due time a red-headed lad
Now known to us as blessed Fechin of Fore.

John and his wife delighted in such salad
Till conjugal duty became a constant sally.

Gay from a spinney, a birded copse, the fauns
Came in a merchant troop. Their shag was fawn.
They chased the white rounds of the nymphs, their hooves
Clicking by privet hedge. They shook the brake
With frisk and fisk. John heard the rascals break
Into the open where the last trail of a Roman
Water-course glittered in grass nearby his home –
A nudist colony. They bandied with dryads
In scrub oak that none had entered for centuries.
The couple marvelled. Thessalian kisses were dry
Between their lips. They listened to the pad of centaurs
And sniffed at times ammoniacal scent,
Then laughed – Greek stable manners were so low
Behind the gate-post of the bungalow.
Cantharides are not more certain when July is out.
So John and Jane had to avoid such lettuce,
Take due precaution with pessary and let,
Pray – lest Priapus show his snout again.

Aisling

Morning had gone into the wood before me,
The drip-drop answering its ray. I saw
Greenness that lettered greener greenness open
With sudden beam as if trees had been sawn down.

Glints echoed from the thickness as I followed
Under the green-brown twistiness by twisted
Fern-rusty paths and, dazzling out of foresight,
A woman rounded whitely from the mist.

Unbraided tresses, gold chasing of her curls,
Encircled her with light that feared no error,
Half hid untouchable breasts as white as curds
Or April snow we see on Errigal
And Nephin, restraining all that glory of swirl.
Her nipples were pinker than the bramble flower.
One slender hand below her navel curved
Lightly to drape her virtue with a cloudlet.

Leaf-stirring in that wood, I asked: 'Are you
A goddess come from Greece, Perimela,
Tella, or dearest of the Nine, Euterpe?
Sky-woman from our land? One of the pair
Who fled to love, the mountain-lost, yew-hidden
Grainne or Deirdre who threw away a sail
North of Loch Etive with a noble youth' –
I frowned – 'their widowed bodies given for sale?'

She smiled and took away her happy hand:
The red-gold curlets changed to modesty.
'Are you the morn personified in handsome
Robes?' 'Veilless, you see again my naked body.
Do you not recognise me now?' she answered,
Unrobed. I heard the ripples of a beck
Repeat the syllables of her high glance
That was all books and every beckoning.

I read her name that held my hushed voice, saying:
'When shall I feel at last upon this brow
Visible comfort of your touch, presage
Of a single leaf plucked from the sacred bough,
Though years of pen and disappointment press age
On it?' She vanished. Suddenly for the taking
I glimpsed Hesperidean fruit beyond our age,
Then, morning emptied my grasp and wakened me.

Eire

(After Ua Bruadair)

Lady of the bright coils and curlings,
    Intricate turns of your body
Have pleased the foreign churls
    Who kept a bodyguard.
Though middle-aged and long a matron,
    The wife of Nial, the fearless,
You played the harlot with men you hated
    And those who loved you dearly.

You smiled at them, calm stately woman,
    Unsmocked your noble limbs,
Conferred with the Saxon, old in statecraft.
    The wife of Eiver — robed as
A young queen in lime-white mansions —
    Cast modesty in a corner,
Betraying the heroes who were vanquished
    By clatter of hide, war-horn.

You were the wife of Lewy the courageous,
    And never lacked a husband.
Cairbre, Cuchullin, the sage Fionn,
    Felim, no bagman in lust,
Had known the bride of Laery the King,
    And Con the Hundred Fighter.
Too late the gleam of coil and of ringlet,
    Is changed into a sigh.

The Normans went under your mantle,
    Whenever a stronghold burned,
And you pushed back their basinets,
    Cathedral mail, spurning
The meadows inching with dew, the thickets
    At dawn, the river harbours,
Hill-bounding of the hunted prickets,
    For wanton snirt and farding.

The Binding

God soon will humble your pride, pucker your cheeks,
And bring the wife of Fintan and Diarmuid – flaxed
With hair-dye – to the church door, ragged, meekly,
Her placket no longer open to the Saxon.

A Jingling Trifle

(After Ua Bruadair)

At Lammas the wealthy snug their joy, then lock up
Mint sovereigns, abuse the wranglesome keyhole
Of trunks. The London girls ungarter their mauve clocks,
Open thin legs for gallants, dangle bare toes.

Sanicle droops beneath the apple-growths
Where hedgehops roll themselves abed in the mould
The fullers brag, toping with saddlers. Late leavers
Gulp from the ale-pot, wipe froth, stumble by corn-sheaves.

Untidy Sive has dropped her apronful of sprouts.
Her husband curses, pulls up her torn skirt
And as she nags him, drags her down and about
To whore her from behind upon all fours.

Crakes are a-speckle in the meadow hollows
Where old men hiding under coltsfoot, wild flowers,
Watch Ragneith, white-bummed in a waiting corner,
Petticoat stained by cramps that clamp her bowels.

Blacksmiths are threading screws with purblind thumbs.
Wash-tubs are iron-ringed as our married women,
And where I stumbled from, straw-footed gaums
Gabble until my daily thoughts are dim.

Unmetrical verse is neither bed nor board.
Whiteboys are hidden safely by the white-thorn.
Mallet is gone that struck the nail into floor-board,
Dutch troops have pinches in their powder horn.

Gib plays with Pit-a-pat in the backroom.
Scholars have wearied of their own conundrums.
Una has bucketed her slops on the landing.
Blanket is warmer stuff that the roll of drums.

False hair in hood is eyeshade for a milch cow.
Chignon for Madam suits her cauldron bottom.
So let the worn-out, the useless, the frayed, the bowed-in,
Patch up the songs that no longer bother me.

The pound is used to falling, the point to boiling.
The rich pass by themselves, all pomp and pump,
The poor still know themselves by blotch and boils:
And dirty water comes first from a new pump.

Bandy-legged, crotchety Sister of our Nine,
Forgive my farrowing words, I've learned to muff
Yet need more delicacies in my decline.
Young Maeve has something better in her muff.

The Binding

Now that no man respects the poetic word
And experience cannot unblind an Irish stare,
Now that the knowledgeable have grown tired,
Jingle-go-jangle is all that I will care for.

The Happy Saint

Lightly noting, Enda sang
A round of psalms at morning-time:
    Virgin had been reborn.
Men sailing by the rocks of Ara
Heard eastward the happy voice that blessed
    The currents of the west.
But jealous saints, the old, the sly ones,
    Were praying that Enda would die.

Lightly humming, Enda smiled
As he washed his face and shaved.
    His head was curly as shavings
Beneath his bench, where he hammered, plied
The plane in his carpenter's shop
    Making a small pent,
While jealous saints, the old, the sly ones,
    Prayed for him to die.

One day, with his monks, he cast the net
As though it dipped into Galilee
    King Herring left the blue lea.
That savoured a broth with shamrock, nettle,
Broiled the fish on a hazel spit
    For a scholar come from Britain.
And the jealous saints, the old, the sly ones,
    Prayed for Enda to die.

All night, three angels looked over his shoulder
As he illumined another Missal.
    Monks tiptoed when he was missing
From Matins, hushed their semi-tones
In chapel. Nobody would wake him.
    Too soon their tears would wake him.
For jealous saints, the old, the sly ones,
    Still prayed for him to die.

Between a psalm and sigh, the young man
Turned weak. Affliction opened the door,
     All scales, bright as Sean Dory.
Tenors were raised; the vespers sung.
Brethren bore him on a litter
     And every wax was lit.
But jealous saints, the old, the sly ones,
     Prayed faster for Enda to die.

Cholera Morbus yellowed his limbs,
Clap burned his sperm with glair and glect,
     Demons beset him, gleeing,
Immodest. Skeleton was limned
Beneath his skin, a brattle of terror.
     Crabs laid in his pubic hair.
Then, jealous saints, the old, the sly ones,
     Prayed louder for him to die.

Tongue out for drop, the stricken sighed
That he was dead. His wits were crazed.
     He clawed stone-bed like a cray-fish.
The body turned upon its side,
Dripped slowly, a corrupted mass
     Of stench that stopped the Mass.
The jealous saints, the old, the sly ones,
     Had known how Enda would die.

The House of Mercy

The beautiful woman is kind, she pleads
For men and their faults, drinking, gambling
And offices against purity.
Her hair is gold as in holy pictures, she wears
A blue-white robe. Ann's daughter, lovely as her mother.
Men fear the torment. The say: 'These two
Console us. We will learn to hate
The body that abuse makes weak.'

Blessed, blessed, to be laid out and carried
In deal to the chapel; happy those
Whose names are read out at Mass.
Had I five pounds to spend
I would change it for my salvation.
Daylight in the House of Mercy, but here
Coughing and wheezing and rheumatism.

Napoleon goes through the snow
And his ballad goes on and on
But the balladmaker is happy at darkfall.
The words are ready in mouth. Hae'pence drop
Into his hat. His stool is next the turf-fire.
Here in the darkness, coughing, wheezing,
And rheumatism. I've put a little by
For tobacco and a pinch of snuff
Hot as the devil's clime from which it came.
The soul, too, comes, from a far place.

Famine has made great clearances
And our language comes to an end.
Beggars wheedle in English at our fairs.
How many coffinships will bring
Emigrants to God's own country?

The Last Irish Snake

Far out to ocean Saint Patrick drove
The snakes from Ireland like a drove
Of shorthorns beyond the Great Blasket
Still clouding, unclouding, mountainous ridges.
He cursed them, tail and blastoderm
And with his crozier, rid
The rocky corners. Coil over coil
Big and small families of outcasts,
Heads still held high, were hurrying,
No time to lay their eggs or cast

A skin, for his Latin lightened, hurled
More bolts at them: chariot-wheels
Rolling downhill from the hub
By bush and boulder as they scattered
With green stripes, yellow dots of charlock,
Land-snakes, water-snakes all hubble-bubble,
Hundreds and hundreds of them scattered by
Jubilant hymn.
                    But one old serpent
Sternly refused to be so servile
And leave Lough Allen, his habitat,
Although it flapped as the holy habit
Of the saint with rage. He showed his fang,
Indignant at these new-fangled ways,
And called to Aesculapius
In vain for he was quickly ousted.
Slowly he scaled and wriggled, eskered
Himself along alluvial soil,
Muddied, a trail of slime. Unsoiled
The water followed with bright reflection
Of intertwining blacks, of golden flecks.
People ten miles away at Roosky
Could hear him unearthing and their roosters
Clapped wings and dropped. The portly monster
Burrowing southward, left Lough Ree.
Wild duck came down, but saw no reeds.
He stopped to untangle at Portumna
And hold a public demonstration.
Scraw, scrub, thornbushes, thistles, briars
Rock, stone, were tossing up and down
As though he were Briarius
Twitched by a hundred dowsing rods,
His only form of rodomontade.
He worked like a huge excavator
With bucketed back digging a cavern
To hide in. Sacred skin was torn
To strips. The water, a brow-white torrent,
Was soon Lough Derg: another lake that
His blood was colouring with lake.
Onward, trundled the great Batrachian

By Foynes, Askeaton, Tarbert, Kilrush
Until the new River Shannon was rushing
South-westward, with small church, shanty,
And farm in flood. He passed Loop Head
And Kerry Head, loop after loop,
Then, left, between those far escarpments,
Day shining on an estuary,
And sank as if he were bedevilled,
Cabling along the ocean bed.

Phallomeda

Aeons ago, before our birth,
The Irish gods, who were coarse and mirthful,
Held their annual sessions on earth.
Late, on a sun-struck day, the Dagda
Strolled into the smoky banquet hall,
Saw on the hook a big cauldron
That twenty black-avised cooks had hauled
 Up, talked with them, bragged.

They poured in bushel and peck of oatmeal
Until the busy flakes silvered, floated.
Wholesome savour and vapour were groating
 As the potstick unsettled them.
He hung there with a gaping mouth,
Appetite blobbing in stirabout
And when it simmered, began to shout
 For an immoderate helping.

With lashings of milk, salt, honey-mingle,
His palate, his gums, were quickly tingling.
He could not be sated by a single
 Helping but called for more.
Spoon was as big as the very ladle,
So fast he swallowed at the table's chin,
Fierce as the Firbogs making a raid
 Till platters piled to a score.

He ate and ate until his stomach
Was swollen as an Orange drum
To which a fife or flute might twurtle.
      And still he ate and ate
More helpings from the pot, gorging
Immortal fondness for thick porridge,
With ladle and spoon, spluttering, splorging
      Plate upon steamy plate.

The gods were watching that banquet
Until the cauldronful had vanished.
The Dagda tumbled into blanket,
      Heavily grunting there.
They heard a Grecian laugh that came
Closer. A naked goddess, shameless
And gamesome, was sharing that shake-down.
      Soon, a gigantic ball,

His stomach was bulging out with gusto
Below her bosom, but his lust
Held him in bonds he could not burst from.
      He clasped her, toppled off,
Rolled over with a double bound
Impatiently trying to mount himself
But was unable to rebound:
      The goddess was on top.

She budded with hope on that mighty paunch,
Pink, white, as he grabbed her by the haunches
So hard that she was scarcely conscious:
      Bonnie bush out of reach.
Then, side by side, they sank. She fumbled
To fire his godhead while he clumsied,
Till she could hear the porridge mumble,
      Slapdash as foreign speech.

Ungracefully, that paradigm,
Who immortalised the glance of Paris,
Lay back again, sprawling her limbs,
      Ready to test tickle

By throb. The huge protuberance
Of gruel diddled her. Tantity
Still held the pair from joy, a yard
     Below, for all her zest.

Peering from doorway, portico,
The gods were laughing at such sport
Until Phallomeda transported
     Herself, in tears, to Greece.
Soon the poor Dagda began to snore.
He dreamed that she was at the doorway,
Smiling. She stripped and tried once more:
     He woke as she succeeded.

So in the words of the Great Mahaffy,
Annalists frolicked with the pen and laughed
At what they saw in the Hereafter,
     Forgetting their horn-beads.
Anticipating Rabelais,
They wrote of the god who lay
With loveliness. I copy that lay,
     Applaud their disobedience.

Impotence

Now that I am almost impotent,
Thought faltering four times out of ten,
And only patience can be tender,
Regular verb is in the past tense.
Disarmed, I lie, a malcontent,
Outside the white-and-crimson tent-flap
Of idle love. I cannot tent
That wound, for all is good intent
And yet desire becomes more wanton
With every failure. Must I want on?
Well, I remember how sinew was tense
And the nearer the kiss, the more intense.

Caresses everwhere prolonged
With come-and-go, all, all, we longed
For. Soon, unable to delay
Smuggle and smugging as we lay
Awake at morning, each second fast
And faster still, we broke our fast
Then sank into a sudden pit,
Knowing that love is but a pittance.
Enwrinkled as the fig-leaf of Cupid,
Bobby can do no more than piddle.
Off clothes: I'll pray to great Priapus,
Although he turn delight to a pus.

A Sermon on Swift and Other Poems

(1968)

A Sermon on Swift

(Friday, 11.30 a.m. 28 April, 1967)

Gentle of hand, the Dean of St Patrick's guided
My silence up the steps of the pulpit, put around
My neck the lesser microphone.

> 'I feel
That you are blessing me, Mr Dean.'

> Murmur
Was smile.

       In this first lay sermon, must I
Not speak the truth? Known scholars, specialists,
From far and near, were celebrating the third
Centenary of our great satirist.
They spoke of the churchman who kept his solemn gown,
Full-bottom, for Sunday and the Evening Lesson,
But hid from lectern the chuckling rhymster who went
Bald-headed, into the night when modesty
Wantoned with beau and belle, his pen in hand.
Dull morning clapped his oldest wig on. He looked from
The Deanery window, spied the washerwomen
Bundling along, the hay carts swaying from
The Coombe, dropping their country smells, the hackney –
Clatter on cobbles – ready to share a quip
Or rebus with Sheridan and Tom Delaney,
Read an unfinished chapter to Vanessa
Or Stella, then rid his mind of plaguey curling –
Tongs, farthingales and fal-de-lals. A pox on
Night-hours when wainscot, walls, were dizziness,
Tympana, maddened by inner terror, celled
A man who did not know himself from Cain.
A Tale of a Tub, Gulliver's Travels, fables
And scatological poems, I pennied them on
The Quays, in second-hand book-stalls, when I was young,
Soon learned that humour, unlike the wit o' the Coffee
House, the Club, lengthens the features, smile hid by
A frown.
       Scarce had I uttered the words,

                                         'Dear Friends,
Dear Swiftians' –
                    When from the eastern window
The pure clear ray, that Swift had known, entered the
Shady church and touched my brow. So blessed
Again, I gathered 'em up, four-letter words,
Street–cries, from the Liberties.
                               Ascend,
Our Lady of Filth, Cloacina, soiled goddess
Of paven sewers. Let Roman fountains, a–spray
With themselves, scatter again the imperious gift
Of self–in–sight.
                    Celia on a close-stool
Stirs, ready to replace her ribs. Corinna,
Taking herself to pieces at midnight, slips from
The bed at noon, putting together soilures
And soft sores. Strephon half rouses from a dream
Of the flooding Tiber on his marriage–night,
When Chloe stoops out unable to contain her
Twelve cups of tea. Women are unsweet at times,
No doubt, yet how can willy–nilly resist
The pleasures of defaulting flesh?
                               My Sermon
Waits in the plethora of Rabelais, since
March veered with the rusty vane of Faith. I had reached
The House of Aries. Soon in the pure ray,
I am aware of my ancestor, Archbishop
Browne, hastily come from Christ Church, to dispel
Error and Popish superstition. He supped
Last night with Bishop Bale of Ossory,
Robustious as his plays, and, over the talk
And malmsey, forgot the confiscated wealth
Of abbeys.
              In prose, plain as pike, pillory,
In octosyllabic verse turning the two–way
Corner of rhyme, Swift wrote of privy matters
That have to be my text. The Lilliputian
March–by of the crack regiments saluting
On high the double pendulosity
Of Gulliver, glimpsed through a rent in his breeches;

The city square in admiration below. But who
Could blame the Queen when that almighty
Man hosed the private apartment of her palace,
Hissed down the flames of carelessness, leaving
The royal stables unfit for Houyhnhnms, or tell (in
A coarse aside) what the gigantic maidens
Of Brobdignab did in their playfulness with
The tiny Lemuel when they put him astride
A pap, broader then the mizzen mast of his
Wrecked ship, or hid him in the tangle below?

Reasonable century of Bolingbroke,
Hume, hundred-quilled Voltaire, Satyr and nymph
Disported in the bosk, prim avenues
Let in the classical sky. The ancient temples
Had been restored. Sculptures replace the painted
Images of the saints. Altars were fuming,
And every capital was amaranthed.
Abstraction ruled the decumana of verse,
Careful caesura kept the middle silence
No syllable dared to cross.
                              Swift gave his savings
To mumbling hand, to tatters. Bare kibes ran after
Hoof as he rode beside the Liffey to sup
At Celbridge, brood with Vanessa in a star-bloomed
Bower on Tory politics, forget
Queen Anne, stride from a coffee-house to Whitehall
And with his pamphlets furrow the battle-fields
Of Europe once more, tear up the blood-signed contracts
Of Marborough, Victualler of Victories;
While in St Patrick's Cathedral the candling clerk
Shifted the shadows from pillar to pillar, shuffling
His years along the aisles with iron key.
Last gift of an unwilling patriot, Swift willed
To us a mansion of forgetfulness. I lodged
There for a year until Erato led me
Beyond the high-walled garden of Memory,
The Fountain of Hope, to the rewarding Gate,
Reviled but no longer defiled by harpies. And there
In Thomas Street, nigh to the busy stalls

Divine Abstraction smiled.
                              My hour, above
Myself, draws to an end. Satiric rhymes
Are safe in the Deanery. So, I must find
A moral, search among my wits.
                                      I have
It.
    In his sudden poem *The Day of Judgment*
Swift borrowed the allegoric bolt of Jove,
Damned and forgave the human race, dismissed
The jest of life. Here is his secret belief
For sure: the doctrine of Erigena,
Scribing his way from West to East, from bang
Of monastery door, click o' the latch,
His sandals worn out, unsoled, a voice proclaiming
The World's mad business – Eternal Absolution.

The Disestablished Church

St Mary's Church is silent now,
As if the window-seeking rays
Of morning came from Paradise Lane
Before a shabby blind had been raised
To show up bedrooms, Sunday parlour,
Easter them with its radiance,
Renew the darts of the Paraclete.
Between the sing-song of sum and noun:

Only the Roman jingle of thirty
Pieces, the crack o' the leather heard
From the Christian Brothers' School around
The corner. Still-framed, the Good Shepherd
Goes on the daily market-round,
Supplying lambs to the butcher, shepping
The trade in brisket, joint and round,
Forgetting the Garden and the Thirst.

(Lashes are red as the long hair of
The Magdalene.) His breeches down,
Boy screams. Another with numbed fingers
Cannot unbuckle his book-strap. Doubt
And fear sit on the bench by numskull,
Exploring with sinful touch the down
Below there, copybook unnumbered.
(Who smears the ointment, faint with longing?)

The punishers in black robes only
Beat harder. One afternoon a bolt
Flooded the gutters. Mysteries
Had fled. I sheltered at the bolted
Protestant church-door: dire misbehaviour.
No angel rolled back the faraway boulder,
A light shone out from misery.
The hand that spared me was its own.

All human-beings will be redeemed.
The clarabella, clavecin,
Are not more sweet to hear in the bout
Of melody when notes are single.
Stuck in that pot of stirabout,
My little spoon at last was singing –
Impudent handle was unbowed,
For consciousness is as we deem it.

Spoon sang the Grace but now would say
Erigena consoled me. Schoolmen
Denounced his arguments as *stultes
Scotorum*. All Europe cried Amen.
Centuries have been stultified
Our broken thought is hard to mend for
The wayward soul can only stutter.
No Council has reached his holy saying.

Bible accompanied elderly ladies
In jetty bonnets, married women
In veils with their alluring sun-spots,
Lace gloves; straw-hatted girls, now dimming

In photographic albums, once spotted
By stare of lens, wore dimity.
Dotage had hidden familiar spots
They gigged to, memory mislaid.

Letters and names, affectionate X's.
Dismounted three times from his ungainly
Horse, William of Orange no longer attracts
A scowl or smile. What did we gain
When ignorance scattered hymn and tract
Beyond the new Border? Who dare gainsay
Our patriotism: plotters untracked,
The stump of Nelson's Pillar exploded,

No Orders itch at night in the hair-shirt.
Saxophone shrieks, guggles the Sabbath
In the military church at Newbridge.
Young fellows and girls, sly savages,
Twist, wriggle hips, as if itch knew
No better. Soldiers, bundling Sabine
Brides, would have mocked at our neurosis.
(St Mary combs her unkissed hair.)

Mark the wall-written thought that spells
Hate in the House where Christ was loaf-slice
And wine. Card-players show their calves,
Shuffle with knave and queen, loafers at
The main-gate British Cavalry
Once left, town-clattering. (Serpent
Unscribes his coils from the capitals
Of the illuminated Gospels.)

Can simple rite be sacrilege?
There is a green dysart, two miles
From where the wider Shannon turns southward.
Runnels are bell-like, west winds mild. The
Ancient Church at Clonfert is soughed
By topmost leaves: like those of Minos
The carven heads on coign, arch. Night-sound
Entered that holiness, ransacked choir.

St Simultas is muffled, cap down.
Moonlighters creep by grave, by vault,
Under the leaded windows of parish
Churches. Slowly the avant-garde
Advances, remembering the parklands
Their fathers had poached. One reckless volley
Of stones contents our partisans.
Darkness unnames the capias.

Ruined Abbey is an urinal
Twice nightly at Ardfert. Leaving
The Abbey Dance-hall, men unbutton
Near Isaac, Bishop, Cross, relieve
Themselves by sculptured lintel, buttress.
Corners are littered with week-end leavings.
They throw the Holy Child their butts.
'Familiar Angel, you're in all

Our Counties. Is morning Service held at
Killester?' 'All bow to knitting machines.'
'The Altar?' 'Hanked like market stall.'
'I see the glinting of chalice.' 'Sheen
Of oil. Factory keeps pew and stall.'
'That girl – Anathema?' 'She knits,
Murmurs a hymn. Straw from the stall
At Bethlehem can often help her.'

(The Woman at Joppa lays down her burden.)
Jumbling of bargains at parish bazaars
Gone. Where are the furnishings, the pews,
The hymn-books of St Barnabas?
The northern preachers of repute
At Baggotsrath? And those pure voices
In Carysfort, alto and basso,
The manuals murmuring the burden?

No clerk will relight the long sixes,
The bells of St Catherine's in Thomas
Street cannot be rung. As children,
My mother, Aunt Ciss, going to Mass

Or sent on messages, were chilled by
That sunless Protestant Church, the massive
Walls, iron spikes, remembered the blood-drenched
Block, Henry the Eighth and his six wives.

The Church Representative Body sold
Furniture, fittings to save arrears.
Methodist firm tramped in with hand-saw,
Hammers, cold chisel, broke down the reredos,
Altar, the gallery rails, the handsome
Pews, eighteenth-century organ. I saw from
A ladder much anguish thrown in the rear,
Knew Christ abandoned to the soldiery.

Here in the tearful street outside,
Bold Robert Emmet was hanged, drawn, quartered,
While balladmakers sold their laments
And printers damped his *Speech from the Dock*.
His blood will spurt in this business quarter
Again, enshrined by glass, cement, steel.
Come all ye British firms with our dockets,
See Catherine staunch his wounded side.

Bird-hating machinery dumps, pounds,
Through suburbs. Catholic Churches, like banks,
Go up. Down damp of tenements
The poor go. Urchins play by the banks of
A fouled canal. Archbishop, sky-tended,
Sprinkles the laid stone. Redemption banks on
Our credit, hands up the mighty tender:
Two hundred and fifty thousand pounds.

Rose MacDowell

The Liberator leaped from tussock
To tussock – Wellington boots, drenched sock –
Still breathless in spiritual struggle,
          Swung with the long pole that
He carried. Sons, grandsons, shouted, coursed
With hounds where the mountain bog-grass coarsens.
Why should they look back? They knew the old man
          Was halfway up the pole.

Morning was smuggling through ocean-cloud
From Gallerus a misty ray
That glimmered on rock bass, pollock, ray,
          Where, guarded by creek or cove,
Tax-free, in caves were foreign kegs
Fit for an Austrian Arch-Duke or Legate,
Haul'd up at darkfall with grapple, arm, leg,
          Over the hills to alcove,

Protestant drawing-room: wine, brandy,
Unrecognisable in brand – from
Spain, Portugal, France – to spread silk fans
          In many a big house
At night. Scent for the ladies, tobacco
For gentlemen. Strange ships dropped anchor,
Halyard. We traded lace, bacon, batches
          Of wool when the wind blew southward.

Still echoing from Derrynane
Below him, dinning like empty pan,
Calling the men to work again,
          He heard the farmbell, faster
And faster as he flapped in his big ulster
Until his aged heart exulted,
Thinking of that young girl in Ulster,
          Forgetful of the fast legend

That followed him. How did it go?
If anybody threw a stone
Over a workhouse wall from Sligo
    To Cahirciveen, it would strike
Without fail an illegitimate son
Or daughter of Daniel O'Connell,
For all the Irish nation was glad
    To see his likeness spread.

The Leader of Catholic Emancipation
Still held his monster meetings. Thousands
Caught up his words in forge, inn, household.
    He stood on the trampled sward
Of royal Tara, called for Repeal,
Defied the batons of the Peelers.
Dublin would hear the church bells pealing
    When he became Lord Mayor.

Wrapped in his cloak, with thick gold chain
Of Office, tri-corned, he left the Chamber,
Cheered by admirers from street and lane.
    The Government arrested,
Imprisoned him. But Rose MacDowell,
Rose, Rose, stepped from a carriage,
Came to the bars. His head was bowed.
    Bad thoughts disturbed his rest.

Through Penal years, he was a student
In Paris, a revolutionary,
Free-thinker, Jacobin. He spent
    Three pious terms at Douai.
He had become a wealthy lawyer,
Respectable Councillor, who awed
The Bench. Old husbands pawed:
    What did they do, eh?

As he crossed on a luckless day to Tarbert,
Shivering under a tarpaulin
He pondered the words of St Paul in
    The Epistles: marry or burn.

Pride wept at night when Thomas Moore
Belittled him in a song – boatmen were mooring –
Young Ireland had blamed his sway, but the common
    People would never scorn him.

At cock-crow, sons with their sons coursed
For hares, ran onward, whooping. Of course
Widowers needed more exercise
    To keep them from pretty faces.
Weak heart would safeguard Derrynane,
Outhouses, private chapel, farm-lands,
Save Dad from a mixed marriage –
    And national disgrace.

Another Protestant Insult

(An extravaganza)

Lingering one day at a book-shop in Patrick Street, Cork,
Intent on the contents of novel and school-text, a Christian Brother
Half-doored himself in surprise before he could say a Hail Mary,
As he backed from an opened page, exclaiming in rage, 'Another
Protestant insult to Our Lady': fire-driven, inhaling
Smoke from below while his pupils scanned the line, 'Let him pluck thee
A cherry who brought thee with child.' Soul showed him its black lining.
His clerical thoughts were bulging with doubt. Gone was his pluck for
A stranger, who smiled at him, held out again *The Cherry Tree Carol.*
Five words rushed out in guilt from the counter with him: 'St Joseph
Suspected the worst!' stopped bicycle, lorry, bus, bread-van, car, all
The traffic signs. Angelus rang out falsehold. Two nuns, Holy Joes,
Sodality women were scattering as his wickedness
Ran to North Monastery.
                The Bishop, the *Cork Examiner*
Must be informed of the blasphemous lyric, the City Fathers
Summoned at once, the bookseller boycotted, made an example
Of, national resolution ayed at a special sitting:
The refectory shook.

That night one brother had a vision
While the community lay in torment.
                                          The relics of
The Waterford merchant, who piously sold the provision shop
His uncle had left him twenty-eight years before our religion
Was fully emanicipated, Edmund Ignatious Rice,
Called, night and noon, by his vocation from the taking of orders,
The weighing scales, the bags of tea, sugar, currants, flour, rice,
Had obtained permission from Rome to found a new teaching Order
Of big strapping fellows to guide, to instruct, young boys at thruppence
A week, shone in the dark as if they were beatified.
Meanwhile the others held in sleep their purple-topped pencils,
As they dreamed of more corporal punishment and longed to be at
Their daily activities. Breeches were down, bums out.
Every crack was a yell. The merciless leather was plied
And muscular arms were tossing to left and to right the bumpers
Of sound until pain and strange pleasure were multiplied.
Lay brothers, tempted in sleep, forgot the Family Grocer,
Their first Superior General, who surrendered his off-licence
For the sale of spirits. Could goodness have guessed that men are made grosser
By the vow of celibacy? Succubi know, lie. Sense
Is oppressed so quickly.
                                  The River Lee was rumouring
Down by the Mardyke. Up Military Hill, up Montenotte,
Gossip came back from the shops to villa, front garden, guest-room,
(Half-hid as a bit of dirt in the umbilical knot.)
From Morrison's Island to Turner's Cross, the North and South Malls,
By Grand Parade, Maylor Street, Merchant Street, the news was busy
The very day that Mickie O'Mahoney quarrelled with Molly
Maguire. In bank, ship-office, it interrupted business.
'Be Jases!' swore burly dockers from the Coal Quay spitting
Beamish through smutty moustaches, while from the cobbles
Of Union Quay, French's Quay, Pope's Quay, respectable
Echoes replied with 'Be Japers!' 'We said so, the very spit
Of his father,' murmured the sons of Crispin, the free-drinking cobblers
True to the last. That evening, in street or snug, cardplayers
Sniggered and asked for the Joker. Jealousy stared
From a broken mirror on Saturday night, as drunkards
Beat up their wives.
                              Near the Dominican Church,

At the open-air shrine, Our Lady of Blackpool, old women recited
The fifteen decades in turn, litanies brought domestic
Peace. But on Sunday at Mass, the congregations were restless,
Uneasy, for news of the hullaballoo had been hurried to Dublin,
And few of our Protestants stole out to the Evening Lesson.
Soon columns were shaking with mirth, newspapers doubled up,
For A.E. had exposed the literary error o' the Devil:
That carol was known in the Middle Ages before the Protestant
Heresy.
      Cork was silent.
           The Angelus rang devoutly:
Noddles were bowed. The Council withdrew its protestations.
Strikers went back to work, the housewives to their bus queues,
Magistrates leaned from the Bench frowning at those accused
Of obscene language and brawling in the slums. Cellophane
Was reverently unwrapped from Madonnas. Booksellers
Smiled. Ignorance was on retreat in its smoky cell.

Ex Trivio

I

Lord Castlereagh
Need not have raised
That cut-throat razor,
Left us the portrait
Of every traitor.
Our final act
Will be an Act
Of Union. Freedom
Waits, feeble, dumb, for
The gallows rope,
When we are europed
From nape to toe-nail,
Scheduled, natoed.

II

Why should we atone for
Molyneux, Swift, Tone,
Emmet, Lord Edward
Fitzgerald?
        Pearse?
           Ward
Politicians, who trade
When all's betrayed,
Salute the Rising
At Easter, rise to
High Office, carpet,
Government car.
Late Ministers, Leaders,
All healthy invalids,
Honoured Directors
Of alien companies.
Unbury old comrades.

III

Seainín O Loíngsigh
Waits in capitals
Of Europe, cap
Crumpled, to beg, whine
For us. So why not
Relearn old manners,
Call Englishman,
West German, Belgian,
When the doorbell
Is answered: 'Your Honour,'
Forget that honour
Has been lynched?

IV

Pray ridiculed port,
Cartooning nose, keep
Sea-limit, port
From British cruisers
And who knows what;
Men called up, air-crews
From the dark night
Of the Disunited
States, our new masters,
Flag at half-mast
The map of Mercator
Bled by the merciless.

V

In Washington,
Pride weighs by the ton.
Bronze Generals
On horseback rally
With raised head, arm,
Federal armies,
Flag soiled, unmoved.
Political moves
Isolate a race
Whose bombers race
On military
Missions from tarmac,
Lease-holds, that pock
The globe now. Pocket
Holds personal gun:
What had begun
As the Whiteskin's right
Is law that re-writes
The unforgettable
Word at Gettysburg.

Dirge

He lies in state,
Though his robust
Soul left in a state
Of disarray
Scarlet robe, hat
Humility raised.
Too late he had flown
The pyx from ice-floe
To jungle war, in
His seventy-ninth year
And dreaming of napalm,
(Dermatic warning),
Met in that nap
Saturnine
Spirits from Hell. Eyed
With helicopters,
He called for more raids
On occupied villages
When troops paraded
Before his lifted
Blessing. The lift
Fires down on devilish
Forests where monkey-
Folk whimper, herds of
Mad elephants
Blow up. He heard,
Far off, phantoms
Of Buddhist monks,
Still burning, sigh: 'Gone!'
As he left Saigon.
Consoled by the Gospel, man
Fears no foe
Who turns to foliage.
Lauded by Church, State,
Cardinal Spellman
Lies in state.

A Jocular Retort

Criticus smiled as he wrote, and remarked
In the Literary Supplement
Of the London *Times* that Mr Clarke was
A garrulous rambling old Irishman.
No doubt I have become too supple
For the links of those boastful manacles
That hold back meaning, but I prefer it
To being a silent Englishman
Who cannot untie his tongue. So I pen
On, pen on, talkative as A.E. was,
When old. Because there is no return fare,
Few friends come out the Isle of AEaea
Where lately my desires have been penned by
A Temple ogre who is one-eyed, filthy.
Whenever Circe has a night-party
And entertains with her famous snake-dance
Clubbable guests that show the kind
Of wallowers they are, when she's half-naked,
She forgets to give us our fill. But I
Have liked her and sometimes she is kind.

Moral Tales

I

They say that Napoleon
Once tried at midnight to pass
A sentry who was napping.
Having forgot the password.
His steps were unheeled but the soldier
Halted the Corsican, ready
For less than a *solde*
To turn his white into red
By doing his duty and shooting

The sneak as a rank impostor.
The Emperor obeyed, saluted
Him; next day raised his rank.

II

Press ran out to photograph,
Interview, Winston Churchill,
Always defiant of the foe,
While the propeller churred
As he walked to or from an air-port
Gate, smoking a stuck-up cigar,
And thinking of brandy, rare port
Or a significant sally,
While the officials cringed
And gathering crowds admired
Him as he boldy infringed
The regulations, addled
The lofty control power. Petrol,
Fuming in tank or can,
Would have been delighted
To ensky the national pet, roll
Up his felo-de-se
With pilot, crew, fellow-travellers.

The New World

I

While others plotted, Jack
F. Kennedy shouted so loud on
The Wall that he tumbled off
Before he was tumbled in,
Despatched, they say, by the slave-traders
No Southerner has betrayed.
There would have been no jack

To lower with him, no cloud
Of mounted skymen, crews shoving
Half-drunken submarines
Around the new Cape Khrushchev
In Cuba, if he had dumped
The bomb, no marshalling
Of sympathisers, only
A world that God disowned:
And the sun, the moon, in a dump.

II

And now his brother
As bloodily slain
In a corridor.

Murderous America.
Mourning with gun
In pocket, moves on.

Galway

I

A stranger can drink in frequented bars
Throughout the week of the Galway Races
Nod, yarn, in backyard, cellar, snug, parlour
And meet himself in the very same place
Beside the quay or the laneway he started
From, only to find the delicate pacers
Unribboned, every starter boxed.

II

His Lordship spoke: 'You men I call on
To raise our great Cathedral, drive pile
Or crane, slap stone into shape, unpile
Vast sums, are ecumenical. I
Maintain the older Faith, the jaunting
Car used in Ireland before Pope John
Had been enthroned. Upon this site,
Long darkened by a British gaol,
A spire will rise, heavenly sight,
To shame the boozers in our bars,
Remind them of Lasting Punishment.'
Therefore to show them what he meant,
The Bishop kept the prison bars.

Drumcondra

They say that trees darken the Palace at Drumcondra
    When scholars from Trinity dine
In secret there with old Dracunculus:
    All wranglers, dialectitians!

The Stump

Half a century has stumped
Away, with much ill done,
Rottenness in the oak-stump
That had scored with green flourishers
A pianissimo air
For Thomas Moore in the Vale of
Avoca. Waters that meet, run,
Gold-seeking for a mile there,
Stir memories of Milesian

Stories. A rock-like stub, cast
In bronze, has been stuck up
Not far from Traitors' Gate,
Wide-stepped in St Stephen's Green
To show the stubbornness
Of William Butler Yeats.
Small crowd at the unveiling
Listened, no doubt, to the stump
Oration on politics, culture,
Art, hoarsened by amplifiers
That had too many ampères,
Up there in the drizzle of leaves.
As the Taoiseach spoke,
I heard the elegiac
Refrain of the faery folk
Away in the West. Occult
Voices seemed to be leaving
The Seven Woods sold for a song –
Five hundred pounds – to Malachi
Bourke by the Forestry
Department; with the great key
Of Coole. So he pulled down
For copper, lead and slate,
A house still remembered abroad,
Untimbered the estate
With cross-cut saw, chain, pulley.
But true to the prophecy
In an old broadsheet,
He failed to make a profit.
Our city trees were impressed.
Woods stood their ground. Press-men
Flashed by. Their cameras bowed.
Umbrellas dripped. Crowd clapped.
Three poets, Eavan Boland,
Brendan Kennelly and I,
Gave out, in turn, a tribute
To what had been Beauty.
But how could I refrain
Hearing that western refrain
And grieving with its notes,

From speaking without notes
About our ancient land,
Soon to become part of
The Continent, remote,
Unfriended: the hated Act
Of Union re-enacted?
The statue of Lord Ardilaun
Went by in a rustle
Of robes and a Cuffe Street bowler
Ran after it on the lawn.
One o'clock jibed as we stumbled
To lunch at the Hotel Russell.
Poetry had been stumped.

Neptune

Here stands the naked Neptune
In bronze, cerulean weeds
Flung off. He hears the inept tune
Our conchs emit so weakly
Yet pardons the ache of reins
As his horses gallop ashore
And he shakes out the reins,
Far from the last bollard
And anchor, his presence assured
Among the Bolognese.
Freshwater nymphs guard closely
Between their sculptured knees
The portly forms of dolphins,
As they envy the women's clothes,
Each hugging her big doll, fin,
Tail, beak. Two naughty boys,
Before, behind him, have tried
To steal, because it is buoyant,
His cod-purse, avoid the trident.
I'll question his shrine at Firenze
Where unsatisfied nymphs strain

Their grip, though fear ends all
As the satyrs lose restraint.
Is this the god that poured
So much from his plenary horn
Of sea-fruit as he pored
Over the breasts of Venezia,
That decadent lady, begging
Her favour like a neat-herd?
All ends, as he begins
To raise that velvet robe,
With her velleity.
Mocked by the net that mars love,
I need the strength of Mars.

Anacreontic

They say that Byron, though lame
In the wrong foot, danced the Sir Roger
To the old-fashioned tune of De Coverly
With Lady Caroline Lamb.
But others had done the same.
The middle-aged banker, Sam Rogers
Twice shared a covering letter
With her. But O when she'd seen the
Translator of Anacreon,
Young Thomas Moore in the wax-light,
Step to her bed without shame,
A naked Cupid, all rosy,
All roundy, no epicene
Lisping in anapaestics,
Softly she blew out the flame-tip,
Glimmered in white, as the moon rose,
And unpetalled the rose-bud from Paestum.

Talaria

Quite early in the morning
From Lower O'Connell Street
By Kapp and Peterson's,
The pipe-shop, Lemon's, all butter-
Drops, lozenges and fondants,
By plate-glass windows, around
The corner of Middle Abbey
Street, often I followed a girl
Whose light brown hair was tied
With a neat school-term bow.
So lovely was her walk,
She might have borrowed gaily
The very talaria
Of Hermes to lift her heels
A millimetre from the
Pavement. Suppose I had come
From the Pillar instead, met her
While passing, what spirit would look
At me from those young eyes?
The simile I had found
Changed into metaphor
Because she had no like.
Could I have guessed that youngster
With the light brown hair, plain ribbon,
Was Christine de Boulay,
The best of our ballet dancers?

Amor Angustus Domi

Come lie with me, Coita,
And let us try to prolong
What cannot last much longer
If our longings co-inhere.
Ultimate moments of pleasure
Dim consciousness by degrees.
So let us deglutinate
Before the great vein has azured
And love becomes corrupt.
Blissing is ready to give
And take us, so forgive, dear,
My haste if I interrupt you.

Stopples

Lifting a hand, I stopple
Ear. Lorries come to a stop:
I pass into silence.
Green acres in their silo:
Those fields that swayed from billhook
In the past, now cess-pooled, built
On. Ghosted by Cypress Grove,
I long for Cecilia, sigh, press
Her lips in my afternoon
Drowse. But at night Affrec
Lies in my arms, supine,
Moon-spent, half bare in a pinewood.
Young wife in her villa on Sunday
Morning, suckling her son,
Does what she knows unsurely,
Less than a moment from pleasure
And as soon as her husband has coupled
With her, brings him a hot cup
Of tea. His goings-on

Continue. Unsatisfied, both go
To Evening Mass, drink whiskey
In *The Blue Haven*. Night whisks key
And Missal from sleepy mind.
I stay at home, minding
Each perfect rhyme. Thought rambles
Beyond their perambulator
To girls, so nebulous,
They cannot take in our lust
Below, my darlings, dawdlers
Who stay with me till dawn.

Orphide and Other Poems

(1970)

Orphide

Clouds held every pass of the Pyrenees
On that February day:
The Pic du Midi, Mont Perdu
Were overshadowed, vapour hid
Cirque, coll, down-drift of snowage glimmered
From massifs, to the unweathered slopes
Of pasturage. Far on the plain
The apparition waited. Cave would
    Bring millions to their knees.

Escaping from boulders to moraine
And gorge, the Gave du Pau, hurtling
With cataract foam through gap, defile –
Faster than superstition – turned
Noisily to the plain, a widening
Tributory of the sky,
Aldering to the little hill-town
On Lourdes. Waves charged the Roman bridge.
    Some were thrown back. More ran.

On that February day, three children
Came from the Rue des Petits Fossés
Under the Château up a side-street
Of Lourdes, sabots a-clatter on the frosted
Cobbles, then down Rue Basse by sleety
Shop-corners. No washerwoman beetled
Blankets below the river-arches,
Antoine, the swineherd, had left the commonage,
    Eagerness stopped there, chilled.

At Massabielle, the unfamiliar
Gloom of forest about them – youngsters
In a folk tale – Toinette Soubirous
And Jeanne, a neighbour's little girl, stirred
In the undergrowth gathering firewood,
Darting as near as breath to ivied
Oak-tree, fearful of seeing a fay,
Nymph beckoning from a damp cave,
    Dwarf, witch with her familiar.

Drawing the white capouche around
Her shoulders, Bernadette Soubirous, the third girl,
Coughed, shivered, waiting by the shelterless
Gave de Pau, unable to work
Like Toinette and Jeanne, although the eldest,
So often her asthma came back by stealth
She heard, as she stooped to tie her garter,
Sound of a runnel, saw in far clouds
    The sun, a sleet-grey round.

Along the cliffs a breeze wintled.
The last gleam of evening had reached
A small cave, made it so fine
With summer hues that it seemed unreal,
Bowering with blossom the eglantine
Above it. Standing there, all shining,
She saw a fair girl who was robed in
White with a blue sash. Yellow roses
    Half hid her bare toes, unwintered.

Envisioned there, the girl of fourteen
Trembled. Was it a river nymph
Or shiny flower-girl from the forest,
About her own age? She wore a simple
Necklace of pure white beads, a chaplet,
Smiled for a moment at Bernadette
And, then, as if she would speak, raised
One hand and faded away. The cave
    Was darker than before.

Bernadette told the others that story
As they were trudging back with their bundles
Across the Bridge to the Place Maréchale;
Bugling, rattlesome, around a turn
The Diligence post-hasted from Tarbes,
Wine-light shone out of taverns.
They reached Le Cachot – once a gaol –
Left Jeanne, ran down with cold bits of flame
    To their home in the lower storey.

At supper Toinette could not hold her
Tongue, so Bernadette had to confess
She had seen a demoiselle gleaming
Within the cave. 'How was she dressed?'
'In white, with a blue sash. On her bare feet
Were two yellow roses.' 'Did she speak?'
'No, Mother, only smiled.' 'Some tale she heard,' said
Her father, 'at Bartres from her aunt or a shepherd.'
    'No, no, the world shall behold her!' –

Her mother thought despite him. Enraptured,
She lay awake that night. Banners
Swayed with high blessings from the Cathedral
As thousands moved with Ave Marias
Towards the Grotto. She had conceived
And borne a saint for France. Her beads
Ivoried. Groping from the bed-warmth,
By table, stool, she touched the bare arm
    Of Bernadette, wrapped her

With raggedness. In bluebell weather
Beyond the chestnuts, in a nook
Bernadette dreamed she was minding her sheep:
A child again, proud of the shepherd's crook
Her uncle had shaped from ash. On the far peak
Of Vignemale, winter was still asleep.
Tink, tonk: from many pasture-lands,
Flocks were climbing up to grasses
    Known by the bell-wether.

O it might have been a holy day
The sun shone so fine, when Bernadette
Her mother and a few friends on the morrow
Reached Châlet Isle. 'Now don't forget
To hold your beads up.' Fear and hope
Divided their thoughts. Some stayed by the grove
Of poplar trees. The small procession
Slowly went on, protected by
    Medallion, Agnus Dei.

At the planks across the stream, heads bowed
While Bernadette gravely approached
The grotto. She knelt and held the beads up,
Her fingers trembling as she showed them,
But sunlight came down at once in greeting.
All knew Our Blessed Lady would speak to
Her: 'Pray for all sinners. Let a great spire
Be raised here.' Above, the eglantine
    Rustled a wintry bough.

'She told me to come on Thursday week,'
Said Bernadette to the other children
That Sunday. As she knelt, Jeanne laughed.
'I'll throw this stone at her.' 'You've killed her!'
They ran from the cave. The invisible gash
Seemed mud until the vision, flashing
Through darkness, shaped itself again.
Bernadette writhed as if from pain,
    Her body, trembling and weak.

At class-time, Sister Philomena
Called out the girl, questioned her.
'What's this I hear? Telling more lies?'
'Sister, it is the truth.' 'Confess
At once. You saw Our Lady?' 'Twice,
Sister.' 'Speak up. What was she like?'
'About my own age, in white with a blue
Sash and chaplet. She wore no shoes, but...'
    'Do you know the meaning

Of what you are saying? Mortal pride
Is wicked. Have you no fear of Hell-fire?
Stand in the corner there till class
Is over.' 'She's always telling lies,
Sister.' Pointer in hand she turned from the blackboard,
Stopped with brows, titter, knuckle-crack.
At recreation time the youngsters teased
The culprit, pulled her hair – all the week,
    Nudged her, pinched her, pried.

'No, no. I'm not guilty of deception –
But pride is wicked so I must take care,'
Thought Bernadette as more than a hundred
Followed her, pious women, bare-headed
Men out of work. They stood in wonder
Where the breeze-white wavelets, half-turning, tumbled
By. At last, unswooning from joy, she
Called out the glorified words: '*Que soy*
        L'Immaculada Concepteio.'

The Church had not been consulted. Père
Peyramale sent in haste for the bold one,
Questioned her severely. 'Now, tell me
Again.' 'A girl of my own age, robed
In white, with a blue sash, Father, a chaplet
And necklace of pure beads. The Gave
Du Pau darkened. I heard her clearly: "Pray
For sinners,"' The little face looked grave. But
        Was every word prepared?

Twice he made the school-child repeat her
Story. 'A girl robed in white with a blue
Sash, Father. Yellow roses half hid
Her bare feet…' 'You stop.' 'I am confused.'
'Think. What was her message?' '"Pray for sinners."
O then, Father, she smiled and added:
"Let a great spire be raised up here."'
She answered the parish priest without fear now.
        He glanced at his gold repeater.

'Child, what is the Immaculate
Conception?' 'Father, I do not know.' 'Yet
That is what the demoiselle called
Herself. You always carry your rosary?'
'Yes, Father.' One hand could feel the horn beads
Praying. He pushed back his calotte.
'Come, Bernadette, kneel down, confess your
Sins.' Soon he quizzed her. 'Back to lessons.
        I mustn't make you late!'

They say the Prefect slowly wrote
Down every word that Bernadette
Said to him. 'The girl was robed in white, Sir,
With a blue sash. Yellow roses half-hid
Her bare feet.' 'Did she speak?' 'She smiled
The first time, sir.' Could it be pride
That sentenced her each time? Thousands
Believed, yet he tried her for an hour.
      Evidence came by rote.

Lourdes was bespelled. Day had been nightmared.
Smoke-demons peered from a fire-balloon
Above the roof-tops. In a white capulet,
Black shirt and blouse, a lassie swooned
Before the Grotto, like Bernadette, then
Unfastened her flannel drawers and let
Them down. At Mass in the Cathedral
Urchins, surprised by a natural need,
      Bolted out, bawling: 'Merde! Merde!'

Rumours came wilder than the waves of
The Gave de Pau. During that bad week,
Thousands with banners stood in mist
Beyond the Grotto. Pallid, weak,
The girl knelt, waiting. What mysterious
Announcement had distorted her features?
'Eat grass now. Find the spring.' She stumbled,
Fell, scrabbed, vomited grass-blades, mud.
      Men lifted her. No banners waved.

That night when the moon was up, good men
Dug at the spot where Bernadettte had
Fallen. The rising gravel-pile
Glittered at them. The ancient caverns
Waited. The Gave de Pau was milling
With sound. Then, slowly, as if surprised,
A spring oozed through the mud. Thousands,
Next day, surrounded it. The mountain
      Echoed their great Amen.

The Bishop of Tarbes spoke from the pulpit:
'Heresy, superstition prevail
And must be stopped.' The Lord Mayor,
In Council, ordered barricades
To be set up around the Grotto
And muddy spring. A bigger throng
Of hymns rose up all day outside
The pale of timbers. That night
     Defiant workmen pulled

Them down. In decade after decade,
Townspeople gathered, stopped in awe.
The spring rose, lily-like, purified
By grace. But faster than trumpet-call,
Squadrons of horse-dragoons were riding
From barrack square, were driving back
Hundreds of hurling hymns. Guarded
By up-flash of sabre, carpenters
     Restored the barricade.

The Paris and provincial Press
Were headlined; RIOTS AT LOURDES. SOLDIERS
ASSAILED BY INFURIATED MOB.
HORSE-DRAGOONS CHARGE STONE-THROWERS.
MANY VICTIMS IN HOSPITAL.
Then lo! The barricades were gone,
Taken down in a telegram
From Biarritz: the brief command
     Of Emperor, plea of Empress.

On Easter Sunday pilgrims made
Their way from townland, hillside hamlet,
In France and Spain. Hucksters filled
Tent, stall, with food and drink, salami,
Roast chestnuts, farm-cakes, lucky dips, flasks.
Wives smiled at the black caps of the Basque men,
Sky-blue berets from Bearne. Beribboned
Beauties from La Provence tripped by.
     All hailed the Maid

Of Lourdes. 'O Thou, full of grace!' they lilted,
Hard patois melting in soft 'e's
Of Languedoc. The bagpipes tilted.
Drums chuckled. Soon jollity increased.
Skirts flying with gavotte, men bibbing.
All, all was baisemain. Bad couples hid
In the forest, oblivious of the gloom
As shirt, loose stays. In her dark room
  Bernadette coughed, cried.

The celebrant, Dean Peyramale
Announced from the altar one fine morning
That the first miracle had happened:
A man, purblind from a cornea,
Shocked into daylight. Church bells rang.
In the vestiarium, brightly shadowed,
The parish priest forgot his snuff-box.
Lourdes would be celebrated, sufferers
  Cured of their maladies.

'So, this chosen girl must be sheltered
By Holy Church, taken from parents
And humble home,' the Bishop said
At lunch to Father Peyramale.
'Your Grace, it shall be as you wish.'
That evening, as he strolled by the potting-
Shed, glass-frames, beyond his rose-plots,
The Dean saw on the path a thrush drop,
  Stubble, a snail-shell, tear

Life out... 'You want to be a servant
Or marry – a girl of your renown?'
'Father, I may have sinned through pride.'
Such conduct would sully the faith of thousands
Who had believed while he denied.
'Too much humility, my child,
Can be contrarious, be still
The voice of pride. Avoid self-will.
  Our Lady has reserved

For you a special grace'… Candles
Were lighted by the little novice
For Benediction. The Convent chapel
Was marigolded at Nevers
One Sunday evening. Could she endure
The glottal redness of the thurible,
The gasp-held tickle of that sweet-smother
Or guess that she was another
        Captive of the Vatican?

'The world of business shall behold her.'
François Soubirous was appointed
Manager of a small cornmill. Soon
Brandy dismissed him from employment.
Poverty zola'd him into truth.
His child of fourteen was the future
Of Lourdes. To her new hospices,
Convents, shops, cafés, banks, offices,
        Hotels were all beholden.

No miracle would ever cure
Arthritis, leukaemia, cancer,
And pox – as he called it – grim diseases.
So many rosaries unanswered,
So many throttled by hope, fatigue,
Anguish, urged on by the cry of steam.
Dear Lourdes, our spiritual resort,
Chips from the saint's door, plaster all-sorts:
        Beads, crosses, curios.

In a white wedding-dress, deeply veiled,
Bernadette stood before the altar
At last, betrothed without a dowry,
At twenty-three: no longer exalted
In soul. Her parents waited, bowed
By tears. She heard, unhearing, the sound
Of Latin: Bride of Christ, unmoved,
Indifferent to her own good,
        Those nuptials unavailing.

Often at night in her small room
She stared at her new name in religion
As if it were written – Marie Thérèse
Bernard. Her fingers fidgeted
Heavier beads. Eyes that had gazed
Upon Our Lady would be raised
No more, voice scarcely heard. Mother
Superior was troubled by her dullness.
　　　All seemed to her a rumour.

'At noon, my sheep will be weary of feeding,'
The ten-year-old child thought. On the north side
Of the chapel, ivy-like shade is best:
The fifteen mysteries inside.'
Dreaming she led them by the Romanesque
Arches, then, turning, saw a speck,
Far off, upon a brink. Rosin
Thickened in rufous stems. It was
　　　The demon-goat, Orphide.

Feverish dreams gave her no rest.
That local legend fled up mist
With her into the alpine passes.
Gigantic rocks were bared. Mistral
Blew. Beard divided, horns rafale'd it:
Orphide pursued her along the trackless.
Fallen on hands and knees in cave-slime,
At Massabieille, she was limed in
　　　The obliterating forest.

Pain, fearful of losing her too soon, held
Body down in that last illness
Of strange deliria. Lourdes water
Given in galling sponge, in sipple,
Special novenas, had not brought
Relief. By day, by night, shriek followed
Moan for the scarlet-black corolla
Of morphine, dismayed the Ursulines.
How could they know Orphide had sullied
　　　All that she once beheld?

Bernadette died of caries
At twenty-nine, irrelicable.
No statue or memorial can
Be seen at Lourdes, no visitors tell
Her grave at Nevers. The candle-grease
Around the miraculous Grotto increases,
While the sick, dipped sorely in sourceful pipe-drawn
Germ-killing-earth-chilled holy water,
    Murmur their Ave Marias.

The Quarry

Holding his glass of whiskey, Father
    O'Donnell stared from the window
At rugged mearing, thrift of oats
    Beneath rock, wind-grey as

The barrenness of Errigal,
    Lurk of the Poisoned Glen
Beyond: soon with the darkness people
    Would gather, pray on bended

Knees, waiting in a disused quarry:
    MacGlynn charged for admission,
Collection plate in a rusty shed
    As though he held a mission,

A fellow with ragged family
    And a boulder'd farm.
The parish priest turned from the bay
    Window. 'The spiritual harm this

Boyo is doing must be stopped
    At once.' The people wanted
To believe in this or that, forget
    Seaweed on soil, their want.

What could he say to them? Consider
　　The annual pilgrimage
To Knock. Thousands went by bus,
　　Excursion train, hymning

Their faith. Sceptics said at the time
　　A magic-lantern had pranked
Its glory on the white-washed gable
　　There, but how could a prank

Have candled such grace for fifty years?
　　A girl from the *Irish Press*
Spoke to the only witness left.
　　Her interview was suppressed.

And what of the bleeding statues
　　In a kitchen at Templemore?
Was it the IRA who bartered
　　Red ooze for rifles? No more

Had been heard of that. Ocean was hazing
　　The forelands of Donegal.
He went to the side-board, hesitated,
　　Drink was bad for his gall-stone.

Who could have foretold that, night after night,
　　Shy words would shuffle uncapped
Or shawled, into the Presbytery
　　As if they had shared a rapture

Unknown to him? An hour ago,
　　Deputy Michael Gallagher,
Respected member of Fianna Fail,
　　Foremost in every gallup

Poll, came. 'Father, I saw Our Lady
　　As clear as the new statue in
Our parish church, with shining halo,
　　Mantle of white and blue. Then

Brats ran about in the dark flashing
    Electric torches, Father.
Not one of them would do the like
    Inside the fairy rath

At Gort, for fear of having a hump clapped
    On his back. After the Gospel
Next Sunday, your Reverence should address
    The congregation. Gossip

And lies are spreading about this wonder.
    All my constituents...'
His voice rose up as if to hold
    A meeting, failed. 'They sent me

To ask you,' he added humbly, 'Whether
    We're worthy of such grace?'
He left. Clasping his breviary,
    Father O'Donnell paced up

And down, then rang for his house-keeper.
    'Mary, I'm going out now
And may be late.' 'I'll leave a tray,
    Father.' She knew his doubt.

He drove along the village street
    Past the nine public-houses.
A tell-tale light leaked: customers
    As usual carousing.

Speed raged him through in-shadowing miles,
    Left tullagh and turlough behind.
Among forgotten hills the Gaeltacht
    Held stories out of mind.

The breeze that blew from Maghera touched
    His brow in cold benediction.
A gun-shot from the quarry, he stopped
    His car. A superstitious

Murmuring came up from rock and quitch-grass.
　　MacGlynn had hurried out,
Searching his cap. Father O'Donnell
　　Nodded, stood by the gate-way. Doubt

Enwrapped him as with soutane. Prayer
　　Had become a solemn hush,
A sweetness of frankincense. Despite
　　His will, he felt the luscious

Feeling below him, for the quarry
　　Seemed aswirl with soft vapour
From which the form of a woman robed
　　In shimmering white was shaping

Itself. Gold of her Claddagh ring shone –
　　He recognised the wife
Of Deputy Gallagher. Smiling,
　　She lifted up her night-dress.

'Hail Queen of Heaven, Mistress of Earth!'
　　Quarry sang. The parish
Priest, half-damned by what he had seen,
　　Struggled from gate to car-door,

Stumbling into hight nettles that hid
　　The dyke. Alarmed, MacGlynn
Ran up to help. He drove off: headlights
　　Cornering rock and whin.

The Dilemma of Iphis

(After the Metamorphoses of Ovid. Book IX, Fable VI)

So the ill-fate of Biblis, that Cretan girl who became a
Fountain in Asia Minor, because of her incestuous
Passion for her own brother, might have disturbed the hundred
Cities of the island had not a pious wonder
Happened soon after at Phaestum, little-known, provincial town
Far from the capital of Minos, that quickly jostled every
Street with its talk, every temple with thanksgiving and sweet smoke;
Our Blessed Lady beholding with compassion a much bewildered
Girl engaged to a girl-friend made a man of her. Sixteen
Years before that miracle occurred, Ligdus, an honest,
Hardworking artisan, petting his wife one night on the bolster,
When she was nearing her time, said:
                                    'Parents as poor as we are,
Cannot afford to rear up a girl until she is marriageable.
Providence never has favoured our daily toiling.'
                                    'But, Ligdus,
What if the infant is a girl?'
                                    'If that be so, the midwife...'
Hands spoke. Cry was stifled. Vainly his wife implored him.
Tears could not change his resolve though they shared their drops together.
They tossed, they turned in their sleep. That night she saw in a vision
Our Holy Mother stand, smiling, beside the bed. Her brow shone
Between the moon-horns. Diadem glittered. She held a golden
Sheaf of Egyptian corn. Vaguely appeared in the shadows
Divine figures of her attendants – dog-headed
Anubis, the cat-like Bubastes, Apis, Harpocrates, silent,
Finger on lip; silent, also, the sistrum, the snakes in
Glimmering bands, twin forks without a hiss.
                                    'Telethusa,'
The daughter of Imachus murmured and her voice, clear in silence,
Seemed but the silence.
                        'Do not weep or despair, for when with mild touch
Lucina has lightened your pangs, disobey the command of your husband,
Bring up your child without fear, be it male or unwanted female.
Mother of all on earth, human or animal, I
Bless and shall protect you.'
                        The portent was gone. In her trouble,

In her joy, Telethusa got up and knelt on the chilled stone-floor,
Thanking Our Lady of Pharos, then dragged herself, slowly, wearied,
Back to the bed and warmed her great belly against her husband's
Thighs as he turned to her in his slumber, feeling his penis
Stir up, inflamed by her nearness.
                                    Next day the young woman
Gave birth to a female infant.
                                In less than a fortnight,
Ligdus performed the familiar rites, naming their first-born Iphis
After her grandfather, a name still used by both sexes.
'Happiest of Omens,' though Telethusa, happily unswaddling,
Bathing her babe every morning when Ligdus had gone to the workshop,
Cautious at night, she would go on tip-toe to the cradle, change nappies
Give suck to her bantling. So when Iphis was two, she dressed her
Neatly in boy's clothes. Later she kept her from tom-play, from street-game.
Told her to fly when a bold urchin pulled out his squirter
Behind an old cart or rubbish heap.
                                    The girl was almost sixteen,
Handsome, tall for her age and dark-haired.
                                            One night after supper.
Ligdus confessed to his wife:
                                'I have promised our son in marriage.'
'And the lucky girl?'
                        She smiled,
                                    'Ianthe, the only daughter
Of –'
        'Telestes.'
                    'The very man. Next week he'll apprentice him
To his own trade.'
                    Now Iphis and the fair Ianthe were loving
Companions from childhood. Both had been taught Natural
History, Arithmetic, Logic, by the same master.
                                                Combing
At bed-time the yellow ringlets that Iphis admired, the young girl
Longed for the nuptial night. Her friend who longed as much for that
pleasure,
So impossible, cried to herself, lying awake, tormented,
Hot with desire, blaming the gods.
                                    'Why am I afflicted,
Alas, with so wicked, so unnatural a passion

As this? Can cow inflame cow? Mare burn for mare? The ram in season
Tups, raddles the ewes. Far in the forest glades the roe-deer
Follow the buck. All creatures mate rightly, in the paddock,
Thicket, air, water. Ruffling their feathers up, the fowl are roostered
At daybreak in turn. No female covers another female.
Why, O why, did Mother confide that secret to her poor child,
When the gods above all cannot be merciful?
                                        Europa
Wanted the bull that carried her across the wave-tops.
So to avoid unnatural forcing, the pang of rupture,
Jupiter changed her into a cow before he mounted her.
Not such – for the gods demand variety – his descent on
Danae in a shower of gold. What deceitful coin of it minted
Her heavenly bliss?
                        Bluster of wing-clap above her frightened
Leda, who was two days pregnant, as she bathed in the local river.
Surprised by a swan, she forgot her obedience to Tyndarus,
Her dutiful Spartan husband, as floating, sustained by the web-feet,
Hover of wing-tips, breathlessly, she rose and dipped with
The god who had hidden excess of his solar rays in the simple
Whiteness of a swan. Hour long conjoined, she drenched, undrenched him
Until his tail-feathers drooped.
                            I need no supernatural
Union, only the thalamus of wedlock. Hail-storms
Hid mountainous Crete, when our Daedalus flashed on those artificial
Wings of the future. Yet had his invention succeeded,
For all his knowledge and skill, juggling with coggle, wire, main-springs,
He could not have made for my pelvis from any material private
Parts that would work. So where can I find in the world a chirugeon
To transplant them at once from the body of a man no longer
Living, graft them on mine?
                            Though my parents and the future
Father-in-law allow us to meet undisturbed, Ianthe,
Beloved Ianthe and I are kept apart by perverted
Love. Fondling my earlobes, she sighs, longs to fill my
Hands and her own with gentle touches. Temptation increases.
Innocence burns as she talks of our nuptials. O how can I
Pluck those rounds that ripen as mine? I thirst at the well-mouth,
Knock at the front door I cannot open. I am a workman
Without the right tool, a torchlit runner who never reaches

His nightly goal. What is our hopeless love but a naked
Encounter of likes? Then why should Venus, Hymenaeus,
Juno, bestow in mockery their blessing on this marriage?'
Anguished as much, Telethusa pretended a sudden fever,
Raving about dire omens, trying to postpone the wedding,
Got up, consulted a haruspex, wasted house-keeping money,
Took to her bed again. Every device had failed. Only
One evening was left to her. So in her wild despair, she hurried,
Veiled in deep black through the rain with Iphis by side-street, by alley,
Entered the temple of Isis in the market place and prostrated
Herself before the High Altar:
                                    'Our Lady of Libya,
Mother of the Mareotic lakes; Patroness of Pharos,
Whose constant ray guides in the darkness, the sounding trireme,
Galley, dhow; Mistress of the nine horns, rising
Subsiding with snow-fed Nilus, cataracted
Beyond the last pale temples of the moon; Goddess,
Whom I have seen at night in a holy vision so clearly,
Then, dimmed as in a dream, thy divine attendants, the unlit torches,
The silent sistrum, the hissless snakes, vouchsafe to hear my
Petition. Have I not done your will, brought up my daughter
Iphis, as a boy? O let her not be punished, derided.
Pity her plight before the morrow.'
                                    In obscurity
The gilded statue of the goddess seemed to stir. The massive
Portals were shaken. The sistrum rattled. In fear, yet hopeful,
The two went past the side-shrines, porphyry images, into the inclement.
Night.
        'Why are you striding like a man?' The mother
Called out to her dearest.
                            'Because I feel like one.' 'Your voice is
Hoarse. You are catching a bad winter-cold and must change every
Stitch, dry yourself, gargle, when we get home.'
                                    The girl stopped, whispered
Tenderly, kissed her mother on both wet cheeks.
                                    Bewildered,
Uncertain of all, Telethusa kept silent. In twenty-five
Minutes they reached their home.
                            Alone in her bedroom,
Iphis kicked off her muddy sandals, unfastened her leather

Belt, pulled the damp chiton and vest over her head, knowing
She had been unbosomed. Her chest was flat, hairy. The nipples
No longer so budlike, were two pink pimples. Something
Had touched her thigh ever so slightly. Then she saw it.
'By Jove, I'm a man at last —'
                    She heard a deep voice exclaiming,
Then cheering of multitudes, far sound of a hymn that struggled onward,
Vison-led, Iphis watched, as last year, the Feast of the Phallica,
Steadied banners, flags flutter, prayed for, borne on
High in front of the chanting priests, newly painted, carven
From the most precious wood, the sanctified image was slowly
Approaching.
           'O look, dear Iphis, at the delicate ivory-tinting,
The great bluish vein, the little violet ones, the crimson
Heart-shaped sex-cap. How proudly it tilts above the masses
Of people.'
           Ianthe cried as phalliphori carried the mighty
Symbol.
          'Come let us follow the crowd or all say it will change to
An angered purple at nightfall. See, torches are flaring, tampling,
The acolytes, clad in pure lamb-skin, their wild locks crowned with ivy,
Half strip their wine-stained limbs as they whirl in fury
Of abstinence, dance to the cymbal-clash, the drum-beat,
Clamouring, cries of women.'
               Joyfully he turned to Ianthe.
'Darling, we are alone,' he murmured. 'This is our marriage night. Cupid
Has drawn the bow-string and his arrows are fledged with kisses
That sparkle!'
           Wondering why her daughter delayed so long in her bed-room,
Changing her clothes, Telethusa listened, quietly opened
The door. There, in astonishment, she saw her husband,
Young again, stark naked, as he gazed down, waiting to show her
The extent of his vigour. But as she stepped forward, burning
For what he held so firmly, she knew that her prayers had been answered
By Providence. Ashamed of her momentary incestuous
Impulse, unseen by her son, she stole from the doorway.

Stranger, read at Phaestum this pious inscription in our temple:
DONA PUER SOLVIT QUAE FEMINA VOVERAT IPHIS

The Trees of the Forest

Stag on the westward ridge, melodious
One, clamourer with your high nodes
Of point and tine. Below, the roe-bucks
Are grazing in a dappled row.

Oak, mighty one, my shelterer,
I lie beneath you, acorn in shell.
Crush of your bark will cure a mastoid,
Swine root among the years of mast.

The water-willow is never hostile.
I pull down sweetness, cross green stile,
Frail blossom of the catkin. Baskets
Are woven, supple as your sap.

The wicked blackthorn, claws sharp as Pangur
Ban's. Each prickle is a pang,
Appetite has been well sustained by
Those berries juicy, darksome, stainful.

The yew-tree, gloomer in churchyard. Coffins
Go under it, funereal cough.
The dewy yew thickens: a sturdy
One. Winds blow strong. It is unstirred.

Aspen, the trembler, leaves a-racing
Fast as competitions in Thrace.
I hear within it the sound of fray.
That whispering makes me afraid.

Hateful the ash, a nub for chariot.
Let every branch above be charred.
Avoid the ash that brings contention,
Quarrel on chessboard, blows in tent.

Apple tree shaken by many hands,
Wide spreader out of pink bloom, handsome
One. Bark for tanning, wealth in garden.
Sweet crop that every man must guard.

Elder, that women strain, boil twice,
The bark will dry the pus in boil
Out of the flowers will come a greenness.
Dyers make the dark and the pale be seen.

Holly, cold light in woods, silver
As winter moon, icedrip from sill,
The leaves are fierce and disagreeable
Although they glitter like filagree.

Pleasant the whiteness of the May,
I smell and pluck it while I may,
Go by it in the twilight, listen
To music coming from rath and liss.

Pleasant, also, the lofty beech
That comes down to the river beach.
Under the shady shade, I drag
My weariness, sore-footed, bedraggled.

Briar, deceitful friend, you hold me
With tiny fingers, unholy one,
Drawing a drop from small or big vein.
I jump away. Your tricks are vain.

Birch, the smooth, the blessed, sent down
From Heaven, with summer grace and scent,
Delicate one: breezes are leaving
Half of your sweetness with other leaves.

Dear Hazel, bring an end to my story,
Pantry of plenty, my winter store.
Sweet, sweet, is the brown-covered kernel:
Good bite for gallowglass and kern.

Stag of the topmost ridge, melodious
One, clamourer with your high nodes
Of point and tine. Below, the roe-bucks
Are grazing in a dappled row.

The Healing of Mis

Along that mountain in the south named after her, Mis,
    The only daughter of Dáire Mor, the King
Of Munster, escaped after the battle near Cahirconlish
    Hurled by Fionn and the Fianna from shingle
To rock against the invaders who had sailed out of Greece
    And Spain. Her fingers a-drip with a father's blood, she
Fled up a forest, echoing foreign cries. Streams
    That passed her ran down to faster flood.

Fear put her in caverns, in greenth of fern, on branches that grieved
    About her and for three centuries her mind
Was lost. A raggedness in thorn-set bramble, in greed
    Of gorse, she sprang from gorge to cave-mouth, hind
Or hare in her claws, devoured it raw. A nakedness
    Blue'd by the sea-gales that blew from Dursey, on freezing
Ridges, she lanked her lengthening hair, a mantle that guarded
    The bushiness above her knees.

In winter when turf was raked under the household cauldron,
    Stories were told of a Geilt that flew over forest top and
Cliff to pray from the sky. Sometimes a shepherd, hatted
    By crack of twig, had a glimpse of hairiness
Crawling from filth and hurried back to safe pasturage.
    Those cloudy cantreds were dreaded and accursed
For a legend endured from the Paps of Dana to Mount Brandon
    Of a lonely sorrow time could not cure.

It happened in the third century that word was brought to Felim,
    The King of Munster, as he came from the boar-hunt in a local
Forest. Riding thoughtfully back to Cashel, he felt
    Such pity that when brands flickered in the banquet-hall,
He offered tribute and tax to any man there who could cure
    The Woe of Mis. 'Greatness, your wish will be fulfilled.'
A harper called, braving from a corner. 'Who's that? 'Duv Ruis.
    She'll listen to strings, but I need a fistful

Of gold and silver coins.' 'Harper, take as much
        As back can carry.' 'And a farl from the royal griddle
Your Grace?' 'It's yours. What else?' 'Nothing. All can touch
        The bottom of female complaint.' 'Hard to unriddle.
Faith-healers like to darken their say. But mine is plain. Let
        My steward be summoned to give this man the sum on credit.
If he fails to perform the feat in three months, he has little to gain,
        For he will pay the debt with his head.'

Laughter unbarred the door: the harper went into the night-rain,
        Journeyed by dysart and dyke, strummed for half-loaf
And the yellowness of ale, sheltered in house or hidy-
        Hole, came to a white battle of waves that broke
Along four promontaries. In a sombre glen
        Between the uphills, he stole into the forest of
Slieve Mis. At times a lonely bird-cry vaulted the silence.
        He stopped, listened from a dry course.

When young beaks had been filled and pickaback insects were safe
        As air, Duv Ruis rested awhile in a sun-scented
Vale, then hastened to spread his travelling cloak in the shade
        Of a blossoming quicken-tree, tossed his ring-coins up,
A silver and golden frolic of profit-making pelf,
        Then arranged them carefully in emblems
Along the cloth-edge, lay on his back to greet the Geilt
        Opened his flap, exposed himself.

Holding his harp, the consolation of his bosom,
        He played a suantree with grace-notes that enspelled
Traditional tunes and, smiling quietly at his ruse,
        Waited. Soon his senses knew that loneliness
Stood by, a bareness modestly draped in tangle-black hair,
        With timeless hands, listening to the special
Melling that drew and soothed her mind as she stared
        In surmise at his rising flesh.

'Are you a man?' she asked. 'I am.' 'What's that you are holding?'
        'A harp.' 'I remember the triangle.' 'Pluck it.'
'You will not harm me?' 'I won't.' She tapped the sounding-board,
        Laughed as it answered her. 'What's this I'm touching

Below?' 'A couple of pouched eggs I like to carry.'
    'Can you lay them as the poult-hen?' 'Only the glair.'
'What's this so high and mighty?' 'Marry-come-up, my dear:
    The wand of the feat as scholars declare!'

He spun the gold and silver pieces into a reel
    Around her temples, an oriental garland,
Faster, faster they went. She clapped. 'I know that gleam
    For I recall the cargoes of bullion from the harbours
Of Tyre and Gaza.' 'Eyes cannot gaze at the feat for it closes
    The lids in bliss.' 'Like this?' She palmed the sun. 'Yes.'
'Perform the feat,' she commanded. Powerfulness held him closely.
    'I cannot. I'm much too hungry.'

'Wait here. I'll bring you venison.' She leaped over
    The quicken-tree with lifted head. He hurried
To pick up kindling in the forest, gather arm-loads
    Of withered branches, fanned them into up-rushers,
Cracklers, with a flick of his flint, set large stones
    For a nearby cooking-pit the Fianna
Had used, then waited, uneasy as his shoes. At last
    She rose above the rowan branches,

Lightly bearing a buck on her shoulder. 'Here's a meal
    For both our bellies… Look, day is aflame on the edge
Of night. Run, run!' 'It's only faggots turned into heat.'
    He poked the stones from the ash and the slope sent them,
Red-hot, into the paven pit. He coiled up
    Each sweeping tress from her filthy body, saw
Her nipples harden into blackberries. 'Bogholes have spoiled them.
    But soon that pair will be redder than haws…

I stumbled on a helmet in sand near to washed-in wreckage,
    Brimmed it from a high cascade, going
And coming patiently to fill your bath.' He sloshed
    Himself as he lathered her down, soaped the skin of her back
With a lump of deer-fat, washed the crack between the slurried
    Cheeks, like a mother, turned her round, picked crabs from
Her sporran, nit-nurseries hidden in tiny flurries
    Through tangled tresses, then began

All over again. He soaped her body, washed it down,
    Drawing the wad of deer-skin to-and-fro
Softly between her glossing thighs, turned her around
    And frizzled her neglected faddle, noticed
It needed a thorough-going cleansing inside and out, scrubbed
    And douched it, cursing her ignorance, lack of care,
Then coiled her tresses neatly after he currycombed them
    As if she was a gainly mare.

'Now canter into dryness, my filly.' She galloped, instead, up
    The smooth slope, became a momentary
Speck on the summit, then flew down again into his arms –
    The favourite no ostler had led across the Curragh
Or mounted yet. 'Lie down with me under the blossoms.'
    He entered so quietly she never felt it
Until a pang shook her. Fearing involuntary loss,
    He waited, obedient as she helped
His through the hymen. Then at the thrusting of the wand,
    Her eyelids closed in bliss. The flowers of the quicken-tree
Were poppies. Both drowsed but how could they stop fingers that wandered
    Until their passion was no longer tender?
'Buck, buck me,' she cried, 'as the stag in rut.' Wildly crouping
    Herself while he husbanded roughly, she spent with him in the spasm
That blurs the sight. They lay without words. Soon limbs drooped
    Towards sleep in the deepening grass.

They woke for late supper. He cut and crusted two fillets in dampish
    Clay, left them to bake until the savour
Called to their mouths. He gave her thick slices of bannock.
                                                        When
    The hot meal was over, she said: 'Why do you delay
The feat of the wand again?' 'We must prepare the bridal
    Bed.' Waist-deep in ferns, he gathered sunny swathes.
She ran to pull the fennel bloom, wildering woodbine
    And made a border of braided daisies.

She did not wake until the sun-god had gone by
    Next day. Hidden in foliage, he could hear
Her lamenting: 'Ba, be, ba, pleasant the gold and silver on
    Our double bed. Pleasant the grace-notes that appeared

Above his breast. But better than money in a ring
      Coining more bright ones, better than skiddle,' she desponded,
As she searched around in vain, hair mantling her from the mist,
      'His pouched eggs and the feat of the wand.'

Climbing down from the leaves to comfort her, he thought: 'I must trim it
      To-morrow.' He held her a minute then led her to the glowing
Branches that waited for her beyond the forest dimness,
      While steaks were broiling, he showed her the honey-comb,
The goat-cheese, the heather-ale, he had bought for the feast at
      A farm near Ventry. After they had eaten, idled
And ale'd, he murmured: 'Tell me about those curious dreams.'
      'How did you guess?' 'From stir and dire cry.'
'High tiers of oars from the Mediterranean were dipping whiteness
      In blueness. Ships swept from archipelagoes
Into surds of sound. Hundreds of bucklers lightened
      Through a conflagatory storm: "Stromboli!" "Stromboli!"
Look-outs were calling down from a red hail of cinders.
            Main-sails
      Were furling as keels hurtled from fumeroles.
Finger-tips of diluvian fire were piling their rains
      On temple, ziggurat, I zigzagged, stole

In another dream through labyrinthine corridors
      Where serpentries of momentary flashes
Reveal the figurative walls, as iron doors
      Clanged at my heels. Clueless in a subterranean
Maze, I reached a hall where darkness was worshipping
      Itself. The unseen, the unheard-of, moved in self-horror
Around me. Yielding to the force of writhesome limbs,
      Unvirgined by the Minotaur –

I knew my father.' 'Wrong dreams are dispelled with the help of music
      And the wand.' Soon Nature showed them more delightful
Ways as they heaved under the mantle. How could he refuse
      The interplay of limbs that orientalised them?
Daily he scrutinised, scrubbed her, rosied all her skin.
      They stayed in the mountain forest twelve weeks or more
Hugging his harp at night he lulled her to sleep. Then, thinly,
      Tried to serve the longing that woke her.

So Mis was healed. Often she hunted in the forest depths
    While he kept house, moss lodge. When rain–clouds hid
All Ireland, and waters ran down their tumultuous steps,
    Unseen, they warmed themselves in a cave by crowdering
Flame. O she might have come from a Sidhe–mound for the gods
    Had made her a mortal. 'I'll examine her future dreams,
Interpret them, find in chance word much she has forgotten;
    Signs and symbols are underneath.'

Early one morning they came down by the turns of a dry course
    And coombe to the highway. Gaily she wore the blue gown,
Shoes and Tyrian cloak he had brought her. A roan horse
    Waited, a servant at the bridle. Her arms were around him
As he rode by ford, rath, to be invested. Goodness
    Blared from the trumpets faring them to the high door
That had laughed him one night from the feast. Blessing,
    Victory, to him who relates this story!

Tiresias: A Poem

(1971)

Tiresias

I

Slowly impelled by invisible prompting beyond the noon-forsook
Slopes of Mount Ida, press of cypresses, dust of pebbling,
Tiresias, staff in hand, toiled below the heights, still snow-written,
Hiding their winter-long tumult in wreathing, in wraithing, of vapour
Pent over cavern, pool. Stopping his wonder to look down
On the groves of lemoning trees, orangeous orchards, Bacchanalian
Vine-stock, Greek fire of the labyrinthine blossom
Sieging with steady rounds of scarlet the hundred cities
Of Crete, the plain of olive woods no more than five thousand
Years old; his mind was divining an underground winter –
Fruiting the whole island with plenteousness from its rock-bound
Cisterns.
   He noticed how mountain flowers had lessened in size, stepped
Into a glory of broom that unsentried his sight, heard far off
Thunderclap. Sky questioning earth. Straightway half-blind from
Preternatural bloom, he became aware of Presences
Aloof yet near. All-powerful Jove had been haranguing
Juno. Bolt rumbled, still echoing among the smaller
Cyclades.
   'Tiresias, tell us both of your experiences,
Changed, as you were, for seven years, into a woman. All Greece
Gossiped, they say, about her, in many-bedded palace, public
Therma, gymnasium. Speak now and be fearless.
Did you enjoy in the consummatory moments of love-making
Greater bliss as woman or man? Phallommeda, –
Pet-name for my dearest wife – has wagered our future
Happiness on this affair. You shall decide for us.'
           'Almighty
Jove, better far to cower from the zodiacal light,
Into the Stygian gloom, than tell my secret, dreading
Sentence beyond the last consonants that spell out nothing.'

'Gods are affable when favonian winds are taking
Fragrance of frankincense skyward. I see from a temple
Courtyard, fifty miles below, the last rings of bead-prayer

Rise in thanksgiving. Tell all.'
                                    'Then, Great Jove, let obedience
Guide me with honesty on the wayward slue of my story.'

II

'Strolling one day, beyond the Kalends, on Mount Cyllene,
What should I spy near the dusty track but a couple of sun-spotted
Snakes – writhen together – flashen as they copulated,
Dreamily! Curious about the origin of species, I touched them.
Tunic shrank. I felt in alarm two ugly tumours
Swell from my chest. Juno, our universal mother, you
Know how easily a child wets the bed at night. Pardon
Frankness in saying that my enlarged bladder let go.
                              "Gods," it
Lamented, "has he become an unfortunate woman, humbled by
Fate, yes, forced twice a day, to crouch down on her hunkers?
Leaf-cutting bee affrights me, Ariadne within her web-rounds."
Timidly hidden as hamadryad against her oak-bark,
I dared to pull up resisting tunic, expose my new breasts –
Saw they were beautiful. Lightly I fingered the nipples
And as they cherried, I felt below the burning answer;
Still drenched, I glanced down, but only a modesty of auburn
Curlets was there. If a man whose limb has been amputated
Still feels the throb of cut arteries, could I forget now
Prickle of pintel? Hour-long I grieved until full moonlight,
Entering the forestry, silvered my breasts. They rose up so calmly,
So proud, that peace – taking my hand in gladness – led me
Home, escorted by lucciole.
                              My mother wept loudly,
Crying, "Forgive me, Tiresias, the fault is
Mine alone for when I carried you in my womb, I
Prayed at the local temple that our Lady Lucina
Might bestow on me a daughter." Tear-in-smile, she hugged me,
Kissing my lips and breasts, stood back with little starts of
Admiration, hugged me again, spread out our late supper:
Cake, sweet resin'd wine, put me to bed, whispered:
"Twenty-five years ago, I chose the name of Pyrrha
For you. Now I can use it at last." She tucked me in, murmured.

"Pyrrha, my latecome Pyrrha, sleep better than I shall."

           Next morning
Gaily she said:
       "I must instruct you in domestic
Economy, show you, dear daughter, how to make your own bed, lay
Table, wash up, tidy the house, cook every sort of
Meal, sew, darn, mend, do your hair, then find a well-off
Husband for you. As a young man you have spent too many
Hours in the study of history and science, never frequented
Dance-hall, bull-ring, hurried, I fear, too often to the stews."
Laughter-in-sigh, she handed me a duster.

           One fine day
During siesta I gazed in reverence at my naked
Body, slim as a nespoli tree, daring to place my shaving
Mirror of polished silver — a birthday gift from my mother —
Between my legs, inspected this way and that, the fleshly
Folds guarding the shortcut, red as my real lips, to Pleasure
Pass. Next day I awoke in alarm, felt a trickle of blood half-
Way down my thigh.
       "Mother," I sobbed.

           "Our bold Penates
Pricked me during sleep."
        "Let me look at it, Pyrrha."

           She laughed then
Said:
      "Why it's nothing to worry about, my pet, all women
Suffer this shame every month."
         "What does it mean?"

           "That you are
Ready for nuptial bliss."
        And saying this, she cleansed, bandaged.
Bound my flowers.
       When I recovered, a burning sensation
Stayed. Restless at night, lying on my belly, I longed for
Mortal or centaur to surprise me.
         One day during
Siesta, I put on my tanagra dress, tightly
Belted, with flouncy skirt, and carrying a blue mantle,
Tiptoed from our home by shuttered window, barred shopfront,
Local temple, took the second turn at the trivium,

Reached a sultriness of hills.
                              I went up a mule-track
Through a high wood beyond the pasturage: a shepherd's
Bothy was there before me. I peeped, saw a bed of bracken
Covered with a worn sheep-skin. I ventured in: listened,
Heard far away *clink-clank, clink-clank* as a bell-wether
Grazed with his flock while master and dog were myrtled
Somewhere in the coolness. By now I had almost forgotten
Much of my past, yet remembered the love-songs that shepherds
Piped among rock-roses to pretty boy or shy goat-girl.
Was it a pastoral air that had led me to this bothy?
Surely I was mistaken. Paper-knife, pumice, goose-quill,
Manuscripts, had been piled untidily together,
Inkstand, wax tablets, small paint-brushes on a rustic
Table.
        "A student lives here,"
                              I thought,
                                        and half half-undressing,
Wearily spreading my cloak along the sheepskin,
Lay on blueness, wondered as I closed my eyelids,
"What will he do when he sees me in my deshabille?"
                                                    Soon
Morpheus hid me in undreaming sleep until dusk. I woke up –
Not in the arms of softness but underneath the gentle
Weight of a naked youth.
                        Vainly I called out, "Almighty
Jove," struggled against his rigid will-power.'
                                              'And yielded?'
'Yes, for how could I stop him when I burned as he did
In what seemed less than a minute, I had been deflowered
Without pleasure or pang. Once more, the young man mounted.
Determined by every goddess in high heaven to share his
Spilling, I twined, but just as I was about to...'
                                                'What happened?'
'He spent.
          O why should the spurren pleasure of expectant
Woman be snaffled within a yard of the grand stand?
While he was resting, I asked him:
                                  "What is your name?"
                                                      "Chelos,
Third-year student in Egyptology. Later
I'll show you rolled papyri, hieroglyphics,

Tinted lettering, sand-yellow, Nilus-brown, reed-green,
Outlined with hawk, horn, lotus-bud, sceptre, sun-circles,
Crescent."
                    He told me of foreign wonders, the Colossus
Guarding the harbour of Rhodes, his cod bulkier than a
Well-filled freighter passing his shins, unfloodable
Temples beyond Assuan, rock-treasuries, the Mountains
Of the Moon, Alexandria and the Pharos –
Night-light of shipping.
                            Soon in a grotto-spring under fern-drip,
Knee-deep, we sponged one another, back and side, laughing.
Chelos faggoted, tricked the brazier from smoke to flame, while I
Found in a cupboard cut of ibex, stewed it with carob
Beans, sliced apple, onion, thyme-sprig. And so we had supper,
Sharing a skin of Aetnian wine until the midnight
Hour, then tiptoed tipsily back to our mantled love-bed.
Drowsily entwined, we moved slowly, softly, withholding
Ourselves in sweet delays until at last we yielded,
Mingling our natural flow, feeling it almost linger
Into our sleep.
                    Stirred by the melilot daylight, I woke up.
Chelos lay asprawl and I knew that he must be dreaming of me
For he murmured "Pyrrha." I fondled his ithyphallus, uncapped it,
Saw for the first time the knob, a purply-red plum, yet firmer.
Covering him like a man, I moved until he gripped:
Faster, yet faster, we sped, determined down-thrust rivalling
Up-thrust – succus glissading us – exquisite spasm
Contracting, dilating, changed into minute preparatory
Orgasms, a pleasure unknown to man, that culminated
Within their narrowing circles into the great orgasmos.
After we breakfasted, he walked with me to the mule-track.
There we lingered awhile, kiss-held, parted.
                                        Weakly I
Cried from a press of cypresses vague with shadow,
"Next week!"
                    Pastoral slope, spinney, went by in a dawn-dream,
Oak alone – even the highway. At last a new villa
Stopped me. I saw in the garden a stone-shape of Priapus,
Girt with long purples, drooped passion-flower, scented night-
Stock. I repeated a hymn to the god, reached the suburbs,

Tiptoed by temple, barred shopfronts, shuttered windows, safe home,
Timidly knocked on the hall-door. It opened softly.
Charico my mother was smiling her fears away.

                                        "A small bird
Twittered just now at the window-sill:

                        Pyrrha is coming!

Pyrrha is coming!"

                        Fondly she remarked at breakfast,
"Heavens above, how your appetite has improved, my daughter,
During the last twenty-four hours!"

                                "Did he whistle
Anything else – that small bird, dear mother?"

                                        She nodded

                                                "Gobble
Another pomegranate, then help me to clear the table.
Have you forgotten so soon that Monday is our washing-
Day?"

                And she handed me a dish-cloth.

                                        Later she added,
"While you were doing your hair just now, I scrubbed four
Whitish stains from your nice new cloak, my careless Pyrrha,
So the marriage arrangements, I spoke of must be completed,
Contract duly signed by the happy bride and bridegroom
After the ceremony. Does my favourite 'niece', Pyrrha,
Understand?"

                        "Of course, dear 'Auntie'. Your loving orphan
Only arrived last week!

                        Who is her husband-to-be?"
"Demetrius, a wealthy merchant of Cydonia,
Trading in copper and other metals with the Phoenicians. He
Has an extensive estate, white-pillared mansion – atrium,
Palm-court, bathing-pool."

                                "And how old is he, dearest 'Auntie'?"
"Fifty-five to a day or so, a tall, handsome
Widower, vigorous still, I can promise you that."

                                                She kept back
An involuntary smile.

                        "He was good to your poor father,
Supped in this house twice a week, whenever he visited
Phaestum – he had a branch-office here at No. Nine, North

Harbour Street. He talked of new business deals, investments,
Rattled an ivory dice-box, pleased when he threw down the winning
Astragal. Now he is coming here by sail in a fortnight,
Eager to find a young bride, insists that his old friend, your 'Auntie'
Charico, make the match for him. So let us consider
Wedding gown shaped in the latest Knossus fashion,
Lace-trimmed lingerie of the lightest serecon, dear,
Not forgetting an elegant pair of Cupido cusps
Eager to show off the paps. No man can resist them. Hands are
Hotheads."
        She went on:
                    "Afternoon frocks, low neck, angle-length,
Waist, tightly belted, two or three travelling costumes, gusseted,
Biased. We'll have an expensive fashion-designer, patterns,
Colours, textures."
           So for a week of deliberation,
Chelos had been only a shade.
               "O, dear, I must see him,
Tell him this very day."
            Pot in hand, I started
Vainly to nard my whole back.
              "Mother," I cried, "come up
Here, please, and help me."
            Charico hurried, stopped in delight.
                            "Oh,
How I have longed to see my baby daughter like this, all
In her skin. Lie down on the bed and I'll anoint you,
Raddle your paps, tint fingernail, toenail, with lac."
                  This done,
Admiration held back her eager kiss.
               "Something else.
Wait a moment."
            Quickly returning, she held on her palm a
Tiny abraxas.
        "What's that, mother?"
                  "A precious rubin.
Close your eyes. Open them. Love-charm has found the right setting."
"Mother, dear mother, redness is darting from my navel."'

III

"'Are you a goddess?" the student exclaimed that afternoon,
As I stood, mother-naked, before him.
                                    "Sea-shelling
Venus herself, whom worshippers call by many place-names,
Surprising the shore-waves?"
                            "Anadyomine?"
                                            "Mechanitis:
She who instructs ignorant men in the Art of Love?
                                        Are
You the lovely Arethusa, coldly pursued downstream
By the son-hot-Alpheus? If so, give me those crimson
Kisses that were denied to him so often."
                                "Of course. So come, mount me,
Mortal. Off with the buskin and be my nympholept. Come!"

Silent-tongued, all that afternoon, we swived, swaling together.
Silent, too, the woods, as we listened, cheek on pillow.
Only the chirr of cicala, grump of tree-frog. In a frenzy
Chelos leaped from our Colchian fleece, darted whitely –
Arrow-red kiss-marks all over his body shouting,
                                        "Hoof off!"
At the doorway.
                "Rascally pimp, self-abuser."
                                        "Who was it?"
"A dirty old satyr. I saw him trotting into the shadowed
Forest reserves."
                "A bad case of satyriasis, dear!
Come back to bed and I'll cure it with the greatest of pleasure.
Women are blamed for being so backward. Look, I am Pasiphae
Wanting her bull."
                Well I remember, Jove, our Pillow
Talk.
        "Why does one of your ticklesome twins, Chelos,
Pollox, – I think – hang an inch lower than its comrade?"

"Theologians assert that Prometheus, a flinty firebrand,
Riled against the gods, declared they were mythical figures.
Men, abandoning the true faith, became his fuming disciples.

Women have always been temple-goers, so priestesses
Wore the white, purple-hemmed vestment that had been discarded.
All the human race was punished by the offended
Deities. Life-giving scrotum, whose simultaneous seed-flow
Doubled by both ducts, as they spurted, and so enabling
Women to share without difficulty the bliss, was altered.
Now they must hurry, Pyrrha."

         I smiled, but kept the secret
No man has suspected, as we turned again to each other.'

IV

'Demetrius and I were married. The celebrant blessed our
Union, invoking with uplifted hands, the grace of Hymen,
Of you, Great Juno, and of all the mighty hierarchy:
Silvering breves, response of the unseen thuribles.
After the wedding-breakfast, spoken healths, tearful
"To the Gods" as our trireme sailed slowly from the harbour.
Odorous breezes, forgotten by Aeolus, followed us, headland
By headland. Nereids waved to us. Dolphins frolicked,
Wavelength to wavelength. Later the horizon was halcyoned. Slaves
Pulled, dipped to the sweeps. Phoebus flamed westward. We sighted
Port.

  Clepsidra warned me at midnight of mother's instructions.
"*Oh! Oh!*" I cried out, when my husband and I were bedded,
"How it hurts... No, no, don't stop, don't stop! I must suffer
Pang without pleasure that I may be truly your loving
Wife. *Ah! Ah!*" I groaned, tightly gripping his loins.

            He
Spent as he kissed me, then, satisfied, lay on his broad back.
Over-excited, shaken by hideous snort, loud snoring,
Vainly I prayed to Somnus. But the god was deep in slumber.

On the third evening Demetrius and I held a banquet:
Guests moved gravely, keeping time to Dorian music.
Then of a sudden – quick tabouring, strum of lyre-strings,
Pizzicato of heel-and-toe rhythm soon married young couples.
Costliest wines latened the feast.

      When the guests had departed,

Demetrius embraced me.
                                    I said in a vinous whisper:
"Dear, I am better now. So carry your Pyrrha, flight
After flight, carefully up the aspiring stone-steps
Within the balistra-defying tower of Babylon to the top-most
Storey lit by Chaldean lampads."'
                                    'What happened then?'
'Metaphorically speaking he did so.
                                    When we were chambered,
I assumed, as they say, the matrimonial position.
Slowly, obediently, I moved with him in the darkness,
Faster yet faster we sped. Determined up-thrust rivalled
Down-thrust – Succus glissading us – soon came successive
Spasms, contracting dilating. They changed to preparatory
Orgasms, a tiny series, as I have said, culminating
Within their narrowing circles in the great orgasmos.

Dutiful husband, ever-obedient wife, willing,
Ready to lie on the bed, night, morning, noon. What more can I
Tell, Great Jupiter?'
                                    'Every titup demanded by our wager.
Every tickle i' the thalamus.'
                                    'Twice a week, then
We performed our marital duty. I lay sideways
Couching in his lap, while he fondled my nipples with careful
Attention. Soon I could feel him perking against me: I turned slowly
Around for our long bilingual kisses until eight jealous
Fingers slide silently along our haunches to what was
Waiting below for us. Be sure we melled several
Times, impatiently urged into bliss by pinch, word, niplet.

After three months, I quickened, told my happy husband.
Still we were dutiful until I had grown too big-bellied…

"Go in unto Zervah, my lovely handmaid, who comes from Tirzah.
Her cruse will comfort you."
                                    He refused.
                                    As a collection
Box in a great temple accepts the coin that a poor pilgrim,
Hesitating with much anxiety over the narrow

Slip, drops in at last: so at times I guided
Demetrius, with gentle hand, to make his deposit,
Promised to reimburse him!
                          The midwife came as I laboured.
Hearing an outcry; swift consolatory favours,
Granted by the Divine Lucina, lessened my sharp throes,
As I gave birth to a baby daughter.
                                I will not speak of
Motherhood, uncradle those memories of milken
Joy.
      So far, all-powerful Jupiter, my story.
During those seven years that I was a woman never
Have I revealed the secret of the sex. Newly
Shapen, newly gladdened, with an eager nymphus,
I have enjoyed those additional love-sensations.
What other man i' the world has ever known the like o' it?'

Broom shone. Tiresias saw the smile of Juno,
Suddenly lift lowered. Words were lost in a new quarrel.
Deluging rain chilled, doused him, as the thunder hurtled
Bolt after bolt. Europa was cumbent: cities were flooded.
Scylla yap-yapped her underdogs, Charybdis divulged
Suck-holes: as Jove's almighty rage expanded,
Leaped by the Pillars of Hercules to those unmappable
Latitudes, where mindless bergs lurk in outmost darkness,
Beyond the ancient limits of all Olympian glory.

                          V

Chelos flung back age, laid down his stylus, exclaiming;
'Thirty-eight years or more, calendared by our sclerotic
Arteries, belong to Chronos. Well I remember that forenoon,
Tiresias.
            Sun-in-mind, I went up the mule-track,
Books in satchel, food, wineskin, to the bothy I still kept on,
When, lo-and-behold, a young girl in a blue mantle
Leaning against a boulder.
                      "Pyrrha!"
                              I cried,

                                        "Divine
Pyrrha!
         What sweet air have you breathed in these seven years?"
Swaying, she trembled into my arms. I bore her to the sheiling,
Laid her down gently on the worn fleece, the bed of bracken,
Noon was silent. Only the chirr of the cicala,
Grump of tree-frog. Silent, also, Pyrrha, tranced in whiteness,
Drawing her skirts up quietly, I saw her auburn
Curlets. Modesty could not conceal the male pudenda,
Mocked by her metamorphosis into a slim youth,
Tear-dazed, bewildered, I groped to her unchanged haunches,
Anus, thought of Ganymede, alyssum-limbed stripling,
Pipe-stopping his father's flock along the slopes of Mount Ida,
Victim of unnatural desire, as yet unravished,
Eagled, unshorn lamb, to Olympus by thunderous wing-clap,
Cupbearer, catamite hated by Hebe, bathed,
Then ambrosially odoured, eiderdowned, be-love-ringed.
Tear-dazed, I mourned for Pyrrha under that blue mantle,
Within reach, yet unpossessible except by perverted
Desire."'
         He turned to Tiresias:
                               'Believe, old friend,
Twice I have grieved for your loveliness.'
                                        And the other:
'Chelos, since that late noon when you deflowered me so quickly,
Always I wore a blue mantle as our love-pledge during those seven
Years.'
         'What has destiny so bound, unbound, bound again, our
Future?'
         'Let the scissors decide.
                               I will dictate now what is
Left of my wandersome story from your last punctum.'
'Continue.'
         'As I have told you, when I wakened and
Found you had put me to bed, I remembered wildly
All that had happened.
                      Demetrius and I had visited
Phaestum. One morning I left our little child toying with
Floor and stool while her grandmother tried to dust, mop up.
Led by invisible prompting, I went to Mount Cyllene,

Saw there at the same mossy boulder a couple of sun-spotted
Snakes — writhen, flashen — as they copulated
Dreamily. I touched them, was metamorphosed once
More. Tear-dazed, bewildered, I could not look at my phimosis.

After a week, then, we parted beneath a cypress alley.
Going down the roundabout track my thoughts kept talking:

"Let your husband, seven-year-old child, and mother believe that
You have been lost. Let remembrance smoke in the temple,
Vasing calamity."
                    My thoughts, still talking, talking,
Hurried me to the draughty quay. There a sea-captain,
Whom I had known, gave me safe passage to Piraeus.
Windbag favoured the full-rigged voyage.
                                    Our ship steered by
Lofty tower-dwellings, anchored in the second basin
Under colossal walls that had often defended Athens.
Daily I strayed from busy street, to byway, stunk alley —
Gutturalising provincials, with guide, at Propylaeum,
Agora — until the drachmas you gave me were handpicked. Sight led me,
Site after site, to the Peloponnese. Villagers
Knew me, bite-and-sup hardened by fists as I laboured
In the little fields, thinking of Crete and its red clay,
Delved, drained, sickled, then revelled among garlands at Thanksgiving
Festivals, coppered the swarms in hiving-time near
Lacedaemon.
                    Fate led me northward through a mountain
Pass to a desolate cross-roads. Twitter of specks flew up,
Crissing an omen no traveller could unriddle. I trudged on,
Saw before me the gold-brown cliffs of Mount Parnassus
Sharing the upper snow-light, came down to a grove of ilex
Shading thin ripples. I stripped, stepped back, tree-hidden,
For a sky-woman lingered, waist-deep in water. She waded
Shoreward until I could see below her navel an auburn
Dazzle. Faint with desire, I stood there, watching.
                                        O why had
Pyrrha not recognised me?
                            With open arms, I came out.
Pulse sang. Peazle burned, purple knob impatient. Body

Wanted its other self.
                           She stooped to her sun-stroked garments
On the bank. Beside them lay a spear, plumed helmet,
Hollowed bronze-round, arm-grips, of the great Medusan buckler –
All the war accoutrement of Justitia.
Darkness surrounded me, clang of words delivered in
Judgment:
                           "Mortal, having looked on what is forbidden,
Blindness must be your punishment, night in, day out.
Yet because you have shown to a goddess such stout admiration,
Take the gift of prophecy and this seemlier
Staff to be your guide."
                           The words of Pallas Athene
Ceased.
          I felt, with all its sacred knowledge, the polished
Cornelwood leading me past the amphitheatre
Slowly, southward, from Delphi.'
                           'What happened?'
                                         'Mind was peopled.
Confusion unconfusing, nameless nations, unfounded
Cities expanding, town within turreted town, future
Happenings, half legendary.
                           Once I glimpsed a big wooden
Horse on rollers, entrailed with armed men, take by surprise
An emptying forum.
                           Once I warned a homeless sea-farer:
"Stopple your crew against the noteworthy sirens, the dreaded
Manatee. The sortes are inimical. Do not
Lassoo the Oxen of the Sun."
                           Too often at night-time, fear
Called up the sappers under thick walls, the scaling-ladder,
Tip-tilt, the rock-abounding-firepot-scalded
Testudo, black flight of the carrion-calling scald-crows.
Peace reigned in seldom dreams.
                           Quiet ferries of coolness,
Aquaducts, plain-arching-hill, refreshing obedience:
Tap-turn, conduit, therma:
                           Benevolent rude. White-robed
Senators, praetors of goodness: a far-off, visionary
   World.

Set it down, Chelos, set it down that hope exulted.'
'Pen is lifted.
                    You came to Thebes –'
                                        'The town where I
Was born –'
                    'And prophesied the rout of the Argive Princes?'

'All that a mortal could carry away as spoil, I
Gave to Eteocles and his general in the war-house,
Plan of assault, counter-assault, as in an historic
Play – *The Seven against Thebes.*
                                Arrogant Argives,
Bloods come from the Bull Feast.
                                    Tideus, the champion,
Hurler of insults, wound-maker, raising his star-studded sky-shield
Against the son of Astacus at Electrae Gate.
                                            Car-borne
Capaneus, torch-litten, opposed by Polypontes
At the West Gate.
                        Huge Hippolomedes, his serpent-rimmed
Shield, figuring mouth-blazing Typhon, driven
Backward by Hypebus, shield-bearer of rayed Jupiter,
Saviour of mankind.
                        At the Neista Gate, footless, headless
Eleoclus, his swaying device a scaling-ladder
Smashed by Magereus.
                            Battle-axed at the North Gate,
Pallen Parthenopaous, the sphinx on his shield, clawless,
Dimmed, unriveted.
                        At the Homoloian Gate, knife-gelded
Chalyb, the Scythian.
                            Ping-ping of death into shriekers, shirkers,
Doom of the battering-rammers.
                                    I heard cries at the Wailing
Wall, the breast-beating chorus of women, fear-raped, their infants
Flung up to spears.
                        Eteocles listened, fire-frowning,
Map in rough hand, until my arrow-spent words had prophesied
Victory.'
            Aureate Apollo descended.

                              Areta, his second
Wife, brought in the timely lamp – gaily enchased with
Brazen Dryades, touched the seven wicks to ivoried
Buds of Colza, smiled as she laid the table:
                                        'A fit meal for
Scholars!
          Cut of swordfish, loaf, goat-cheese, melon and shaddock.'

                              VI

Over the wine-pug, the ageing pair still talked of wonders,
What were their purpose? The lost sight of Tiresias blinked at
Preternatural bowering of broom on Mount Ida.
                                        'Often
Innermost thought brings back the years of my womanhood:
Red-tinted nipples, red-infolding labia, desirous
Body so apt for hot pursuits, so ready to wait on
Hands and knees. Dream of the mounting Centaur. Dream of
Snubby, white-horned, shaggy-thighed, capifigging
Pan.
       Keep the secret, Chelos. I attended once the
Eleusinian Mysteries. Fragrant myrtling in forest
Groves, kettling, lightly-fingered flute, danced procession
Flaring from temple-steps, women undoing calyptra.
I, too, leaped among the hairpin-scatterers, divesting
Themselves for the limb-gleaming whirlabout of maenadic
Love-embrace. Broached, lined, by the wine-men. I sank through the last
Shudder of bliss into the Divine.
                              Enough of that now!
What have I become?
                      An augurer, Chelos.
Soothsayer, swing-door of the future, that old cedar
Box in which our hope flutters under the swarth ills.
Mano, my kind unmarried daughter, is my constant
Eye-opener, divining the throw of chuck-stone, dib, knuckle-bone,
Searching the swerve o' the swallows, cloud-turn, smoke-pile, to discover
Lost ring, stolen saucepan, purpose a pimple, ringworm,
What is behind an itch.
                      Mano reads palm, mug-dregs.

So we tell fortunes, the black or fair stranger, unexpected proposal,
Legacy from abroad.
                    Simple gifts content me,
Basket of apricots, string of dried onions, olive
Oil, a pint for that wine-jar over there on the table.
Can it all be superstition? Syrup of figs from the oldest
Tree in the world?'
                  'But you have called up the Manes.'
                                  'Yes. They
Manifested themselves at times from the oblivion
Below us, obscurities, unmaterialised vacua
Wavering as the sulphurous fumes that dampen
Phlegeton, the fire-breaks of Acheron, our own
Selves hereafter. Oimoi!
                  Chill of cerements clad me.
Blaze of cremation ashed me.
                  No more. I'll speak, old friend of
Insight, shown by an inner seeing.
                  Let us consider
Twofold mind, present-in-future: the act of day, busy
Travelling of the arch-wise sun, peopling of gardened
Suburbs, low-lying without the Mediterranean
Cities: Asian hubbub, spreading hordes of incessant
Beings. Such my happiness. Such my affliction.
Such my vatic bondage.
                  Marching legions of future
Rome, highway men carrying the bundle of their lawmakers
Throughout Europe. I count the expeditionary forces,
Hear consular names that farsight will not mention.
Famous sieges, taking of citadel, mole, dragon
Snap of catapultic engines, rockage crashing from
High ballista, moving wheel-towers, over-reachers,
Focal flashes: Archimedean refractors,
Mathematical precision instruments, aimed by silence,
Sweeping the sea five leagues from Syracusan
Bases, leaving a wake of sun-burned galleys, charry
Smoke.
          I stood awhile in Carthage, saw far-sea-gone
Cargoes, ware-housing quays, fortune in bond, successive
Trade wars, grapnel of greed, hauling of luxury

Ships, mainsails torn into flags of distress, blockaded
Ports, rivalry reconnoitring the rock; fleets
Night-manoeuvring in the Straits.
                              Peninsular War.
                                        At last
Africa invaded. Punic cities burned down, rebuilt by
Flames of mercantile pride.
                          O then I saw, far northward,
Boreus besoming from an Alpine pass the elephantine
Tracks going down to the hot-foot plains of Trebia
Ready for a Roman rout.
                      The vision faded,
Long afterwards –
                  Our Greece surmastered.
                                        Phalanxed
Squares, unshielded, the running din of beaten pile,
Vexilla, piling of cuisses, leather cuirasses, dinted
Blades defeated by Punic faith. Mind-flitting fantasies
Goggled me and a century of shadow-fighting
Dragged past in my slumber; shouts of the Roman victors
Echoed from Pydna, sobbed along the Macedonian
Plain. Glint of helmet, thrown up, caught again on
Javelins, camp fires pissed out, flickering dreams of the
Future.
        I saw the final annexation before our
Art was moulded again, sculpted; caryatides carried
Greater care and our philosophy was walked away with.
Greece and Rome divided by a military alliance.
Soon, I witnessed the last act –
                                a sea-battle near Epiros,
Figure-headed by a Queen bedaubed with terror; sixty
Galleys, with gull-white flashing of sweeps – no Roman blood on
Them – followed her arse as she squatted to pump ship.'
                                'What then?'
                                            'A hundred
Years of peace. History surprised by our planet, stands still.
Ceres will smile on the unblooded earth and the altar poppies
Flickering in her temples, flamelets of Aetna, be a wonder,
Nature obey her, seasons fold their own twelve. No hay blight,

No sunburn. Heat for a century will never catch cold,
Quickly rotating crops yellow the plain, the upland: clustered
Hazel-nuts bow to them. Terminus, wreathed with acanthus
Rule, undisputed boundaries.
       During the Harvest
Festivals flamens will carry the sacred flame-bearers,
Basket-crowned girls bring medlar, apricot, melon:
Pure rites of Pomona keep all pious matrons
To the wrong side of the blanket while their husbands
Sober their desire with mulling draughts. All that rises,
Swells, bulges out, peels, will pour libation,
Magnify the Horn of Plenty.
        Dip your pen in
Human blood, Chelos, or the smut of fire-entered
Villages, set down the decline and fall of the Roman
Empire.
    Men, in their ignorance, will worship a jealous
Deity, no other gods before him. He will condemn his
Stepson, a healer, riding on a donkey, brimming wine-casks,
Filling the nets of poor men. His priests will wear the toga
At new altars, sacrifice the invisible.'
         'You mean?'
            'All
Blurs again, confuses. Barbarian hordes at every
Gateway, Rome untenemented, cohorts thrown, flame smoke-sacking
Flame.
    Sometimes, I hear a din of disputation,
Rostra in arms, religious wars in the Dark Ages
To come, aiai!'
      Chelos had gone.
         The seer stood at the open
Door, wondering if Minerva had mocked him with a useless
Gift. Was the peplos of old age but a pretention?
Had not the higher mathematicians, Hipparchus, Ptolemy,
Thales and others surmised in abstract sums the cosmic
System?
     'When I was young, I gazed at the slow-sky-wheeling
Galaxy, laughed, fancied those scattered silver bits were
Minas flung out in extravagance by the Great Gambler.

Will the compelling patience of a future science
Save mankind from the peril of fire, flood, famine, disease and
Plague? Enmity of atoms, suspected by Anaxagoras,
Cast our hope out of space?'
                              He sighed.
                                        Suddenly Momus,
God of pleasantry, raising his carved grin, confronted the second
Sight of Tiresias and chuckled a warning.
                                          'Diarist, take
Care what you dictate for Jupiter has deceived you.'
'Why?'
       'In order to win his wager.'
                                    'How?'
                                           'Guess.'
                                                    'Thought is
Getting hotter…
                I have it!
                           You mean that little
Series of…'
            'Yes.'
                   'I'll question my wife to-night in our pillow
Talk.'
      'By your sebum, don't do that, old man! No wife has
Ever blabbed about her bliss, even on the bolster,
Even when she is lying on her back.'
                                     'But, Momus,
Joking apart…'
               The chuckler was gone.
                                      He heard Aretes
Calling him.
             Gentle hand was touching his elbow.
                                                  'Come in, dear
Friend, for the purple-robed hours pass by. Luna has led her
Star-flocks home – and your cup of hot milk waits on the table.'

Collected Poems

(1974)

The Wooing of Becfola

On a Sunday morning, the wife of Diarmuid,
High King of Ireland, got out of bed and
Put on her clothes.

        'What is it, Dear?
Where are you going?'

            'By rath and bell-tower
To Glen-na-Scail.'

            'What do you need there?'
'Embroidered cloaks, three diadems,
Nine antique brooches, filagree'd,
Bestone'd, part of my dowry.'

            'Come, lie
Beside me again. A Sunday journey,
They say, is unlucky, perilous,
And bed is better than a wrong turn in
A wood.'

      'I go because I must.'
'You cannot travel alone.'

          'My handmaid
Is coming with me.'

      Southward the pair
Hurried from Tara. They gossiped, strayed
By paths of sunwort. Legend hid them
That night in a Munster forest. Eyes stared
At them, waited for the kill. But
Becfola climbed into an oak, clung
There, felt the hot breath at her heels as
The wolf-pack whimpered for the next meal.
Fear closed her eyes. Fear opened them.
Heart beat again. The wolves were gone.
She wept, despaired, for the bones of
Her maid had been gnawed.

          Then something shone like
Her joy to come. Within a hollow
She saw a young man lightly cloaked
In purple silk with circlets of silver
And ruby on the two long plaits

That reached his muscular shoulders, a ball
On each of them. She tried to call out,
Though voice was weak. That sword-hilt embossed
With precious stones, that curving shield-rim
Would save her from evil-doer, loss
Of virtue, when her new champion wielded
Them. Bracelets, rings, were alight as he tended
A cooking-pot, went about the flame.
She ran, stumbled: he caught her tenderly.
Drew her to the fire, gazed at
Her, spoke no word. More faggots piled
Themselves under the pot. Amazed,
She shared the meal with him. In silence
He brought her to a nearby brook, where
She dipped her hands with his, wet, dried
Her mouth and followed him. She looked back —
The fire had vanished. Her surprise
Stopped her again. They were at a lake-shore
A copper boat was moored to an islet:
He drew it to the bank by cable
And creak of rack-wheel, pointed, smiled,
Guided it to the water-steps of
That island house. She saw fine beds there,
But never a soul. Without a word,
They stripped together like man and wife.
Without a word, she lay between him and
The wall.
             Twice in the night they woke,
Turned to each other, but did not deceive
The High King of Ireland.
                              Next morning he spoke:
'You are my wife now but cannot stay.
Return home, wait till I send the unholy
Sihn.'
          'How can I go alone? My poor maid
Was killed in the forest.'
                              'She is unharmed,
Cherished by an unreal fire.'
So wife and maid returned to Tara —
All that happened had lasted less than

A minute.
                    Becfola quickly undressed,
Lay down by her husband. He turned
To her.
                    'You took my good advice
And now you are like a honey-bush.
All May and murmur as if you had hid in
A raid of kisses. Why is it, I wonder?'
She felt his mounting warmth. She slid
Under his arms with a lay sigh,
Stretching her own. She heard the dawing
In the elms outside and smiled.
                                        'Because
My Dear, I am your obedient wife.'

Austin Clarke's Notes on the Poems

A couple of years ago, Robert Frost was given an Honorary Degree at Oxford University and, on his way back to the United States, stopped in Dublin to receive a similar honour from the National University of Ireland. After the Conferring, I had the pleasure of being introduced to him and, as we sat together on a comfortable sofa in Newman House, he asked me what kind of verse I wrote. Having been rarely asked such a question, I was confused and then, suddenly, thinking of the 'strong man' whom I had often seen on his 'pitch' near St Martin's in the Fields, replied: 'I load myself with chains and try to get out of them.' 'Good Lord!' exclaimed the wise octogenarian poet, 'you can't have many readers.'

When these poems were first published in small semi-private editions, some prosodic notes were included and it now seems best to retain them. Although *Pilgrimage and Other Poems* was included in *Collected Poems* (1936), I have decided, after some hesitation, to use it as an introduction, romantic in mood, to the later poems and satires. It was written in exile, when the future of our new State seemed so hopeful that Irish writers could delay for a while in the past. Turning from our early myths, I wanted to explore imaginatively a little of the Celtic Romanesque era and historical periods neglected and almost forgotten except by Gaelic scholars and other specialists. The lapse of years between two of the small collections here was due to the fact that I found intense pleasure in the writing of verse plays (*Later Poems*, 1961).

The Vengeance of Fionn

Grainne is approximately pronounced (Grawnya), Fionn (Finn), Oisin (Usheen).

P.3   Almhuin (Aloon) – The Hill of Allen, on the great plain, the site of Fionn's chief rath.

P.4   Rath Ghrainne. The Rath of Grainne, Corrain, Sligo.

P.5   Beann Gulbain, a mountain in Sligo, on the borders of Donegal, now called Benbulbin.

P.13   Grianan, a sun-room, set apart for women. Pronounced (green-awn).

P.15   Knocknerea, a mountain cape in Sligo, haunted by the sidhe (shee, 'faeries'), the burial place of Queen Maeve.

P.15   Cailleach, an old woman, Grainne's foster nurse.

P.21   Cailins – girls. Pronounced (colleens).

P.21   Creels, baskets.

P.21   Luss, the foxglove.

P.23   Dowth, a great tumulus in the green valley of the Boyne. The great stone chambers engraven with hieroglyphs, wherein the Druids brooded and buried the dead, can still be visited through a long deep passage in the hillside. There, around the Boyne, the spirit of Aongus – the unseen protector of Diarmuid – was.

P.23   Temair, Tara of the Kings.

P.23   (VI) Scene. Donegal.

P.30   The forests, in the Gaelic Legend called Doire dha Bhoth (the word of the two bothies).

P.31   The Lakes of Len, now Killarney. Len was one of the mysterious *De Danaans*; and wrought like Mulciber and Tubal Cain.

P.32   Lovers. Aongus, the Irish god of Love.

P.34   Cromlech, a boulder (lit. a crooked stone), usually applied to stone circles, or dolmens, which are known as *Leabthacha* Dhiarmuda, known as the Beds of Diarmuid and Grainne to this day.

P.37   Bacach – a blind man, a beggar.

The Sword of the West

P.57   *Concobar.* Uladh, Ulster (Ulla).

P.80   *The Music-Healers.* Based on a story preserved in a seventeenth-century MS, one of the epic tales in which are described the events preceding the hero's tragic end.

P.84   Calitin. An enchanter.

The Cattledrive in Connaught

P.111   *Induction.* Mannanaun Mac Lir, The Son of Lir, the sea-god. Cf. the tale, Ceithearnach Ui Dhomhnall (O'Donnell's Kerne) and Silva Gadelica. He was wont thus to ramble in the character of a prestidigitator or a professor in divers arts, one that on all and sundry played off tricks of wizardry, until now at last he is vanished from among us without leaving us more than his bare report, even as all other magicians and artists that have ever been are vanished; likewise the Fianna, and all classes of people that since that date have appeared, or for all time shall appear, and in the long run ourselves along with them.

P.111   *Ceilidhe.* A dance gathering. Magheraroarty (maher-a-ro-arty). The Waves of Tory, a pattern dance.

P.112   *Blessing.* Rann, a verse or song.

P.113   *Secrecy.* Lines suggested by the Book of Kells.

P.113   *Silver and Gold.* Harp, head; terms used in the game of pitch-and-toss played in every village on Sunday. The harp is the Irish equivalent of the English tail of a coin. This is a survival from Georgian times when the Irish penny had a harp on the obverse side. The harp has now been restored to our coinage.

P.114   *The Itinerary of Ua Clerigh.* O'Clery, the original form of the writer's surname. Itinerary poems were favourite forms among the later Gaelic poets.

     O'Clery, i.e. Clarke.

     Tirnanogue, the Land of the Ever Young.

     Curoi Mac Dara, one of the Tuatha De Danann or divine race. His fortress is at Cahirconree, in Kerry.

P.115   The late Padraic O Conaire, Gaelic storywriter, was one of the pioneers of the language revival.

P.116   Curoi Mac Dara, one of the Tuatha de Danaan. His fortress is at Cahirconree in Kerry, but the southern cycle of myth which surrounds his name has been lost.

P.116   *The Pedlar.* This was suggested by an essay in *An Crann Geugach,* (The Branchy Tree), by Padraic O Conaire. On the theory that the ass, being a desert animal, has an atavistic dread of rustling leaves, the essayist substituted branches for the proverbial carrot, achieving better results by contrary means.

P.117   *The Fair at Windgap.* A free, abbreviated version of *Aonach Bhearna Na Gaoithe,* composed by Tomás O'Modhrain, at the beginning of the last century.

P.119   *The Lad Made King.* This is based on one of the fragmentary episodes, which are associated with the epic tales of Conary Mor, and deal with his early years.

P.120   *The Lost Heifer.* This is the mode of the Jacobite Songs. The lines were written during a period when our national idealism suffered eclipse. The Heifer or Silk of the Kine is a secret name used by the Jacobite poets for Ireland.

P.120   *The Son of Lir.* Mannanaun Mac Lir, the Son of Lir, the sea-god.

P.122   *The House in the West.* The most westerly house in Ireland, the legendary mansion of Mór, the sun's daughter. Mór was the wife of Lir, the sea-god, and was originally a rain-goddess. Her name is found in the place-name Tivorye, at the foot of Mount Eagle, in West Kerry. Jeremiah Curtin, in *Hero-Tales of Ireland*, mentions that Dunmore Head was called Mary Gearane's House, a corruption of *Tigh Mhoire ni Greine,* the house of Mór.

P.124   *The Frenzy of Suibhne* (Sweeney). This is merely a glimpse of *Buile Suibhne,* a middle-Irish romance of a king who, cursed by a saint, wandered in madness, through the woods. The story, published by the Irish Texts Society for the first time in 1913, has escaped attention. George Moore regarded it as one of the great stories of the world.

P.127   Midna. A magician who played slumber-music on a reed outside the camp of the Fianna.

     Although most of these lyrics are based on assonance and feminine, or stopped, rhyme, they are not necessarily an attempt to suggest the intricate prosody and sound of Gaelic verse.

P.128   *The Circuit of Cuchullin* (Ku–hull–in). The hero of the Northern cycle of Sagas. The episode of the taming of the elemental horses occurs in the *Briccriu Flend*, or *Feast of Briccriu*. In triple time blank verse.

P.131   *The Cattledrive in Connaught*. Based on 'The Pillow Talk at Cruachan', the prologue to the *Táin Bo Cuailgne*, the great prose epic of the wars between the northern and western kingdoms.
Eochaid (Yohee).
Ailill (alyeel).
Cruachan (kru–hane).
Crotal, a yellow dye from lichen.
Minn, an ornament for the head worn by women.

Pilgrimage

Assonance, more elaborate in Gaelic than in Spanish poetry, takes the clapper from the bell of rhyme. In simple patterns, the tonic word at the end of the line is supported by a vowel–rhyme in the middle of the next line. Unfortunately the internal patterns of assonance and consonance in Gaelic stanzas are so intricate that they can only be suggested in another language.

The natural lack of double rhymes in English leads to an avoidance of words of more than one syllable at the end of the lyric line, except in blank alternation with rhyme. A movement constant in Continental languages is absent. But by cross–rhymes or vowel–rhyming, separately, one or more of the syllables of longer words, on or off accent, the difficulty may be turned: lovely and neglected words are advanced to the tonic place and divide their echoes.

P.151   *Pilgrimage*. Beaded plains. The plains of Galway are covered with countless field–walls of loose stone and boulders forming a strange pre–historic landscape, fascinating when the light of day is seen through the myriad chinks.
Ara, the Aran Islands.
Pins are still placed near the wishing–wells and rags tied to the guardian tree.
The holy mountain is Croagh Patrick, and once a year it is still crowded with pilgrims and penitents.

P.154   *The Confession of Queen Gormlai*. This cultured woman 'made many pitiful and learned ditties in Irish' when her third husband, Nial, was slain by the Ostmen on a ridge near Dublin. A distressing vision which caused her lonely death, as told in an old book, may symbolise a conscience wounded by others.

P.159   *The Scholar*. A free paraphrase of an anonymous poem, *An Mac Leighinn*, discovered at Maynooth Library.
The Scholar and *The Cardplayer* are taken from *The Son of Learning*, a poetical comedy first produced at the Cambridge Festival Theatre in November 1927.

P.162   *The Cardplayer.* The Red Lake is Lough Derg, or St Patrick's Purgatory, to which great annual pilgrimages are made, as in the Middle Ages.

P.161   *The Young Woman of Beare.* The episodes of this allegory are fanciful, the Old Woman of Beare, or Berehaven in Kerry, is a well-known figure in country stories. She had seven periods of youth before the climacteric of her grief. She speaks in a famous and classic poem: 'the lament of an old hetaira who contrasts the privation and suffering of her old age with the pleasure of her youth when she had been the delight of kings' (Kuno Meyer). Dr Hyde thinks she was an early Nino de l'Enclos or else a mythic personage euphemised by the romancists. In Glendalough, that holy place, a man told me of a poor crone who had lived in the ruined settlement below the abandoned mines. She refused even the consolations of religion, for she remembered with great anger her own times of merriment and the strong mortals she had held, when silver and lead were brought down the mountain-side, more than half a century ago.

The drama of racial conscience, as strange to the previous Celtic school as Gaelic art, has become intensified. The immodesty of present-day female dress is denounced in virile Pastorals and Parliament passes laws against temptations.

P.168   *The Marriage Night.* The religious Confederacy of Powers in the seventeenth century sustained defeat at Kinsale, and culture submitted to iconoclasm.

P.169   *The Planter's Daughter.* In barren Donegal trees around a farmstead still denote an owner of Planter stock, for in the past no native could improve his stone's-throw of land.

P.170   *Aisling.* The Aisling or Vision poem reached its pitch, as an art form, in the seventeenth and eighteenth centuries. There is a wonderful chapter on that form in Daniel Corkery's literary history of the period, *The Hidden Ireland.*

Night and Morning

P.186   *Repentance.* The Confession poem was a recognised literary form in Gaelic and lasted till the eighteenth century.

Ancient Lights

P.195   *Celebrations.* In *The Oxford Book of Irish Verse*, one of the editors, Donagh MacDonagh, thought it necessary to add a note when including this poem so he wrote in his introduction: 'Here it is necessary for reader or critic to know that the "Celebrations" with which the poem deals are the Dublin Eucharistic Congress of 1932, that the Papal colours are yellow and white, with crossed keys, while the Irish flag is green, white and yellow.' The following details may be added: the Rebellion started on Easter Monday, 1916. Over the gateway of Dublin Castle there is a statue of Justice. During the Civil War, seventy Republicans were executed by the Provisional Government. Between 1936–46, when the Republican Government was in power, of the small group of political intransigents, four were shot without trial, four were shot by firing squad, one was hanged by Pierrepoint, and three died on hunger strike.

P.196 *Three Poems about Children* (III): This orphanage was at some distance from the main convent building and the sixty children, trapped in an upper dormitory, without fire escape were in the charge of an elderly lay woman. All perished. The lines were inspired by a statement of the local bishop.

P.202 *Mother and Child.* As Minister of Health Dr Noel Browne practically rid our country of tuberculosis by his energetic and rapid organisation of hospitals and grants. Later his courageous attempt to introduce further welfare measures was opposed by the Hierarchy, the Government and wealthy medical specialists. He is now one of our Socialist deputies.

P.202 *Inscription for a Headstone.* James Larkin was a prominent Labour leader. During the Lockout of 1913, 200 people were batoned on Bloody Sunday at a public meeting which had been prohibited by the British authorities. This led to the formation of the Citizen Army. The leader of the Dublin capitalists was William Martin Murphy, a newspaper owner and ruthless clericalist.

P.203 *The Blackbird of Derrycairn.* Based on *Lon Doire an Chairn*, one of the early Ossianic lays.

P.204 *Vanishing Irish.* Raftery, a Connaught poet of the early nineteenth century. The reference is to his well-known poem, *Brighdin Bheusaidh* (Breedyeen Vesey). The lover in this mock-classical poem descended into Hades.

Too Great a Vine

A great-grandfather of mine, who was a skinner, lived in the Liberties of Dublin and had a tannery in Watling Street, near Usher's Quay. In his later years he seems to have become eccentric for he wore wigs of different colours during the week. He amused himself by writing occasional verses of a satiric kind about his fellow-traders and got the ballad-singers from Thomas Street to recite these outside their shop-doors. As I have few personal interests left, I have concentrated on local notions and concerns which are of more importance than we are, keep us employed and last long. With the exception of the sonnet and the little experiment in *rime riche*, these pieces came to me quite unexpectedly, last August, in little more than a fortnight. This explains, to some extent, the continuity of mood. In their notice of *Ancient Lights: Poems and Satires. First Series*, a few critics suggested that some of the pieces were too mild to be called satires. I hope that I have made amends.

P.209 *Abbey Theatre Fire.* Despite wide-spread reports at the time the Abbey Theatre was not seriously damaged by the fire. That plain building, which was good enough for Yeats, Synge and Lady Gregory, was demolished by order of the Directors – all for the sake of an imposing façade and a hundred extra seats. The tune is – *King Stephen was a worthy peer*.

P.210   *Wolfe Tone*. The father of Irish Republicanism and leader of the United Irishmen is now regarded with suspicion. When I was a student, there was a marked site for a memorial to him outside St Stephen's Green. Seumas O'Sullivan wrote a poem about it in 1918, but the tablet had long since disappeared. A similar site for a Thomas Davis statue has been kept for some years at College Green opposite the eighteenth-century Houses of Parliament. I wrote these lines on the morning that the fine Gough Monument in the Phoenix Park was blown up.

P.210   *The Trial of Robert Emmet*. All the arrangements had been made for the mock-trial, when this sonnet was published in *The Irish Times*. As the court-house is not large, high prices were to be charged for the seats. Fortunately the Judiciary protested and, after some weeks of patriotic delay, the Minister for Justice stopped the project.

P.211   *Past and Present*. During the Penal Days, the clergy, perforce, were educated abroad.

P.212   *Miss Marnell*. The actual facts were even more distressing. In this poem, *Miss Marnell*, and the following one, I have tried to express wheat I would feel, if I were one of the 'minority'.

P.213   *Local Complainer*. According to a newspaper report, both Catholics and Protestants subscribed. Some time ago this statue was mutilated but the matter was hushed up. It is said that the outrage was committed by a local Catholic of feeble mind. A few days later a couple of Dublin schoolboys were arrested for shooting at a similar statue with an air rifle. As the result of wide organising, religious statues have been erected in many towns and villages, by the roadside, on hilltops, outside factories, quarries and mines, and in the poorer districts of Dublin. Most of these are painted plaster casts, supplied by enterprising firms. They may prove our public piety, but certainly display our total lack of artistic taste.

P.214   *The Loss of Strength* was suggested by a dangerous illness and by Coleridge's poem, *Youth and Age*.

> This body that does me grievous wrong
> O'er aery cliffs and glittering sands
> How lightly then it flashed along.

P.218   As Aer Lingus aeroplanes are all named after Irish saints, the machine might have been any one of the following: St Brigid, St Patrick, St Brendan, St Colmcille, St Laurence O'Toole, St Malachi, St Finbar, St Finian, St Kevin, St Fabinn, St Senan, etc.

P.220   *Pilgrimage*. The day after I had written these lines, the Archbishop of Dublin flew to Lourdes to welcome the main contingent of pilgrims. I quote from a newspaper report of his speech. 'He would ask them to accept with patience whatever inconvenience or pain came their way. "Our suffering is small beside the sorrow of our invalids."'

The Horse-Eaters

P.225 *Intercessors.* This sonnet, 'Irish-American Dignitary,' and 'The Flock at Dawn,' now slightly amended, were published in Rome in the *Transatlantic Review* towards the end of the year. Somewhat upset by my own indignation, I was much relieved when, shortly afterwards, the Pope forbade the clergy of his diocese to gad about and indulge in daily amusement. He warned them, too, of the danger of becoming televisionaries. His reform received little attention in our newspapers and indeed, a few weeks later, *The Irish Press* proudly displayed a large photograph of our missionary nuns in England receiving the gift of a scooter to speed them on their rounds.

P.225 *Irish-American Dignitary.* The date of this memorable visit: 26 August, 1958.

P.226 and p.233 *Knacker Rhymes* and *The Hippophagi.* Traffic in these sensitive creatures had been quietly and discreetly increasing for some time, but on 17 December 1959, the loss of forty-eight horses at sea during a storm drew public attention to what had been going on. Protection Societies, both here and in Great Britain, have chosen the lesser of two evils, thereby showing shortsightedness and remarkable stupidity. Instead of advocating total abolition of this new slave trade and appealing to decent citizens, they ask for an export trade in horse meat and are even raising subscriptions to start this new industry. Cars now carry the brutal slogan: 'Stop exporting horses. Start meat factories here.'

'Tinahely Horse Fair is not what it was. Buyers, working for the export market, were offering £45, £50, £60 for fit horses, feeling each beast in the way that a cattle breeder runs his hands over a well-nourished animal.' *The Irish Times*, Report, February, 1960.

P.228 *Christmas Eve.* These disturbances, which might have been averted by tact and a sense of humour, were reported briefly and vaguely in the local press, but full accounts were cabled by enterprising correspondents to New York. No enquiry was held. Later a question was asked in the Dáil but was met by an indignant denial.

P.229 *The Flock at Dawn.* Multiplication Table: this is a reference to a well-known book on the Safe Period by a Jesuit. It is kept under the counter in religious bookshops.

'Nor are those considered as acting against Nature who, in their married life use their right in the proper manner although on account of natural reasons of time or of certain defects, new life cannot be brought forth.' Pope Pius XI.

Young married couples are encouraged to think that the Safe Period is ninety percent effective, but a clerical student tells me that *interruptio, pollutio,* and other sinful practices are increasing. As many wives are not strong enough for constant child-bearing and are frequently in danger of death, marriage in Ireland has greater risks than in many other countries.

P.230   Archbishop Browne. According to my maternal grand-father, whose name was Browne, this much abused ecclesiastic, who burned the National Relic, was one of our ancestors.

P.231   *In the New Statesman Office*. When I was writing this poem, I did not know that the Society of Jesus had recently obtained a Lottery Licence at the Dublin District Court. A few days after I had completed the lines, I picked up from the gutter, hesitantly, a rather soiled brochure entitled 'St Francis Xavier Draw'. The details were rewarding: Weekly Draws for Cash, Sweep Tickets, Television Sets and Superb Saloon Car. Daily Draws for £5 cheques. Generous Bonus to Promotors for Advance Payments.

P.232   *Early Unfinished Sketch*. Cf. Herrick: *The Vine*.

P.233   *The Hippophagi*. Alphonsus Liguori. In his *Theologia Moralis,* the eighteenth-century saint enumerated conscientiously and with mediaeval frankness the physical intimacies permitted or forbidden in the married state. He was lenient in some of these matters and D.H. Lawrence would have agreed with his answer to the enquiry: *Quaeres an, et quando liceant tactus, aspectus, et verbia turpia inter conjuges?* In his seventies the saint was occasionally levitated although crippled with arthritis, but in his ninetieth year, he was tormented by 'diabolical apparitions' and 'fearful temptations against every virtue.'

P.237   Audeon, who was the patron saint of the Bristol traders in old Dublin, is said to have come from Rouen.

P.237   Lowry Lorc. The Legend of Lowry Lorc, a provincial Irish king, resembles that of Midas, for he was horse-eared.

P.237   Tulyar. An international sire, was bought by our Government for £250,000.

P.238   This Maynooth episode is well-known for it was mentioned by James Joyce in *The Portrait of the Artist as a Young Man*. I have ventured to use it because it was often mentioned during the Sinn Fein period when I was growing up.

Forget Me Not

This poem was commissioned by the Arts Council of Great Britain for the Poetry at the Mermaid Festival, London, 1961.

Flight to Africa

In recent years many universities of the USA have done much to help and encourage poets. All the poems in this book, with the exception of three, are due, indirectly, to the patronage of a leading American university, which enabled me to visit Mount

Parnassus. Shortly after my return I experienced for ten weeks a continual, voluptuous state of mind during which the various pieces arrived with such joyful ease that I suspect some to be Greek gifts. The three poems written previously are 'Flight to Africa', 'The Stadium', 'Forget Me Not'.

P.256   *The Wounds of Fodhla.* 'Pilallo,' a Cromwellian expletive used in a seventeenth century Gaelic poem. The word occurs in a Cornish story by A. Quiller-Couch.

P.257   *Flight to Africa.* 'The Nuncio said that Ireland was represented in Nigeria at the moment by the Taoiseach, Mr Sean Lemass, and that was a very significant fact. Dr Lucey: "I am not one who takes kindly to emigration. I do not think that we can always afford in the spiritual world to send out boys and girls as priests and brothers and sisters abroad: that is the part of Christian Charity, but the right place for an Irishman is in Ireland."' *The Irish Times,* 27 September 1960.

'At a reception given to him in Cork during Patrician week, the Papal Legate said that emigration from Ireland was an act of Divine Providence and went on to say that the Church in Britain, the USA, and indeed the entire English-speaking world, would be in a sorry plight but for emigration from this country.' *The Dublin Evening Mail.*

P.258   Our Merchant's Son, a Jacobite 'secret name'.

P.259   *Precautions.* Monsignor Lambruschini of the Pontifical Lateran University; Fr F. Hust, SJ, of the Gregorian University, Monsignor Palazzini, Secretary of the Vatican Conciliar Congregation. Their recent conclusions, which seem cynical, were printed in *Studi Cattolici* and reported in English and American newspapers, but suppressed here. Apparently Irish parents must not be warned of the danger to which their daughters may be subjected in remote regions.

P.263   *From a Diary of Dreams.* Line 1: I lost my way on a rainy night in Cambridge, and suddenly, at a corner, under a street-lamp, saw the name 'Jesus Lane' on a blank wall. A private symbol.

P.275   *Corporal Punishment.* See *Punishment in our Schools* published by the School Children's Protection Organisation, and *Corporal Punishment in Irish Primary Schools: Three senate speeches,* by Owen Sheehy Skeffington.

P.278   *Richmond Hill.* Re: concluding stanza of this limerick. Last December I took up in shame an old copy of Thomas Moore's *Collected Poems* to read again the *Fables for the Holy Alliance* – that forgotten 'Common Market' – because the birth-place of the poet had been demolished a few weeks previously by order of the Dublin Corporation. The page opened at an earlier satire unknown to me, and I caught sight of these lines:

Made Ireland first, in wild, adulterous trance,
Turn false to England's bed, and whore with France.

Our National Poet, in a similar image, was referring to the purchase of the Irish Parliament and denouncing as buyers both the Whigs and Tories. His lines are a reminder that we have a precedent for our present hasty wish to sell abroad our limited freedom.

P.289   *On the Mountain Tops.* Father Murphy, a leader of the 1798 Rebellion, was hanged. There is still a statue to his memory at Tullow on the West Wicklow border. In Nenagh, recently, a memorial to the 'Croppies' was dragged down ignominiously by means of a tractor and replaced by a statue of Christ the King.

P.291   *Beyond the Pale.* This old-fashioned descriptive poem was suggested by the *Walks and Gig Drives* of Victorian parson-poets. *See English, Scottish and Welsh Landscape Verse,* chosen by John Betjeman and Geoffrey Taylor.

P.295   *Eighteenth Century Harp Songs.* Free variations on Gaelic songs by Turlough O'Carolan (1670–1738), poet, harpist, composer. His harp tunes were influenced by Geminiani and Corelli.

P.299   *A Vision of Mars* and *Aisling.* From *Aisling Meabhuil* (A Deceptive Vision) and *An Aisling* by Egan O'Rahilly (c. 1670–1726).

P.300   *O'Rourke's Feast. Pleraca na Ruarceach* by Hugh Mac Gauran, set to music by his contemporary, O'Carolan. Mr Donal O'Sullivan has reprinted in *Songs of the Gael* the vigorous version by Charles Wilson (1758–1802). The brief, semi-parodic version by Dean Swift is well-known: but why did that temperate drinker choose the poem and – with a by-blow – father the stage-Irishman of yesterday and today?

P.301   *Cock and Hen,* Cf. *Amhrain Mhuighi Seola* (Songs of Mayo), collected by Mrs Costello.

P.302   *Rustic Match-Making.* Cf. *Songs of the Gael.*

P.303   *The Adventures of the Great Fool.* Variation on a strange Gaelic poem used as an intermediate Course text when I was at school. I found it absorbing as our master could not explain its theme.

P.306   *How Coveteousness Came into the Church.* This traditional tale was set down by Douglas Hyde in *Saints and Sinners.*

P.309   *Songs of the Books.* Suggested by *Amhran na Leabhar* by Tomás Rua O'Sullivan (1785–1848). A similar stanza form is used here. These poor laymen, long forgotten, were the pioneers of popular education.

A friend, Professor David Krause, of Brown University, urges me to write a note on the occasional use of *rime riche* in these poems and satires. I do so hesitantly, for several French scholars were unable to tell me the history of this device. I learned from a note in an old schoolbook that Victor Hugo was the first to use it extensively and his example was followed by De Musset, Gautier, Verlaine. *Rime riche* is the perfect rhyme, since two identical words, with separate meaning, are in accord: *la tombe, qui tombe.* Variant*: belle, rebelle.* Examples:

Waterloo! Waterloo! Waterloo! morne plaine!
Comme une onde qui bout dans une urne trop pleine...
Hugo

Sculpte, lime, cisèle:
Que ton rêve flottant.
   Se scelle
Dans le bloc résistant!

Gautier

In English the second homonym seems at times to be ironic in effect, and in composite self-rhyme may lead back, perhaps, to the mood of *Pacchiarotto and How He Worked in Distemper*, in which the rhyme becomes a running commentary.

Old-Fashioned Pilgrimage

P.358   *Robert Frost*. This occurred at Newman House, Dublin, after an honorary degree had been conferred on the poet by the National University of Ireland.

P.364   *Pablo Neruda*. I met him first at the International PEN Congress in Jugoslavia in 1965.

P.364   *The Paper Curtain*. When I set down these impressions after the PEN Congress at Bled, I was not aware that a Jugoslav writer had been held for years in captivity.

P.368   *Letter to a Friend*. Ireland's Eye, isle, from Norse. Cf. 'eyot'.

P.372   *Nova et Vetera*. Title of a study by George Tyrrell.

P.376   *Pigeon Pie*. Suggested by a pamphlet written by the present incumbent of Dunster.

P.377   *Custom House Official*. Friends have told me that expensive art books which they ordered from London were held up at the Customs and some illustrations removed. Taking a hint from Yeats's poem about an ideal fisherman, I tried to imagine an ideal gauger.

P.381   *More Extracts from a Diary of Dreams*. Some of these dreams, as indicated, were in colour.

P.381   Brian O'Nolan, a brilliant satirist, who wrote both in Irish and English, and use the pen-name Myles na gGopaleen, died in 1965. He was dismissed from the Civil Service by the Cabinet with a small pension, owing to his satiric and witty comments on our Tammany methods in political life.

The Echo at Coole

P.393   *The Labours of Idleness*. Thomas Love Beddoes was a nephew of Maria Edgeworth.

P.394   Waxies. A name for shoe-makers, because they used waxed thread.

P.398   *The Echo at Coole.* Carroll O'Daly (Cearbhall O'Dálaigh), a fifteenth-century poet from Corcomroe in Co. Clare. His Echo poem is one of the earliest of its kind. Suggested by the draft of the poem 'A prayer for my daughter', printed by Jon Stallworthy in *Between the Lines. W.B. Yeats's Poetry in the Making.*

> And after to the garden on that side
> Where the Katalpa's grow (growing) and call
> Until an echo in the wall
> Above Maecenas' image had replied.

P.418   *Black, White and Yellow.* In June 1966, I saw about two hundred demonstrators kept on a traffic island near Times Square, New York, by a large posse of armed police. These peaceable people were carrying posters and banners in protest against the war in Vietnam and the conscription of the young. The temperature was at 100 degrees.

When Telefís Éireann wished to send out a group of journalists to observe conditions in North and South Vietnam, the Government intervened. The Minister for External Affairs, who had championed frequently the cause of small countries at UN meetings, pointed out that such an investigation would prove embarrassing to a Great Power, which he did not mention by name.

P.431   *The Subjection of Women.* Sidhe (Shee), Fairy folk.

P.443   *Eire (A Bheith na Lub).* Daithi ua Bruadair, c. 1625–1698.

P.444   *A Jingling Trifle (Guagan Gliog).* In the last line of the fourth stanza, the onomatopoeic words 'cramp' and 'rump' were borrowed derisively from the speech of the Planters:

> 's is gnáth crúmpa 'san rúmpa Raghnaite

P.450   *Phallomeda.* I have changed this ancient tale slightly by introducing a well-known Greek goddess into it, instead of an Irish one. In several stories of the Fianna, a champion arrives from Greece to challenge all.

Orphide

P.495   *The Quarry.* Based on a private report circulated among the Hierarchy at the time.

P.504   *The Trees of the Forest. Buile Suibhne*, a mediaeval saga in prose and verse about a king who was cursed by a saint and wandered in madness throughout the forests of Ireland and Britain.

P.506   *The Healing of Mis.* Mis is pronounced Mish. Ruis is Ruish. *The Romance of Mis* was edited by Brían O Cuív. This ancient story seems to anticipate the curative methods of Freud. I am indebted to Professor David Greene for his translation. I have ventured to add a few stanzas about dream-analysis.

P.506   Geilt. A mad person.

P.507   Suantree. A soothing song.

Tiresias

P.515   In a poem entitled 'Tiresias', Tennyson has depicted the seer in gloomy terms. T.S. Eliot, in the well-known lines,

> And I, Tiresias, have foresuffered all,
> Enacted on this same divan or bed,

expresses his own Puritanism. In our new permissive age I have tried to present a cheerful account of the experiences of Tiresias as wife and mother.

In this poem, the first syllable of Tiresias is accented.

The incident is taken from Ovid's *Metamorphoses*: 'They tell that Jupiter, by chance, well drenched with nectar, laid aside all weighty cares, and engaged in some free jokes with Juno, in her idle moments, and said: "Decidedly the pleasures of you, *females*, is greater than that which falls to the lot of us males." She denied it. It was agreed between them to ask what was the opinion of the experienced Tiresias. To him both pleasures were well-known' (translated by Henry T. Riley, 1851).

Bibliography

Poetry

The Vengeance of Fionn (Maunsel and Company) 1917
The Fires of Baäl (Maunsel and Roberts) 1921
The Sword of the West (Maunsel and Roberts) 1921
The Cattledrive in Connaught and Other Poems (Allen and Unwin) 1925
Pilgrimage and Other Poems (Allen and Unwin) 1929
The Collected Poems of Austin Clarke, with an introduction by Padraic Colum (Allen
    and Unwin) 1936
Night and Morning: Poems (Orwell Press) 1938
Ancient Lights. Poems and Satires: First Series (The Bridge Press) 1955
Too Great a Vine. Poems and Satires: Second Series (The Bridge Press) 1957
The Horse-Eaters. Poems and Satires: Third Series (The Bridge Press) 1960
Later Poems (Dolmen Press) 1961
Forget Me Not (Dolmen Press) 1962
Flight to Africa and Other Poems (Dolmen Press) 1963
Mnemosyne Lay in Dust (Dolmen Press) 1966
Old-Fashioned Pilgrimage and Other Poems (Dolmen Press) 1967
The Echo at Coole and Other Poems (Dolmen Press) 1968
A Sermon on Swift and Other Poems (The Bridge Press) 1968
Orphide and Other Poems (The Bridge Press) 1970
Tiresias: A Poem (The Bridge Press) 1971
Collected Poems (Dolmen Press) 1974
Selected Poems, edited by Thomas Kinsella (Dolmen Press) 1976
Selected Poems, edited by Hugh Maxton (Lilliput Press) 1991

Novels

Austin Clarke wrote three novels, all of which were banned by the Irish Censorship
Board:
The Bright Temptation: A Romance (Allen and Unwin) 1932; republished Dolmen
    Press, 1965
The Singing-Men at Cashel (Allen and Unwin) 1936
The Sun Dances at Easter: A Romance (Melrose) 1952

Memoirs

First Visit to England, and Other Memories (The Bridge Press and Williams and Norgate) 1945

Twice Round the Black Church: Early Memories of Ireland and England (Routledge and Kegan Paul) 1962; republished Moytura Press, 1990

A Penny in the Clouds: More Memories of Ireland and England (Routledge and Kegan Paul) 1968; republished Moytura Press, 1990

Plays

Austin Clarke wrote twenty-one verse plays.

The Son of Learning: A Poetic Comedy in Three Acts (Allen and Unwin) 1927; republished Dolmen, 1964. *The Hungry Demon* (a version of *The Son of Learning*) was performed at the Gate Theatre, Dublin, 27 September 1930

The Flame: A Play in One Act (Allen and Unwin) 1930

Sister Eucharia: A Verse Play in Three Scenes (William and Norgate and Orwell Press) 1939

Black Fast: A Poetic Farce in One Act (Orwell Press) 1941

As the Crow Flies: A Lyric Play for the Air (The Bridge Press and Williams and Norgate) 1943

The Viscount of Blarney and Other Plays (The Bridge Press and Williams and Norgate) 1944

The Second Kiss: A Light Comedy (The Bridge Press and Williams and Norgate) 1946

The Plot Succeeds: A Poetic Pantomime (The Bridge Press and Williams and Norgate) 1950

The Moment Next to Nothing: A Play in Three Acts (The Bridge Press) 1953

Collected Plays (Dolmen) 1963, includes all the above

Two Interludes, Adapted from Cervantes: 'The Student from Salamanca' and 'The Silent Lover' (Dolmen) 1968

The Impuritans (Dolmen) 1973

The Visitation: A Play. A Comedy in One Act (*Irish University Review*, Austin Clarke Special Issue, Vol. 4, No. 1, Spring 1974)

The Third Kiss: A Comedy in One Act (Dolmen) 1976

Liberty Lane: A Ballad Play of Dublin in Two Acts with a Prologue (Dolmen) 1978

Selected Plays of Austin Clarke, chosen and introduced by Mary Shine Thompson (Irish Drama Selections 14; Colin Smythe) 2005

Bis in Nocte: A Medieval Comedy in Three Scenes (unpublished).

Criticism

Austin Clarke wrote reviews for several British newspapers and literary magazines when he went to England in 1922. On his return to Ireland in 1937 he began reviewing books for the *Irish Times* and for a six-year period during the 1960s for the *Irish Press*. He returned to review for the *Irish Times* and was contributing reviews to it up until the time he died in 1974.

Poetry in Modern Ireland (Three Candles Press) 1951
The Celtic Twilight and the Nineties (Dolmen Press and Dufour Editions) 1969
Reviews and Essays of Austin Clarke, edited by Gregory A. Schirmer (Irish Literary Studies 40; Colin Smythe) was published in 1995 and consists of almost fifty essays and reviews.

Recording

Beyond the Pale (Claddagh Records, 1962). Readings, with commentary, of Clarke's own poetry, with an introduction by John Montague.

Publications about Austin Clarke

Austin Clarke: His Life and Works by Susan Halpern (Dolmen Press) 1974
Austin Clarke: A Study of his Writings by G. Craig Tapping (Academy Press) 1981
The Poetry of Austin Clarke by Gregory A. Schirmer (Dolmen Press) 1983
Austin Clarke: A Critical Introduction by Maurice Harmon (Wolfhound Press) 1989

★

Austin Clarke's library, part of the Poetry Ireland Collection, is housed in University College Dublin Special Collections and may be accessed via www.ucd.ie/library.

Index of Titles

Index of First Lines

COLLECTED POEMS